MW01119558

Youth and Inequality in Education

The transition to adulthood for many is mediated by class, culture, and local/global influences on identity. This volume analyzes the global injustices that create inequities and restrict future opportunities for young people during this transitional time, including poverty, unemployment, human rights, race, ethnicity, and location. It critically examines global instances of youth discrimination, offering positive strategies and practices such as youth work that successfully remediate these injustices. With international contributions from Australia, England, Malaysia, Peru, Philippines, Portugal, Morocco, Jordan, Aotearoa New Zealand, and the U.S., this volume is particularly important to researchers and scholars in the fields of youth studies, education, and social work.

"Heathfield and Fusco have orchestrated an international assemblage of voices speaking to the issues facing contemporary youth, particularly youth at the margins of society. The approach of the contributors is mostly qualitative, providing intimate views of the realities of young people's lives rather than statistical abstractions. These case studies are well informed theoretically and take up political questions about inequality in a refreshingly straightforward way. This book will be appealing to students (and teachers and activists) seeking to 'make a difference' in the world and to do so in a principled way."—*Professor William New, Beloit College, USA*

"In this courageous and compelling book, Heathfield and Fusco have modeled the very practices they hold up as central to youth work that is transformative and that illuminates and interrupts inequality. Not only have they put young peoples' voices, experiences, and relationships at the center of this volume, they have also developed a volume that is radically and globally inclusive. Youth work, as elaborated within this text, is a diverse but immensely collaborative bridging of people, practice, policy, and ideas for our mutually successful futures. In embedding the very local and contextually grounded stories of these young people (and their adult allies and partners) within the broader framing of global in/equality, Fusco and Heathfield have not only provided a path forward for a more unified global youth work agenda but also helped to cultivate and prepare the soil so that the seeds germinated within these chapters can take hold and thrive."—*Professor Stacey Horn, University of Illinois-Chicago, USA*

Michael Heathfield is Associate Professor of Social Work and Youth Programs at Harold Washington College, USA.

Dana Fusco is Professor of Teacher Education at CUNY, York College, USA.

Routledge Research in Educational Equality and Diversity

Books in the series include:

Identity, Neoliberalism and Aspiration
Educating White Working-class Boys
Garth Stahl

Faces of Discrimination in Higher Education in India
Quota Policy, Social Justice and the Dalits
Samson K. Ovichegan

Inequality, Power and School Success
Case Studies on Racial Disparity and Opportunity in Education
Gilberto Q. Conchas and Michael A. Gottfried
with Briana M. Hinga

Youth and Inequality in Education
Global Actions in Youth Work
Edited by Michael Heathfield and Dana Fusco

Youth and Inequality in Education

Global Actions in Youth Work

Edited by Michael Heathfield and Dana Fusco

NEW YORK AND LONDON

First published 2016
by Routledge
711 Third Avenue, New York, NY 10017

and by Routledge
2 Park Square, Milton Park, Abingdon, Oxon OX14 4RN

Routledge is an imprint of the Taylor & Francis Group, an informa business

Library of Congress Cataloging-in-Publication Data
A catalog record for this book has been requested

ISBN: 978-1-138-80829-4 (hbk)
ISBN: 978-1-315-75066-8 (ebk)

Typeset in Sabon
by Apex CoVantage, LLC

Printed and bound in the United States of America by Publishers Graphics, LLC on sustainably sourced paper.

Contents

Tables and Figures

TABLES

FIGURES

Foreword

By the time this book is published, the 2nd European Youth Work Convention, held during Belgium's Chairmanship of the Council of Europe, will have come and gone. I cannot anticipate its conclusions at this juncture, but its theme will have been "Finding Common Ground." This is an agenda in stark contrast to the European Youth Work Declaration that followed the 1st European Youth Work Convention, also held in Belgium in 2010. At the heart of that Declaration was the celebration of the diversity of youth work—including the diverse work of self-governed youth organizations, the responsive practice in open youth work, dedicated projects with young people, and street-based 'detached' youth work. While we, as youth workers, see huge merit in our adaptability and responsiveness to the many issues identified or presented in young people's lives—and how that adaptability shines through in the contributions to this text—we can also look chaotic and unfocused, as if 'anything goes.' As the editors of this volume rightly say in their conclusion, "the risk in this adaptability is that youth workers become all things to all people and valued by no one." The quest for common ground that anchors the diversity of youth work may be elusive but must not be abandoned. For Dana Fusco and Mike Heathfield, as they reflected on the contributions they have brought together, the common ground is clear. Youth work in all its forms shares, for them, a common mission to illuminate and interrupt inequality and injustice achieved through connecting with young people; connecting young people to their communities, traditions and generations; and forging connections between agencies and other practitioners who, too often, otherwise engage with young people in atomized and isolated ways. In those different ways, they illuminate and challenge the inequity and unfairness that is endemic in the lives of young people and interrupt it in partnership with, and through the participation of, young people in order to establish practice and action that will broaden horizons, extend experience and opportunity, and construct new prospects and pathways for the young.

So many thoughts, at so many levels, came into my mind as I read through the contributions to this book. Any book of this kind will, inevitably, produce that effect: the broad concepts invoked ('youth,' 'inequality,' 'youth work') in a debate at a *global* level cannot fail to do otherwise.

The consequence in any foreword will, of course, be a broad-brush commentary, posing questions, highlighting issues, advancing observations. The first is to do with the notion of inequality in a world currently suffering from the proclaimed triumph of neo-liberalism and through which rampant free market capitalism produced the global economic crash of 2008. Yet it is a world also rebalancing its resources—perhaps—on account of the growing economic and demographic power of the 'BRICS' countries.

Whatever the complexities of these macro-analyses of the production and distribution of resources, one thing is reasonably clear—it is the young who have disproportionately borne the brunt of contemporary economic, demographic, health- or faith-based uncertainties and unpredictabilities in life across the globe. All this, coupled with the environmental dangers that are more and more apparent (not least in terms of their effect on food, water, and energy scarcity) have, arguably, produced greater general inequality yet, paradoxically, perhaps a greater sense of equality amongst the young who share the prospect of having to deal with these legacies.

But as every youth studies textbook spells out resoundingly, the young are not a homogenous group. While some young people are relatively protected from precarity and challenging futures, many more are experiencing, albeit in different ways, a sense of social dislocation that, as research routinely confirms, leads frequently to a spectrum of pyschosocial disorders, from offending and suicide to bulimia and depression.

One asks, then, how young people—in their many different contexts, with their very different economic and personal resources—can be supported in confronting and navigating the challenges they face. The answer, an increasing number of voices assert, is youth work. But whose voices, and what kind of 'youth work'?

Both adult professional protagonists for 'youth work' and their younger counterparts from representative youth bodies may sometimes, if quite inadvertently, fail to give sufficient voice to those groups of young people positioned so far on the margins that their needs and aspirations are silenced: LGBTQ young people, street kids, those leaving public care systems, young people with disabilities, young people in geographically remote areas (like those on Gaya), those within youth justice systems. Youth policy initiatives, including the development of many forms of youth work, may—whatever their expressed intentions around 'reach' and social inclusion—patently fail to get anywhere near those groups, the resources sucked up instead by other young people who are more alert to the opportunities presented and more eager to take part. When that happens, inequalities are exacerbated, not reduced. This is what Filip Coussée has described as the youth work paradox: Youth work, too often, works for those young people who arguably do not need it, and fails to reach those who do. We should also not forget that 'youth work,' like 'youth policy' more generally, is not necessarily an intrinsic good. As I said at the 1st Global Forum on Youth Policies in 2014, my own interest in the idea of 'youth policy' started when I witnessed young people in my youth center experiencing the effects of the intentional, but negative, policies developed in 1979 by Margaret Thatcher's UK government towards young people. Punitive measures were put in place; positive initiatives were curtailed or withdrawn. Likewise, at the 1st European Youth Work Convention in 2010, the image of youth work as a 'dog' (looking for a home) was projected. But what kind of 'dog': companion, defender, guide? A general consensus was that, whatever young people wanted, public authorities were looking for a 'retriever'—to go out and find 'disaffected' youth and return them to the fold. That is hardly the youth work that progressive practice seeking to address and perhaps even redress multiple forms of inequality aspires to.

But it doesn't have to be like that. Street work, issue-based work, advocacy and advice work, and project work under the broad banner of youth work can, if approached appropriately, extend its reach in order to ensure communication and contact with young people on the margins. It can help those young people to make more sense of their predicament, equip them with capacity and self-belief to realize individual potential as well as connect them to the collective struggles that their particular group, and those with shared experiences of oppression and exclusion, will have to endure. As with all forms of youth work, that engagement can struggle with and juggle the tensions of providing both a *forum* for association and self-discovery and a *transit zone* on the pathways to adulthood.

Youth work should not rest on the back foot. Too often, I hear it being defended for its preventative value (in reducing school exclusion, criminality, or substance misuse), and too little do I hear it being lauded for its promotional role (in fostering engagement with civil society, equipping young people with a range of pro-social skills, and contributing to social change). Anyone involved in direct youth work (as I was, as a part-time paid youth worker for 25 years, preceded by some 10 years as a volunteer) knows it delivers a variety of impacts, albeit differentially, on different groups, on different issues, and over time. Funders and politicians invariably cry 'prove it,' and we embark on the quest for the holy grail: the basket of indicators that will evidence our outcomes.

Funders and politicians completely miss the point. The obsession with 'outcomes' is misguided and misplaced. The journey taken by youth work with young people is a complex, incremental journey shaped both by extraneous pressures and the internal dynamics and demands of the groups concerned. The journey, at different points, melds groups, issues, methods, and contexts—relocating setting, taking on new participants and losing others, introducing new topics, and so forth. We should accept that poor youth work—practice that cannot twist and turn, professionally and reflectively, to this multiplicity of demands—will very likely produce poor outcomes. Equally, however, we need to assert and advocate philosophically that good youth work is unlikely to produce poor outcomes but holds the promise of making a contribution, sometimes relatively minor and modest, sometimes of considerable significance, to the personal life trajectories of individuals, their engagement with communities, civil life and citizenship, and their participation in the labor market. At the heart of such professional, reflective practice lie the values of social justice, equality, democracy, mutuality, and reciprocity.

Michael Heathfield and Dana Fusco, together with the contributors to this book, have taken their particular lens to these and other questions and issues. They invoke the idea of youth work as a prism through which, depending on how the light is refracted, the practice produced gives rise to differential attention to themes such as morality, development, community, democracy, and—in an increasingly unequal globalized world—challenging oppression and injustice.

The book provides, as Heathfield outlines, "global stories about effecting change when adults and young people work together on shared agendas for positive change." Other remarks throughout the text particularly resonated with me, striking a chord with both my intellectual and academic commitment to youth work and with memories of my own modest practice at a local, community level in the second-largest city in England. Importantly, it is noted that youth work rejects the dominant discourse of adolescence (of young people as trouble, needing to be contained and excluded from mainstream participation) and embraces young people as active agents in their own (and others') lives. The choice of the term 'youth' is, as Sercombe argues, "significant, deliberate and political." Elsewhere in the book, it is stated that "youth are both the products and agents in which they engage, and these reciprocal processes provide a basis for development—both their own and that of others." They are both taught, and take, the knowledge and skills to understand the challenges and inequities they face.

We have to be careful not to overstate the capacities of youth work; there is a risk of it becoming "overspun but undersung," as a colleague of mine once described the UK's reforms in youth justice at the turn of the millennium. Civic actions may flow from youth work practice that raises consciousness, but these may ultimately have limited effect on overall structures and processes of oppression and inequality. That should not devalue the role of 'youth work'; as Fusco registers, so long as further critical questions are asked, the contribution of youth work is in fact elevated—even if concrete answers to those questions are elusive or, indeed, impossible to determine. Youth work may often be shaped, to some extent, by funding that is inextricably tied to wider social, economic, and political contexts, but that is part of its challenges and dilemmas: to understand and 'purposefully consider' the broader context in which youth work and specific programs and practices are situated.

The way these things play out through youth work in different parts of the world is the substance of the narratives and analysis in this book. As the long-standing Organisational Secretary of the global network of youth researchers (International Sociological Association Research Committee 34), I am delighted that so many of our members have contributed to the debates in this volume, and I thank my good friends and colleagues, Mike and Dana, for their energy and dedication in seeing the manuscript through to its completion. The book should be read as a powerful reminder and wake-up call about the place and role of youth work in building services by, with, and for young people, cultivating the possibilities and potential of civic and political activism, and contributing to economic and social development. And at its heart must always be the need to confront the 'deeds of dismissal,' where young people's capacities, competencies, and contributions are so often summarily and cursorily devalued and dismissed, to which many of the authors, some explicitly, others more implicitly, allude.

Howard Williamson
Treforest, Wales, February 2015

Acknowledgments

Mike Heathfield would like to thank Pete and Betty, who provided a childhood home brimming with love, lessons, and learnings on equality and justice.

Section I

Understanding Young People, Inequality, and Youth Work

1 Youth and Inequality

Weaving Complexities, Commonalities, and Courage

Michael Heathfield

Without courage, we cannot practice any other virtue with consistency. We can't be kind, true, merciful, generous or honest.

—*Maya Angelou (1928–2014)*

Maya Angelou found the courage. After dropping out of school at age 14, she went on to courageously meet her potential, becoming a master of six different languages, a Civil Rights activist, a world-renowned poet, a recipient of a Presidential Medal of Honor, a recipient of a Presidential Medal of Freedom, and a Grammy Award winner, to note just some of her accomplishments. She went on to give to the world her gifts, even when the world was not so sure it wanted them.

It is both a complex and simple world in which we live. While some things remain much the same, other aspects of our world make rapid changes or illusionary shifts. There are global gifts and risks, but these are neither shared globally nor with much equity. Indeed, for some young people, real lives are constrained by circumstances beyond their control. The rich and powerful demonstrate increasing reach into everyday lives across the borders of simple geography, while surprising numbers of young people have never had the opportunity to leave their own neighborhood, village, or country, either physically or virtually. Alongside lack of opportunity comes self-doubt and loss of hope. Those who have, believe they deserve even more; those who don't have, believe the world belongs to 'others.'

Inequality is not an equal opportunity player. The warp and weft of inequality matches the complexity of our human tapestry and weaves an uneven cloth of diverse coarseness. As Stewart (2013) notes:

> Race is the basis for clearly significant groupings in the United States and Brazil, indigeneity in Guatemala and Peru, religious differences in many Middle Eastern countries, and ethnicity and religion in many sub-Saharan African countries. Quite often multiple groupings are relevant in which case inequalities need to be assessed along these multiple demarcations—for example, religion, ethnicity and gender may all be highly pertinent groupings in some countries. (p. 15)

Diversity can be acknowledged and celebrated. Sometimes it is. Yet, it is also often the site of injustice and discrimination, the bedrock on which many inequalities are built. Human heterogeneity sources the social structures, the communal and personal capabilities, and the outcomes around which both social progress and vast arrays of inequalities coalesce in complex ways. Yet, it also strikes us that inequality has a consistency in the ways in which it impinges on lives in that inequality often resides in three locations: it can reside within, between, and across peoples. We have learned that often all three locations can be in operation at any one time. Inequality can reside within the self, and for many people a conscious and deliberative process is required to uncover, name, and guard against this enemy within. Internalized self-hatred is a subjugating force of considerable power and reaches into many lives in hugely differential contexts. In her essay, "Eye to Eye: Black Women, Hatred, and Anger," Audre Lorde explores how racism, sexism, and homophobia have led to Black women "metabolizing hatred like daily bread" (Lorde, 1984, p. 152). Yet, our identities and experiences are rarely individual, even if that is how they are perceived, and most importantly, judged by others. Research that emphasizes "individuals' experiences with these social identities, rather than the systems of power and oppression that shape these experiences" (Nunez, 2014, p. 85) has been sharply criticized for leaving a gap in our understanding of how hegemonic structures influence life opportunities.

Our lives are predominantly lived in relationships, making and sustaining connections that build our communal humanity beyond our own internal processes and biology. These connections between selves are a second site in which inequalities can thrive and wound, whether at the family, group, or larger social level where social capital is accrued (Putnam, 2001). Yet these social groupings can also sustain and visit injustice on their own people and those who are judged to be 'other.' Being both an outsider and insider is a common duality that resides within many. At the largest scale, injustices premised across selfhoods provide us with a human history littered with mass discrimination and oppression. In the early 1800s, the U.S. government enforced a westward march of 16,000 Native Americans known as the 'Trail of Tears' (Cherokee Nation, 2014). Thousands of people from numerous tribes had their ancestral lands taken from them; thousands did not survive the march to what is now Oklahoma, and the newly designated 'Indian Lands' provided an inhospitable home for the original Americans. Unfortunately, our human history is littered with parallel examples of mass subjugation and denial of rights and violence. Worse, many of these examples target and/or directly impact young people who then can never meet their potential even when they maintain, as Angelou inspires, their courage to be 'kind, true, merciful, generous or honest.'

The weave of inequality, in both its complexities and its commonalities, needs to be deeply unpacked if we are to make any social progress henceforth. Multi-level analysis is critical, particularly in understanding relationships between inequality, poverty, oppression and violence.

The weave is thick, coarse, and not always put together in predictable patterns. For instance, we understand that violence and poverty are often intertwined. Yet, homicide is more closely associated with poverty and income inequality than rape and robbery are (Hsieh & Pugh, 1993). Further, we can find among the poorest of cities very low homicide rates, e.g., Kolkata in India (Sen, 2008). As Amartya Sen (2008) reminds: "Given the co-existence of violence and poverty, it is not at all unnatural to ask whether poverty kills twice—first through economic privation, and second through political carnage" (p. 8). Over a decade ago, Kenneth Maton, in his presidential address of the Society for Community Research and Action, stated: "The social problems of our day—violence, children living in poverty, children raising children, school failure, divorce, and demoralization—are each deeply embedded within multiple levels of the environment" (Maton, 2000, p. 26). To truly begin to understand the base of inequality requires consideration of multiple factors and identities, including understanding how social categories are interrelated given the multiple and sometimes fluid identities that people hold, understanding arenas of influence or embodied practices, and understanding the history of both (Nunez, 2014).

It is with this backdrop of understanding, as well as with courage and humility, that we approach this text, attempting to uncover the interconnected, intersubjective underpinnings of social injustice in the context of youth, youthhood, and social education practices with young people. In this opening chapter, we uncover for transparent interrogation our response to three questions: Why inequality? Why youth? Why now? Fusco will explore youth work in greater detail in a following chapter examining whether youth work is, has been, and can be a powerful response to youth's location in inequitable social and economic arrangements.

WHY INEQUALITY?

Aspects of identity and social/cultural location provide the nexus for human growth and development. They are also key coordinates around which unequal treatment is intentionally and unintentionally focused. Inequalities founded around capital, gender and sexuality, ability, race, and ethnicity have taken much different journeys and traveled with uneven speeds. There have been substantial shifts around some fundamental inequalities, while others have moved at a much slower pace. Some of these shifts are transnational in their nature, while others are more clearly bounded by their specific geography and culture.

Unequal Capital

Beyond doubt, the most significant transnational shift has been the huge transfer of wealth from the poor and middle classes to an increasingly small financial elite. Breaking historic records, the top 10% of employees in the United States earned more than half of the country's entire income in 2012 (Saez, 2013), with similar patterns in other westernized areas. The World Economic Forum (2014) predicted that widening income disparities was the second greatest worldwide risk in the coming 12 to 18 months. The startling headline of 2014 was that 1% of the world's population owns almost half of global wealth.

Concentrated wealth has a dehumanizing impact on the minimal few who receive it and the mass of people who toil in its creation. This is a global pattern defining the nature of our globalized economy and the result of neoliberal policies that have found a welcoming home in many westernized democracies. They are also policies promulgated by financial institutions with transnational reach and are attached to Western capital when it is offered to support post-colonial countries seeking to grow their economies. Deregulated global markets have a deeply penetrating reach that disregards many notions of statehood and independence. The increasing wealth gap dominates all else because it is a key driver of many social ills and injustices. Much of the current societal ills are occurring in relation to policies and politics that privilege marketization over collective responsibility, purchasing power over distribution of power, and individualism over community and citizenship.

We are not alone in expressing concern for the lives affected by this relatively new and unprecedented shift in the global concentration of wealth. Global capital has always transcended the simple boundaries of geography and culture. But now the pace of wealth transfer to the very few is exponential. In 2014, the newly elected Pope spoke to his worldwide flock of some 1.2 billion Catholics, placing this income disparity in a religious frame in which a 'new tyranny, is born from the ideologies defending the absolute autonomy of the marketplace. Whatever new religious messaging is now emanating from the Vatican, it is abundantly clear that the espoused ideology will have a sharper focus on poverty and inequity, wherever it is found. The impact of concentrated capital on poor communities and how highly contextualized social justice imperatives can both mediate and challenge injustice is a key concern for this text. Income inequality is a foundational issue, but it is always also entwined with other significant social factors that lend vital importance to the specific contexts and cultures in which people strive, thrive, or struggle to survive.

We often assume poverty is the cause of society's ills: that those who grow up poor are more likely to become pregnant as a teenager, drop out of high school, have mental health issues, be obese and prone to violence. But, poverty is a proxy for a complex and interwoven tapestry of factors including lack of access to public transportation, affordable and safe housing, jobs, and the centrality of a quality education. As UNICEF data (2013) indicate, wealth is not the best indicator for predicting social wellbeing. This conclusion is consistent with other recent research that has revealed that negative social outcomes such as violence, drug abuse, and mental illness are most likely to occur not in poor countries but in less-equal ones, i.e., in societies with the largest gaps in wealth equality (Pickett & Wilkinson, 2011). However, we hesitate to rely on economic explanations alone.

Unequal Gender and Gender Preferences

A second marker of inequality that has also moved with unprecedented speed in some contexts is the legal and social recognitions afforded lesbian, gay, bisexual, and transgendered people. This is an inequality in which culture, context, and geography do indeed set boundaries that seem more impermeable. As a global inequality, framed through a lens of human rights, this issue has moved the arc of equality much faster in some democracies than any other social movement has achieved over much longer periods of time. In some corners of the globe, lesbian, gay, bisexual, and transgender rights are on the agenda, but the agenda is one of state-sanctioned violence and the denial of the basic right of survival. Concurrently, we have nation states that have broken the monolithic power of heterosexuality to confer childrearing, pension, estate, and marriage rights to same-sex couples (*The Guardian*, 2014).

Inequalities around sexual identities are always enmeshed within patriarchy and the policing of highly gendered expectations, and we can see that both first-wave and second-wave Western feminism have impacted inequality in uneven and unexpected ways. America has yet to have its first female president, a gendered ceiling that has been broken in many countries and continents for some considerable time. Despite decades of equal-pay legislation, American women still earn considerably less than their workplace equivalent male counterparts, are under-represented in national government, and have barely penetrated the upper echelons of the business community. This pattern is also one that replicates itself across the globe. Sexual violence against women such as rape, gang rape, forced prostitution, and genital mutilation are global ills that tragically are still subject to male-dominated policing and judicial system prejudices that decimate the lives of victims for a second time if they attempt to seek justice and equality. This still-dominant reality for women sits alongside the progress that some nations have made in workplace and familial policies that support family lives, broadening opportunities for both men and women to transcend more traditional boundaries. Inequalities by gender are differentially experienced by women of different race, ethnicity, class, and sexual preference.

Unequal Race and Ethnicity

The recent American political experience has also taught that investing hope heavily through one simple aspect of inequality, such as racial identity, has proven that change is a much more complex operation. Entrenched systems of power maintain, regroup, and react and thus are always also at play in maintaining a status quo that serves their interests. We have yet to see if gender will also distract from the complex fundamental changes required to begin to reduce inequalities that impact millions across the globe. What you see is only one aspect of what you get. As will be seen in this text, race and ethnic identities are boundaries that seek to define future pathways for many young people across the globe. The tracks of colonialism have carved deep fissures in many nations, with racial and ethnic groups subject to numerous injustices that resonate beyond their specific contexts because they have unfortunately familiar contours. Yet, some of the same racial and ethnic identities are global in their utilization of these very same identities for building communities, resisting injustices, and building capacities that prejudice self-determination, ownership, and shared social progress. There are global commonalities, for example, with gender, identity and statehood. In Germany, the complex balancing of dual identities plays out for Turkish youth (Koydemir, 2013) and young women in Bolivia build stronger identities through their human rights work (Gervais, 2011). In Canada, values are transmitted through motherhood roles for immigrant Salvadorian young women (Carranza, 2012).

This is not an unremitting picture of gloom. Nor are we fatalists about the power and impacts of these large systems and their hegemonic reach. In this text, we highlight global stories that indicate change can occur at the internal, group, and national level when adults and young people work together on shared agendas for positive change, when they find the courage to build pathways for meeting their own potentials.

WHY YOUTH?

We grown folks have a very long and rather well-documented history of messing up things for our offspring and future generations in general. On a global scale, it seems unclear if the grown folks can do enough to stop the whole planet from overheating and destroying all of us. Hundreds of years of industrial progress has given us a catastrophic carbon legacy while there are some of us still challenged to even acknowledge the scale of our damage. Despite seniority and wisdom on our aged team, it is debatable whether we can truly muster the scope of responses required to stop, let alone reverse, the impact of our neglectful actions. This is a global risk that transcends boundaries and will pay little attention to the age of its victims. Yet, we do little to open pathways for our young to be agents of their own lives, let alone agents of social change.

Youth represents an unequal age. On its own it can be a source of inequality and ageist practices. Add to it any of the above social factors and the picture becomes increasingly difficulty to sketch. Lareau's (2003) well-known text *Unequal Childhoods* places social class as a key factor in understanding inequality. Her intensive case-study approach with Caucasian and African American families revealed that regardless of ethnicity, middle-class parents place priority on what she calls 'concerted cultivation'—or the cultivation of children's talents through a variety of structured activities. Through this 'cultivation,' dominant values, such as time management and teamwork, are also learned. Yet, we also know that in many locations survival takes precedence over cultivation.

According to the World Health Organization (2011), 41% of annual homicides globally occur among youth between 10 and 29 years of age, with young males in particular as both the perpetrators and victims. Sexual assault among young females is also a huge concern, with up to 24% of females reporting that their first sexual encounter was forced. Often, such violence among and between young people is surrounded by hostile and volatile adult worlds. Driven by culture, religion, and ethnicity, old wounds seem barely healed and provide subcutaneous damage that can quickly be opened to revisit past carnage. The crisis in Gaza in 2014 provides a vivid illustration that the subjugation of one culture by another can never result in social justice, and adults on either side will continue to engage in heinous and violent acts against humanity.

Yet, it is often the young who are the focus of our attention and gaze. There are global patterns to be found in the specific labels applied to young people, for example, 'at risk' young people in Israel (Krumer-Nevo, Barak & Teichman, 2007) and Hong Kong (Chui & Chan, 2012). 'NEET' young people (not in education, employment, and training) have transcended their European ancestry and can be found throughout the UK (Jones, 2012) and now in South Africa (HRDSA, 2014). 'Delinquent' still has global currency that reaches from Japan (Matsuura, 2011) to the U.S. (Office of Juvenile Justice and Delinquency Prevention, 2014) and into Africa through colonial powers (Fourchard, 2006). Unfortunately, such labels (and the programs that follow) have been insufficient in describing the issues they are attempting to explain, are based on a perspective that privileges deficits and additive solutions over more complex calculative understandings, and are woven together as universal solutions with little youth or community participation.

For both of us, *Youth and Inequality in Education* demonstrates that there is considerable global injustice that singles out young people, as an externally proscribed class of people, for immoral treatment with regard to resources, voice, opportunity, and real change. These are the deeds of dismissal. In many countries, the rights and needs of young people are dismissed with a common range of tools that have always been used by those with power to control and disappear those judged not worthy of full citizenship, potential, and contribution. The deeds of dismissal limit potential, deny rights, silence voices of protest, segregate, label, dehumanize, and enshrine a distribution of power in which compliance appears the only means to escape the consequences of hegemonic resistance. We also see that such dismissal often occurs within the guise of adult protection.

Too many adults cling to the power and status that is culturally endowed to their adulthood without a critical awareness that this sense of being has an etiology not enshrined in biology or natural development. As we will see, segregated age categorizations, with attached and assumed characteristics, are historical and cultural artifacts with surprising malleability as well as confounding consistency (see Sercombe, this volume). Biology has very little to do with some of the common assumptions and prejudices that we attach to humans segregated by age. But many of these assumptions maintain their cultural power across historical periods and geographic boundaries. Many of them focus on young people and the transitions they make from childhood to adulthood. Many of them are simply erroneous.

We know that too many young people experience their transition to adulthood with considerable uncertainty, compromise, challenge, and contradiction. Anxiety among young people is at an all-time high (Twenge, 2006). Young people's experience of this transition to adulthood is, of course, mediated by class, culture, location, and the complex interplay of aspects of identity compounded by both local and global influences. But, there are also broader social realities at play. There is a long and dominant history in some cultures of dismissing the young, especially those who may be fast approaching the permeable boundaries of adulthood within distinct cultures. There is also a long and dominant history in some cultures of embracing the young, coaching them and providing them with intentional apprenticeships for their future roles and responsibilities. As we shall see in this text, industrialism and imperialism are larger forces more likely to eradicate some of these transitional processes and dismiss localized cultures that have long-embedded traditions in which young people are worthy community participants with key roles and responsibilities.

The adult world builds professional and semiprofessional responses to militate against a panoply of injustices at the individual, group, and structural levels. Again, here there are patterns in the language, signs, and symbols used to label, investigate, and discuss the initial youth phenomena and the diverse responses, their methodological bases, and their differential impacts. Human systems of 'care' for children and young people register very strongly in this respect (see Stark, Bancroft, Cholid, Sustikarini & Meliala, 2012 for a study of community-based Indonesian systems; Wessels et al. (2012) for Sierra Leone; and Mears, Singletary and Rodgers (2011) for Kenya). Programmatic local responses to young people from adult systems also have a reach beyond profession and geography. We can find mentoring programs in Rwanda (Makubutera, Bizimana, Owoeye & Nzayirambaho, 2013), teen-pregnancy hotlines in Taiwan (Wei, Chen, Su & Williams, 2010), and hip-hop interwoven with feminism in Austria (Franz, 2012).

Racial and ethnic groups, gender identifications, neighborhoods, and class origins are often intertwined with ascribed labels and their attendant stereotypical characteristics. Thus, in youth work with specific groups of dismissed young people, language, identity, and voice also become common characteristics of practice that reach across vastly different contexts and communities. In youth work that is embedded with a commitment to social justice, a critical analysis and practice of more liberating power dynamics is central. This indeed may be another characteristic that transcends hugely different contexts in which 'an ecology of adversity' (Kabiru, Beguy, Ndugwa, Zulu & Jessor, 2012, p. 13) is an appropriate descriptor concealing a vast territory of difference.

The political and professional responses to the deeds of dismissal now frequently include newer strategies for 'inclusion.' It appears that any critical exploration of the dominant social order, which systemically excludes so many young people, is largely absent from these initiatives. The Pathways for Youth (2013) initiative seeks to coordinate U.S. federal programs and outcomes for the most disadvantaged youth. This policy includes a 20-item list of issues facing young people. Poverty and injustice do not appear in this list of social ills. They remain unspoken while they are hugely present among these articulated youth issues. So Pathways for Youth, intending to spur a new focus on coordinated federal intervention, fails to name the primary social contours that constrain the lives of so many young people. This, of course, should perhaps not be unexpected, since 'Hope' and 'Change' were hugely successful political marketing slogans. As Noam Chomsky articulately notes, there was never an intention to identify hope 'for what' or change 'what to' (Chomsky, 2009).

In short, young people not insulated by social and economic capital look out upon the world and see environmental and economic tragedies, health and education crises, and failed political systems. They see that this is the world adults have created and are leaving to them. These are the very same adults who simultaneously ask young people for their trust in that they will be cared for, their patience for life-long learning, and abeyance for youths' vulnerability. These are the very same adults who have created the devastating social and political conditions that have created crisis, poverty, and increasing inequality, systemically removing significant pathways to secure and successful futures for many youth.

How do we expect them to know themselves and their futures and to trust in their own courage to undertake those futures with some measure of success in such an adult landscape?

WHY NOW?

A watershed moment has been reached in the U.S. context in which the generational progress guarantee has been broken for young people. For the first time in U.S. history, a generation is not likely to do better than the generation of its parents. Despite having skills and credentials in hand, Generation Y is not likely to find the positions that will secure their futures. In fact, average incomes for individuals of this generation have been falling since 2008 (see http://www.westernjournalism.com/evidence-the-next-generation-will-not-be-better-off/). Successful young people completing higher education in the U.S. are saddled with unprecedented levels of debt that may never be paid off (Chopra, 2012).

There is no greater depository for the turmoil of injustice than in the lives of children and young people. There is no greater hope for action and change than in those very same lives. A staggering 43% of the world's population is under the age of 25. In countries with the lowest economic growth, the youth bulge has been the greatest (ICDP, 2014). If we use the Population Reference Bureau's (2014) definition of youth as those aged between 10 and 25, the proportion of the youth population in the countries represented in this text is as follows: Portugal (16%); United Kingdom (18%); United States (20%); Australia (20%); New Zealand (21%); Peru (28%); Morocco (28%); Malaysia (28%); Philippines (31%); and Jordan (32%). Beneath these numbers are future trajectories. In many countries across the world, these young people have two significantly different future pathways. As Hanan Morsy, lead economist of the European Bank for Reconstruction and Development, noted in a recent speech, "Youth are the engine of growth for the future" in many countries while also being hugely more impacted by economic crises and thrown into "the vicious cycle of poverty and social exclusion" (Morsy, 2014).

To frame many young people only as victims of systems of injustice would also be a partial and erroneous portrait of the realities of many young lives. Globally, however, the power of young people to impact change on the social order of their nation has taken many forms recently and provides a reminder to powerful adults that, en masse, young people can provide the energetic catalyst for change (Herrera, 2014; Laiq, 2013; Taft & Gordon, 2013). Laiq (2013) uses rich case studies of Egyptian and Tunisian young people who have played significant roles in their respective revolutions against oppressive regimes. She also captures the challenges they face when seeking to participate in civil society or government organizations to sustain the important move towards social justice they have been instrumental in creating. What this research points to is the tension between the immediacy of street activism and the slow pace of institutional reform when young people are systemically included. Young people were at the heart of the largest-ever street demonstration in Hong Kong in July 2014, expressing their concern about independence from Chinese rule and the requirement for voting rights (Bradsher, Forsythe & Buckley, 2014). Young people's groups were very well represented in The People's Climate March of September 2014, which coordinated over 2,000 separate marches across the globe (see Mech, 2014) for a Canadian example of coordinated activism and participation). The inclusion of 16- and 17-year-olds in Scotland's recent referendum on independence from the United Kingdom helped achieve an amazing voluntary voter turnout rate of 85%, with young people being one of the largest demographic groups voting a somewhat surprising 'no' on the question of independence (BBC, 2014).

In the U.S., the 2011 Occupy Wall Street protest did not have one simple mission because it encompassed so many concerns about our postmodern neoliberal society. Occupy Madison Build is now building houses for the homeless in Wisconsin, while Occupy Wall Street members are still pursuing legal cases against the NYPD for their actions in Zuccotti Park. Indeed, the City of New York has now paid out over $1 million to Occupy activists to settle court cases arising from police actions. An amazing coalition of New York law school clinics provided the detailed analysis of these egregious infringements of the human right to protest and free assembly (Knuckey, Glen & MacLean, 2012). A Democratic mayor of New York was elected in 2014 by a staggering 73% of those voting on a platform that expressly emphasized the huge disparities of wealth evident in a 'tale of two cities' and a need to change oppressive stop-and-frisk policing policies that were disproportionately used against New York's young people of color.

Young people have been at the heart of many recent movements to challenge dominant orthodoxies and oppressive regimes (Bloom, 2012; Ginwright, Noguera & Cammarota, 2006; Harvey, 2013; Welton & Wolf, 2001). Some movements clearly begin in reaction to 'mega-capitalism': the Occupy Movement, the Tiny House movement, free shared media, open-source software, and even bike lanes in urban areas. Most of these begin as individuals seeking liberation from the cost (fiscal as well as spiritual cost) of living and end up as trends and then movements. These groups of people with common concerns begin to live beyond 'markets' and then create new 'markets' defined around their own collaborative ideologies. Youth involvement and activism has not just been driven by reaction to vast economic injustice. There have been numerous drivers, often pulling together various strands of protest around the panoply of collective human concerns. In Eastern Europe, the collapse of the Soviet empire brought many changes across the region, and in many of these newly independent nations young people played significant roles in protest, activism, and making demands for far-reaching change. Here again uniformity of view, purposes, and outcomes is hard to find, and young people across the region had different views and values about the formal collapse of Soviet domination (Nikolayenko, 2011). Nor should we pretend that young people are only agents for change in the service of a more just world. In a recent speech, "Youth and the Politics of Disposability in Dark Times," Henry Giroux (2013) stated that today's "youth are facing a crisis unlike that of any other generation" due to market fundamentalism as an erroneous ideology for solving social problems. As Van de Walle, Coussée and Bouverne-De Bie (2011) note, the complex realities of young people's lives do not necessarily support this simple transition, nor unearth the deeply embedded capitalist meme.

Dismissed young people have also been recruits in oppressive movements and can still be pressed into this reaction, especially as cultural or ethnic differences are utilized as a popular tactic for inciting animus and violence. Disconnection from family and community can also lead young people to join groups which intentionally provide identity, structure, and belonging while serving oppressive and violent purposes (Mann, 2005). This is also a global pattern that unfortunately continues to repeat itself. So the explicit purpose of youth activism becomes exceptionally important. The European elections of May 2014 saw the rise of both right-wing and left-wing parties as older, more established parties lost their luster for an increasing percentage of the European electorate.

There is a movement in the literature, and in practice, which establishes a more complex lens of how social justice, change, and national progress can be made and assessed. Amartya Sen's writing addresses complexity and reframes inequalities or 'unfreedoms' on a global scale while establishing that there are baseline freedoms from which all others emanate or are eliminated. Concepts such as social cohesion, wellbeing, and social progress are now receiving considerable attention and are able to provide more meaningful quantifications that progress our understanding of the complexities of the world in which we live. All of these move away from the simpler economic formulas and measures through which progress has been traditionally measured. Sen's work (1999, 2008) provides the fundamental groundwork on which newer frames provide stronger analytical devices to capture complex social constructs, such as social progress. These newer multifaceted concepts and their associated tools should serve as more appropriate measures for capturing the shifts in a range of common inequalities. The Social Progress Imperative uses complex data sets to produce fascinating findings, presented as their Social Progress Index (Porter, Stern & Green, 2014). Indeed, this very new initiative is used as an important organizational structure for key elements of this text.

The world, unfortunately, offers far too many examples of how little value is placed on the lives of children and young people. Yet, this occurs alongside examples of how significant change can occur when power, politics, and people work together to solve what may seem like intractable human problems. Mozambique's continued economic growth, reduction of poverty rates, reduced infant mortality, and increase in school participation shows changes can occur (World Bank, 2014). Malawi has had great success with a program that brings into the teaching profession more women who are committed to teaching in rural environments where the need is greatest (UNESCO, 2014). Over 1,500 women, including Ivo Morales, the president of Bolivia, attended a G77 (representing the governments of 133 nations) meeting in which the call to end discrimination, inequality and injustice was centrally located within extending the rights of women and girls (Puri, 2014).

It seems to us that the time is now to raise the issues: that 'youth' is a social category decided upon by adults and resting on ageist assumptions, rules, and policies that young people have had no role in designing or deciding upon; that interwoven inequalities hit young people the hardest, directing and re-directing lifelong and generational trajectories that are often associated with categories of race, gender, and class; that at least some young people are tired of the world that their entrusted adults have created and are reclaiming spaces locally and globally that they can transform for new futures and possibilities; that youth work offers renewed possibility as a credible player in allying with young people to reshape the future (see Fusco, this volume); and that we have found interesting stories globally that tell a complex and fascinating tale that we hope is just one in a large body of literature currently emerging with inequality in its headlights.

CONCLUSION

Our concern here is with the warp, the weft, and the utilization of the human tapestry.

Our warp comes from parentage, heritage, and biology and links our past, present, and future together in ways we can learn to understand once we begin to explore the threads that tie us to our past culture. Our weft is the connections we build, the links and relationships we make as we manufacture our own life story beyond that which is given to us. While vertical and horizontal strands are the central substance of all cloth, they are never alone in how the material is made, looks, used, or judged. There is artistry, craft, and purpose within each bolt of material in which commonality and difference coexist. The roughest cloth may provide shelter against nature's wildest elements, and the finest silk may only be used to display wealth and status to all who observe. We must understand the human histories of these weaves, but more so we must understand that to make social progress, to start a new human tapestry—one that is built on diversity, acceptance, and courage—we will require a new loom. Inequality will one day be understood as the complex interplay among multiple drivers, including economic, political, cultural, institutional, religious, ethnic, gender, and social class, but the end game will only be reached when we have the courage to remember that "considerations which are relevant to a claim for inequality are moral considerations, they are special moral claims" (Raphael, 1946, p. 122).

REFERENCES

Adamson, P. (2013, April). *Child well-being in rich countries: A comparative overview* (Innocenti Report Card 11). Florence, Italy: UNICEF Office of Research.

BBC. (2014). *Generation 2014*. Retrieved from http://www.bbc.co.uk/programmes/p01gf7rb

Bloom, D.E. (2012). Youth in the balance. *Finance & Development, 49*, 6–11.

Bradsher, K., Forsythe, M., & Buckley, C. (2014, July 1). Huge crowds turn out for pro-democracy march in Hong Kong, defying Beijing. *The New York Times*. Retrieved from http://www.nytimes.com/2014/07/02/world/asia/hong-kong-china-democracy-march.html?_r=0

Carranza, M.E. (2012). Value transmission among Salvadorian mothers and daughters: Marianismo and sexual morality. *Child and Adolescent Social Work Journal, 30*(4), 311–327.
Cherokee Nation. (2014). *Cherokee nation*. Retrieved from http://www.cherokee.org/
Chomsky, N. (2009). Crisis and hope: Theirs and ours. *Brecht Forum speech*. Retrieved from http://www.democracynow.org/2009/7/3/noam_chomsky_on_crisis_and_hope
Chopra, R. (2012). *Too big to fail: Student debt hits a trillion* [Web log post]. Retrieved from http://www.consumerfinance.gov/blog/too-big-to-fail-student-debt-hits-a-trillion/
Chui, W.H., & Chan, H.C. (2012). Outreach social workers for at-risk youth: A test of their attitudes towards crime and young offenders in Hong Kong. *Children and Youth Services Review, 34*, 2273–2279.
Fourchard, L. (2006). Lagos and the invention of juvenile delinquency in Nigeria, 1920–60. *The Journal of African History, 47*, 115–137.
Franz, B. (2012). Immigrant youth, hip-hop, and feminist pedagogy: Outlines of an alternative integration policy in Vienna, Austria. *International Studies Perspectives, 13*(3), 270–288.
Gervais, C. (2011). On their own and in their own words: Bolivian adolescent girls' empowerment through non-governmental human rights education. *Journal of Youth Studies, 14*(2), 197–217.
Ginwright, S., Noguera, P., & Cammarota, J. (Eds.). (2006). *Beyond resistance! Youth activism and community change: New democratic possibilities for practice and policy for America's youth*. New York, NY: Routledge.
Giroux, H. (2013). *Youth and the politics of disposability in dark times*. Speech presented at McMaster Centre for Scholarship in the Public Interest, Ontario, Canada.
The Guardian. (2014). Lesbian, gay, bisexual and transgender rights around the world. Retrieved from http://www.theguardian.com/world/ng-interactive/2014/may/-sp-gay-rights-world-lesbian-bisexual-transgender
Harvey, M. (2013). *How long will I cry: Voices of youth violence*. Chicago, IL: Big Shoulders Books.
Herrera, L. (Ed.). (2014). *Wired citizenship: Youth learning and activism in the Middle East*. New York, NY: Routledge.
HRDSA. (2014). *Challenges facing youth who are Neither in Employment, Education nor Training (NEET) in South Africa*. Retrieved from http://www.hrdcsa.org.za/latest/content/challenges-facing-youth-who-are-neither-employment-education-nor-training-neet-south
Hsieh, C., & Pugh, M. D. (1993). Poverty, income inequality, and violent crime: A meta-analysis of recent aggregate. *Criminal Justice Review, 18*, 182–202.
ICDP. (2014). *ICPD global youth forum*. Retrieved from http://icpdbeyond2014.org/key-events/view/13-icpd-global-youth-forum
Jones, H. (2012). Youth work practice in England. In D. Fusco (Ed.), *Advancing youth work: Current trends, critical questions* (pp. 157–172). New York, NY: Routledge.
Kabiru, C. W., Beguy, D., Ndugwa, R. P., Zulu, E. M., & Jessor, R. (2012). "Making It": Understanding adolescent resilience in two informal settlements (slums) in Nairobi, Kenya. *Child & Youth Services, 33*, 12–32.
Knuckey, S., Glen, K., & MacLean, E. (2012). *Suppressing protest: Human rights violations in the U.S. response to occupy Wall Street*. New York, NY: NYU School of Law, Center for Human Rights and Global Justice. Retrieved from http://chrgj.org/wp-content/uploads/2012/10/suppressingprotest.pdf
Koydemir, S. (2013). Acculturation and subjective well-being: The case of Turkish ethnic youth in Germany. *Journal of Youth Studies, 16*(4), 460–473.

Krumer-Nevo, M., Barak, A., & Teichman, M. (2007). Inclusion and its implementation: Youth workers' perspectives on an experimental social-business initiative for 'at-risk' youth in Israeli community centers. *Vulnerable Children and Youth Studies*, 2(3), 257–260.

Laiq, N. (2013). *Talking to Arab youth: Revolution and counterrevolution in Eygpt and Tunisia*. New York, NY: International Peace Institute.

Lareau, A. (2003). *Unequal childhoods: Class, race and family life*. Berkeley, CA: University of California Press.

Lorde, A. (1984). Eye to eye: Black women, hatred and anger. In A. Lorde, *Sister outsider: essays and speeches* (pp. 145–175). New York, NY: Crossing Press.

Makubutera, A., Bizimana, J. D., Owoeye, O., & Nzayirambaho, M. (2013). Correlates of psychosocial outcomes among youth heads of households participating in mentoring programs: A study among Rwandan youths from Bugesera District. *Vulnerable Children and Youth Studies, 8*, 49–59.

Mann, M. (2005). *The dark side of democracy: Explaining ethnic cleansing*. Cambridge, UK: Cambridge University Press.

Maton, K. (2000). Making a difference: The social ecology of social transformation. *American Journal of Community Psychology, 28*, 25–57.

Matsuura, M. (2011). Youth corrections in Japan: Family-like settings for delinquents with the experiences of child maltreatment. *Child and Youth Services, 32*(4), 281–285.

Mears, M., Singletary, J., & Rodgers, R. (2011). Strategies for supporting orphans and vulnerable children: An exploratory study of an exemplary model of care in Kenya. *Child and Youth Services, 32*(4), 286–302.

Mech, K. (2014, September 9). *Why Canadian youth are participating in the People's Climate March* [Web log post]. Retrieved from http://tarsandssolutions.org/member-blogs/why-canadian-youth-are-participating-in-the-peoples-climate-march

Morsy, H. (2014, 25 March). *Marginalization and inequalities facing youth* [United Nations Webcast]. Retrieved from http://webtv.un.org/search/marginalization-and-inequalities-facing-youth/3391083602001?term=marginalization#full-text

Nikolayenko, O. (2011). *Citizens in the making in post-Soviet states*. New York, NY: Routledge.

Nunez, A. M. (2014). Employing multilevel intersectionality in educational research: Latino identities, contexts, and college access. *Educational Researcher, 43*(2), 85–92.

Office of Juvenile Justice and Delinquency Prevention. (2014). *About OJJDP*. Retrieved from http://www.ojjdp.gov/about/about.html

Pathways for Youth. (2013). *Draft strategic plan for federal collaboration*. Retrieved from http://www.findyouthinfo.gov/docs/Pathways_for_Youth.pdf

Pickett, K., & Wilkinson, R. (2011). *The spirit level: Why greater equality makes societies stronger*. New York, NY: Bloomsbury Press.

Population Reference Bureau. (2014). *Youth data sheet 2013*. Retrieved from http://www.prb.org/pdf13/youth-data-sheet-2013.pdf

Porter, M. E., Stern, S., & Green, M. (2014). *Social progress index 2014*. Washington, DC: Social Progress Imperative.

Puri, L. (2014, June 9). First decolonisation, now depatriarchilisation. *Inter Press Service News Agency*. Retrieved from http://www.ipsnews.net/2014/06/first-decolonisation-now-depatriarchilisation/

Putnam, R. (2001). *Bowling alone: The collapse and revival of American community*. New York, NY: Simon & Schuster.

Raphael, D. D. (1946). Equality and equity. *Philosophy, 21*, 118–132.

Saez, E. (2013). *Striking it richer: The evolution of top incomes in the United States*. Retrieved from http://eml.berkeley.edu/~saez/saez-UStopincomes-2012.pdf

Sen, A. (1999). *Development as freedom*. New York, NY: Anchor Books.

Sen, A. (2008). Violence, identity and poverty. *Journal of Peace Research, 45*, 5–15.
Stark, L., Bancroft, C., Cholid, S., Sustikarini, A., & Meliala, A. (2012). A qualitative study of community-based child protection mechanisms in Aceh, Indonesia. *Vulnerable Children and Youth Studies, 7*, 228–236.
Stewart, F. (2013). *Approaches towards inequality and inequity: Concepts, measures and policies* (Office of Research Discussion Paper No. 2013–01). Florence, Italy: UNICEF Office of Research.
Taft, J.K., & Gordon, H.R. (2013). Youth activists, youth councils, and constrained democracy. *Education, Citizenship & Social Justice, 8*(1), 87–100.
Twenge, J. M. (2006). *Generation me: Why today's young Americans are more confident, assertive, entitled—and more miserable than ever before*. New York, NY: Free Press.
UNESCO. (2014). *Education for all global monitoring report*. Retrieved from http://www.unesco.org/new/en/education/themes/leading-the-international-agenda/efareport/reports/2013/2013-report-epub-en/#256
Van de Walle, T., Cousée, F., & Bouverne-De Bie, M. (2011). Social exclusion and youth work—from the surface to the depths of an educational practice. *Journal of Youth Studies, 14*(2), 219–231.
Wei, H., Chen, L., Su, H., & Williams, J.H. (2010). A multi-method evaluation of the teen pregnancy hotline in Taiwan. *Journal of Child Adolescent Social Work, 27*, 213–229.
Welton, N., &Wolf, L. (2001). *Global uprising: Confronting the tyrannies of the 21st century: Stories from a new generation of activists*. Gabriola Island, BC, Canada: New Society Publishers.
Wessels, M.G., Lamin, D.F.M., King, D., Kostelny, K., Stark, L., & Lilley, S. (2012). The disconnect between community-based child protection mechanisms and the formal child protection system in rural Sierra Leone: Challenges to building an effective national child protection system. *Vulnerable Children and Youth Studies, 7*(13), 211–227.
World Bank. (2014). *Success stories from Africa*. Retrieved from http://blogs.worldbank.org/africacan/african-successes-one-pager#1
World Economic Forum. (2014). *Global agenda outlook*. Retrieved from http://www3.weforum.org/docs/WEF_GAC_GlobalAgendaOutlook_2014.pdf
World Health Organization. (2011). *Youth violence: fact sheet*. Retrieved from http://www.who.int/mediacentre/factsheets/fs356/en/

2 Youth in a Global/Historical Context

What It Means for Youth Work

Howard Sercombe

In 1986, almost thirty years ago now, Ian Hacking wrote a classic essay entitled "Making Up People" (Hacking, 1986). The argument was that human identities are not 'natural,' but that from time to time social processes—perhaps political, perhaps administrative—call into being a new kind of person, or a new possibility of 'how to be' for people. The argument is an extension of Michel Foucault's analysis of 'the constitution of the subject' (Rabinow, 1991), which suggests that human beings live through a sense of self and subjectivity that then shapes their lives and their responses and relationships. These selfhoods or subjectivities emerge within particular historical and political locations and are formed in the context of relations of power, which will allow, facilitate, even demand certain ways of being, and proscribe, condemn, or marginalize others.

Youth is like that. Youth is not a 'natural' category, if there are any such categories. Some societies, it appears, have not felt the need to have a youth category at all (Epstein, 2007; Seig, 1976). For those that have, youth has meant different things (Schlegel, 2009a). The point of entry and the point of exit from the youth category has been different, both with respect to age and the symbolic indicators that mark the individual as now a youth, now no longer or not yet a youth. The roles and duties of young people have been different. Their deemed attributes and capacities have been different. The connection with other social roles and institutions has been different. Even within a particular society, these things are subject to change (often rapid change) over time. If there is anything biological about youth/adolescence, it is not the biology that determines what it means to live as a young person in any given social and historical context.

A discussion of youth and youth work, especially one that attempts to think globally, needs to be located within an understanding of the historical and political contingency of its subject. The meaning of youth, and therefore the meaning of youth work, changes constantly. In a globalizing and modernizing world, societies that may have had well-established, even ancient traditions for welcoming the rising generation face radical changes in the nature of what it means to be young and in the relationship of the young to the society as a whole. To the extent that these are a function of modernization, they may reproduce the processes that occurred in the 19th and 20th centuries in the industrial economies of the West. But the nature of the globalized economy in the 21st century will also present particular challenges, not the least of which will be the pace of change itself. Especially (but not only) for the BRICS economies (Brazil, Russia, India, China, South Africa) this change is happening over decades, not centuries.

For Foucault, the constitution of any subject population involves several parallel processes. The population in question needs to be separated from the rest of the population in order for the distinction to become stabilized. In the medieval period, for example, madness (Foucault, 1961) was understood either in terms of demonic possession or through the identity of the fool or village idiot and generally tolerated as a sometimes amusing, sometimes annoying part of community life. In the 17th century, during a process he calls 'the Great Confinement,' mad people, along with various other populations such as street prostitutes, orphans, people with disabilities, alcoholics, the destitute, or the unemployed, were cleared off the streets and put into workhouses or asylums. Once the subject population is separated out from the general population, they are available for inquiry, for the development of knowledge about them. Driven by the Royal Societies and the new culture of scientific discovery, ways of life that had always evoked curiosity were now contained in the fishbowl of the workhouse. 'Gentleman' scholars built reputations and wrote books on the scientific nature of a range of human conditions, and madness gradually became reconfigured as mental illness, treatable by a new specialism in medicine, that of psychiatry.

Finally, the subject identity is adopted by the subject population (Rabinow, 1991). The emergence of a subject identity and the containment of a population within a subject identity is never a one-way process imposed from the top or impressed by a ruling class (Foucault, 1984). No process of power ever is. It is a function of extended negotiation in which the subject population collaborate (not necessarily willingly) in their subjection, in the constitution and adoption of the subject identity. A mad person learns how to be a mental patient and what is required of them in that role.

Each of these movements is constituted in discourse: in Foucault's example, the discourse of psychiatry. Other discourses survive or co-exist: the discourse of demonic possession is still active, and there is still a range of practitioners who will do exorcisms or 'deliverance ministries' with mad people. But psychiatry becomes the official discourse, its practitioners are credentialed, and it is able to make extensive claims on social resources to support the continuing work of psychiatry. The constitution of youth as a subject follows the same kind of process (Sercombe, 1996). Notwithstanding the cultural and historical diversity noted above, throughout the 19th and 20th centuries, through the Industrial Revolution and the massive political, scientific, and cultural changes that came with the emergence of capitalism, a standard way of 'doing youth' has emerged in the West. With the global penetration of capitalism and modernity, that way of 'doing youth' interacts with, absorbs, and rolls over other social and cultural forms.

THE CREATION OF A YOUTH CATEGORY

> The adolescent was invented at the same time as the steam engine. The principal architect of the latter was Watt in 1765, of the former Rousseau in 1762. (Musgrove, 1964, p. 33)

So Frank Musgrove begins his chapter on the historical development of adolescence, entitled "The Invention of the Adolescent." The date of origin is, of course, a contrivance: modern notions of youth emerged fitfully and gradually amidst the fractures and innovations of the Industrial Revolution. The notion of the 'invention' or 'discovery' of adolescence (employed also by Epstein, 2007; Gillis, 1974; Griffin, 1993; Magarey, 1978; Muncie, 1983; Springhall, 1984) serves rather to indicate that adolescence was one of those innovations: that a historical break occurs in the concept of youth around about this time. In Europe, the timing of this break coincides in a general way with the gradual transformation from feudalism to capitalism.

To speak of the 'invention of adolescence' is not to say that there was no conception of youth, and no youth problematic before 1762 (Schlegel, 2009b). Natalie Zamon Davis's (1971) work on the behavior of groups of apprentices in the preindustrial period notes the concerns about rowdyism and public nuisance that such groups evoked. Pearson (1983) likewise discusses complaints about delinquency and misrule back to the 17th century. Springhall (1984) references the opinion of Shakespeare's shepherd in *The Winter's Tale*, that "there were no age between sixteen and three and twenty, or that youth would sleep out the rest, for there is nothing in between but getting wenches with child, wronging the ancientry, stealing, fighting" (p. 21).

But this was not 'adolescence.' In medieval France, according to Aries, "people had no idea of what we call adolescence, and the idea was a long time taking shape" (1962, p. 29). 'Youth' referred to a much longer phase, to the prime of life, to the period between childhood and old age, to the age of vitality and productivity. Like Aries, Gillis describes a stage of youth in the preindustrial period significantly different from modern conceptions. Concentrating more on socioeconomic than cultural data and picking up a four-stage life span as typical, he suggests that,

> imprecise as youth's boundaries were, there being no universally recognised age-grading as in today's society, its sociology was relatively clear. Beginning at what seems to us to be a very young age, children began to separate from their families and to go to live in other households. By 14, a great majority would be living in a state of semidependence, either as servants in households, apprentices living in their masters' homes, or students boarding away from their families. It was precisely this detachment from family that gave preindustrial youth its peculiar structure and meaning. (Gillis, 1974, p. 2)

The major institutional component of the preindustrial family, as writers like Gillis, Kett, and Pearson have described it, is the practice of apprenticeship or service. Young people lived in the household of their employer until they could establish an independent household by marriage or inheritance, usually in the late 20s for men, late teens for women. This institution, established by law (young people without any visible means of support could be forcibly placed into apprenticeship under Poor Law provisions) constituted the major 'dividing practice' concerning youth in the preindustrial period, under which the young were kept dependent and subservient and excluded from full membership of the commonwealth. It follows that the prerequisite for the emergence of modern concepts of youth is the erosion of this institution.

The Emergence of School and the Erosion of Intergenerationality

Gillis (1974) suggests that this happens on several fronts at once. Middle class families were the first to abandon the practice of 'sending out' their children to live and work in others' households. The motivation was that the increasingly socially mobile and therefore status-conscious middle classes had much to fear in the association of their offspring with servants, especially when the servants were (as was increasingly the case) 'hired help.' Increasingly, in the early 19th century, the children of the middle classes were being kept at home: girls until they married, boys until they went to university or some professional apprenticeship could be negotiated for them. But birth rates among the middle classes as well as others were still high and places in the professions or in education expensive and scarce. There was therefore a chronic oversupply of candidates for too few positions.

Faced with a crisis of unemployment among the educated young, and attendant moral panics around 'bohemianism' and political rebellion in the 1830s and 1840s (at least for young men), the middle classes increasingly began to exert control over their young. The major institution for achieving this was the school. In the early to middle 19th century, this discipline was mostly applied to young men. At this point, although local private schools for girls existed, girls were still usually controlled within the patriarchal home, perhaps with a private tutor (Dyhouse, 1981). Increasingly, however, towards the end of the 19th century, boarding schools for the daughters of the middle classes were also becoming popular. Kett's study of adolescence in America records equal numbers of girls and boys in the lower grades of early 19th-century elementary schools, though numbers dropped radically once girls entered their teens (Kett, 1977). However, teaching as a profession itself was rapidly emerging as an acceptable occupation for young women, and Kett records that by the end of the 19th century, girls outnumbered boys in the secondary schools because of the gateway to school teaching that secondary education provided.

As the role of the school in controlling a now extended period of dependence, *in loco parentis*, became critical, schooling itself became standardized and subject to official control. In effect, the reformed boarding school of the 19th century (which became the model for the establishment of schools more generally) was a total institution, guaranteeing the discipline of the bodies of the sons of the middle classes. This 'dividing practice,' this confinement of the bodies of young men in an institution dedicated to their control and training, was an essential component of the constitution of youth.

Among the children of the working classes, the 19th century followed a different, but parallel history (Gillis, 1974). Factory manufacture, by the provision of an independent wage, offered opportunities for young people to establish independent, landless households and to enter into marriages of their own volition. The ability of older children to move out and establish independent households was limited only by their earnings, and the Factory Commissioners in England in 1842 reported that many fourteen-year-olds were independent in this way. These social and economic changes were recognized in the law, which abolished compulsory apprenticeship in England in 1814, thus signaling the demise of the dominant technique for the control of youth in the preindustrial period (Musgrove, 1964).

The early period of mechanization required the labor of children and young people in large numbers. However, as technology improved, labor inputs decreased, and a higher skill level was required of those workers that were employed. Increasingly, positions of skilled labor were monopolized by adult men, and while the unskilled labor of women and juveniles was still required, it became more dispensable (Musgrove, 1964). Youth unemployment, and the attendant anxieties about social disorder, began to loom larger in the public consciousness (Magarey, 1978).

Meanwhile, upper-middle-class social reformers began to intervene in the administration of government as it applied to the children of workers. The Factory Acts of 1833 in England required "that no child under the age of 9 was to be employed in cotton mills or factories and hours were to be limited to eight hours a day for those under 13 and twelve hours for those under 18. They also stated that factory owners should provide some elementary schooling . . . for their juvenile employees" (Muncie, 1983, p. 32).

For a long time, these measures were evaded or actively resisted both by employers and parents. However, as the technological advances in manufacturing towards the end of the 19th century began to take root, juvenile unemployment became more and more of a concern as the combined influence of the Factory Acts and changing work practices meant that a significant and growing number of young people were neither at work or school. With most working families needing both parents at work, "a growing number [of children] were thrown onto the streets to become vagrants or to engage in petty criminality" (Muncie, 1983, p. 32). "They are idling in the streets and wynds; tumbling about in the gutters; selling matches; running errands; working in tobacco shops, cared for by no man . . . " said James McCosh in 1867 in a paper to the National Association for the Promotion of Social Science (cited in Musgrove, 1964, p. 76).

As the 19th century progressed, the middle-class solution to the youth problem was increasingly and coercively applied to the working classes. Compulsory, universal education (to the age of 13) was instituted in 1870 in Britain. At first, this set of practices, as it applied to the working class, only affected younger children, and even them only erratically, when schools could be provided and their labor spared. Over the age of 13, many young people were workers (Bessant, 1993). Notions of age were still out of focus, as schools themselves dealt often with students of all ages in one classroom on an individual tuition basis (Barcan, 1988). As in America (Kett, 1977), elementary school and secondary school populations were not distinct, 7- and 17-year-olds were in the same class, with no guarantee that the 17-year-old would be further advanced in his or her studies.

The expanding reach of elementary schools, larger schools, and the adoption of class methods of teaching progressively clarified age-cohorts: 9-year-olds studied with 9-year-olds, 11-year-olds with 11-year-olds. At the level of discourse, this division was accompanied by an increasing discrimination between different ages, a more elaborated and structured 'age-system' (see Gesell, 1956) that increased its reach with every extension of the school-leaving age.

However, the real moment in the establishment of the division of adolescence was the secondary school. While schools had separated children and young people from adult life, secondary education separated youth from children. As the 20th century progressed, the school-leaving age was progressively extended to 14 (in 1918 in England, mostly in response to fears about working-class delinquency (Barcan, 1988) then to 15 (1947 in England). Fees for secondary education were abolished in Britain in 1944 (Roberts, 1983), leading to a significant growth in the number of young people staying at school, especially in the groups which had been marginal to the secondary school experience—the working class, and young women. The age of compulsory education has been progressively raised in the 20th century, first to 14, then to 15, and in Britain, to 16, largely in response to moral panics over the rate of juvenile crime or as a way of mopping up excess youth labor (Lawson & Silver, 1973; Polk, 1993). The establishment of secondary schools and the institutionalization of working-class young people within them were not finalized until the post-war period. Curiously, this was the point at which the new discourse of the 'teenager' became established (Doherty, 1988).

Since the late 1980s, in most Western jurisdictions, the school-leaving age has been increased to 18 either by law or by a combination of inducements (like the payment of allowances) and penalties (e.g., increasing credentialism, making employment difficult for young people without upper high school education). With each policy move to increase the effective school-leaving age, the length of time spent in adolescence increases. With it, the collateral damage arising from the ever-increasing delay and ambiguity in achieving adult status and from the marginalization of those young people who for whatever reason are not able to successfully bind to the school as a system and as a means of progression also increases.

The construction of youth in the modern sense is, then, an effect of the secondary school. The secondary school divides young people from other adults and from children, weakening relationships across generations and strengthening age-peer relationships. It isolates young people from economic and political processes, creating dependency. Participation in these processes is through simulation: the simulations of student representative councils and youth parliaments, the simulations of real-world problems through school curricula, the simulation of reproduction through dating and the high school romance. The artificial construction of age-graded cohorts in an institutional environment creates a distinct youth culture, disconnected from the economic and political processes of the wider society and limited to resolving its tensions through the 'magical' expression of subculture (Cohen, 1980).

THE CREATION OF YOUTH WORK PRACTICE

Youth work emerges within this process as a response to social problems created by it. It is significant that the precursors to modern youth work practice emerge precisely during the period we have been discussing: the Glasgow Young Men's Society in 1821 (Anon, 1837), the YMCA in 1844 (Stern, 2011), and the Boys Brigade in 1883 (McFarlan, 2000). Their purpose was inextricably tied to the processes of the industrial revolution: the growth of cities and the independent movement of young people to the cities to work; the disconnection from traditional kin and clan relationships and from long-standing rural traditions; age-streaming and the strengthening of peer relations; the displacement of younger teenagers from the workforce and the problem of young people who were neither in school or at work. They provided recreational space, resources such as libraries or reading rooms for informal education, opportunities for adventure and the possibility of looking beyond the limited horizons of inner-city industrial slums, the opportunity to organize and generate resources, and the absorption of excess time and energy on the part of young people now under-employed and economically displaced. Sometimes a product of the initiative of young people themselves, sometimes an intervention in order to mitigate social damage or distress, youth work is characterized by its attempt to restore a sense of agency for young people and to work with them within their social context to negotiate their ambiguous and often prejudiced economic and political status. (This is not to say that youth work has not been part of the process of containment and control of the young, or that alone among the institutions youth work has been a beacon of liberation and democracy for young people; but in the commitment to young people's agency, there is a structural limit to the extent to which youth workers have been able to be part of repressive policy.) Movements such as the YMCA and Scouting caught on rapidly—we might now say virally—across the industrializing world. The conclusion that they did so because they were (and are) socially necessary is difficult to avoid.

The idea that youth or adolescence is constructed by processes of *exclusion* is one which gradually becomes more common in work around the youth question through the 1960s and 1970s. Eisenstadt's *From Generation to Generation* (1956) (probably the most developed functionalist analysis of the youth question) argues that age differentiation and the existence of age grades is not a "universal, biologically conditioned (inescapable) fact" (p. 21) but that the social organization around age grades is culturally specific and functional for each society. Eisenstadt is therefore specifically concerned with the social conditions for the emergence of youth groupings rather than the youth category as such. Briefly, according to Eisenstadt, the role of age groupings in universalistic (i.e., non-kin-based) societies is to integrate familial structures with broader political and economic structures, a role which has become necessary because kin-based and familial institutions have become private, divorced from economic and political functions and therefore at risk of social disintegration. However, their efficacy in doing so depends on a number of preconditions:

> (a) the extent of harmony between the values and orientations of age groups and the basic institutional norms and values of the social structure—compatibility which manifests itself in . . . smooth interaction with other generations, (b) the extent to which the identity evolved through participation in age groups is adequate for attaining full social status; and (c) the extent to which fully institutionalised roles are allocated to age groups (Eisenstadt, 1956, p. 276/277).

In other words, 'youth' as a social structure is functional if the age grouping has clear economic, political, and ceremonial roles. Eisenstadt argues that failure in any of these areas will result in deviant youth groupings, including unorganized or organized groups of delinquent youth, youth organizations of revolutionary movements and parties, and rebellious (countercultural) youth movements. Further, he suggests that the above prerequisites routinely do not obtain in modern societies: values are heterogeneous, youth groups do not guarantee adult accreditation, and youth groups have no clear social role. In other words, youth groups are excluded from economic and social participation. As a result, youth groups have routinely become deviant. However, Eisenstadt argues that this deviance may "make youth groups one of the most important channels through which the numerous changes of modern societies takes place" (1956, p. 323).

There are generational effects also. Generational analysis, pioneered by Karl Mannheim in the 1920s (Mannheim, 1952/1923), looks at how birth cohorts are shaped by the particular social-historical environments in which they grow up. Conceptually, a generational structure is different from an age structure: you grow out of an age grouping while you are part of your generation for life: the baby boomers are an example. Generations are located in particular points of history, under particular conditions of social change, and this can create particular dynamics in the relationship between adults and the young. For example, Musgrove (1964) agrees with the general analysis that modern adolescence is a product of the practice of excluding young people from economic and political life. But in particular circumstances the age-structure effects of this (in which structures systematically exclude young people from participation) may be compounded by generational effects (in which the generation that holds the power at a particular historical moment excludes and represses the rising generation). Often, the social force behind this, he argued, is demographic. In the period in which he was interested (the inter-world-war period) decreasing mortality led to a kind of bottleneck in the circulation of positions of political and economic power: incumbents were simply living much longer than they used to. This created pressure from below, and the older generation, in order to protect their own positions, instituted controls of various kinds to artificially keep young people in positions of economic and political dependence. At different points, this might include extending the qualifications required to take up positions (including compulsory minimum ages for qualification), extending qualifying periods, establishing quotas of various kinds, requiring other kinds of service such as compulsory military service, or creating different classes of employment, so that members of the rising generation are kept in insecure, mobile, poorly resourced, or temporary positions.

While the establishment of youth work as a practice is universal across modern societies, its resourcing and institutional location has been highly variable. In many places, youth work has operated predominantly (sometimes almost exclusively) within the voluntary sector, often within faith-based organizations, while parallel professions such as teaching and social work have moved to the center of state-based governmental processes. Where youth work does have official recognition and professional training can be variously located within social work, sport and recreation, education, and health or justice systems, inhibiting the development of international collaboration and a consolidated professional discourse, organization, and knowledge base. Youth work is variably seen as a separate and distinct entity or a subset or specialism within other professional identities such as social work or education. Levels of official recognition and support vary, and even in places such as the United Kingdom, where official support for youth work practice has been comparatively high, youth work is seen officially as optional in a way that school-based education is not. Notwithstanding this uneven profile, and the fragmented discursive landscape through which youth work is constituted as a practice, it is possible to recognize practices and organizations across all modern societies that support work that is recognizably youth work and descriptions of the practice that consistently return to the principle of the young person as agent and that engage young people within their social environment.

YOUTH AS A SCIENTIFIC OBJECT: THE DISCOURSE OF ADOLESCENCE

The structural and institutional forces that progressively divided young people from the rest of their adult contemporaries and confined them in age-streamed cohorts created particular kinds of objects: the 12-year-old, the 15-year-old, the high school student. The institutions which contained them—the secondary school, the juvenile reformatory, the boys' club—also created opportunities for their observation and for the development of scientific knowledge about them. It was in this matrix that a new kind of person was made, to use Hacking's phrase: the adolescent.

The story of the development of the discourse of adolescence has been told by several commentators on the youth question, including Arnett (2002), Atwater (1983), Brake (1980, 1985), Epstein (2007), Griffin (1993), Muncie (1983), Murdock and McCron (1976), Muuss (1996), Smith (1976, 1981, 1983, 1984) and Springhall (1984). Universally, the story begins with G. Stanley Hall (1844–1924), and the publication of his two-volume work *Adolescence: Its Psychology and Its Relations to Physiology, Anthropology, Sociology, Sex, Crime, Religion and Education* in 1904. Muuss points to Hall as the "first psychologist to advance a psychology of adolescence in its own right" (1996, p. 20). Steinberg considers Hall "the 'father' of the scientific study of adolescence" (1993, p. 460). Atwater suggests that the "modern scientific study of adolescence began with . . . Hall" (1983, p. 20). While discourses of the lifespan and of youth were by no means absent from the preindustrial and pre-20th-century scene, Hall brings the subject of youth under the control of scientific discourse, claiming the term 'adolescent' to represent its new scientific status. In the process, the understanding of youth/adolescence is transformed from a category that is essentially social in character (to do with family, to do with economy, to do with status) to a category that is presented as an object for analysis and control. The publication of Hall's work may be seen as a historic moment in a discursive shift, which established a scientific discourse about youth, the scientific basis for the professional appropriation of the youth category (Murdock & McCron, 1976; Muuss, 1988; Smith, 1983; Springhall, 1984). Developmental psychology became the scientific basis for regimes of youth regulation in the school, the reformatory, and the modern family.

There is a degree of historical accident about how this process happens, and it could have happened differently. The new discipline of psychology was just emerging. Hall was granted the first American PhD in psychology, in 1878, after a number of years spent studying in Germany. Hall had a strong literary bent, and there were a number of literary and folk traditions about young people current in Germany at that time, including the *Wandervogel* movement and a number of angst-ridden teenage heroes in the literary works of authors like Goethe and Schiller. The key notion that adolescence is constituted by *Sturm und Drang* (storm and stress) originates in those sources. Hall's interests in education (his first job was as a schoolteacher, and his first lecturing position was in psychology and pedagogy) brought the new discipline powerfully into mesh with the expansion of the high school, which Hall himself actively promoted. As the first president of the American Psychological Association and the founder of the American Journal of Psychology, he was in a strong position to promote his ideas. There were other contenders: Sociology was emerging as a discipline at pretty much the same time, and anthropologists (notably Margaret Mead) were strongly interested in the teenage years and particularly in the social context of growing into adulthood. But the new discipline of developmental psychology became dominant in understandings of young people, and it continues to be.

Hall's theory was based on a popular (but spurious) idea from embryology that the development of the human fetus retraced the process of evolution. As the theory goes, the human embryo first resembles a single-celled organism, quickly develops into a multi-celled organism, then develops into progressively different members of the evolutionary tree like the fish and the monkey until the fetus becomes recognizably human. Hall extends this idea beyond birth, arguing that human behavior is ape-like in early childhood and hunter-gatherer-like in middle childhood. Youth/adolescence is the threshold of civilized manhood, in which the individual moves from the barbarian phase of adolescence, through a great deal of turmoil, into the pinnacle of evolution: civilized, European man.

The theory did not survive well. The biological assumptions were wrong, and the psychological elements were quickly overtaken by the experimental psychology movement and by Freudianism. But the key constitutive ideas (Foucault calls them the 'founding axioms') not only survived but also continue to shape our conception of the youth category. In a nutshell, the foundation left by Hall was a concept of adolescence as *a universal stage of human development, characterized by great struggle, in which the child metamorphoses into the civilized adult*.

Three axioms embodied in this foundation have been the subject of continued debate within psychology and also within sociology, which entered the discursive contest with the anthropological work of Margaret Mead. The first is the notion that the life span is a series of discrete stages, each qualitatively different, through which human beings pass in immutable order (though the timing is variable), and that adolescence is such a stage. The second is that this stage is characterized by turmoil, by struggle, by *Sturm und Drang*. The third is that this stage is inherent within the human and is thus universal across human societies. These three axioms have constituted the core of the discourse of adolescence, which has come to dominate the constitution of youth as a subject in professions like education, law and jurisprudence, social work, and psychology. Hall's contribution has also established psychology, specifically developmental psychology, as the dominant discipline for understanding the young.

What this means is that 'adolescence' cannot be said without invoking the idea of a discrete stage, biologically determined and characterized by trouble. Of course, it is possible to speak of youth without implying these things. There is a substantial research literature that shows that a discrete youth category is not universal across societies, that development is usually continuous rather than subject to big qualitative shifts and discrete stages, and that young people are usually pretty happy and get on well with their parents. But to speak of young people as regular people, with normal, rational reactions to their social circumstances, and who generally have good relationships with their friends and with the adults in their lives, places the speaker outside the dominant discourse. And while speech outside the dominant discourse may get a hearing, it generally struggles for traction and remains marginal, an interesting side dish.

Youth work has generally either rejected the discourse of adolescence or remained deeply ambivalent about it. The fact that the practice is called youth work rather than adolescent work and that we name our client as 'young people,' not adolescents, is significant, deliberate, and political. It also places us outside the main stream of power-talk about youth. Not that youth work is not about containment and control: it is. But the terms of that control (in principle at least) lie in the young person's own agency rather than in compulsion and repression.

The overall argument, then, is this: While many societies have institutions and practices that treat young people differently from children and from other adults, modernity has created a specific form in which young people are marginalized from economic production and compulsorily contained in age-specific cohorts within the secondary school. This containment has been progressively extended by the extension of the legal leaving age and by ever-increasing demands for credentials, which means that the effective leaving age now stretches into the late teens and 20s. Alongside this, the scientific discourse of adolescence has created a conception of youth as a discrete, biologically determined stage of life, characterized by turmoil and trouble. This discourse justifies the maintenance and extension of exclusionary structures, including differential pay rates and employment regulations, curfews, legalized age-based discrimination against the young, prejudicial policing, and a range of other practices. Youth work, in recognizing the personhood of young people beyond their objectification, works with young people to enable them to manage the conditions of their disenfranchisement, to both challenge those conditions and to achieve agency even while they stand. As such, the practice remains marginal to power and to official resourcing, especially compared to cognate professions in social work, teaching, and juvenile justice.

GLOBALIZATION

The discussion so far has centered on the development of modern concepts of youth and modern institutions for their containment and control, which emerged gradually over the 19th and 20th centuries in the West in response to the emergence of industrial capitalism and its attendant political and cultural expressions. It is important to recognize that the situation for young people in the West continues to change, to move. While the nominal youth population shrinks in the West as the population ages, the shift to a knowledge economy extends adolescence as the period of effective compulsory education increases into the 20s and 30s (Sercombe, Omaji, Drew, Love, & Cooper, 2002). 'Choice biographies' obscure structural inequalities faced by the young and hold them individually responsible for their own conditions through the choices about self-advancement that they have individually made (Woodman, 2009). The disproportionate impact of the global financial crisis (and attendant government austerity) on young people create new intergenerational tensions, especially in countries like Spain and Greece, where a relatively educated youth population faces 40%–50% unemployment (Population Reference Bureau, 2013). Even without the recession, intergenerational transfers from the young to the old through escalations in education fees and payments, generous welfare and pension benefits, rising housing prices, and the deferred cost of climate change create intergenerational tensions which are yet to manifest in open political conflict.

Globalization can mean a lot of different things. In this context, I want to draw attention to the process by which modern conceptions of youth as adolescence, created through the establishment and reach of secondary schooling and the scientific discourse of adolescence, are expanding across the world. In the process, a wide variety of established social forms involving young people and the process of welcoming young people in to the commonwealth are destroyed or compromised, and established codes for intergenerational relations are dismantled (Durham, 2004). It is not my intention to argue that these forms are superior to the modern form, or better for young people, or more conducive to human flourishing: Some will be, some won't, and at the level on which this paper operates, it is impossible to generalize. But we do know about the weakness of the modern construction and organization of the youth category and therefore for its wholesale adoption on a global basis. Briefly, some of those weaknesses are:

- The disconnection of young people from economic life and economic contribution
- The disconnection of young people from other workers of different ages

- The infantilization of young people, the contraction of their deemed capacities and amplification of their pathologies and risks
- The lack of a meaningful social role for young people, and their alienation from key social institutions
- The general pathologizing of young people, and the equation of youth and trouble
- Legal limits on young people's rights and powers
- Prejudicial treatment of young people in policing, justice, housing, employment, incomes, and social policy
- The scapegoating of young people for problems that belong to the social order as a whole
- Schooling as the only competent means of education
- The further marginalization of young people who do not do well at school or who for whatever reason do not fit the school as an institution and schooling as a process
- Indeterminate and ambiguous means of graduation out of the youth category.

The modernization of the youth category is happening unevenly globally. For example, 5% of girls and 11% of boys in Somalia are enrolled in secondary schooling. In Mauritius, the equivalent numbers are 89% and 90% (Population Reference Bureau, 2013). While increased enrollment in secondary schooling seems to be a key development goal everywhere, governments routinely struggle to keep the figures moving in an upward direction (The World Bank, 2013)—as, indeed, they did in the West until World War II. Nevertheless, the widening reach of secondary schooling, and through it the institutionalization of modern adolescence, is undeniable (Cole & Durham, 2007).

Other factors distinguish the contemporary global modernization process from that of the 19th and 20th centuries described above. The first is the speed of change. A process that took centuries in Britain and North America is happening in decades now. Traditional forms for the integration of young people are being dismantled at a similar rate, though of course many will continue to coexist with the institutions of modern adolescence, and communities will find adaptations and compromises (Durham, 2004). The second is the sheer size of the youth population. 200 years ago, the European population was still relatively small. The current global population is not. Young people between the ages of 10 and 24 comprise about 25% of the world's population: some 1.8 billion people. The ageing profile of Western nations, in which the 10–24 year old population averages around 17%, contrasts with Africa, where it averages 28% and is expected to double by 2050. Even in China, where the one-child policy has reshaped the demographic profile, 22% of the population is between 10 and 24: that's 300 million young people (Population Reference Bureau, 2013).

I have argued that the disenfranchisement of young people occurs across a wide range of contexts. However, as a gross measure of alienation and exclusion, the rate of unemployment and the numbers of young people neither in work or school is useful. Globally, the unemployment rate for 15–24 year olds across the five years from 2005–2010 was around 15%. But in places like South Africa, with 29% of its population between 10 and 24, around half are unemployed. Particularly interesting is the convergence between high unemployment rates and high levels of education. Among young people of university age in South America, 45% of young women and 34% of young men are enrolled in tertiary education. South America also lives with a rate of around 19% youth unemployment. I have already mentioned the situation with Greece and Spain, where tertiary enrollment rates of around 90% for Greece and 73% for Spain coincide with unemployment rates around 40%. South African tertiary enrollment is lower, but secondary school enrollment is high, and unemployment for its 15 million young people sits at around 50% (Population Reference Bureau, 2013).

I have argued above that youth work emerges as a socially necessary mechanism for addressing some of the problems created by the modern organization of youth and their downstream consequences. The current organization of the profession is firmly rooted in national, or even sub-national, prerogatives and has been resistant to internationalization. If the modernization of the youth category is, as I have argued, proceeding rapidly and globally, youth work will need to go global also.

REFERENCES

Anon. (1837). The Glasgow young men's society. *Young Men's Magazine, 1.*

Aries, P. (1962). *Centuries of childhood.* London: Cape.

Arnett, J. (2002). The storm and stress debate. In J. Arnett (Ed.), *Readings on adolescence and emerging adulthood* (pp. 6–16). Upper Saddle River, NJ: Pearson Educational.

Atwater, L. (1983). *Adolescence.* Eaglewood Cliffs: Prentice-Hall.

Barcan, A. (1988). *Two centuries of education in New South Wales.* Sydney: NSW University Press.

Bessant, J. (1993). *Constituting categories of youth: towards the 21st century.* Melbourne: National Centre for Socio-legal Studies, La Trobe University.

Brake, M. (1980). *The sociology of youth culture and youth subcultures.* London: Routledge and Kegan Paul.

Brake, M. (1985). *Comparative youth culture.* London: Routledge and Kegan Paul.

Cohen, S. (1980). *Folk devils and moral panics* (2nd ed.). Oxford: Robinson.

Cole, J., & Durham, D. (Eds.). (2007). *Generations and globalisation: Youth, age and family in the new world economy.* Bloomington, IN: Indiana University Press.

Davis, N. (1971). The reasons of misrule: Youth groups and charivaris in sixteenth century France. *Past and Present, 50,* 41–75.

Doherty, T. (1988). *Teenagers and teenpics: The juvenilization of American movies in the 1950's.* Boston: Unwin Hyman.

Durham, D. (2004). Disappearing youth: Youth as a social shifter in Botswana. *American Ethnologist, 31*(4), 589–605.
Dyhouse, C. (1981). *Girls growing up in late Victorian and Edwardian England.* London: Routledge and Kegan Paul.
Eisenstadt, S. (1956). *From generation to generation.* London: Routledge and Kegan Paul.
Epstein, R. (2007). *The case against adolescence: Rediscovering the adult in every teen.* Sanger, CA: Quill Driver Books.
Foucault, M. (1961). *Madness and civilisation.* London: Tavistock.
Foucault, M. (1984). *The history of sexuality: An introduction.* Harmondsworth: Penguin.
Gesell, A. (1956). *Youth: The years from ten to sixteen.* London: Hamilton.
Gillis, J. (1974). *Youth and history: Tradition and change in European age relations 1770-present.* New York: Academic Press.
Griffin, C. (1993). *Representations of youth the study of youth and adolescence in Britain and America.* Cambridge: Polity.
Hacking, I. (1986). Making up people. In T.C. Heller, M. Sosner, & D. Wellbery (Eds.), *Reconstructing individualism* (pp. 222–236). Stanford: Stanford University Press.
Kett, J. (1977). *Rites of passage adolescence in America 1790 to the present.* New York: Basic Books.
Lawson, J., & Silver, H. (1973). *A social history of education in England.* London: Methuen.
Magarey, S. (1978). The invention of juvenile delinquency in early nineteenth century England. *Labour History, 34*, 11–27.
Mannheim, K. (1952/1923). The problem of generations. In P. Kecksmeti (Ed.), *Essays on the sociology of knowledge* (pp. 276–322). London: Routledge & Kegan Paul.
McFarlan, D. (2000). *The Boys' Brigade: The adventure begins here.* London: The Boys' Brigade.
Muncie, J. (1983). *The trouble with kids today.* London: Hutchinson.
Murdock, G., & McCron, R. (1976). Consciousness of class and consciousness of generation. In S. Hall & T. Jefferson (Eds.), *Resistance through rituals* (pp. 203–207). London: Hutchinson.
Musgrove, F. (1964). *Youth and the social order.* London: Routledge and Kegan Paul.
Muuss, R. (1988). *Theories of adolescence.* New York: McGraw-Hill.
Muuss, R. (1996). *Theories of adolescence* (6th ed.). New York: McGraw-Hill.
Pearson, G. (1983). *Hooligan: A history of respectable fears.* London: Macmillan.
Polk, K. (1993). Reflections on youth subcultures. In R. White (Ed.), *Youth subcultures: History, theory and the American experience* (pp. 99–106). Hobart: National Clearinghouse for Youth Studies.
Population Reference Bureau. (2013). *The World's Youth: 2013 data sheet.* Washington: Population Reference Bureau.
Rabinow, P. (Ed.). (1991). *The Foucault reader: An introduction to Foucault's thought.* London: Penguin.
Roberts, K. (1983). *Youth and leisure.* London: George Allen and Unwin.
Schlegel, A. (2009a). A cross—cultural approach to adolescence. *Ethos, 23*(1), 15–32.
Schlegel, A. (2009b). Cross—cultural issues in the study of adolescent development. In L. Steinberg & R. Lerner (Eds.), *Handbook of adolescent psychology: Contextual influences on adolescent development* (Vol. 2, pp. 570–598). New York: Wiley-Blackwell.
Seig, A. (1976). Why adolescence occurs. In H. Thornburg (Ed.), *Contemporary adolescence: readings* (pp. 39–45). Monterey: Brooks/Cole.

Sercombe, H. (1996). *Naming youth: The construction of the youth category*. PhD thesis, Murdoch University, Perth.

Sercombe, H., Omaji, P., Drew, N., Love, T., & Cooper, T. (2002). *Youth and the future: effective youth services for the year 2015*. Hobart: National Clearinghouse for Youth Studies.

Smith, D. (1976). The concept of youth culture: a reevaluation. *Youth and Society*, 7(4), 347–366.

Smith, D. (1981). New movements in the sociology of youth: a critique. *British Journal of Sociology*, 32(2), 239–253.

Smith, D. (1983). Structural-functionalist accounts of youth. *Youth and Policy, 1*(3), 1–9.

Springhall, J. (1984). The origins of adolescence. *Youth and Policy*, 2(3), 20–35.

Stern, M. (2011). Real or rogue charity? Private health clubs vs. the YMCA, 1970–2010. *Business and Economic History On-Line, 9*. Retrieved from http://www.thebhc.org/publications/BEHonline/2011/sternpdf

The World Bank. (2013). *Progression to secondary school.* Retrieved from www.data.worldbank.org/indicator/SE.SEC.PROG.FE.ZS?display=default

Woodman, D. (2009). The mysterious case of the pervasive choice biography: Ulrich Beck, structure/agency and the middling state of theory in the sociology of youth. *Journal of Youth Studies, 12*(3), 243–256.

3 History of Youth Work

Transitions, Illuminations, and Refractions

Dana Fusco

> . . . In the spirit of those to whom social equality has become a necessity for further social development, so we are impatient to use the dynamic power residing in the mass of men, and demand that the educator free that power. (Addams, 1905, p. 53)

Inequality, and the disparities it creates, is often considered a matter rooted in economics, and it is. Yet, there is an uneven and complex relationship between a nation's wealth and opportunities that create more equitable social arrangements. Wealth alone might account for a society's provision of basic needs, basic education, and basic healthcare, but the picture gets far more complicated when issues of rights, freedom, and inclusion enter the scene (Porter, Stern & Green, 2014). Stated another way, *wealth does not guarantee that nations turn their economic success into social progress to make the lives of citizens sharply better than before, nor does it guarantee the creation of inclusive governance and civic structures that guarantee and protect those rights*. Those interested in a world that continuously strives towards more equitable and inclusive social arrangements must ask: If not wealth, then what? As an educator, my concern lies in the role of education as an awakener of critical consciousness, imagination, and deep intellectual pursuit. Education's role as a strategy for unraveling the complex entanglements that perpetuate inequalities and injustices is by no means a new or radical proposal. Educational models have for years been designed to put one on a path towards greater clarity around social issues: e.g., the Freedom Schools' aim to enhance the political participation of African Americans living in the oppressive South of the United States (McAdam, 1990); the critical pedagogy movement grounded in the work of Freire (1970); the Modern School tradition in many parts of Latin America beginning with Escuela Moderna in 1901 (latter Ferrer Schools in the United States—see Avrich, 1980); the 'unschooling' method (Holt, 1977); democratic schools in the United States like Sudbury Valley (Greenberg, 1992); and settlement houses, like Chicago's Hull-House (Addams, 1905), to name a few. These educational models support intellectual pursuit as a common tenet for individual freedom and choice, though some more explicitly use that freedom towards greater social good. Informal educational models run a similar gamut from promoting individual to collective development (Austria, 2006). Here, I ask specifically whether and how youth work, as an informal education strategy, plays a role in untangling the coarse weave of inequality such that young people are propelled towards imagining and then creating brighter, more inclusive tapestries for the future.

Hurley and Treacy (1993) define youth work as "the social education of young people in an informal context" (p. 1). That simple definition generally holds up well today. Yet, over its 200-plus years of anglophonic history, youth work has also shifted in both aim and approach. These shifts have largely been characterized as 'transitions' in the history of youth work (Butters & Newell, 1978). This chapter is specifically interested in how such 'transitions' illuminate (or not) inequality; that is, how over time youth work has framed the causes of inequality, how that framing has mattered for those who work with young people, and how youth work can be reclaimed as a powerful response for addressing and resolving inequalities and injustices in the lives of young people. The intent is not to protect youth work or to re-invent it as the modern hero, but rather to regenerate and elevate its capacity to reach its own potential as an important player in human/societal transformation. I consider how youth work at times in history refracts or illuminates social issues in relationship to its work with young people. In the sections to follow, I review the sociological analyses that have propped notions of 'transitions' as critical in youth work history. I then ponder how the notion of illuminations and refractions allow issues of in(equality) to be more intentionally maneuvered into and out of our frame of sight. I conclude with what this means for practitioners who are interested in keeping inequality illuminated.

YOUTH WORK: SOCIOLOGICAL ANALYSES

In the broadest sense, youth work has been characterized as falling into one of two sociological approaches: either as a strategy that aims to support young people to become productive members of existing society or as a strategy aimed towards changing the societal structures and oppressive mechanisms that recapitulate inequalities in the lives of younger generations (Butters & Newell, 1978; Cooper, 2012; Cooper & White, 1994; Hurley & Treacy, 1993). Functionalism and interpretivism are two main sociological theories that have been used to explain the first view, both with the expressed goal of maintaining social order (sociology of regulation). Radical humanism and radical structuralism operate out of the latter ideology representing the sociology of change. These four main paradigms in sociological thought (Burrell & Morgan, 1979) have been associated with various youth

Table 3.1 Sociological Underpinnings of Various Youth Work Models

	Sociology of Regulation		Sociology of Change	
	Functionalism	*Interpretivism*	*Radical humanism*	*Radical structuralism*
Butters & Newell, 1978	Character building	Social education repertoire	Radical paradigm	
Cooper & White, 1994	Treatment	Reform; advocacy	Non-radical empowerment	Radical empowerment
LISTEN, Inc., 2000	Youth services	Youth development	Youth leadership and civic engagement	Youth organizing

work practices (see Table 3.1). More recently, LISTEN, Inc. (2000) proposed a continuum of youth engagement from youth services (at the lowest end of engagement) to youth organizing (at the highest end of engagement). This more recent continuum also readily maps onto prior sociological analyses and helps draw out themes from the past to present-day youth work. Together, these taxonomies offer rigorous content and context for the analysis of practices with young people, practices that are often implemented without the benefit of broader and comparative critical awareness.

The Sociology of Regulation

According to Durkheim, the father of functionalism, education should help young people develop the skills and abilities needed to participate in a given political society (Durkheim, 1956). This socializing role of education supports social cohesion, assuming a stability of thought and behavior from one generation to the next through rational human action (Burrell & Morgan, 1979). One of the main youth work models that resides within this frame of understanding is character building (Butters & Newell, 1978; Cooper & White, 1994; Hurley & Treacy, 1993). Character building has long and deep historical roots in the United States. As early as 1872, Charles Loring Brace, founder of the Children's Aid Society in the United States, wrote of the concern of child poverty: "those who have much to do with alms-giving and plans of human improvement soon see how superficial and comparatively useless all assistance or organization is, which does not touch habits of life and the inner forces which form character . . . Education is a better preventive of pauperism than charity" (Brace, 1872, p. 350).

The times were tumultuous. Things were changing fast, and the period of youthhood was for the first time being created. Educating in order to "touch . . . the inner forces which form character" was a direct response to these times. The Industrial Revolution, urbanization, child labor laws, Romanticism, and the emergence of leisure all framed the real and perceived problems of working-class young people and fast-growing urban poverty. Organizations like the YMCA, founded in 1844 in London, and the Children's Aid Society, founded in 1853 in New York, provided food and boys' lodging to many who flooded the urban areas in search of work as well as newly arrived immigrants to the cities. Like the YMCA, the Boys' Brigade, founded in 1883, was a Christian organization. Robert Baden-Powell, vice president of the Brigade, later became founder of Scouting in 1907. Whether the YMCA, Brigade, Scouts, or Boys' Lodging Houses, the practice of the day was the provision of basic living necessities, education, religion, and discipline (Sheldon, 1922), all steeped in supporting the moral values of the dominant ruling society and ensuring young people have contact with adults of good moral character (Hurley & Treacey, 1993).

Influenced by Edward Livingston's (1831) report on reform and prison discipline, the prevention of crime, which was linked to poverty, was also a strong motive for building young people's character. Brace states, "my great object in the present work is to prove to society the practical truth of Mr. Livingston's theoretical statement: that the cheapest and most efficacious way of dealing with the 'dangerous classes' of large cities [The 'dangerous classes' were American-born children of Irish and German immigrants] is not to punish them, but to prevent their growth (Brace, 1872). In New York City, lodging-houses for boys were the first non-formal settings for intentional social interventions that would address urban poverty. "Eventually they are drawn into the neat and comfortable Boys' Lodging-houses, and there find themselves, imperceptibly changed into honest and decent boys" (Brace, 1872, p. 630).

It is within this notion of 'doing unto' that criticism of a non-participatory modality of working with young people later emerged. The difference is represented as "doing something *for* children and youth to doing things *with* children and youth" (Gibbons, 1950, p. 363). 'With' implies new notions of 'child' and understandings about their capabilities to participate and marks a historical transition from 'youth services' to 'youth development' (LISTEN, Inc., 2000). Larger social organizations and institutions, like school and family, must still function in an orderly fashion but do so by consensus and negotiation of the people engaged there. Unlike functionalism, interpretivism does not script what society's function shall be but rather relies upon the subjective experience of those who live it. People have voice and choice to alter and redesign actions within an overall structure that remains intact. Youth work that focuses on personal development is an example of working within this paradigm and, like character building, has roots as far back as the late 1800s, when new seeds of thought about human development as occurring ontogenetically and culturally (as opposed to only biologically) were sown. In the latter case, one could set development in the right direction through education. Development was a result of lived experience and so should be crafted for the outcomes desired. This view of development was consistent with later sociocultural views that emerged such as those of Lev Vygotsky and Jerome Bruner and was in stark contrast to competing maturational views that relied on Darwinian understanding of nature as unfolding over time.

In the last 20 years, certainly within the U.S. context and its broad reach, the genre of youth work as 'personal development' has moved away from its phenomenological (subjective and experiential) roots to 'youth development,' which instead relies on objective, scientific research in its design of evidence-based youth programming. Since the 1970s, developmental theories gained traction as legitimate scientific explanations of human behavior and more recently have provided the empirical bricks and mortar of youth development programs in the United States (National Research Council and Institute of Medicine, 2002). Youth development programs by design should be consistent with developmental research to include features such as physical and psychological safety, appropriate structure, supportive relationships, opportunities to belong, positive social norms, support for efficacy and mattering, opportunities for skill building, and integration of family, school, and community efforts (National Research Council and Institute of Medicine, 2002). This set of developmental imperatives emerged from several bodies of research. First, in the early 1990s, research by the Search Institute found that the more 'developmental assets' young people reported, the less likely they were to be engaged in drug and alcohol use, violence, and sexual activity, and the more likely they were to succeed in school, exhibit leadership, and engage in pro-health behaviors (Scales & Leffert, 1999). Developmental assets, of which there are 40, are those "skills, experiences, relationships and behaviors" that are the foundation to healthy development (see http://www.search-institute.org/research/developmental-assets). Second, a science of positive psychology was launched as a challenge to the overreliance on pathological explanations of human behavior of the times (Seligman & Csikszentmihalyi, 2000). The field of positive psychology is about valued subjective experiences such as wellbeing, hope, and happiness (Seligman & Csikszentmihaly, 2000). Such experiences are the result of nurturing strengths rather than fixing deficits and pathologies. From this nascent field grew the positive youth development (PYD) movement in the United States, with its focus on nurturing those aspects of human nature that predict 'thriving' behaviors among young people. For Lerner and colleagues, PYD includes 'five C's': competence, confidence, connection, character, and caring (Lerner, Phelps, Forman & Bowers, 2009).

While early character building focuses on the individual learning (and molding of) young people, youth development takes an ecological-relational approach, creating 'contexts' wherein character and other intrapersonal qualities are developed interpersonally. Illuminated is the social milieu of young people, not just the internal traits and behaviors, though individual growth remains in focus. Institutions of family, school, and community should be working collaboratively to provide young people with the right types of foundational opportunities for their future. In youth work parlance, youth development lines up to what Butters and Newell (1978) dub 'the Social Education Repertoire.' The goal of youth work from this stance is to help young people become healthy, well-adjusted adults through the successful accomplishment of life tasks in which strengths and assets are accumulated. While the theory also purports that the lack of external assets (e.g., caring neighbors, positive family communication, caring 'educative' school climate) is equally related to poor youth outcomes, it offers little contextualization for the sociopolitical and economic factors that play a role in family, school, and community wellbeing. Structural factors are ignored, leading to a micro-contextual grounding of development and no implied methodology for community action or activism. This is in stark contrast to community movements such as Hull-House in which activities were civic as well as educational, political as well as familial. There is also a distinction to be made between youth work models derived from education and psychology versus those derived from the traditions of social work—a statement that warrants further deliberation.

The Sociology of Change

As character building emerged as a distinct practice, there were other youth/intergenerational organizations of the same time period that sprung up in critique of the capitalist project and resultant poverty. Some were influenced by socialist thinkers like William Morris, others by writers like Karl Marx. Clarion Scouts, for instance, emerged from the former. Rather than teach youth 'discipline' as a trait of character, these collectivist micro-societies were interested in alternative ways of being and being together "outside the toil and drabness of the world of work and crowded urban living" (http://www.wcml.org.uk/contents/creativity-and-culture/leisure/clarion-movement). Theirs was a pursuit of leisure that included cycling, singing, and rambling as well as Socialist Sunday schools: creative endeavors that redefined work as play. Here, faith (and Christianity) is replaced by sociopolitical ideology and the creation of a new type of society that was interested in responding to the resultant poverty of the industrial revolution by re-defining how people live, work, and play, communally.

The university settlement houses were also places of redesigning community emerging as a holistic and collaborative set of interventions to the piecemeal solutions to poverty until then. Canon Samuel Barnett founded Toynbee Hall in the East End of London in 1884, bringing together affluent volunteers from around the world to live with (rather than serve) those who were poor. The idea spread. In 1889, Jane Addams and Ellen Gates Starr started the famous Hull-House in Chicago as a communal space where immigrants lived together, ate together, talked together, and created community solutions to urban problems. The accomplishments of the residents of Hull-House at that time were impressive: the Immigrants' Protective League, the Juvenile Protective Association, the first juvenile court in the nation, and the Institute for Juvenile Research, to name a few. Not unlike the 'character builders,' Addams's vocational choice to begin Hull-House was deeply influenced by her quest for moral purpose (Hunt, 1990). Growing up in Judeo-Christian culture of the American Midwest during the 1880s, Addams had a deep sense of moral responsibility for others (Hunt, 1990). She also grew up during a time of 'Lincolnian democratic ideals' and was steeped in values of self-sacrifice and community. Alongside this, her professed Quaker father taught her to regard "religious certainty with skepticism" (Hunt, 1990, p. 232). It was on her second trip to Europe that she learned of Toynbee Hall in London. As she began Hull-House, she insisted on being free from 'professional doing good,' which she perceived was less authentic. She observed that it was "the men of practice, despite their uncertainty of theory" who produced effective solutions to social problems (cited in Meiklejohn, 1960, p. 254). The settlement houses reflect an amalgam of social, humanitarian, and Christian beliefs and ideals, but as Addams insisted were not "philanthropy" but "the instrument of freedom" (Meiklejohn, 1960, p. 255). There was a political and democratic necessity of supporting young people to do what they do as if all else was equal (Shields, 2006).

Radical paradigms provoke social change by challenging oppressive social systems. According to Butter and Newell's (1978) typology, one cannot operate in more than one paradigm at a time. Moving towards radical understanding requires "a critical break" from the paradigm of social regulation. Based on conflict theory, these paradigms view dominant structures and regulation as counter to individual freedoms. Youth work then is "concerned with raising young people's awareness of the effects of the dominant value system and how it serves to inflict damaging consequences on them as a group of people and as a consequence impede their personal development" (Hurley & Treacy, 1993, p. 40). The concerns here are deeply humanistic ones. At another level of 'radicalism,' the focus goes beyond individual freedom to collective action and activism and an insistence on the need to address structural disadvantages embedded in the societal core: an aim that the provision of social services cannot achieve (Butters & Newell, 1978). Through concerns raised in the context of everyday life, people achieve true critical consciousness that is otherwise masked by participation in dominant hegemonic structures (Friere, 1970).

In short, youth work, like most social practices today, rests on a complicated set of understandings about youth and society, inequality, social progress, and education. These different paradigms have implications for how youth are seen, the types of programs and interactions with young people that ensue, and the overall goals of the practice. If one presumes that a lack of social progress results from lack of civic engagement and that citizens who are disengaged are those most likely marginalized from the hegemonic structures, then social progress can be made through inclusionary and pluralistic practices. This is in sharp contrast to practices aligned with a sociology of regulation, which tend to leave structures standing while focusing on the individual character and personal growth of those who reside within those structures. In this latter view, equality is achieved through individual achievements and changing one's circumstance. The stories of young people who have overcome all odds to be successful are heralded as evidence of its possibility.

Youth work resides in both places, marking 'the great divide' in the field. One way to bridge the divide is to recognize that each lives in the other and that the dialectical relation between regulation and freedom is a modern invention that is not disappearing any time soon.

TRANSITIONS AND REFRACTIONS

As stated, according to Butters and Newell (1978), practices within the sociology of regulation act to preclude radical youth work practice and emancipatory aims. They argue that 'a critical break' is needed to move towards a radical paradigm of youth work because regulation functions to replicate the dominant social order and thus 'expel' any movement towards radical change. Looking at youth work historically allows one to frame the past according to these 'breaks.' However, like ocean waves that hit the shoreline, transitions break not like shards of glass, distinct and separate, but as one, rolling into another even as they split into separate movements. This leads to a false understanding that once a transition occurs remnants of the prior period are left behind. In the case of youth work, and likely most social and cultural phenomena, this might not be the most accurate representation of reality. Alternatively, prior perspectives, methods, and values are simply rendered invisible, for the moment, through refractions that bring other characteristics momentarily into the light. Much like a prism, some facets come into full view while others are hidden depending on one's vantage point and illumination. Seen this way, youth work too has multiple facets, refracting some while holding others in plain sight.

Facets are what we see on the surface, or the surface explanations for engaging with young people. Four facets are readily identified so far in youth work's history: the moral obligation, the developmental imperative, the call to community action, and the political and democratic necessity. To describe youth work practice globally means that all four facets of the prism are always present, expressed differently and illuminated or not by particular ways of thinking and practice, through linguistic frames of reference and representations, in certain moments in history, and through certain social and cultural (and funding) priorities. The question is: When certain facets are illuminated, in what ways are the social causes of inequality made visible or invisible?

Youth work has not always aimed to illuminate oppression explicitly. If we go back to an earlier definition: Youth work is "the social education of young people in an informal context" (Hurley & Treacy, 1993, p. 1). There is no mention of youth work that would explicitly represent a sociology of change, and yet this definition is quite applicable to today's context. More recently, the Council of Europe defined youth work as a practice "guided and governed by principles of participation and empowerment, values of human rights and democracy, and anti-discrimination and tolerance" (2010, p. 2). Here, an explicit valuing of empowerment and rights, which illuminates another facet of youth work, is also very much alive and applicable to today's context but perhaps not explicit enough in triggering systemic change. 'Global youth work' adds a fifth facet (see Figure 3.1) and is perhaps most explicit in its purpose of ending oppression; in particular, it focuses on North/West dominance over Southern globe societies (Sallah, 2014). Global Youth Work (GYW) was first coined in 1995 by Bourn and McCollum of the Development Education Association and has been most widely accepted in the U.K. (see Sallah, 2014 for a description of the history). Unlike Development Education, GYW focuses not just on new knowledge (or consciousness raising) but on the application of knowledge at a community level. GYW also begins from the lived experiences of the young people themselves, who then co-create the agenda for action (Sallah, 2014). Change begins in the personal but, according to Sallah (2014), can and should move towards local, national, and global understandings. In fact, Sallah is explicit in his desire to see global youth work as rooted in a social justice that reverses domination and exploitation of the South.

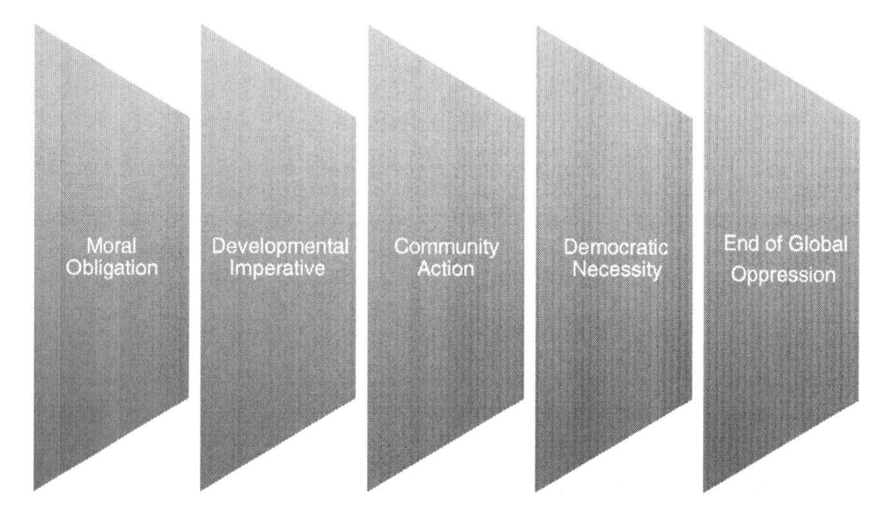

Figure 3.1 Facets of Youth Work

Reading Cases as Refractions

Imagine, then, viewing youth work practice through the notion of refractions. Which facet is most illuminated? Who illuminated it? Why? When that facet is illuminated, where are conversations about inequality? What are the spaces afforded for young people to name issues that are not originally part of agenda, program, or funding priority? How do adults respond when young people reclaim those spaces and/or resist adult-driven agendas? Do injustices get named and challenged or swept under the proverbial carpet? What other facets become illuminated at different moments in this lived negotiation of space?

The following recent practice description provides an interesting case in point. Gervais (2010) describes human rights workshops for adolescent girls that took place in Cochabamba, Bolivia over a three-year period. The workshops were led by adult community educators from the local women's outreach center. "The goals of the workshops were to equip the participants with theoretical elements and practical tools regarding the promotion and defense of citizenship rights and duties, human rights, gender equality, and a culture of peace" (Gervais, 2010, p. 198). The workshops explicitly focused on the girls' experiences of victimization and not the adult's own preconceived notions of injustices based on gender. As a result of the workshops, the girls were "able to name, analyze, and seek to change" their circumstances (p. 204). They discussed issues of discrimination and violence that ensued even within their own families due to their gender and the construction of 'female' as subservient. The workshops also helped the girls "claim, access, and defend their rights" (p. 207). As is common within projects that begin with a raising of consciousness, new civic actions mushroom from the original project; in this case, some of the girls shared their knowledge with others who did not attend the workshops, organized post-workshop group events to raise awareness, and wrote letters to government officials. The authors are in full recognition of the lack of structural change towards which the project is aimed. Though some girls were compelled towards action as a result of the workshops, we do not know that their actions will penetrate the male-dominated hegemonies nor do we know that greater consciousness does not itself provoke unintentional and negative consequences and backlash for the girls. As the authors conclude:

> it is precisely because structural change is so lacking that the empowering feelings of dignity, self-worth, and solidarity derived from the workshops may serve as one of the few sources of comfort and strength that the girls may be able to draw upon in order to overcome any abuse, rejection, and denial that they may encounter in the future . . . What remains to be seen is the extent to which the girls will continue to claim their rights in interpersonal and institutional spaces over the long term, as well as to engage actively and enduringly in collectively

> based women's advocacy that seeks to transcend the structural impediments to women's equal participation in all aspects of Bolivian society. (p. 211)

The promotion of human rights casts this practice automatically within a radical paradigm, the facet of ending oppression of girls and women being most illuminated in expressed purpose. However, two additional observations are warranted. First, such practices do not illustrate a transitioning away from prior purposes like character building (here defined as 'strength') or personal development (here defined as 'empowerment') in order to engage in action and activism at a community, social, or political level. In fact, attention to individual experiences with and responses to gender-based violence are critical to the girls' intellectual understandings as well as psychological healing. Second, even when we are operating under a radical paradigm, we should recognize that we also concurrently live within and perpetuate mechanisms of social control. In today's funding climate, often it is adults who receive funds to offer particular types of services for children and youth. It is the adults who have the power to 'engage' youth. Or, stated another way, youth participate in adult-defined projects, and the space for 'voice' is within a structure (design, objectives, methods) defined by adults. Master practitioners will also recognize that young people's resistance to adult agendas (and power) is manifested in many different ways. Learning how to read the signs of resistance is critical to effective youth work. Then, we could ask: Who illuminated the issue? Did the girls decide that this issue was important to them? Did they help design the workshops (the content and the pedagogy), or were they passive recipients of an important yet adult-driven message/agenda? Which girls were *not* present and why? If the girls were not involved in the distributed power for such arrangements, then is this case really operating from a radical paradigm, or is it a more advanced model of social control, and how do we discern the difference? These questions are not meant to criticize or negate the work but rather to elevate the youth work contribution.

The interconnectedness of these facets and how they become illuminated or not by different frames of reference is both a challenge and an opportunity for youth work practitioners. Youth work is always about a starting point that is different from almost all other starting points in other adult-youth interactions. Youth work starts where young people are. However, this purist notion is just that; it is the ideal that we hold onto while we await spaces to reclaim. A key question for us is whether we can recognize in our own practice which facet might be receiving the most illumination and whether we can self-critically spin the prism in order to create both a fuller spectrum of possibility and one that never keeps invisible issues of inequality or injustice.

On an individual level, youth workers are always operating from a set of beliefs that are formed by their experiences, theoretical understandings, cultural and sociopolitical awareness, biases, skill sets, and more. Practitioner 'use of self' is critical in working intentionally and relationally with young people to bring forth human change (Fusco, 2012). At an organizational level, there is an additional set of factors that drives the work. Many program imperatives are dictated by funding mandates that are themselves tied to larger social, economic, and political contexts. To not be keenly aware of these contextual factors is to miss the fact that youth workers do not operate in a silo; they are part of an interconnected field and profession that illuminates (or not) different facets of the work at different times and for different reasons. At the same time, it is also within the reach of practitioners to purposefully consider the broader context in which youth work and specific programs and practices are situated. And so we must ask: Which facet is most illuminated by the funding to improve minority participation in STEM careers, to promote social and emotional competencies among young people, to ensure college and career readiness among older youth? And then which facet is momentarily invisible, and does that matter to the young people whose wellbeing I am entrusted with?

Alternatively, we can rethink youth work to be citizen space unrestricted by funding that ties our hands to particular outcomes. There are some successful models of organizations that are creatively managing their funding streams while keeping youth in the lead and allowing their issues to always navigate the agenda. Engaging youth in *their* issues might mean engaging them in finding the funding to support those issues as well. The recommendation is not an either/or solution; rather, it is at least a critical awareness of the imperatives we have illuminated.

CONCLUSION

It is educators who have the capacity to free the power that resides within us all and is in need of awakening when the wellbeing of people (and young people) is at stake. We live in a world that does not self-perpetuate that awakening but needs constant reminders and wake-up calls. Youth work is often such a reminder; it is often a strategy that names and then acts upon inequality. Framed as the sociology of change, youth work as a 'radical' paradigm is not content with individual change or development in isolation from larger structural factors that perpetuate injustice. However, youth work is also a strategy that illuminates other (individual or personal) facets of being-ness: personal safety, general health, individual character, discipline, social and emotional competencies, strengths, preparedness, leisure, engagement, belonging, and confidence, to name a few, sometimes with little attention to larger systemic issues and sometimes alongside 'radical' endeavors. Collectively, then, youth work operates from various imperatives, some named here: moral obligation, the developmental imperative, a call to community action, political and democratic necessity, and an end of oppression. These imperatives are refracted at different times for different reasons, sometimes intentionally, often not. How and whether we choose to illuminate various facets is within our reach if we have the state of mind to critically reflect on our work, the imperative being driven, the causes of the drive, and the impact on the young people with whom we work.

REFERENCES

Addams, J. (1905). *Democracy and social ethics.* New York: The Macmillan company.

Austria, R. S. (2006). Toward a movement: Uniting organizers and direct service provides in a movement for juvenile justice reform. *Afterschool Matters, 5*, 30–40.

Avrich, P. (1980). *The modern school movement: Anarchism and Education in the United States*. Princeton: Princeton University Press

Brace, C. L. (1872). *The dangerous classes of New York: and twenty years' work among them.* 1973. Reprint: NASW classic series.

Burrell, G., & Morgan, G. (1979). *Sociological paradigms and organizational analysis: Elements of the sociology of corporate life*. Burlington, VT: Ashgate Publishing Company.

Butters, S., & Newell, S. (1978). *Realities of training: A review of the training of adults who volunteer to work with young people in the Youth and Community Services*. Leicester: National Youth Bureau.

Cooper, T. (2012). Models of youth work: A framework for positive skeptical reflection. *Youth & Policy, 109*, 98–117.

Cooper, T., & White, R. (1994). Models of youth work practice. *Youth Studies Australia, 13*(4), 30–35.

Council of Europe. (2010, July 7–10). *Declaration of the 1st European Youth Work Convention.* Ghent, Belgium. Retrieved from http://www.coe.int/t/dg4/youth/Source/Resources/Documents/2010_Declaration_European_youth_work_convention_en.pdf

Durkheim, E. (1956). *Education and sociology*. New York: Free Press.

Freire, P. (1970). *Pedagogy of the oppressed.* New York: Herder and Herder.

Fusco, D. (2012). Use of self in the context of youth work. *Child & Youth Services, 33*, 33–45.

Gervais, C. (2010). On their own and in their own words: Bolivian adolescent girls' empowerment through non-governmental human rights education. *Journal of Youth Studies, 14*(2), 197–217.

Gibbons, I. L. (1950). Character building agencies and the needs of Negro children and youth. *The Journal of Negro Education, 19*(3), 363–371.

Greenberg, D. (1992). *The Sudbury Valley school experience.* 3rd ed. Fram ingham, MA: Sudbury Valley School Press.

Holt, J. (1977). *Growing without schooling: A record of a grassroots movement.* Boston: Holt Associates.

Hunt, J. B. (1990). Jane Addams: The Presbyterian connection. *American Presbyterians, 68*(4), 231–244.

Hurley, L., & Treacy, D. (1993). *Models of youth work: A sociological framework.* Dublin: Irish Youthwork Press.

Lerner, J. V., Phelps, E., Forman, Y. E., & Bowers, E. P. (2009). Positive youth development. In R. M. Lerner, L. Steinberg, R. M. Lerner, & L. Steinberg (Eds.), *Handbook of adolescent psychology, Volume 1: Individual bases of adolescent development* (3rd ed., pp. 524–558). Hoboken, NJ: John Wiley & Sons Inc.

LISTEN, Inc. (2000). *An emerging model for working with youth* (Occasional paper series on youth organizing, No. 1). Washington, DC: Funders Collaborative on Youth Organizing.

Livingston, E. (1831). *Introductory report to the code of reform and prison discipline*. Quebec: Thomas Cary.

McAdam, D. (1990). *Freedom summer*. Oxford: Oxford University Press.

Meiklejohn, D. (1960). Jane Addams and American democracy. *Social Service Review, 34*(3), 253–264.

National Research Council and Institute of Medicine. (2002). *Community youth programs to promote positive youth development*. Washington, DC: National Research Council and Institute of Medicine.

Porter, M. E., Stern, S., & Green, M. (2014). *Social progress index 2014*. Washington, DC: Social Progress Imperative.

Sallah, M. (2014). *Global youth work: provoking consciousness and taking action*. Dorset: Russell House Publishing.

Scales, P., & Leffert, N. (1999). *Developmental assets: A synthesis of the scientific research on adolescent development*. Minneapolis, MN: Search Institute.

Seligman, M., & Csikszentmihalyi, M. (2000). Positive psychology: An introduction. *American Psychologist, 55*, 5–14.

Shields, P. M. (2006). Democracy and the social feminist ethics of Jane Addams: A vision for public administration. *Administrative Theory & Praxis, 28*(3), 418–443.

Sheldon, F. M. (1922). The congregational education society. *Christian Education, 6*(3), 163–165.

Section II

Social Progress Through Youth Work: Welfare and Wellbeing

4 Intergenerational Partnership and Youth Social Justice in a Malaysian Fishing Village

Steven Eric Krauss, Dzhuhailmi Dahalan, and Shepherd Zeldin

Civil associations contribute to the effectiveness and stability of democratic government both because of their internal effects on individual members and their external effects on the wider polity (Hyden, Court & Meese, 2003; Kwon, 2004). Within this framework of civil society, youth organizations have become prominent players in many developing countries. In addition to addressing the basic needs of large youth populations, which most developing countries boast, there has also been a recognized need to develop future leadership and human capital, which are seen as essential to the future success of development efforts. In developing democracies like Malaysia, youth organizations are considered important stabilization agents that contribute to social stability, which in turn ensures national sovereignty thus enabling ongoing development to take place (Nga & King, 2006). Toward this end, Malaysia has made substantial commitments to its youth sector, which boasts over 8,000 registered youth organizations including international bodies such as Girl Scouts and St. John's Ambulance to local sports, uniform and religious bodies, clubs and youth councils. This structure forms a strong foundation of youth involvement in civil society that began during the pre-independence period of the mid-20th century. At that time, education- and skills-training-related groups were formed alongside the uniformed bodies, recreation, community service, and religious organizations transplanted from the colonial power, Great Britain (Nga, 2009).

Through their roles as providers of non-formal education, recreation, leadership, and community development programs, youth organizations have the potential to address development gaps arising from uneven wealth creation and distribution (Ginwright & James, 2002; USAID, 2012). Indeed, Malaysian youth organizations are often recognized for their efforts in providing valuable programs and services. Historically, they are also known for their role in the political activism of the 1970s when they were on the forefront of efforts protesting against poverty and inequality, especially among the Malay population (Nga, 2009). Since then, however, few have portrayed Malaysian youth organizations in a social justice role. Do such organizations exist? If so, what are their strategies to bring about change? How do they use youth programs to address marginalization and economic inequality? How do they interact and engage with communities and adults to carry out such work? To address these questions, we present a case study of BESUGA—the Youth and Sports Association of Gaya Island—a Malaysian youth association that has been a catalyst for community-based economic and social development in the East Malaysian state of Sabah.

The chapter begins by describing Gaya Island and the many challenges confronting its low-income traditional fishing villages. We provide a brief overview of Malaysian youth associations, followed by a profile of BESUGA. We follow with the 'BESUGA story,' a discussion of the work and evolution of the organization and how it went from a rather ordinary youth development program provider to an agent of social change within a span of only five years. Finally, we conclude with a discussion of challenges the organization still faces and offer a new way of thinking about youth-adult partnership across multiple generations as a result of the lessons learned on Gaya Island.

GAYA ISLAND, SABAH

Ten minutes off the coast of Kota Kinabalu (KK), the capital of the State of Sabah in East Malaysia, lies Gaya Island, the largest of the five-island Tuanku Abdul Rahman (TAR) Marine Park. With a total area of 12,185 acres, Gaya Island is home to several upscale beach resorts as well as marine park resources and tourism and coastal activities such as diving, snorkeling, island hopping, deep sea fishing, and beach activities (Said, 2011). With its pristine beauty and prime location, Gaya Island is a popular destination among tourists.

Despite the large numbers that visit Gaya each year, few pay much attention to the island's eastern and southern shores, where 11 low-income fishing villages span the beachfront on a series of interlocking docks. These are the traditional communities of Kampong[1] Lok Malom, Kampong Lok Urai, Kampong Lok Baru, Kampong Lobong, Kampong Kasuapan, Kampong Selamat, Kampong Ubian, Kampong Lok Parru, Kampong Simalak, Kampong Pondo, and Kampong Pulau Gaya. Comprising a substantial population of approximately 10,000, the majority of the inhabitants of these villages are 'Bajau Laut,' known by the locals as 'sea gypsies' for their skills in seafaring (Said, 2011). Gaya's Bajau are predominantly Muslim, having originally sailed from the Philippines in the mid-19th century. In addition to the Bajau, small minorities of Malays, Bisaya, Kagayan, Rungus, and Chinese as well as Suluks, Ubian, and other Filipinos dwell among Gaya's 11 villages.

Given their close proximity to KK, the residents of Gaya provide the city with a supply of cheap labor (Said, 2011). The vast majority of Gaya's residents lack formal education beyond a basic primary level and thus work as laborers, selling at the eateries and outdoor markets or in other unskilled jobs. Their main sources of supplementary income derive from fishing and harvesting marine resources such as sea cucumber, clams, shells, and others as well as industries such as boat making and boat transport services. Others work at the hotels on the other side of the island. Most adult women are homemakers that do mat weaving and craft-making from shells and sea produce. Many sell their products at Tamu (farmer's markets) or the famous Pilipino market in Kota Kinabalu. For Gaya's young people, employment opportunities outside of fishing are limited on the island, encouraging them to leave their villages to look for jobs outside (Said, 2011).

Gaya's fishing villages sit along the island's beachfront. Their houses are traditional wooden homes built on pillars erected from the ocean floor. It is common for immediate and extended families to stay together in one house, which can result in more than seven people living together (Said, 2011). The arrangement of houses, with their multiple docks jutting out into the South China Sea, facilitates the island's fishing activities and the residents' transportation back and forth to the mainland. Water taxis running between the island and KK are abundant and, for just a few ringgit[2], provide the main source of transportation for those working on the mainland.

Marginalization of Gaya and Its People

Gaya's traditional villages are mostly ignored by the tour companies and internationals that visit KK and the Marine Park. Their shanty coastal houses are viewed more as an eyesore than a tourist attraction. Mainland Sabahans often warn visitors to avoid Gaya Island due to alleged illegal immigration and drug smuggling. The negative perceptions of Gaya are largely based on the erroneous belief that many of the island's residents reside there illegally. Although historians dispute the exact dates of the Bajau people's settling on the west coast of Borneo, their presence there has been well documented since the mid-19th century (Miller, 2011). In line with this history, our study participants contend that the Bajau have lived on Gaya Island for decades and that close to 80% of the residents reside there legally.

These negative perceptions have played a major role in shaping public opinion about Gaya. In fact, while in KK, when we asked several mainlanders about Gaya Island they immediately warned us against going there. Perceptions about the island have only added to the geographic and economic marginalization experienced by the residents. Few private companies consider Gaya's traditional fishing villages as a worthwhile attraction for tourists. Political leaders have shied away from investing in Gaya because it is perceived as a bastion for illegal residents.

Gaya's Greatest Challenge

The greatest challenge for Gaya's residents has been their struggle to survive without basic infrastructure. For decades, the villages were denied running water and electricity despite being ten minutes from the state capital, sharing the island with world-renowned resort hotels, and being unwavering supporters of the ruling government. Their ongoing pleas for support, however, have fallen on deaf ears. To survive, the villagers have relied on expensive potable water shipped from KK and stored in tanks behind their houses (it is noteworthy that most other Malaysians pay almost nothing for water) and expensive gasoline-powered generators for electricity. Most families struggle to meet their monthly financial responsibilities.[3] Furthermore, the island still lacks many other basic resources.[4] For one, there are no doctors or medical clinics on the island; to get medical or dental treatment, residents have to travel by boat to the mainland.

In brief, Gaya Island and its people have been systematically marginalized—socially and economically—for decades. Over the past six years, however, the situation has begun to change for the better. A string of events resulting from community advocacy has brought about substantial upgrades to the island's physical infrastructure, resulting in a wave of hope among the Island residents. These improvements are due in no small part to the work of an unexpected group of activists—the island's very own youth association.

YOUTH ASSOCIATIONS IN MALAYSIA

Youth associations in Malaysia are voluntary non-governmental organizations headed, administered, and comprised of young people between the ages of 15 and 40, as stipulated in the country's Youth Societies and Youth Development Act (2007, Act 668, Section 2). Malaysia's official definition of youth being 15 to 40 is considerably wider than most other countries and international bodies.[5] When youth organizations first started out in Malaysia, there were no formal restrictions of age for members. Malaysian officials felt that an age limit could be useful to encourage young people to contribute and to expose potential talent and leadership. Others contend that the definition is designed to reduce intergenerational isolation by facilitating cooperation and interaction between adolescents and young adults (Nga, 2009). The law has its share of critics, however, who claim that the definition marginalizes 'real' youth (namely, those between the ages of 15 to 25), excluding them from important developmental experiences such as meaningful organizational roles and leadership responsibilities (Hamzah, Suandi & Tamam, 2002).

As of 2010, there were approximately 3 million members of youth associations in Malaysia out of a total youth population of nearly 12 million (Malaysian Institute for Research in Youth Development, 2011). Youth associations have always been defined broadly to include local and grassroots as well as international organizations. Unlike their Western counterparts, the vast majority of Malaysian youth associations are not independent from government. Although informal or unregistered organizations exist, most associations register with the national Registrar of Youth (ROY) office under the Ministry of Youth and Sports. Registration with ROY ensures support from the government in the form of involvement in state-sponsored trainings, workshops, and programs as well as operational funds. This support is vital to the start-up and survival of many grassroots organizations, especially in the initial stages of their development. Registration with the ROY also allows associations representation in the state youth council, which is a leadership body comprised of representatives of all the registered youth associations in the state. Critics point out, however, that too much involvement by the government in the sector detracts from the ability of the associations to stand on their own and become self-sustaining. Hamzah et al. (2002) have pointed out that, rather than devising creative ways of raising funds, many Malaysian youth organizations have failed due to an inability to sustain themselves.

Successful examples exist, however, that deserve attention not only for their size or popularity but also for the impact they have had on their respective communities. Few such cases have been documented in Malaysia. To address this gap, we set out to study one such association, the Youth and Sports Association of Gaya Island (*Belia Sukan Gaya*), also known as BESUGA. The chapter focuses on key youth workers—the organization's leaders led by the President and co-founder Sadja Nori Susulan and the other Executive Committee, or 'Exco,' members. Despite facing significant economic, political, and social inequalities, BESUGA has successfully brought together three generations of Island residents for recreation, sports, instruction, and social action. Moreover, the association has successfully organized diverse stakeholders to bring electricity and fresh water infrastructures to the island. Through an analysis of their work and leadership, we attempted to shed light on the organization's role in bringing social justice to Gaya Island.

Our story is presented in the form of an exploratory case study. We collected data through focus groups, interviews, phone conversations, and emails. In addition, we interviewed adult residents from the island, reviewed documents about the island and BESUGA such as historical white papers, PowerPoint presentations made to government bodies, and photographs of programs and activities, and made several trips to the island for observation. Our trips to Gaya allowed us to meet with community leaders such as the island's school headmaster.

The Youth and Sports Association of Gaya Island (BESUGA)

BESUGA was established in 2007 as a sports-based association. Founded by Sadja, the current president, and Alamin Abd Rashid, the organization started out with 17 members and has since grown to 414 youth. The organization is governed by a 15-member Executive Committee, of which members are elected each year. 70% of the members are male. This is due mostly to the fact that a majority of the programs are still sports-based; however, there are several young women on the organization's Exco. These young women play vital roles in the work of the association, which are further discussed later in the chapter.

BESUGA's mission is to enhance the overall health and wellbeing of its members and, by extension, the entire Gaya Island community. The main objective of the association's youth development work is "to educate the members in order to prepare them to contribute back to their community and the nation." Towards this end, BESUGA's activities are provided in two core programming areas referred to as 'general youth development' and 'sports.'

The youth development program consists of regular activities in the areas of education and public speaking, travel and tourism, expedition, culture, welfare, and religion designed to enhance members' mental, physical, and spiritual competencies. In 2012, BESUGA ran over 40 programs, earning it recognition as one of the top youth associations in Sabah. The sports programming area consists of hosting regular tournaments in football, volleyball, netball, chess, and other sports. The sports tournaments help to increase awareness and interest in the association and the other activities it provides with the goal of getting the members more engaged in the other educational and leadership activities. Sports, aside from being effective as a recruiting tool, also help to develop physical/health competencies and motivation among the BESUGA members.

To ensure that financial limitations are not a barrier to participation in the association, initial registration fees are kept at a minimum of only one ringgit, and the same amount is charged as a monthly membership fee. To support the organization's programs and activities, as an officially registered association under the ROY office under the Ministry of Youth and Sports, the state government provides an annual subsidy of RM5,000 for operating expenses. This is in addition to entry fees collected from programs such as soccer and volleyball tournaments that the organization hosts several times per year. Occasional sponsorship from outside entities such as the local technical college also helps subsidize program costs.

As with many Malaysian youth associations, the age range of 15 to 40 translates into different roles and expectations of the members. All youths from the ages of 15 to 40 from the island are eligible to join the association. Within this larger group, however, three core sub-groups with different responsibilities and expectations coincide. The first consists of adolescents—those 15 to 18 years old who comprise the majority of the general membership. This group is predominantly comprised of secondary-school-age program participants. The second group consists of emerging adults—those 18 to 30 years old. The emerging adults in BESUGA are the most active members of the organization and comprise much of the Exco. This group also acts as a bridge between the adolescent members and adults both within and outside of Gaya. Those aged 30 to 40 are the smallest group in number and tend to take on more adult roles, acting in advisory and supportive capacities as organizers and intermediaries. This group also plays a vital role in the association's leadership development and outreach work. Once an Exco member has completed his or her term, he or she becomes an organizational 'ambassador' in his or her respective village and works with the adult community leaders in that village to recruit youth to join BESUGA.

THE EVOLUTION OF BESUGA AS AN AGENT OF SOCIAL CHANGE

The majority of Malaysian youth associations focus on their primary role as providers of youth programs. Like similar associations found elsewhere, they often play peripheral or supportive roles in social change efforts (Camino & Zeldin, 2002). In the case of Gaya Island, however, BESUGA was the main driver in bringing about essential improvements to Gaya Island's residents, specifically water and electricity. Our analysis indicates that this social-justice-oriented work, initiated in 2006, occurred in four phases: (1) youth development program provider, (2) organizer of community stakeholders, (3) intermediary linking the needs of Gaya's villages to important resources outside the island, and (4) community educator.

Phase 1: Start-Up—Providing Education and Sports Programs

In 2006, following their successful hosting of the Sayo Nara I-Team soccer tournament, 17 youth from Gaya Island decided to form BESUGA. The tournament, which brought together 25 teams from Gaya and nearby Kota Kinabalu, was one of several hosted by the group. Attempting to capitalize on the Gaya youths' intense interest in sports, the organization initially registered with the state as a sports-based association. From the beginning, however, the association's mission was education and positive youth development. BESUGA leaders set out to utilize sports as the main vehicle to engage youth in island-based activities in an attempt to enhance their physical wellbeing, motivation, teamwork, and leadership competencies.

As a poor community, there are few facilities on the island. Prior to BESUGA, young people had to travel to the mainland for organized activities and were afforded little in the way of organized programs. Well aware of these challenges, BESUGA's leaders decided to host regular competitive sports tournaments that did not require expensive equipment or facilities (e.g., soccer, netball, volleyball). To increase association membership, the tournament registration fees were also counted as membership fees, making it easy for the young people to join the association. This approach allowed BESUGA's membership to grow with each program held.

Building on their initial success, the leaders of BESUGA began to recognize other opportunities for providing knowledge, skills, and competencies to the youth of Gaya. By utilizing the talents and abilities of those within the association, BESUGA began to expand its programming by offering classes and training in areas including sewing, cooking, and English. The common theme cross-cutting all of the programs was the development of competency, connectedness, and preparedness for adult roles.

Within only a few years, BESUGA's activities steadily increased. By 2012, they were running 30 organized activities annually in addition to the other informal services they were providing such as community programs on environmental awareness and vocational/technical education with nearby colleges. BESUGA's membership and reputation grew with each program. One adult resident commented:

> *Since the existence of BESUGA there have been a lot of changes on the island. Other than the electricity supply, what I see is the movement and cooperation amongst the youth. As an example, before this, from this area until to that end of Lok Kurai village, there were tons of trash everywhere. But because of the Youth Association, he [i.e., Sadja] introduced BESUGA here and spread the environmental issue throughout Gaya Island.*

These efforts and early successes helped BESUGA achieve the honor of being named the fourth-best youth association of 2012 by the state Ministry of Youth and Sports. It was a significant achievement for an organization only five years old and gave the entire island a newfound sense of pride and accomplishment.

Phase 2: Forging Key Community Partnerships

BESUGA's focus on education and program provision facilitated its growth into the realm of community engagement and organizing. Following a successful start-up period in which it increased its membership through sports and education programs, it began to broaden its scope of work, building on the visibility and legitimacy it had gained in the eyes of adult community leaders. Various parties in the community such as school officials, parents and village leaders, began to look up to BESUGA. Even adult residents with no ties to the organization began to notice that BESUGA was sparking greater cohesion among the island residents. One resident shared his observation:

> *From the cultural perspective, for one year I lived in Kesuapan village. I noticed that with BESUGA's existence in the community, cooperation among the villagers was stronger . . . Before, our culture was based on our race. We are Bajau. Bajau tend to keep to themselves. However,*

> *after BESUGA came along, there was greater cooperation among the people.*

As alumni of the island's only primary and secondary schools (which serve over 2,000 students), BESUGA's leaders' popularity helped them develop strong working relations with the headmaster of the secondary school. This has allowed Azman, as the head of BESUGA's education programs, to work closely with parents of problematic students. Like other low-income communities throughout the world, many Gaya adults lack formal education. Many parents do not see the value of their children's education, especially when the children are old enough to work and support their families. Azman and the other youth leaders try to emphasize the importance of education, using themselves as examples and pointing out the many career opportunities that exist for children who complete school. As a result of this work, the school started inviting BESUGA's leaders to provide regular motivational programs for the students in which the group's leaders encourage them to study hard and explain the different opportunities available to them once they complete their studies. Through these efforts, BESUGA began to earn the respect of school leaders and parents and was able to facilitate stronger linkages between the two parties.

As BESUGA becomes more influential, it now faces the challenge of serving a large population spread across 11 villages. This means that all of the villages are represented in BESUGA programs. It also means that there are many more community leaders with whom to network and forge relationships. In rural Malaysian culture, the role of the village head (also known as *ketua kampong*) is particularly significant, and it is vital to get his permission to conduct any activity within his respective village. Garnering the village head's support essentially ensures the subsequent support of the village residents. Culturally, village heads retain significant status in the eyes of their residents, who put their trust in the head to manage village affairs. To run programs in the different villages on Gaya, BESUGA requires each village head's approval. Some heads are more supportive of youth-led programs than others, however. For this reason, Sadja and the other leaders go out of their way to include the village heads in the planning and execution of programs. In most cases, their efforts at garnering support have been successful. Sadja recalled BESUGA's special working relationship with Abdul Hashim, Village Head of Kampong Kasuapan and others:

> *So, we help him (village* head) *from the procedural aspects of the water and electricity projects. He is very proud because there are still a group of young people who are concerned about what is happening in the village.*

Through collaboration and partnership, BESUGA has been able to overcome many of the challenges that often derail the efforts of other Malaysian youth associations. Such challenges often include getting—and keeping—adult community members involved and finding meaningful roles for them. When we talked to adult residents on Gaya, there was a strong desire to support what the association was doing. Several of the residents mentioned that much of the adult support for BESUGA comes in the form of energy and manpower. For example, one Exco member gave the example of how the adult residents helped the association meet its need for a stage to conduct its cultural programs:

> *We have a lot of programs but don't have a stage. Every time we have a program, we have to set up a makeshift stage. The people involved in doing this are mostly the older people. Every time, they will build a new stage for us, and help us lift the timber. They don't ask for money. They are volunteers; they help with everything. It is a big sacrifice by the older people for BESUGA.*

The BESUGA youth leaders recognize the sacrifice and support of the adults in the community and the partnership that the two groups have. As poor fishermen with little formal education, many of the adult residents help in relatively simple ways that are proportionate to their resources and abilities. This often takes the form of physical labor, as illustrated in the above quote. For example, Mr. Ghani and Mr. Alawi, older Gaya residents, offered their time and money to take the lead on building a volleyball court in their village knowing that volleyball is a popular activity among the Island's youth. In brief, BESUGA's building of relationships with the village heads, parents, and other adults effectively made them partners in the organization's work. This proved to be a critical strategy that later paid huge dividends in the effort to bring water and electricity to the villages.

Phase 3: Organizing to Bring Resources and Change to the Community

Despite years of neglect, the residents of Gaya Island have been unbridled supporters of the ruling Barisan National (BN) government. Prior to 2008, they had unsuccessfully tried to capitalize on this support by lobbying their representatives at both the federal and state levels, focusing on their most pressing needs of running water and electricity. Slowly, an infrastructure was funded, most notably a school and a police station. Nonetheless, progress on water and electricity was slight.

The political context changed in 2008, however. For the first time in Malaysia's history, the ruling government experienced a near-defeat in the country's general election. Popularly called the 'political tsunami of 2008,' the upheaval put every BN representative on notice and gave the residents and community leaders the courage to make unprecedented demands of their political leaders. In Sabah, although the BN won the state elections, its representatives knew that they had to change the way they governed. The support of community groups and their ardent patrons could no longer be taken for granted.

Things began to change. Realizing that the time was ripe for action, the leaders of BESUGA, motivated by their own growing popularity and string of recent successes, took the lead in lobbying their representatives. This time, however, they decided on a different approach that would go beyond a mere request. Using an organizing and partnership approach, BESUGA enlisted the support of influential members from the Kota Kinabalu area to help in the lobbying efforts. These included academic leaders from nearby University of Malaysia-Sabah (UMS), representatives from Kota Kinabalu City Hall, and those from the state electric company, among others. BESUGA then called for a program inviting the different parties and local politicians to attend. Sadja explains:

> *We set up a program and invited the Village Heads, the YB (local political representative), the Kota Kinabalu City Hall (DBKK) and the school leaders in addition to all the local community members. During the program we asked the leader (i.e. YB) why electricity and water supply is not provided here. We gave our opinion and together put pressure on him (the YB).*

After listening to the different viewpoints from community, academic, and business leaders, the government finally agreed to provide electricity and running water to the island. This was a major victory for Gaya's residents as well as BESUGA. It also marked an important step in the organization's evolution, that of becoming an intermediary agent capable of linking the Gaya community with outside resources. According to our participants, the association's advocacy efforts had a transformational effect on the adults in the community, resulting in more positive perceptions of the youth as well as a stronger desire to contribute their own time and energy. One of the adult residents commented:

> *A meeting was held to bring electricity to Gaya; I still remember young people and adults sitting together. We have no problem with it, we are always willing to see what problems they face* [BESUGA/youth] *and we are always ready to give them help.*

While many of the adults in the community became more inclined to play active, supportive roles in BESUGA's programs, others began to see young people in a different light. Sadja elaborated:

> *The youth are now going into Kampong Lok Kurai and Kampong Lok Baru. They go in with Mr. Muslim* [older Exco member]. *So the people there see something different, because the ones managing the electricity*

> *installation project are the young people. The contractor is named Amin. As a young person, he is helping the village to get their electricity supply. . . . So, it's like that—the community's perception on Gaya Island is anchored to the youth.*

Phase 4: Educating the Community

After the agreement by the state government to provide running water and electricity to Gaya, BESUGA, at the request of the community leaders, took the lead in coordinating the transition effort. As a youth association, this was a role it was not prepared for. Association leaders knew little about the process and what it would take to make the transition to a more sophisticated infrastructure. The young leaders of BESUGA soon realized that, first and foremost, community education was needed to help the villagers understand what having electricity meant. For most, it was the first time in their lives that they had centralized power in their homes, and there was much that they needed to learn. To meet this need, BESUGA created a special Exco position for Zuraidah, a 21-year-old female leader who volunteered to head the electrification transition project. One of her first tasks was to make sure that the residents understood what was required of them during the transition process. For this, she had to go door-to-door in every village answering residents' questions and explaining about monthly costs, fees for installation, and how to fill out the necessary paperwork. She said:

> *First, there is a form that I made for them about how many lights and how many socket plugs that they want to use for the house. And then I give them a reasonable price. The price is from the contractor. I had to negotiate with the contractor for a cheaper price, so now the villagers get the cheapest prices! If it was more expensive they probably would not be able to afford it. The second issue, in terms of the meter application, they cannot understand. So, the villagers will ask, "What is the procedure? What about the meter? How about the wiring?" What I tell them is that we do the wiring first and then after the meter is in we will proceed with the wiring. That's my way to help them understand.*

Much of Zuraidah's work targeted changing false perceptions, which proved challenging. For example, many of the villagers thought that once the electricity was installed, it would be free every month. Others did not realize that they had to pay extra depending on the number of lights and sockets they wanted installed. When told what these would cost, many accused BESUGA and the contractors of trying to make money off them:

> *Most of the residents didn't understand anything about electricity management, at least in the beginning. Some of them thought that it was*

> *free, whereas before they had to pay for the gasoline generator, and others thought that somebody wanted to run a business with it. I need to tell them how it works, get their cooperation, and give them the consent form in order to have it installed.*

Through helping the residents understand what was required to properly manage their new resource, Zuraidah became a well-known figure in the Gaya community. Moreover, many island youth who did not know BESUGA before the project became aware of the organization through Zuraidah's work. The establishment of strong community relationships by BESUGA has been important during the transition period to new electric and water supplies. To date, electricity has been installed in several of the villages, with the rest expected to be completed within the next year. The water infrastructure is still being installed and is also near completion. These are major projects that take time, especially given the size of the population, the area being served, and the type of non-traditional housing in which the residents live. The length of the process has resulted in complaints from residents, to which BESUGA, and Zuraidah in particular, have had to respond through massive education efforts about the magnitude of the projects.

DISCUSSION

BESUGA's Challenges

Despite BESUGA's successes, the organization faces critical challenges that must be addressed to realize its vision of becoming a full-fledged education provider for the Gaya community. A key strategy toward fulfilling its goal revolves around plans to establish the GITC (Gaya Island Training Center) for training community members in computer literacy (and other programs) and a homestay (bed and breakfast) to be run by the association. To expand their work and make the GITC a reality, the leaders identified four core challenges. The first is the ongoing struggle to spread awareness about the importance of the association. Despite their accomplishments, the leaders insist on the need for greater awareness among the island youth about the importance of the association. The leaders feel that many youth cannot yet appreciate BESUGA's role in the community beyond its sports programs. This has led to difficulty in recruiting and grooming new leaders. With several of the Exco members being close to 30 years old, there is a need to develop the leadership capacities of the younger members, particularly those 15 to 20.

According to Sadja, developing new leaders has been challenging for several reasons. Although the organization has had little difficulty mobilizing the island's youth for programs, it has had less success attracting younger members to play substantive leadership roles in the association. While youth participation is often emphasized as a main ingredient for successful community organizations, the challenge of recruiting young people into such roles gets less attention. Research shows, however, that this is a concern shared by many youth-serving organizations, not only in Malaysia (Larson & Walker, 2010).

Despite support from village leaders, BESUGA has faced what leaders describe as instances of 'turf' issues with village heads that have arisen following their successful penetration into the villages. According to Rani, a former BESUGA president, village heads often feel threatened when 'outside' groups like BESUGA are embraced by their residents. BESUGA has attempted to address this issue by emphasizing its desire to have strong relationships with all village leadership. It has repeatedly emphasized its desire to serve the villages and help the heads in any matters relating to the youth. Most heads have responded positively, yet a small number remain distrustful of BESUGA's intentions. Funding remains a challenge for BESUGA. Working in and on behalf of low-income communities has proven difficult in terms of fundraising for programs. It often conducts programs on shoestring budgets, covered mostly by the RM5,000 provided by the State Ministry of Youth and Sports each year and occasional sponsorship from outside groups. Leaders commented that finding long-term sponsors is a major challenge, as many do not want to support programs on Gaya out of fear of negative publicity.

Lastly, the demands on Exco members have resulted in a significant amount of stress. Role diffusion among Exco members who are also full-time employees, parents, and spouses has taken its toll on many of the organization's leaders. Despite their love for the community and passion for BESUGA, the responsibilities seem endless. Furthermore, their successes have raised the bar of expectations, amounting to a growing scope of work. Therefore, the need to involve more BESUGA members—especially the younger ones—in the running of the organization has become a priority.

Social Change on Gaya: Programs, Partnerships and Intermediary Work

Youth are both products and agents of the settings in which they engage, and these reciprocal processes provide a basis for development—both their own and that of others (Brandtstader, 1999; Zeldin, 2004). Less emphasis has been placed on youth development programs as foundations for social action that result in concrete community change and social justice, particularly in traditional societies. From the BESUGA experience, we identified three processes through which the youth brought social change to Gaya. The first is the provision of high-quality, well-attended sports and education programs that are conducted regularly, are well-promoted and managed, and meet the needs and interests of the youth. Second, the successful and regular implementation of BESUGA programs garners support from adult residents as well as village heads, leading to stronger working relations. This has strengthened a sense of community cohesion and ownership for youth programming and for the next generation of young people. Third, the establishment of strong community partnerships opens up greater opportunities for leveraging key resources from outside the community that not only strengthens their youth development efforts but also brings valuable resources to the community as well. BESUGA continues to evolve. After leading the effort to obtain electricity and water, the association is now overseeing the transition process and is actively teaching the community about these new resources. The association has therefore extended its role beyond that of program provider to community organizer, intermediary organization, and community educator. All of these roles are critical to its success in bringing about social change to Gaya Island.

Conceptualizing Youth-Adult Partnership in Traditional Societies Through Multi-Generational Partnership

We found that, in the case of BESUGA, it is the emerging adult group—those between 18 and 30—which plays a crucial bridging role in fostering inter-generational connectivity between adults and adolescents in the community. Because they are closer in age to the secondary school youth—they play sports and share similar interests—it is easier for them to connect with adolescents. This helps motivate the adolescent members to be more engaged in the organization and play meaningful roles; they have more in common with leaders who are closer to them in age (Center for the Study of Social Policy, 2007). At the same time, because emerging adults are older and have begun to embrace adult roles in terms of post-secondary education, employment, and family, they are also able to relate to and garner the respect of adult residents. This has helped to forge effective working relationships between all three groups, which is a key ingredient for bringing vital services and benefits to communities (Zeldin, Larson, Camino & O'Connor, 2005). This differentiation of roles fits Malaysian culture. In this context, youth-adult partnership is not a dichotomous construct but one involving three generations. The emerging adults are at the center; they provide programming to the adolescents and organize support from (and with) older adult residents and community leaders. In Malaysia, it is uncommon for adolescents to play formal leadership roles in youth organizations as the secondary school years are mainly devoted to academic pursuits for most students. These developmental and vocational expectations limit adolescents' leadership involvement. This is in contrast with Western culture, in which youth tend to take on leadership opportunities by the time they are in high school and often earlier (Camino, 2000; Mitra, 2008).

For youth associations to be effective partners with adults in traditional societies, culture dictates deference to adult leaders (Tyson, Jeram,

Sivapragasam & Azlan, 2011). As organizational leaders, the emerging adults in BESUGA must find a balance in both sharing power with and leading older adults. BESUGA recognizes this by requesting permission of village heads and soliciting their ongoing feedback. Similarly, BESUGA must find a proper balance in partnering with adult residents. While the adults seem comfortable with BESUGA taking the lead in change efforts, their tacit support and willingness to pitch in (build stages, construct playing fields) is vital to the work.

CONCLUSION

The lessons from BESUGA's work highlight the potential that youth associations have in bringing greater social justice to traditional, underserved communities and the key role that youth-adult partnership across generations can play as a strategy for mobilizing for change. Given the social, ecological, and political challenges that face our world today, the next generation cannot wait until they are full-fledged adults to begin the work of building a more cooperative and sustainable world (Ginwright & James, 2002). In organizations like BESUGA, young leaders are not just being taught about leadership; they are taking leadership roles and learning by doing—thus making their communities more accountable and effective. In response to reports of decreasing participation in youth organizations, the BESUGA example offers initial insight into how youth organizations can become relevant again and how youth and adults working together can respond to a wide array of community needs.

NOTES

1. 'Kampong' means 'village' in the Malay language.
2. Currency of Malaysia, equal to approximately .32 USD
3. The average household income of a Gaya Island family is approximately RM500 per month.
4. At the time of writing, the villages had electricity but the water system was still in the process of being installed in the villages and they were still relying on holding tanks.
5. The United Nations define youth as those between the ages of 15 to 24 years; the Commonwealth Youth Program uses 15 to 29 years as its official youth age (The Commonwealth, 2015).

REFERENCES

Brandtstadter, J. (1999). The self in action and development: Cultural, biosocial, and ontogenetic bases of intentional self-development. In J. Brandtstadter & R. Lerner (Eds.),

Action and self-development: Theory and research through the life span (pp. 37–67). Thousand Oaks, CA: Sage.

Camino, L. (2000). Youth-adult partnerships: Entering new territory in community work and research. *Applied Developmental Science, 4*(1), 11–20.

Camino, L., & Zeldin, S. (2002). From periphery to center: Pathways for youth civic engagement in the day-to-day life of communities. *Applied Developmental Science*, *6*(4), 213–220.

Center for the Study of Social Policy (2007). *Engaging youth in community decision making. The Anne E. Casey Foundation.* Retrieved from http://www.cssp.org/community/constituents-co-invested-in-change/other-resources/engaging-youth-in-community-decision-making.pdf

The Commonwealth (2015). *Commonwealth Youth Programme (CYP) fund established.* Retrieved from http://thecommonwealth.org/history-of-the-commonwealth/commonwealth-youth-programme-cyp-fund-established

Ginwright, S., & James, T. (2002). From assets to agents of change: Social justice, organizing, and youth development. *New Directions for Youth Development, 2002*(96), 27–46.

Hamzah, A., Suandi, T. & Tamam, E. (2002). *Persatuan belia di Malaysia : Perkembangan & penyerlahan potensi (Youth organizations in Malaysia: Development & potential).* Serdang: Universiti Putra Malaysia Press.

Hyden, G., Court, J. & Mease, J. (2003). *Making sense of governance: The need for involving local stakeholders.* Overseas Development Institute (ODI). Retrieved from http://www.odi.org.uk/publications/3135-making-sense-governance-need-involving-local-stakeholders

Kwon, H.K. (2004). Associations, civic norms, and democracy: Revisiting the Italian case. *Theory and Society*, *33*(2), 135–166.

Larson, R.W., & Walker, K.C. (2010). Dilemmas of practice: Challenges to program quality encountered by youth program leaders. *American Journal of Community Psychology*, *45*(3–4), 338–349.

Malaysian Institute for Research in Youth Development. (2011). *Malaysian Youth Index 2011.* Retrieved from http://www.ippbm.gov.my/v3en/index.php/component/content/article.html?id=253

Miller, M.T. (2011). *Social organization of the west coast Bajau.* Retrieved from http://www.silinternational.com/silewp/2011/silewp2011–009.pdf

Mitra, D.L. (2008). Balancing power in communities of practice: An examination of increasing student voice through school-based youth–adult partnerships. *Journal of Educational Change*, *9*(3), 221–242.

Nga, J.L.H. (2009). The roles of youth organisations in Malaysia's political development. Unpublished PhD thesis. University of Leeds, UK.

Nga, J.L.H. & King, V.T. (2006). Youth organisations' participation in the nation building of Malaysia. Working paper—Department of East Asian Studies, The University of Leeds, UK. Retrieved from https://c.ymcdn.com/sites/www.istr.org/resource/resmgr/bangkok_papers/ngaking.pdf

Said, H.M. (2011). Promoting community based tourism in Bajau Laut community in Kampung Pulau Gaya, Sabah. *Universiti Tun Abdul Razak E-Journal*, 7(2), 46–57. Retrieved from http://www.unirazak.edu.my/research/ejournal/cases/SUSTAINABLECULTURALTOURISMINPULAU_GAYAFinalSubmit31012012.pdf

Tyson, A.D., Jeram, D., Sivapragasam, V., & Azlan, H.N. (2011). Ethnicity, education and the economics of brain drain in Malaysia: Youth perspectives. *Malaysian Journal of Economic Studies*, *48*(2), 131–146.

USAID. (2012). Youth in development: Realizing the demographic opportunity. Youth Policy Toolkit. USAID: Washington, D.C.

Zeldin, S. (2004). Youth as agents of adult and community development: Mapping the processes and outcomes of youth engaged in organizational governance. *Applied Developmental Science*, 8(2), 75–90.
Zeldin, S., Larson, R., Camino, L. & O'Connor (2005). Youth-adult relationships in community programs: Diverse perspectives on good practice. *Journal of Community Psychology, 33*(1), 1–10.

5 Success Stories from Youth Suicide Prevention in Australia

The Youth Work Contribution

Trudi Cooper, Catherine Ferguson, Brooke Chapman, and Shane Cucow

The most intractable social problems, the so-called 'wicked problems,' (Churchman, 1967) cannot be resolved successfully by simple, single-profession or single-jurisdiction programs of intervention. Suicide prevention provides an example of a 'wicked' social problem of this type. Suicide was one of the earliest topics of sociological inquiry in the 19th century when Durkheim (1897) identified that cultural patterns of suicide could not be explained by popular contemporary explanations based upon a purely individual etiology (such as insanity, heredity, or race). In this chapter, we look at how a focus on the sociology of suicide can usefully inform discussion about the role of youth work in suicide prevention.

Durkheim (1897) asserted that suicide was a sociocultural phenomenon strongly influenced by dominant cultural norms. Using this assertion, he developed a typology that still influences contemporary discussions. He proposed that there were three distinct social patterns of suicide: egoistical suicide, altruistic suicide, and anomic suicide. He argued that egoistical suicide was more prominent in societies and subcultures in which extreme moral individualization was normalized and there was weakened connection and commitment to others beyond the self. Altruistic suicide, he argued was more likely under the opposite social conditions, in which moral individualization is completely subsumed and commitment to the good of others at the expense of the self was normalized or might even constitute a duty in some circumstances. Anomic suicide, he argued, became more likely when normal patterns of social expectation were disrupted, when the expected social roles and positions that provided meaning and social status in patterns of people's lives were not achievable. Durkheim asserted that this could occur with economic disruption, such as increased or decreased prosperity, or when social roles were in flux.

Durkheim's key contribution, that suicide had a strong cultural component, is now generally accepted even though there are a number of criticisms of his method of statistical comparison. The main criticism of his method asserts that the statistics from which he derived his theory are unreliable because of varying reluctance of coroners and doctors to record a suicide when alternative explanations might be possible (Hassan, 1996; Jones, 1986; Wasserman, 2001). Despite such critiques, Durkheim's contribution can be summarized as follows: He opened discussion about the relationship between sociocultural conditions and suicide; he countered the prevalent assumptions in his era that suicide was purely an 'individual trouble' that occurred independently of sociocultural norms; and he demonstrated the complexity of the relationship between sociocultural norms and suicide rates. His typology was not deterministic; it did not predict which individuals would commit suicide. Instead, he focused attention towards the relationship between suicide and sociocultural norms, social roles, social structures, and social connection. He discussed how social change that brought freedom and prosperity could, under some circumstances, increase the prevalence of suicide. For example, he argued that sociocultural norms, such as individualism, made egoistical suicide more likely but also brought social benefits, such as greater freedom and autonomy, and that anomic suicide was sometimes prompted by expanding horizons and greater social and economic opportunity and more varied social roles, which many people consider valuable. He argued that altruistic suicide is facilitated by social norms of solidarity and selflessness that are highly valued in many other circumstances (Jones, 1986). These insights have consequences for social policy in suicide prevention because it means there are no easy quick fixes.

This chapter outlines the origins and development of a coordinated government approach to suicide prevention adopted by the Australian government between the mid-1990s and still current in 2014 and discusses the youth work contribution to the initiative. In this chapter, we contend that youth work has a vitally important role to play in prevention of youth suicide but that, for success to be realized, it is essential that other professions understand and facilitate what youth workers can achieve. In addition, the youth work contribution will be most effective if youth work is supported by a whole-of-government coordinated-policy approach to suicide prevention that includes other interventions.

ORIGINS OF AUSTRALIAN SUICIDE PREVENTION POLICY

The impact of youth suicide is especially pronounced for family, for friends, and even for other people who are not intimately connected to the young person. Concern about the prevalence of youth suicide led to the issue becoming a policy priority in Australia in the mid-1990s. Male youth suicide had risen sharply since the 1960s even though suicide rates had declined across other age groups (Hassan, 1996). Similar concerns were expressed through a government report produced in the late 1980s (Ministerial Council for Suicide Prevention in Western Australia, 2009) and the findings of the Royal Commission into Aboriginal Deaths in Custody (Johnston, 1991), which specifically addressed concern about Indigenous youth suicide in custody.

For the purposes of this chapter we used the Australian Bureau of Statistics definition of suicide: A death is considered a suicide if it has been established by the coroner that the death was the result of a deliberate action of the deceased and that the deceased intended the action to end his or her own life (Australian Bureau of Statistics, 2010).

The Australian National Suicide Prevention Program was implemented as a whole-of-government suicide prevention policy, commencing in 1995. Australia was one of the first countries to develop a whole-of-government policy to prevent youth suicide with the introduction of a national strategic approach, developed and implemented in 1995–1996. Three key strategic commitments informed policy: collaboration, mental health literacy, and 'gatekeeper training' (Commonwealth of Australia, 2011). Collaboration was interpreted very broadly to include vertical collaboration between all levels of federal, state, and local government; horizontal collaboration between different departments and portfolios within government; collaboration with industry; and collaboration with young people. The principle of mental health literacy refocused discussion on mental health away from stigmatizing language of 'mental illness and deficiency' and towards 'wellness and recovery.' 'Gatekeeper training' aimed to increase support to at-risk young people by educating people who had regular contact with them, so they could recognize and respond positively to early signs of lack of wellbeing and risk for suicide. Between 1995 and 1999, a total of AUD31 million was allocated for the establishment and implementation of a national youth suicide prevention plan. This was a policy supported by the Council of Australian Governments (COAG)—the body that oversees joint federal-state policy initiatives in Australia. In 2000, the National Youth Suicide Prevention Strategy was expanded to become the Living Is For Everyone (LIFE) strategy (Commonwealth of Australia, 2008). Youth suicide prevention has continued to be a priority for Suicide Prevention Australia (SPA), the national 'peak' (advisory) body for suicide prevention in Australia, which advises federal and state government on suicide prevention (Suicide Prevention Australia, 2010a).

Policy Success

The success of the sustained national program is indicated by national data on youth suicide (15–25 years old) in Australia. Since the commencement of the program, there has been a sharp decline in suicide rates among young men aged 15–25, especially those living in urban areas. A more modest decline occurred in suicide rates for young women aged 15–25, which commenced at a much lower baseline (see Figure 5.1). However, the suicide rate for rural and remote Indigenous Australians remains much higher. The rate for Indigenous Australians living in urban areas has been reduced, reversing the previous patterns in which there was a higher suicide rate for young people in inner city areas. The ABS does not publish statistics for suicides by

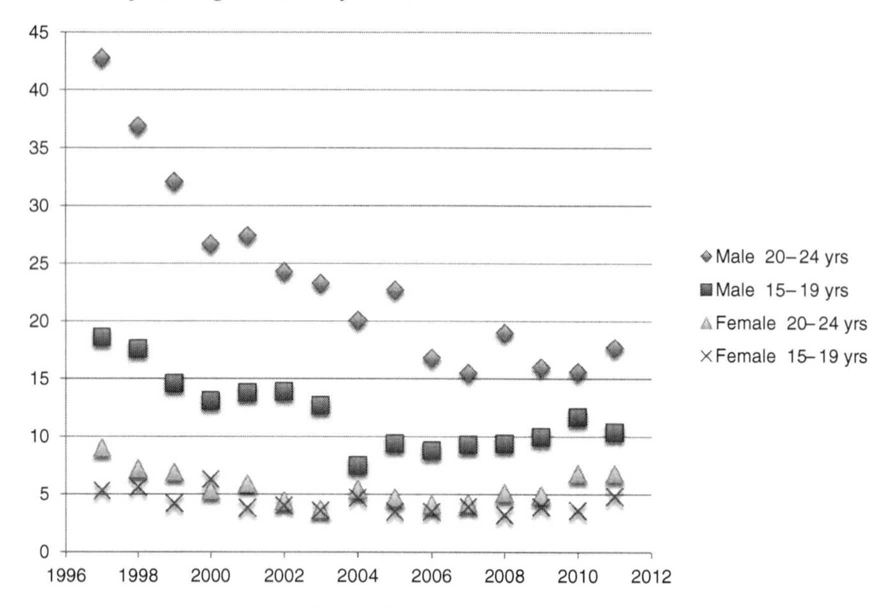

Figure 5.1 Australian youth suicides, 1997 to 2011 (per 100,000 of population)

young people under 15 years old, because the number of such deaths is low (ABS, 2010) and because such reporting may increase distress to families of the deceased. However, the 2011 House of Representatives Standing Committee on Health and Aging has recommended that data be collected for suicide for young people under the age of 15 (Commonwealth of Australia, 2011). In addition, available statistics do not differentiate the method of suicide across age groups, and it is also acknowledged that if there is the slightest doubt about the intention of the individual to commit suicide the coroner will provide an alternative determination. This particularly applies when the deceased is young (ABS, 2010). Figure 5.1 shows the ABS data youth suicide rates for 1997–2011.

Variation Between Youth Populations

Youth suicide rates vary considerably between different youth populations. The male youth suicide rate remains higher than the female youth suicide rate (3–4 times greater risk of completed suicide for young men than young women) and the greatest reduction has been achieved in the highest risk group (young men). Other groups of young people at higher risk of suicide include Indigenous Australian young people (4–6 times greater risk of completed suicide for young people aged 15–19). A similar elevated risk of suicide has also been reported for other First Nation people living in Anglo-Celtic societies, including the Inuit population in Canada and the Maori population in New Zealand (Centre for Suicide Prevention Canada, nd; Ministry of

Health New Zealand, 2012). This is considered to be a response to on-going marginalization and compounded by historical dispossession, cultural disruption consequent to colonization (Hassan, 1996). In Australia it is difficult to obtain accurate national trend statistics for Indigenous Australians (McNamara, 2013) because of historic under-identification of Indigenous status.

Other groups with higher risk include LGBTQ young people (3–14 times greater risk of completed suicide), considered to stem from homophobia and fear of rejection (Macdonald & Cooper, 1998); homeless young people and young people who have been subject to sexual, emotional, or physical abuse as children; unemployed young people; young people who abuse drugs and alcohol; young people who are bullied either at school, work, or in their leisure time, including cyber-bullying; young people in custody; and recently arrived migrants (Hassan, 1996).

Reliable national data is not separately reported for most youth populations. Many of the risk factors are interconnected; for example, young people who have been sexually abused are more likely to become homeless (MacKenzie & Chamberlain, 2008), and homeless young people are more likely to be unemployed (Barker, 2012). Both unemployment and homelessness are more likely to lead to depression and mental health problems (Muir, 2012), and mental health problems are strongly associated with problematic drug and alcohol use (White & Wyn, 2013). In addition, drug and alcohol use is an acknowledged response to pain and trauma, and unemployment and homelessness may be compounded by intergenerational exclusion (Wyn, 2009), racism, or homophobia (Macdonald & Cooper, 1998). Some common threads are marginalization, fear of rejection, trauma, and lack of positive adult support. Notwithstanding the success of the suicide prevention program and the relative infrequency of youth suicide, it remains the second most common cause of death, after road trauma, for young men in Australia, and hence is still a policy concern.

Youth workers are uniquely placed in their capacity to contribute positively to suicide prevention policy. First, a central purpose of a youth worker's role is to support young people to reach their fullest potential as human beings in all facets of their life, including wellbeing. Second, youth work methods focus on supporting young people to build on their strengths. Third, youth workers are 'cultural workers' who aim to enhance peer support and to challenge peer culture that oppresses or bullies. Finally, youth workers are more likely to have contact with higher risk and 'hard-to-reach' (authority-avoiding) youth populations.

YOUTH SUICIDE PREVENTION STRATEGIES IN AUSTRALIA

Interventions to address suicide can be categorized as universal, selective, or indicated (Gordon, 1983). Many school-based programs and in particular those focused on mental health literacy fall into the category of universal interventions because of the (near) universal involvement of young people with school. Youth services provide an example of a selective intervention because not all young people access youth services but youth workers are more likely to have access to some young people who may be at high risk of suicide and who avoid mainstream services. These 'hard to reach' populations include many young people who have a statistically elevated risk of suicide, including homeless young people, LGBTQ young people, young people who have been removed from parental care or are estranged from their families, young people who are engaged in problematic substance abuse, and young people not in education or employment. Indicated interventions are those that are provided for individuals who are at severe and immediate risk of suicide or self-harm. These include individual young people who have already self-harmed or attempted suicide and those who have disclosed suicidal ideation.

Youth suicide prevention strategy in Australia seeks to adopt a two-pronged approach by addressing social and environmental factors that contribute to risk as well as interpersonal and intrapersonal factors that support wellbeing. Social and environmental factors include the way the media reports suicide and self-harm, the availability of lethal means, and levels of social inclusivity and cultural acceptance of difference. Interpersonal factors include the web of personal relationships that surround the individual—for example, whether a person believes they are valued by those around them and can rely on support from family and friends or whether they fear rejection, taunting, bullying, and exclusion. Intrapersonal factors (those unique to or within the individual) relate to factors of psychological distress, such as past trauma, depression, and other mental health difficulties, and differing degrees of individual ability to overcome difficulties.

The holistic, 'whole-of-governments' policy approach developed in the mid-1990s focused upon seven strategies, summarized in Table 5.1. The methodology for this chapter first collated primary documentation about the policy and its implementation (government policy documents, reports of practice, evaluations of practice). The youth work role within policy was acknowledged but not generally explicated. The authors used their knowledge of youth work practice and standard texts on youth work to make explicit some of the tacit elements of youth work practice in suicide prevention policy so that other professionals gain a better understanding of the youth work contribution to the success of the suicide prevention policy.

The next section discusses the strategies in more detail and the youth work contribution to each of these strategies.

Strategy 1: Regulation of Media Representation of Suicide

In 1999, the Australian government introduced the Mindframe National Media Initiative, in response to concerns that prominent, glamorized, or

Table 5.1 Summary of Key Suicide Intervention Strategies

Strategy	Purpose	Life domain	Government level
1: Regulation of media representation of suicide	Prevent copycat suicides	Media	Federal government
2: Availability of lethal means	Restrict access to guns and poisons	Safety	Federal government
3: Youth friendly support services	Encourage help-seeking	Social support and health and well-being	Federal government State government Third sector
4: Collaboration with industry	Prevent workplace bullying	Awareness-raising	Federal government Private sector
5: Gatekeeper training	Training people working with young people	Training	Federal government State government Third sector
6: School policy to prevent bullying in school	Prevent bullying at school	Education policy, culture, and in-school support	State government Third sector
7: Anti-homophobia policies	De-criminalization and support for LGBTIQ young people	Rights, legislation, social support	State Government Private sector Third sector

sensationalized reports of suicides, especially if they included descriptions of method, may normalize suicide as a response to problems and increase likelihood of cluster or 'copycat' suicides (Mindframe, nd). "Suicide clusters are identified by the occurrence of a greater number of deaths by suicide than would be normally expected in a particular location and/or time period (i.e., the observed suicide rate is exceptionally higher than the expected rate in the underlying population)" (Cheung, Spittal, Williamson, Tung & Pirkis, 2013, p. 1). These concerns also extended to media portrayal of mental illness, with suggestions that negative portrayal may contribute to community stigmatizing attitudes and discrimination towards those suffering a mental health condition. The Mindframe National Media Initiative encouraged "responsible, accurate and sensitive media portrayal of suicide and mental illness" (Pirkis, Blood, Dare & Holland, 2008, p. 3) and the standards were designed to promote reporting "that raises public awareness about the issue of suicide without it leading to a risk of imitation" (Machlin et al., 2012, p. 46). In 2002, the Mindframe website was funded by the Australian Government under the National Suicide Prevention Program developed as a resource to support appropriate standards of reporting (see http://www.mindframe-media.info/).

Evaluation of the effects of this initiative compared reporting of suicide and mental health before implementation of the new standards with reporting in 2006-2007. Pirkis et al. (2008) found positive changes in how suicide and mental health were reported. Both issues were presented in more sensitive and appropriate ways compared to before the standards were developed. Machlin, Pirkis and Spittal (2013) reported that only about 1% of suicides were reported in the Australian media in 2006-2007. Suicide was only reported in the media when there was some other public interest concern. In the second part of their report, Machlin et al. (2013) considered the quality of the reporting and found that in some cases there were still considerable opportunities for improvement. They found the most extensive and inappropriate suicide media coverage related to the deaths of two young women in Melbourne, Victoria in 2007. The report recommended inclusion of mental health telephone support line numbers when reporting on suicide and/or mental health issues. This recommendation has now been adopted by the media. Excessive detail was the main problem identified, especially in celebrity suicide, as was inappropriate descriptions of mental illness. Concern was also expressed about descriptions of well-known suicide sites in some news reports.

On a positive note, the media has reported the recovery of several well-known Australians, providing reinforcement for the potential transient nature of mental illness and the good prospects for recovery. The Mindframe website includes information developed by Romeo et al. (2008) to sensitize Australian undergraduate journalism students to the issue of reporting suicide. Australian journalism in controlled media (e.g., radio, newspapers) follows reporting guidelines on suicide and mental health. However the uncontrolled media, such as Facebook, Twitter, Tumblr, and other social media, are used by young people and do not adhere to the guidelines. Christensen and Griffiths first raised concerns about social media in 2000 when it was less diverse.

On balance, regulation of media reporting of suicide seems to have been effective in the 'controlled' media but has had no effect on uncontrolled media. Most young people engage extensively with uncontrolled media. This means it is important for youth workers to be aware of suicide discussion and reporting in the uncontrolled media relevant to young people with whom they have contact. This includes what is happening on 'tribute sites' if a suicide has occurred in the peer group. Youth workers must be prepared, if necessary, to counter perceptions and commentary on uncontrolled media, to discuss non-lethal solutions to life problems, and to directly support young people who may be adversely affected by representations and discussions of suicide on the Internet and in social media.

Strategy 2: Availability of Lethal Means

Access to lethal means is acknowledged as an important factor in facilitation of suicide. Policy to control public access to firearms was introduced in

1996 in response to Australia's only mass shooting, in Port Arthur, Tasmania. This was not part of the suicide prevention strategy but occurred at the time when the strategy was being implemented and contributed to suicide reduction. Research has shown that use of firearms as a suicide method has reduced since 1996 and does not appear to have been displaced by others methods (Chapman, Alpers, Agho & Jones, 2006). The most common methods of suicide were hanging, strangulation, and suffocation, accounting for just over half of suicides. The tools available to enact these methods are generally available in the community, making it difficult to restrict availability to these means. Drugs and poisoning were the next most common methods of choice. In many instances, these methods require planning to enact suicide. Policy in Australia limits the prescription of drugs in a number of ways, including prescribing guidelines, restrictions on quantity and use, and frequency of repeat prescriptions. Similarly, over-the-counter drugs, which may be lethal, are sold in limited quantities (limits on both quantities in each package and the number of packets per purchase). The acquisition of poisons also requires effort, and suppliers are required to seek purchaser identification and record the sale of poisons. Other suicide methods include drowning and jumping from a height (ABS, 2011). In these instances, the installation of physical barriers at sites regularly used for suicide have had promising results, with a reduction in suicide and some evidence that the suicide is not displaced to another method (Cox et al., 2013).

Youth workers can do little to directly influence young people's access to lethal means. However, gatekeeper training has been made available to youth workers working with high-risk populations of young people. Trained youth workers are more aware of the signs a young person may be planning suicide, such as gathering the means, giving away valued possessions, or sending farewell messages. They can offer support, encourage help seeking, mediate in conflicts, and support referral. If they are working with high-risk peer groups, they can also educate other young people to be aware of adverse indications, can advise on how to seek help, and can normalize help seeking. Youth workers can contribute to reducting risk of young people accidentally overdosing when suicide is not their intention through programs that raise awareness of early symptoms of poisoning and by facilitating programs, such as the Red Cross 'Save a Mate' program, that develop young people's knowledge about peer first aid for youth populations in which drug overdose and poisoning pose a higher risk.

Strategy 3: Youth-Friendly Support Services

Good mental health literacy and access to support services can prevent suicide. Part of the suicide prevention strategy is to improve mental health literacy of young people and to make mental health services more 'youth friendly.' Mental health literacy is described as "a person's knowledge, beliefs, and abilities that enable the recognition, management or prevention of mental health problems" (Commonwealth of Australia, 2011, p. 43), and mental health literacy is still considered low in the Australian population (Jorm, 2012). School-based initiatives that targeted mental health literacy included KidsMatters (for primary schools) and Mindmatters (for secondary schools) (SPA, 2010b). It has been recommended that "the Australian Curriculum, Assessment and Reporting Authority include social development education and mental health as a core component of the national curriculum for primary and secondary schools" (Commonwealth of Australia, 2011, Recommendation 8). This has implications for the training of teachers, who may require additional training to present age-appropriate health-related curriculum. In an analysis of current school-based mental health literacy programs, Wei, Hayden, Kutcher, Zygmunt and McGrath (2013) reported relatively low effectiveness of these programs. In one Australian program, results showed increased knowledge but only a moderate impact on reducing stigma and a weak impact on intentions to seek help (Rickwood, Cavanagh, Curtis & Sakrouge, 2004)

The suicide prevention strategy funded several national and state-based youth-focused organizations to offer mental health and wellbeing services. These programs were designed to be acceptable to young people (SPA, 2010b) and included youth organizations such as Headspace, Youth Connections, ReachOut.com by Inspire Foundation, Youth Focus, youthbeyondblue, Kids Helpline, and National Centre Against Bullying (SPA, 2010b). It was recognized that mental health literacy could be facilitated by increasing use of appropriate web pages (Christensen & Griffith, 2000). Youth Focus operated structured peer-support weekends for young people identified as at risk of suicide. This program has been designed to develop participants' coping strategies and improve their overall mental health and wellbeing (SPA, 2010b).

Online services form an important component of suicide prevention and early intervention, offering young people the ability to access support throughout the day and night in regions where face-to-face services are impossible to access locally. Delivering services online allows young people to connect with youth work programs on their own terms in the places where are they intuitively looking for information (Metcalf & Blake, 2014). In addition, the ability to remain anonymous while using a service opens pathways for young people who otherwise would not seek professional help. One of the youth services that targets mental health literacy is ReachOut.com by Inspire Foundation, and the next vignette describes how ReachOut.com staff use youth work methods in an online service, a form of 'virtual detached youth work.'

CASE STUDY: REACHOUT.COM

ReachOut.com is Australia's oldest online youth mental health service, having operated for 16 years as of 2014. It is a health promotion and early intervention program provided via website, online forums, and mobile applications. The service targets young people 14–25 years old, inclusive of those showing early signs and symptoms of mental health difficulties, those at risk of developing mental health difficulties, and all young people regardless of mental health status. ReachOut.com contributes to the reduction of youth suicide by supporting large numbers of young people in understanding mental illness and acting early to prevent its progression. ReachOut.com assists young people with recognizing, understanding, and acting on signs and symptoms of mental health difficulties. This is achieved through the provision of practical information and personal stories, online discussions with peers and mental health professionals, and through the development of online tools/mobile applications for building mental health literacy and resilience skills. Giving guidance and tools for building preventative factors (such as mental health literacy, self-awareness, communication and problem-solving skills) helps young people to interrupt or prevent the progression of mental illness. Through the use of social media and peer-moderated asynchronous forums, ReachOut.com also aims to foster a sense of social belonging and social connectedness—key resilience factors. Together, these strategies provide recognition and self-help options for young people, allowing them to start the journey from distress to action for emerging mental health difficulties.

ReachOut.com receives over a million unique visitors each year. Young people accessing the service are predominantly from a younger cohort, early in the age range of onset for common mental illnesses. 2013 annual user survey statistics indicated that 7% were aged under 14 years, 29% 14–15 years, 37% 16–18 years, and 26% 18–25 years. Of those visitors, 26% identified as lesbian, gay, bisexual, trans*, or intersex. 21% lived in rural and regional areas of Australia, which demonstrates good reach into areas where face-to-face services can be scarce. 56% of surveyed users access ReachOut.com between 5:00 p.m–9:00 p.m., when face-to-face services are traditionally closed.

Most users present with high levels of psychological distress (76%) and have not previously accessed mental health care (51%). While the majority of young people are looking for support with issues related to their mental health, their needs are very diverse. For visitors surveyed, the main topics of information they sought include depression (19%), anxiety (9%), and self-harm (6%) as well as suicide, eating disorders, abuse and violence, bullying, and a range of other life and mental health issues. The dominant reasons for visiting include going through a tough time and looking for help (71%), looking for general information (51%), and looking for tips on improving wellbeing (51%). Twenty-eight percent visit because they know somebody else going through a tough time and are looking for information on how to help.

For young people currently or previously visiting during a tough time, 66% indicated ReachOut.com helped them feel more able to deal with their issue. Importantly, 65% also reported that ReachOut.com helped them feel like they are not alone. Of the 77% of young people who scored high or very high on the Kessler K10, 44% had not previously sought clinical support. Of those who hadn't sought clinical support, 46% said they were more likely to seek help from at least one type of mental health professional after using ReachOut.com. A 21-year-old female reported, "I get general information and answers from real people. I feel normal and like there are other people going through similar things. I don't feel alone about issues."- 21-year-old female from QLD

Strategy 4: Collaboration with Industry

There are very few documented programs that involve collaboration with industry, despite the fact that employment in some industries increases young people's risk of suicide. The construction industry has been identified as an industry that increases suicide risk for young people. Broadbent, Corney, du Plessis and Papadopoulos (2013) reported on a successful Australian intervention to improve the mental health literacy and help-seeking behavior of apprentices in the construction industry. This program was designed and presented by youth work staff in collaboration with the construction union and employers. There is scope for more industry-based programs, especially in fields of youth employment where risks are elevated.

One promising program that is being promoted in Western Australia as part of the Western Australian Suicide Prevention Strategy (One Life) (Department of Health, 2009) is that of Pledge Partners (http://www.onelifewa.com.au/partner-with-one-life/pledge-holders/). This program is not specifically designed for youth, but involves businesses and other employer organizations signing a pledge to support suicide prevention in the workplace. These organizations include a range of industries and pledge to provide suicide prevention information and activities. Systematic evaluation of both these programs has yet to be completed.

Strategy 5: Gatekeeper Training

Gatekeepers are described as individuals within a community who can be trained to recognize the warning signs of suicide, know how to ask appropriately about suicidal ideation, and can support someone in seeking professional help (Tompkins, Witt & Abraibesh, 2010). 'Gatekeeper training' programs vary in philosophy, content, and length (Rodi et al., 2012; Wallack, Servaty-Seib & Taub, 2013) and are considered effective. Research suggests that gatekeeper training is most successful when part of a comprehensive suicide prevention program (Christensen & Petrie, 2013; Isaac et al., 2009; Wallack et al., 2013; York et al., 2013). Mandatory training in mental health awareness and suicide risk assessment for teachers was one of 10 recommendations made by the House of Representatives Standing Committee on Health and Aging in 2011. Gatekeeper training is offered to teachers (but is not mandatory) and others who have regular contact with most young people, including youth workers, especially those working with higher risk groups.

In the vignette that follows, a school-based youth worker reflects on how she works with young people on suicide prevention issues.

CASE STUDY: A YOUTH WORKER'S EXPERIENCE OF SUICIDE PREVENTION IN A SCHOOL

I was a professional youth worker at a college that served a low socioeconomic community in the southeastern suburbs of Perth, Western Australia. I worked with many young people who indicated suicidal ideation. Here I describe the helping relationship I had with many students to show the value of dialogue and trust that was shared during difficult times of their lives when they thought of suicide. Many talked about and showed deep sadness while describing a sense of loss and emptiness within because they felt they did not belong or feel connected to someone or something in life they could rely upon when they need to feel loved, accepted, and safe in the world. They also gave incredible insight based on their perception of their place in the world in context of family, friends, and the added burden of feeling alone. As a youth worker based in a school, the approach I use is grounded in specific helping skills. I use both the observational data available and listen for the common cues that are associated with suicide ideation. If I am unclear of anything that has been said to me, I seek clarification to eliminate any doubts I may have about risk factors coming from the young person. These may need to be reported to referral agencies (also sometimes to others such as school principals), who will expect a clear account of why you think a young person is suicidal. Clarifying means asking questions, repeating back, or summarizing what the young person has said to check you have understood the conversation correctly and as a way to engage with the young person; it is important to affirm your readiness to listen and give attention as they confide in you. Establish an immediate (same day) response by the end of the informal counseling session. Sensitivity is important. The response to students will differ depending on how serious they are about ending their lives. This involves considering a young person's formal and informal support systems and whether they are active or could be reactivated if needed.

Strategy 6: School Policy to Prevent Bullying in School

Bullying has been shown to increase risk of suicide. The National Safe Schools Framework is a collaborative effort by the Australian Government, State and Territory governments, non-governmental school authorities, and other key stakeholders to promote a national approach to addressing bullying, harassment, violence, and child abuse and neglect in a sustained and positive approach (http://education.gov.au/national-safe-schools-framework-0). A manual and resources kit has been made available to all schools to support development of appropriate programs to promote student wellbeing. The commitment to address bullying in school is a positive beginning. Where youth workers are employed in school, they can be involved in processes to resolve interpersonal conflict that underlie bullying. Youth workers are useful in this context because bullying often occurs out of school, as well, and youth workers are able to bridge both worlds as part of their role.

Strategy 7: Anti-Homophobia Policies

When the youth suicide prevention policy was introduced in the 1990s, homophobia still had legal sanction because the age of consent for sexual activity between young men was still set at 21 years old in most states in Australia. For young men who were gay, this meant that they still risked legal or welfare action if they came out. A qualitative study of young men's coming out experiences conducted in 1996 found that, of the six young men interviewed, three had seriously contemplated suicide to the point of making plans, and one had attempted suicide (Macdonald & Cooper, 1998). During the period since the implementation of the suicide prevention strategy, the age of consent was equalized to be the same as for heterosexual sex (16 years old in most Australian states), so legal barriers have been removed. The lower age of consent is significant for youth work because it is much more politically acceptable to offer support services to young people when they are engaged in legal activity and to fund youth agencies to provide support. As part of the suicide prevention strategy, specialist youth agencies receive funds to support LGBTQ young people. A more recent study confirmed the findings of the earlier study that the average age for the first suicide attempt is 16 years old, which is often before 'coming out' (National LGBTQ Health Alliance, 2010).

The school environment is important because attendance is compulsory, and most young people do attend. A positive school environment supports the wellbeing of students, including those who identify as lesbian, gay, or bisexual (Birkett, Espelage & Koenig, 2009), and suicide rates are reduced where school policies include specific anti-homophobic policies (Hatzenbuehler & Keyes, 2013). A kit produced in New South Wales in 1996, "Resources for Teaching against Violence," which included information to combat bullying, violence, and homophobia, was provided to schools; however, evaluation showed that in the early years of the policy, homophobia was not appropriately addressed within schools, either in terms of bullying prevention or education to reduce prejudice of students (Desmarchelier, 2000; Ferfolja, 1998; Smith, 2000). More recently, Michaelson (2008) found similar issues in Queensland, despite attempts by the State Education

Department to address homophobia. One of the barriers to reduction of homophobic attitudes and behaviors within the school environment is that the policies are 'hidden' within bullying policies, whereas research found homophobia needs to be addressed specifically (Jones, 2013; Michaelson, 2008). This has been rectified in NSW, according to a recent state government report (NSW Government, n.d.). Internationally, there is evidence that teachers are not well equipped to address homophobia (Clark, 2010). Clark reported that homophobic taunts were stopped, but no allies provided support for LGBTQ students. Clark considered the stopping of taunts alone to represent a neutral, apolitical stance. Jones reports that some schools have begun to adopt specific policies to address homophobia (Jones, 2012), but outcomes have not yet been evaluated.

Youth workers have potential to counter homophobia both in school and out of school and are well placed to act as allies to LGBTQ students. Specialist community-based youth agencies, such as the Freedom Centre in Western Australia, offer support to young people that is not available to young people anywhere else. The Freedom Centre was established in 1994 to offer peer support to LGBTQ young people (http://www.freedom.org.au/). The Freedom Centre was founded at a time when there were no other specialized support services and when homophobia was either unaddressed, or sometimes even condoned, in schools. The Freedom Centre is now part of the National Suicide Prevention Strategy and receives public mental health funding.

Since the commencement of the suicide prevention policy, mainstream community attitudes to homophobia have changed, as illustrated by a recent poll that indicates 64% of the Australian population support same-sex marriage (http://www.australianmarriageequality.org/); however, acceptance is not uniform. In some cultural, sub-cultural, and religious groups, active support for LGBTQ young people is still essential because homophobia is intense and the risk of suicide remains high.

INDIGENOUS[1] SUICIDE PREVENTION POLICY

For the period 2001–2010, suicide rates of Aboriginal and Torres Strait Islander peoples were twice that of non-Indigenous Australians (ABS, 2012). In June 2010, the Senate Community Affairs References Committee (SCARC) recommended that ". . . the Commonwealth government develop a separate suicide prevention strategy for Indigenous communities within the National Suicide Prevention Strategy . . ." (SCARC, 2011). A National Aboriginal and Torres Strait Islander Suicide Prevention Strategy was published in 2013 (Commonwealth of Australia, 2013). Indigenous suicide has been linked to a range of specific factors such as colonization, dispossession, racism, and social marginalization, as well as grief and the intergenerational effects of 'stolen generation' policies that weakened family ties and kin-support systems (Closing the Gap Clearing House, 2013). Many of the strategies within mainstream suicide prevention policies are relevant to Indigenous Australians, but the Senate committee identified the need for additional culturally specific approaches (De Leo, Sveticic, Milner & McKay, 2011), and this led to the National Aboriginal and Torres Strait Islander Suicide Prevention Strategy document that was produced in May 2013. The key premise of the strategy is that risk factors for suicide for Aboriginal and Torres Strait Islander people include not only risk factors shared by the non-Indigenous population but also the consequences of historic circumstances that have an adverse impact on social and emotional wellbeing and mental health of Aboriginal and Torres Strait Islander people. The strategy incorporates an Aboriginal view of health, which favors community-focused, holistic and integrated approaches to suicide prevention with an emphasis on investment in "upstream" prevention efforts to build community, family and individual resilience and on restoring social and emotional wellbeing. This is a holistic perspective that encompasses mental, physical, cultural, and spiritual health and is often referred to as social and emotional wellbeing rather than mental health.

> The social and emotional wellbeing concept is broader than this and recognises the importance of connection to land, culture, spirituality, ancestry, family and community, and how these affect the individual. Social and emotional wellbeing problems cover a broad range of problems that can result from unresolved grief and loss, trauma and abuse, domestic violence, removal from family, substance misuse, family breakdown, cultural dislocation, racism and discrimination and social disadvantage (Social Health Reference Group, 2004, p. 9).

Key principles of the strategy include focusing upon strengthening communities and respecting Indigenous cultural values. Action plans should be developed through genuine partnerships with Indigenous people, take a holistic approach, and incorporate values that build upon cultural perspectives on healing and spirituality; programs should also be high quality, evidence-based, and delivered in culturally appropriate and safe ways. Programs include connectedness with culture and an emphasis on inter-generational support and a role for elders to teach young people about culture and cultural identity.

Suicide prevention in Indigenous communities still has not achieved parity with other cultural groups because racism and the effects of dispossession and cultural denigration have not yet been addressed at a societal level in Australia. Youth workers have a useful contribution, especially in challenging the racism of non-Indigenous Australians. Youth workers may also have a role in supporting cultural connection and pride in young Indigenous Australians; however, as Chauhan (n.d.) argued, for success, cultural pride and integration needs to be accompanied by strategies that address racism and inequality. The message from Chauhan's seminal work is that youth workers should not limit their work to celebrations of culture that make it an exotic spectacle but must prioritize actions to address racism and promote genuine respect by non-Indigenous people for Indigenous people and their cultural values.

DISCUSSION: THE YOUTH WORK CONTRIBUTION

Risk for suicide is elevated by factors that are intrapersonal, interpersonal, and structural. These factors include oppression (racism, homophobia), (fear of) social rejection, social exclusion, social isolation, lack of support (family/friends), early-life trauma or separation, bullying and threat of physical or emotional violence, inability to achieve culturally sanctioned social roles (when homeless or unemployed), overwhelming emotional pain, social inequality, self-reliance and reluctance to seek help, and the unavailability of culturally suitable services. Durkheim's typology can be used to explain how, at a societal level, diverse socioeconomic policies can elevate or reduce suicide risk. In the Australia suicide prevention approach described, youth workers have a role within a multi-professional approach in the following ways:

- Youth workers are able to make contact with young people in the young person's environment, including some who would not have contacted mental health services. This includes online support, which is 'where young people are' and informal support in the school environment.
- Youth workers are able to offer information and support, assist young people with resolving problems, provide supported referral of young people to specialist services, and often have contact with young people who avoid authority.
- By the 1990s, mainstream youth work in Australia had adopted anti-oppressive values and were able to publicly support LGBTQ young people and reject racist stereotypes when many other professionals, including teachers and mental health services, were staying silent (see, for example, the Freedom Centre in Perth).
- Young people experience no stigma discussing their concerns with a youth worker, and the young person is often able to raise his or her concerns obliquely and test the response, whereas most others services do not facilitate informal contact and use may be stigmatized (see, for example, the first and second case studies in this chapter).
- Youth workers work directly with peer groups to make homophobia, sexism, and racism less acceptable and to challenge negative stereotypes, stigmatizing attitudes, and bullying (see, for example, the second case study).

- Youth workers are able to work through informal education methods to help young people find meaningful social roles in their lives even when their aspirations are disrupted or blocked. These approaches are explained in many basic texts on youth work (see, for example, Jeffs & Smith, 2005).
- Some youth workers are able to provide material support through emergency accommodation, support for entering education and employment, or linking young people to appropriate services (see Jeffs & Smith, 2005, or any basic text on youth work).
- Some youth workers offer support to reconnect with family and heal relationships (see any basic text on youth work).

The authors contend that while the contribution of youth workers is significant, in some instances the effects of youth work intervention are palliative to counter the effects of social phenomena such as, racism and homophobia. These interventions would be less needed if the cause of oppression were removed. Likewise, a youth worker can support a young person to seek help, but this will only lead to successful outcomes if the young person feels comfortable with the services offered.

The whole-of-government approach requires all parts of government to be aware of their contribution to suicide prevention. The next three examples illustrate how youth work intervention in suicide prevention can be enhanced by other initiatives and why continued success of suicide prevention depends on integrated whole-of-government, or even whole-of-society, approach.

- Oppression, inequality, intolerance, and marginalization contribute to suicide in some high-risk youth populations, especially Indigenous young people and LGBTQ young people. This means challenging institutional tolerance or support for racism and homophobia in schools, by the police, by employers, and in everyday life. To some extent this has occurred, but high suicide rates in the most oppressed youth populations indicate there is room for further improvement. Legal and policy barriers still remain (e.g., welfare policies that differentially affect Indigenous people, marriage inequality). These signal that oppression is sanctioned.
- Symbolic actions can reinforce equality (or inequality) and provide what Garfinkel (1956) would call 'ceremonies of elevation.' Many youth and community organizations have their own ceremonies that recognize achievements of young people who rarely receive praise. These can be very effective for the individuals involved. At a cultural level, these need to be supplemented by symbolic actions, such as the Rudd government apology to the stolen generation (Indigenous children forcibly removed from their parents because of their race), the Gillard government apology to victims of child migration and forced adoptions and those abused by church and state-care services.

These actions cost little and have been helpful, but there is room for more action here to reinforce the unacceptability of racism, sexism, homophobia, and other forms of oppression.

- Self-reliance, help-seeking, and mental health stigma: there is a normalized reluctance to seek help in Australian culture generally and this is heightened specifically within hegemonic masculinity. Youth workers can provide youth-friendly services face-to-face and online, and can locally influence reluctance to seek help. However, youth workers can only challenge stigma about mental illness/health in a very limited and local way. Other services and the media are the main drivers of social change. There is evidence that the media reporting rules, plus the willingness of politicians and celebrities to discuss their recovery from depression, have begun to change cultural values. There is still some way to go on this, and it is important that the experience people have with mental health services is sufficiently positive and respectful that they choose to continue to engage with them.

Successful Collaboration Partnerships

Many professions outside youth work have an incomplete idea of what youth workers do. They observe that youth workers engage with young people but do not understand the processes used in youth work or the conditions that youth work requires for success. Other partners in inter-professional collaborations need better understanding of the methods used by youth workers and must respect professional judgement of youth workers for partnerships to succeed. This means the 'terms of engagement' for youth work have to be controlled by youth workers. Youth workers should not be expected to prioritize other organizations' goals above their own or to align their practice with the methods, policies, or procedures of other professions. For example, it is not possible for youth workers to operate effectively if other professions demand they must share all young people's conversations without the young person's permission. By the same token, it is very important that youth workers are absolutely clear with young people about the limits to the confidentiality they can offer. Youth workers and youth work educators still have work to do in educating the public and other professions about the nature of youth work because other professions do not understand youth work. Youth workers also need an excellent understanding about the conditions that are essential for effective youth work, especially the importance of methods of work that maintain young people's trust and confidence.

CONCLUSION

Youth work has an important and unique role to play in response to many social issues. Many of the 'big' education, health and welfare issues facing societies would also benefit from a well-researched, multi-faceted and coordinated whole-of-government approach. This should also include organizations and service providers in the not-for-profit and for-profit sectors. This review on youth work and suicide prevention strategies showed that the Australian initiative achieved a high level of success because it coordinated a multi-faceted response. It is important that the potential role of youth work is well understood by other professions. For this to occur, youth workers need to be able to explain to others their values, their methods, and the pre-conditions for success in their work. It is equally important that other professionals respect this while understanding that youth work methods will be different from their own and their normal assumptions and preconditions may not apply. Youth workers should not be disheartened if they alone are unable to solve intractable social problems. Their efforts will be less effective in the absence of supportive policy across government. A mature profession has a clear understanding of its contribution and how this can be helped or hindered by policy in other domains of government.

NOTE

1. The terms 'Aboriginal' and 'Indigenous' are used interchangeably in this Chapter. Many of the Australian documents use the term Aboriginal and/or Aboriginal and Torres Strait Islander both of who are considered as the Indigenous population within Australia.

REFERENCES

Australian Bureau of Statistics. (2010). *Causes of death, Australia, 2008* (Catalogue No. 3303.0). Canberra, ACT: ABS. Retrieved from http://www.ausstats.abs.gov.au/ausstats/subscriber.nsf/0/E8510D1C8DC1ACCA2576F600139288/$File/33030_2008.pdf

Australian Bureau of Statistics. (2011). *Causes of death, Australia, 2009* (Catalogue No. 3303.0). Canberra, ACT: ABS. Retrieved from http://www.abs.gov.au/ausstats/abs@.nsf/0/EBA9606492CEFC61CA25788400127CEB?opendocument#

Australian Bureau of Statistics. (2012). *Causes of death. Australia, 2010* (Catalogue No. 3303.0). Canberra, ACT: ABS. Retrieved from http://www.ausstats.abs.gov.au/ausstats/subscriber.nsf/0/E39670183DE1B0D9CA2579C6000F7A4E/$File/33030_2010.pdf

Barker, J.D. (2012). Social capital, homeless young people and the family. *Journal of Youth Studies, 15*(6), 730–743.

Birkett, M., Espelage, D.L., & Koenig, B. (2009). LGB and questioning students in schools: The moderating effects of homophobic bullying and school climate on negative outcomes. *Journal of Youth and Adolescence, 38*(7), 989–1000.

Broadbent, R., Corney, T., du Plessis, K., & Papadopoulos, T. (2013). Using generalist youth work practice in suicide prevention: A program for young construction workers. *Youth Studies Australia, 32*(1), 46–54.

Centre for Suicide Prevention Canada. (n.d.). *Canada's aboriginal communities and suicide: Called to listen, called to understand*. Retrieved from https://suicideinfo.ca/LinkClick.aspx?fileticket=JEM4FDfgWtA%3d&tabid=618

Chapman, S., Alpers, P., Agho, K., & Jones, M. (2006). Australia's 1996 gun law reforms: Faster falls in firearm deaths, firearm suicides, and a decade without mass shootings. *Injury Prevention, 12*, 365–372.

Chauhan, V. (n.d.). *Beyond steel bands 'n' samosas: Black young people and the youth service*. Leicester: National Youth Bureau.

Cheung, Y. T. D., Spittal, M.J., Williamson, M.K., Tung, S. J., & Pirkis, J. (2013). Application of scan statistics to detect suicide clusters in Australia. *PLoS ONE, 8*(1), 11.

Christensen, H., & Griffiths, K. (2000). The Internet and mental health literacy. *Australian and New Zealand Journal of Psychiatry, 34*, 975–979.

Christensen, H., & Petrie, K. (2013). Suicide prevention: signposts for a new approach. *Medical Journal of Australia, 198*(9), 472–474.

Churchman, C.W. (1967). Wicked problems. *Management Science, 14*(4), Guest Editorial.

Clark, C.T. (2010). Preparing LGBTQ-allies and combating homophobia in a U.S. teacher education program. *Teaching and Teacher Education, 26*(3), 704–713.

Closing the Gap Clearinghouse (AIHW & AIFS). (2013). *Strategies and practices for promoting the social and emotional wellbeing of Aboriginal and Torres Strait Islander people* (Resource sheet no. 19). Produced for the Closing the Gap Clearinghouse. Canberra: Australian Institute of Health and Welfare.

Commonwealth of Australia. (2008). *Living is for everyone (LIFE) framework*. Canberra: Department of Health and Aging. Retrieved from http://www.livingisforeveryone.com.au/Research-and-evidence-in-suicide-prevention.html

Commonwealth of Australia. (2011). *Before it's too late: Report on early intervention programs aimed at preventing youth suicide*. Canberra: House of Representatives, Standing Committee on Health and Aging. Retrieved from http://www.aph.gov.au/parliamentary_business/committees/house_of_representatives_committees?url=haa/youthsuicide/report.htm

Commonwealth of Australia. (2013). *National Aboriginal and Torres Strait Islander suicide prevention strategy*. Canberra: Australian Government, Department of Health and Ageing. Retrieved from http://www.health.gov.au/internet/main/Publishing.nsf/Content/305B8A5E056763D6CA257BF0001A8DD3/$File/Indigenous%20Strategy.pdf

Cox, G.R., Owens, C., Robinson, J., Nicholas, A., Lockley, A., Williamson, M., & Pirkis, J. (2013). Interventions to reduce suicides at suicide hotspots: A systematic review. *BMC Public Health, 13*(214), 12. Retrieved from http://www.biomedcentral.com/1471–2458/1413/1214

De Leo, D., Sveticic, J., Milner, A., & McKay, K. (2011). *Suicide in indigenous populations of Queensland*. Mt. Gravatt, Queensland: Australian Institute for Suicide Research and Prevention.

Department of Health. (2009). *Western Australian suicide prevention strategy 2009–2013*. Retrieved from http://www.mentalhealth.wa.gov.au/Libraries/pdf_docs/WA_Suicide_Prevention_Strategy.sflb.ashx

Desmarchelier, C. (2000). Teacher's understanding of homosexuality and body image: Habitus issues. *Journal of Men's Issues, 8*(2), 237–253.

Durkheim, É. 1897. *Le Suicide: étude de sociologie*. Paris: Alcan. Tr. 1951a.

Ferfolja, T. (1998). Australian lesbian teachers—a reflection of homophobic harassment of high school teachers in New South Wales government schools. *Gender and Education, 10*(4), 401–415.

Freedom Centre. (2014). How we work at Freedom Centre – the peer model. Retrieved from http://www.freedom.org.au/index.php?option=com_content&view=category&layout=blog&id=36&Itemid=55

Garfinkel, H. (1956). Conditions for successful degradation ceremonies. *American Journal of Sociology, 61*(5), 420–424.

Gordon, R.S. (1983). An operational classification of disease prevention. *Public Health Reports, 98*(2), 107–109.

Hassan, R. (1996). *Social factors in suicide in Australia* (Trends and Issues in Criminal Justice No 52). Canberra. Australian Institute of Criminology.

Hatzenbuehler, M.L., & Keyes, K.M. (2013). Inclusive anti-bullying policies and reduced risk of suicide attempts in lesbian and gay youth. *Journal of Adolescent Health, 53*(1 Suppl.), S21–S26.

Isaac, M., Elias, B., Katz, L.Y., Belik, S.-L., Deane, F.P., Enns, M.W., . . . The Swampy Cree Suicide Prevention Team (12 members). (2009). Gatekeeper training as a preventative intervention for suicide: A systematic review. *Canadian Journal of Psychiatry, 54*(4), 260–268.

Jeffs, T., & Smith, M.K. (2005). *Informal education: Conversation, democracy and learning* (3rd ed.). Nottingham: Education Now Publishing Co-operative Ltd.

Johnston, E. (1991). *Royal commission into Aboriginal deaths in custody*. Canberra: Commonwealth of Australia.

Jones, R. A. (1986). *Emile Durkheim: An introduction to four major works*. Beverly Hills, CA: Sage Publications, Inc.

Jones, T. (2012). *Discrimination and bullying on the grounds of sexual orientation and gender identity in Western Australia*. Perth: Government of Western Australia: Commissioner for Equal Opportunity. Retrieved from http://www.eoc.wa.gov.au/Libraries/GBTI_project/2012-GBLTI__Tiffany_Jones_report.sflb.ashx

Jones, T. (2013). *Bullying in schools*. Retrieved from http://www.latrobe.edu.au/news/articles/2012/article/bullying-in-schools

Jorm, A.F. (2012). Mental health literacy: Empowering the community to take action for better mental health. *American Psychologist, 67*(3), 231–243.

Macdonald, R., & Cooper, T., (1998). Youth suicide and young gay men. *Youth Studies Australia, 17*(4), 23–27.

Machlin, A., Pirkis, J., & Spittal, M.J. (2013). Which suicides are reported in the media and what makes them newsworthy crisis. *The Journal of Crisis Intervention and Suicide Prevention, 34*(5), 305–313.

Machlin, A., Skehan, J., Sweet, M., Wake, A., Fletcher, J., Spittal M., & Pirkis, J. (2012). Reporting suicide: Interpreting media guidelines. *Australian Journalism Review, 34*(2), 45–56.

MacKenzie, D., & Chamberlain, C. (2008). Youth homelessness 2006. *Youth Studies Australia, 27*(1), 17–25.

McNamara, P. M. (2013). Adolescent suicide in Australia: Rates, risk and resilience. *Clinical Child Psychology and Psychiatry, 18*(3), 351–369.

Metcalf, A., & Blake, V. (2014). *2013 ReachOut.com annual user survey results*. Sydney: ReachOut.com by Inspire Foundation.

Michaelson, M.T. (2008). Inclusion and social justice for gay, lesbian, bisexual, and transgender members of the learning community in Queensland State schools. *Australian Journal of Guidance and Counselling, 18*(1), 76–83.

Mindframe. (n.d.). *Facts and stats about suicide in Australia*. Retrieved from http://www.mindframe-media.info/for-media/reporting-suicide/facts-and-stats

Ministerial Council for Suicide Prevention. (2009). *History of Ministerial Council for Suicide Prevention* [Internet]. Retrieved from http://www.mcsp.org.au/abouthistory

Ministry of Health New Zealand. (2012). *Suicide facts: Deaths and intentional self-harm hospitalisation 2010*. Retrieved from http://www.health.govt.nz/publication/suicide-facts-deaths-and-intentional-self-harm-hospitalisations-2010

Muir, K. (2012). Walking a well-being tightrope: Young people in Australia. *Journal of Population Research, 29*(4), 293.

National LGBTI Health Alliance. (2010). *Suicide and LGBTI people*. Retrieved from http://www.lgbthealth.org.au/sites/default/files/Alliance-LGBTI-Suicide-20101118.pdf

NSW Government. (n.d.). *Inclusion of anti-homophobia in school bullying policy.* New South Wales: South Western Sydney Local Health Network. Retrieved from https://www.nswtf.org.au/files/inclusion_of_antihomophobia_in_school_bullying_policy.pdf

Pirkis, J., Blood, W.R., Dare, A., & Holland, K. (2008). *The media monitoring project: Changes in media reporting of suicide and mental health and illness in Australia: 2000/01–2006/07.* Canberra, ACT: Commonwealth of Australia. Retrieved from http://www.mindframemedia.info/__data/assets/pdf_file/0018/5166/Pirkis,Blood,Dare-and-Holland,-2008-MediaMonitoringProject.pdf

Rickwood, D., Cavanagh, S., Curtis, L., & Sakrouge, R. (2004). Educating young people about mental health and mental illness: Evaluating a school-based programme. *International Journal of Mental Health Promotion, 6*(4), 23–32.

Rodi, M.S., Garraza, L.G., Walrath, C., Stephens, R.L., Condron, D.S., Hicks, B.B., & McKeon, R. (2012). Referral patterns for youths identified at risk for suicide by trained gatekeepers. *Crisis, 33*(2), 113–119.

Romeo, M., Green, K., Skehan, J., Visser, A., Coan, L., & Hazell, T. (2008). Researching and reporting on suicide or mental illness: A student perspective. *Australian Journalism Review, 30*(1), 123–131.

SCARC. (2011). *National Aboriginal and Torres Strait Islander suicide prevention strategy.* Retrieved from http://www.health.gov.au/internet/main/Publishing.nsf/Content/mental-pub-atsi-suicide-prevention-strategy

Smith, V. (2000). Youth roundtable member finds homophobic abuse too often ignored at school. *Youth Studies Australia, 19*(4), 54–55.

Social Health Reference Group. (2004). *A national strategic framework for Aboriginal and Torres Strait Islander Peoples' mental health and social and emotional wellbeing 2004–2009.* Retrieved from http://www.naccho.org.au/download/aboriginal-health/social_and_emotional_well_being_framework_20042009.pdf

Suicide Prevention Australia (SPA). (2010a). *Position statement on youth suicide prevention.* Retrieved from http://suicidepreventionaust.org/wp-content/uploads/2012/01/SPA-Youth-Suicide-Prevention-Position-Statement.pdf

Suicide Prevention Australia (SPA). (2010b). *Submission to House of Representatives Standing Committee on Health and Ageing—Inquiry into youth suicide* (Submission 11). Leichhardt, NSW: Suicide Prevention Australia.

Tompkins, T.L., Witt, J., & Abraibesh, N. (2010). Does a gatekeeper suicide prevention program work in a school setting? Evaluating training outcome and moderators of effectiveness. *Suicide and Life-Threatening Behavior, 40*(5), 506–516.

Wallack, C., Servaty-Seib, H.L., & Taub, D.J. (2013). Gatekeeper training in campus suicide prevention. *New Directions for Student Services, 141*, 27–41.

Wasserman, D. (2001). A stress-vulnerability model and the development of the suicidal process. In D. Wasserman (Ed.), *Suicide: An unnecessary death* (pp. 13–27). London: Martin Dunitz.

Wei, Y., Hayden, J.A., Kutcher, S., Austin Zygmunt, A., & McGrath, P. (2013). The effectiveness of school mental health literacy programs to address knowledge, attitudes and help seeking among youth. *Early Intervention in Psychiatry, 7*, 109–121.

White, R., & Wyn, J. (2013). *Youth and society: The social dynamics of youth experience.* South Melbourne: Oxford University Press.

Wyn, J. (2009). The changing context of Australian youth and its implications for social inclusion. *Youth Studies Australia, 28*(1), 46–50.

York, J., Lamis, D.A., Friedman, L., Berman, A.L., Joiner, T.E., Mcintosh, J.L., & Pearson, J. (2013). A systematic review process to evaluate suicide prevention programs: A sample case of community based programs. *Journal of Community Psychology, 41*(1), 35–51.

6 The Istambays and Transition Crises

Locating Spaces of Social Sufferings and Hope in the Philippines[1]

Clarence Batan

While youth unemployment as a social issue remains pervasive worldwide (Population Reference Bureau, 2013; UNDESA, 2012), in areas of the Global South, such as the Philippines, the problem of the search for and lack of work seems to produce a more complex degree of precariousness that negatively impacts Filipino youth's transition to adulthood. One fascinating manifestation of this unemployment issue in the Philippines is a phenomenon locally known in the country as 'istambays' (on standbys) that represents a loosely organized sector of relatively young Filipinos who are 'waiting for employment.' Although the concept of istambay is negatively laden as an individualized problem, the istambay phenomenon straddles the personal and the social (Batan, 2012), which directs attention to how popularly perceived individual-based negative stereotypes coalesce with significant social contexts of varying istambay lives.

The main thesis of this chapter argues that the istambay phenomenon in the Philippines is a manifestation of the deeply rooted structural defects in both the systems of economy and education in the country. As an attempt to unravel the 'social' in the lives of the istambays, this chapter narrates the layers of transition crises that directly impinge on their development towards gaining a legitimate status. These are: (a) poverty of families, (b) institutionalized cultural capital crisis, and (c) social mobility crisis. These transition crises, as experienced by istambays, lead to understanding a complex process of negotiation between their 'waiting status' and their social environments. This negotiated process brings forth two interesting research themes related to the youth's wellbeing and transitional issues. On the one hand are the protective ethic among Filipino families, observed to be rooted in value formation of the collective culture of Philippine society, and the ethic of sharing in the practice of religious faith. On the other is the apparent disconnection of istambay youth with the state, which is expressed in their distrust of the Philippine government's lack of accountability, particularly in terms of generating employment for them—a critique of government's educational and employment programs and initiatives, which seems perceptually unrecognized and unfelt by these istambays. This chapter ends by explaining how these transition crises may be reversed through an analysis of both the social sufferings and spaces of hope that these istambays share, negotiate, and anticipate.

ETYMOLOGY AND LOCAL DEFINITIONS OF ISTAMBAY

Etymologically, the Filipino term 'istambay' is derived from the English idiom 'on standby' (Almario, 2001; Vicassans's Pilipino-English Dictionary, 2006). English as a language and as an official form of communication was introduced in the Philippines during the U.S. occupation in the early 1900s, and the evolution of the term istambay and its usage by present-day Filipinos appears to be a by-product of this colonial period. Istambay is a localized version of standby, which over the years has developed a set of peculiar characteristics that signify a particular subsector in Philippine society. Evidence of the foregoing observation is the inclusion of the term istambay in two local dictionaries published by well-known universities in the Philippines. One definition explains istambay as "a person who does not have work and who usually hangs-out on street corners" (Almario, 2001, p. 385). This definition also recognizes the use of 'tambay' as an accepted abbreviated form of istambay. Another definition of istambay comes from a Pilipino-English dictionary (Vicassans's Pilipino-English Dictionary, 2006), which offers a more lucid characterization of the negative stereotypes attached to being an istambay. This dictionary defines istambay as "(1) an act of spending one's time unprofitably; idler; (2) a person who spends his time unprofitably; idler; (3) inactive; not being used, as machines" (p. 209). This definition also suggests the Filipino terms 'paglalakwatsa' (gallivanting), 'taong tamad' (lazy) and 'di ginagamit' (not being used) as synonyms for istambay.

Despite the similar negative emphasis of these local definitions, these conceptions of istambay reflect two differing yet related themes. The latter (*Vicassans's Pilipino-English Dictionary*) describes the istambay as troubled, deficient, and delinquent, but the former (Almario, 2001) reflects more of the social aspects of being istambay, that is, 'not having work' and spending time in 'kanto,' or street corners.

YOUTH TRANSITION STUDIES AND THE ISTAMBAY PHENOMENON

Studies of transition issues among the Filipino youth (e.g., Miralao, 2004; Natividad, 2004; Raymundo & Cruz, 2004) emerged in the early 2000s, directing attention to varied growing-up patterns that may be reflective of precarious development processes navigated and negotiated by young Filipinos in a variety of social spaces (from local/physical to global/virtual communities). In a developing country like the Philippines, demographic youth bulge (Xenos, 2001) is expected to impact one contentious transition issue known among youth sociologists as school-to-work. Seminal works on this subject matter, especially in the Global North, have appeared over the past decades (e.g., Brown, 1980; Coté & Allahar, 1994; Galaway & Hudson, 1996; Hogan & Astone, 1986; Kerckhoff, 1990; Lehmann, 2007; Thiessen & Looker, 1999a, b; West & Newton, 1983; Willis, 1977; Wyn & White, 1997), focusing their analyses on the nature, challenge, and variety of precarious youth employments (and the lack thereof) argued to be navigated in multiple economies (White & Wyn, 2008). While the general nature of this transition problem may be shared by young people in areas of the Global South such as the Philippines, the varied forms of inequalities, marginalization, and social exclusion in developing countries present theoretical challenges.

In recent youth literatures, one specific transitional problem known as youth inactivity (International Labour Organization, 2006) drew attention as a separate area of study from youth unemployment and underemployment. In the Philippines, an obvious manifestation of youth inactivity is the istambay phenomenon, which, arguably, is publicly visible and observable. Films (e.g., Cabreira, 1979; Santiago, 1963) and songs (e.g., Bartolome, 1992; Camo, 1997; Enchi, 2005) commonly portray them as those who are neither in school nor working.

Interestingly, Filipino youth istambay seem to share the experiences of fellow inactive youth worldwide, who have been given names such as 'NEET'('Not in Employment, Education, and Training') (Bynner & Parsons, 2002; Coles et al., 2002; Furlong, 2006), 'status zero' (Williamson, 1997, 2004), 'idle youth' (Edelman, Holzer & Offner, 2006; Ericta, 2003), the 'economically inactive' (Franzén & Kassman, 2005; International Labour Organization, 2006), and the 'hikikomori' (Furlong, 2008) in Japan. In the same vein, conceptual descriptions of contemporary young people, such as 'prolongation of youth' (Arnett, 2002), 'arrested adulthood' (Côté, 2000), and 'generation on hold' (Coté & Allahar, 1994), seem to direct attention to the phenomenon of youth inactivity even in North American and European contexts.

Another set of literatures closely using 'waiting' as a metaphor is found in studies conducted in South America (Auyero, 2011) and Africa (Ralph, 2008). These studies direct close attention to 'time' as a salient element of analysis in understanding the lack of productive work among marginalized sectors, and to 'youth,' as seemingly may be seen as social sufferer to adverse impacts of 'waiting,' especially in the context of finding work.

In the Philippines, studies directly relating stories about the Filipino youth istambays are rare (e.g., Jocano, 1969; Margold, 1995). In recent years, a body of relevant research has generated newfound interest in both the academic and policy circles capturing salient elements of Filipino istambays' lives (Aldaba & Ang, 2010; Canlas & Pardalis, 2009). These sample studies, mostly supported by the International Labour Organization (ILO), aim to address and develop sound employment strategies and policies, particularly for young Filipinos. Locally, the official state agencies, such as the National Youth Commission (NYC) and the Technical Education, Skills, and Development Administration (TESDA), since being established in the mid-1990s have implemented policies, programs, and projects on wide-ranging youth-related issues (e.g., Philippine National Youth Commission, 2005, 2012) as mandated by laws (Republic Act No. 7796, 1994; Republic Act No. 8044, 1995). The NYC serves as the official youth policy agency in the country and strategizes to promote rights-based strategies and rights-based standards for the youth, capacity-building of youth, and organizations towards participation and development. TESDA's mission is providing policies, programs, and standards towards quality technical education and skills development of Filipino youth.

Yet, even with these state agencies doing more than a decade of work on youth policy, employment vulnerability of marginalized Filipinos, in the context and form of youth inactivity (International Labour Organization, 2006), such as in the case of istambays, has remained pervasive and has not yet gained policy attention. While this discourse on state-driven, privately led, and civil society NGO-initiated youth services merits careful examination, what this chapter offers is only a glimpse, yet a salient one, on how youth policy may be not only directed toward the economic dimensions of youth unemployment but also addressing and including the issue of inactivity along the nexus of educational-employment dispositions and structures that these istambays negotiate as both individuals and citizens. What this chapter provides are narratives and voices of Filipino istambays that may lead to new insights on how youth services and youth work may be reframed and re-imagined amidst current shifts in contemporary labor economies worldwide.

HYPOTHESES AND METHODS

The substantive hypotheses in which the istambay thesis was first explored (Batan, 2010) operated under Mills's notion of sociological imagination (1959), which suggests unraveling the intersection between the history and biography in understanding a social phenomenon, and Bourdieu's theory of practice (1977, 1984, 1986), which articulates the notions of fields, forms of capital, and habitus. Theoretically, I find the use of this Mills-Bourdieu approach engaging in demonstrating varying elements and strategies on how the istambay phenomenon is perceived and how the life histories of istambays may be contextually and meaningfully understood.

Data reported here is part of an ethnographic study of Filipinos born in the 1970s that monitors and documents life histories from 1994 until the present. Specifically, qualitative data used in this paper were generated from observations and interviews during fieldwork conducted in 2005 and

2007. The two case study sites included a fishing village in Talim Island and an urban-poor barangay (village) in Manila; both communities are in Luzon Island. Primary study respondents were considered youth at the time of interview (between the ages of 18 and 30 years old). To allow intergenerational discourse, also included in this paper are voices of selected mothers and teachers of respondents. These qualitative data were electronically recorded and transcribed, coded and organized using both manual and computer-assisted Atlas.ti software program, and employed thematic analysis and narratives as analytical techniques. Interview schedules were generated using Filipino language; the English translation is provided by the researcher. Ethical consent was secured in the entire conduct of the research process. To protect confidentiality and anonymity, all research participants reported here were given pseudonyms.

ISTAMBAY AND THE WEB OF TRANSITION CRISES

A powerful metaphor to understand the concept of transition positions is young people as travelers who are set to journey different routes using life vehicles, like the 'train-car' metaphor employed by Furlong and Cartmel (1997) in their analysis of British youth's life trajectories in the 1990s. They explain that, in the past, youth journeys may be likened to boarding railway trains on which, once boarded, the youth will have a slim chance to change directions. They could upgrade; however, Furlong and Cartmel insist that the journey of youth would still be limited because the general direction of the train is predetermined. But at present, the train is overtaken by cars, which, as Furlong and Cartmel suggest, has allowed youth to have a lot of individual choices. This gives these youth some sense of control to go to a specific life direction.

Utilizing this powerful youth transition metaphor in the Philippine context, I find that istambays are situated in a relatively different life journey. First, the inactivity of istambays means that they are temporarily not on board any type of life vehicle, whether it is a train, bus, local jeepney, or boat. They are standing by fish ports and train, bus, and jeepney[2] stations patiently waiting for their chance to board. Second, it is not that istambays do not want to travel. They just do not have the means to pay for the journey, especially the least educated and most vulnerable. Third, if some educated istambays have the means to travel, they discover that their vehicles have engine problems, and they lack enough gasoline to take them to the destination of full adulthood. Fourth, because in the Global South all the life vehicles available for disadvantaged istambays are generally public transportation, they do not have a car to allow them to make personal choices on the route to reach their destination. Istambays' journeys, if ever they get on board, are determined by the institutions that structure them. Although restricted, istambays' main interest is to have the chance to cease waiting, to move on, and to travel, so that they can continue their life's journeys with their families.

Understanding the transitional crises of Filipino youth istambays, in its most vulnerable form, starts with having a sense of the adverse impact that inactivity brings into their lives not as individuals but rather informed by the sentiment that they burden their respective families. For instance, I remember my interview with Araw, which was colored by a series of silences, sad pauses, and tears. When I approached him in 2005 for another interview, he was hesitant at first because, according to him, "Nothing happened in my life since." His narrative articulated a common anatomy of istambay life: for almost seven years since my last interview, Araw had waited for his chance to board either the boat of education or the jeepney of employment. In the following interview excerpts, Araw explains a possible reason behind his inactivity:

> *I think this is a manifestation, directly related to the problems in the Philippines! . . . Today, it is so difficult to find work. Of course, one should not be istambay, one should be working . . . One needs to earn to spend for the needs of the family.*

Araw's commentary relating his inactivity with the apparent unemployment problems of the Philippines and his desire to find a job in order to assist his family reflects the underlying conditions of how istambay is possible in Filipino society. In the narratives of the case study respondents, 'trabaho' (work, job, or employment) is positioned at the core of istambay discourse. Initially, it is the lack of trabaho that characterizes istambay. However, I argue that, with the issue of unemployment, the phenomenon of istambay in the Philippines is constituted by a combined crisis of identity and a web of crises that ultimately hinder a smooth transition into acquiring legitimate status. These transition crises are, on the one hand, mitigated by the culture of protection working within the observed familial-faith dynamic in the lives of case study respondents. On the other, these crises manifest a sense of disconnection with the state, reflecting distrust of the government and the ailing state of Philippine economy. This begs more interesting questions on what policies, programs, and projects might best respond to these crises.

The web of transition crises this study found significant in understanding the istambay phenomenon are: (a) the poverty of families, (b) the institutionalized cultural capital crisis, and (c) the social mobility crisis. These three are interrelated, build on each other's weaknesses, and, to a certain degree, predict the extent of istambay vulnerability. Due to social reproductive mechanism, those case study youth respondents who are the poorest acquire the least educational capital and thus are the most vulnerable. Consequently, these youth are the most restricted in their journey along transitional routes. In Bourdieu's terms, the amount of capital (economic, cultural and social) and the extent to which this capital is converted into economic and symbolic goods determines how one is able to be socially mobile. Success in using this capital means gaining legitimate status, a symbolic capital that defines one's position in society. Failure to do so denotes a conversion crisis. In this study, I argue that these transition crises serve as focal points for understanding more meaningfully the istambay phenomenon.

Poverty of Families

During fieldwork (2005–2007), the Philippines was experiencing economic crisis (de Dios et al., 2004; Wallace, 2008) as reflected in some interviews where youth respondents, as well as their mothers and teachers, discuss the impacts of poverty. Most of the respondents were aware of the economic crisis of the country through personal experiences of poverty of their own families. For example, Luming, a mother respondent, expressed this sentiment, saying, "I could deeply feel poverty because of the expensive cost of basic commodities."

It appears that, indeed, this experience of poverty in case study sites is not new but rather has been shared across generations. Rey recalled the poverty of his parents and how they struggled with work and going to school. He also grew up experiencing the same poverty, which was especially important in his school experience.

> *Poverty, you see whenever they talk about their lives, they being my parents, they really found going to school very difficult. So, it was a hard life for them. When my father was a child, he said that he sold pandesal (short bread). My mother struggled going to school, even if she only had few pieces of clothes, she went to school; even if she did not have any school allowance. She told me that she used to pick up the peelings of santol fruit, just to show her classmates that she has something to eat. So, it is the same with my experience, just like them.*

Comparative statistics on the quality of life in the Philippines between 2000 and 2007 confirms the worsening condition in the country (see Table 6.1). According to the government poverty estimates, in 2007, 1.73 million more people have become poorer compared to 2000 estimates. In comparison with the Social Weather Station's (SWS) self-rated poverty indicator (a private non-profit research agency), the total estimate of those who self-rated themselves as poor has remained virtually the same, from 43.5 million in 2000 to 43.6 million in 2007. The national budget for education has been further reduced to 6% less of what was allocated in 2000. In the Human Development Report of the United Nations, the Philippines slipped from the 70th to the 90th rank, suggesting that the quality of life has indeed worsened in 2007, as compared to 2000.

Table 6.1 Selected Quality of Life Indicators Philippines 2000 versus 2007

Indicators	2000	2007	Remarks
Poverty	23.8 M, 30%	25.5 M, 33%	1.73 M more
Government SWS self-rated	43.5 M, 56.5%	43.6 M, 49.5%	No improvement
Education as % of budget	17.4%	11.4%	6%
UNDP human development ranking	70th out of 162 countries	90th out of 177 countries	Slipped 20 places
Unemployment	3.5 M, 11.2%	2.6 M, 7%	Reduced labor force under 2007 definition
Underemployment	5 M, 19.9%	6.6 M, 19.7%	1.6 M more
Degree of hunger	10.8%	17.9%	Worse

M = Millions

Interestingly, the unemployment rate had been reduced to 7% in 2007, but this reported lowered estimate was due to the change in the definition of unemployment. Correspondingly, the additional 1.6 million underemployed in 2007 indicates another significant defect in the Philippine labor economy. In this debate on the changing definitions of who are unemployed or underemployed, I argue that istambays are lost in these statistics. For instance, the new definition appears to have excluded those istambays who have given up looking for work, which further marginalize them as individuals with no conceivable category in labor statistics. That is, it fails to capture the subtleties constituting disadvantaged people, such as the istambays, whose fluid, inactive experiences make them less appealing to become part of reported statistics.

Institutionalized Cultural Capital Crisis

Directly related to the economic difficulties experienced by the families of youth case study respondents is their struggle towards attaining college education. Despite glaring poverty, Filipino families are observed to place high value on education because it is regarded as a means of social mobility (Castillo, 1979). Thus, college education among Filipinos has become a tool to combat poverty, especially among the lower class. In such a context, education functions like a capital whose conversion into employment is the foremost profit.

Bourdieu's notion of cultural capital (1984; Bourdieu & Passeron, 1990/1977), as a conceptual tool, provides a good framework to illustrate how the educational credentials of case study youth respondents fail to deliver the expected employment outcomes. This notion of cultural capital shows its relationship with social class and class fractions and how it is systematically structured in institutions like the educational systems. Cultural capital has been further refined into three forms: embodied, objectified, and institutionalized (Bourdieu, 1986). In this istambay study, it is observed that, among these forms, it is this institutionalized form of cultural capital, the accumulation of educational qualifications of case study respondents, which was central in their lives. Education is seen as an investment and as a family project. Thus, it is the conversion of this institutionalized cultural capital into another form, preferably an economic one (employment), that is crucial to the lives of these youth. The failure to convert means a credential crisis (Collins, 1979).

For most of the youth case study respondents, earning this institutionalized capital did not come easy. Their struggle to study was mainly due to the economic difficulties of their families. In fact, it is both their poverty and their desire to improve the quality of life of their respective families that motivate them to study harder. Thus, the educational route is an ideal pathway to take, especially among lower-class Filipinos, to improve their lives. However, this ideal is also convoluted by a complex set of factors that create another crisis, which the varying istambay experiences of the respondents embody. This is what I call the *institutionalized cultural capital crisis*, which is rooted in the youth respondents' failure to use and convert their educational capital into employment that would secure their earnings and livelihood. This crisis is observed to work differently between the meso and the most vulnerable istambays.

Table 6.2 provides an overview of the educational attainment of both youth and mother respondents. Here, the generational shift in educational attainments between youth respondents and their mothers' education is apparent. This is most notable among the least and meso-vulnerable youth where all of them have virtually exceeded their mother's educational attainments. However, for the least vulnerable group, only slight educational change is observed, which reflects the extent of their relatively early withdrawal from the school system.

In the Philippines, the education of children, especially at the tertiary level, is a family project. Because most of the tertiary educational institutions are privatized, the primary responsibilities for carrying the cost of education rest on the parents. While the Philippine government offers scholarship programs, they are mostly acquired by academic achievers. Unlike most governments in developed countries, the Philippines has yet to evolve a system of educational loans that will assist students to pursue higher education. Thus, I find it fascinating that most of the young people in the Talim community, who accompanied me in the first round of my research, finished their college education. This was substantively different from almost 20 years ago when the community registered only a handful of college graduates. Rex was among them, and he shared with me how his parents helped him reach

Table 6.2 Youth Respondents and Mothers' Education

Typology	Name	Education	Mother's education
Least vulnerable	Rey	College graduate	Elementary undergraduate
	Gilda	College (on-going)	College undergraduate
	Love	High school graduate	Elementary graduate
Meso vulnerable	Camille	College graduate	Elementary graduate
	Coy	College graduate	Elementary graduate
	Rex	College graduate	High school graduate
	Siza	College graduate	College graduate
Most vulnerable	Mon	Vocational undergraduate	College undergraduate
	Jepoy	Vocational undergraduate	High school graduate
	Araw	College undergraduate	Elementary graduate
	Emong	Elementary undergraduate	Deceased
	Jemma	High school undergraduate	High school undergraduate

his dream to finish college. Responding to my question, "How did you finish college?" Rex narrates:

> *I persevered, with the help of, with the sacrifices of my parents, I worked hard. I motivated myself that I will graduate! And I did it without any problem . . . this was through the help and determination of my parents, as well as my siblings.*

Whereas familial support was available to assist the educational needs of some case study respondents, the litmus test to determine the impact of educational investment, or the lack thereof, is to understand the social mechanism on how such institutionalized cultural capital hinder, shape, or reproduce the positions these Filipino youth occupy in Philippine society. As reflected in the educational trajectories of youth respondents, the istambay phenomenon appears to be first constituted in the educational field, where these respondents initially experience varying degrees of inactivity due to delays in their studies. For some, this study delay, which may be considered as their first istambay waiting experience, was just temporary. But for others, it was longer, like in the cases of Araw and Jepoy, who still expressed their desires to return to school if the opportunity arose. In other cases, such as the married respondents, Mon and Jemma, they passed on their educational hopes to their children and thus did not see themselves as studying again. Emong, on the other hand, due to extreme poverty, accepted early on in life that his educational inactivity was permanent.

Metaphorically, educational attainment is like a 'ticket' that one pays for and shows at the train, bus, and jeepney stations or fish ports before boarding a specific employment route. This ticket determines the distance and destination of the young passenger. Having a college degree promises a better destination compared to a high school undergraduate whose credential limits the choice of destination. However, in the context of the istambay phenomenon, the problem with this 'ticket' is that it appears to lose some of its credential value. This is because the actual journeys are restricted to a privileged few who have the special cultural stamp on their tickets that allows them to travel to their employment destination.

There is a long-standing consensus among academics and policymakers that the best way to prepare the youth for the future is to provide them equal access to educational and employment opportunity structures (International Labour Organization, 2006; UNESCO, 2010; United Nations, 2007). However, as this istambay study suggests, despite the Philippines' well-developed education system and high literacy rates, the persisting economic crisis furthers the difficulties of poor families to access education, as seen in the two case study sites. While it is expected that those who did not invest more in education would have limited work choices than those with college degrees, joining the ranks of the unemployed and underemployed casts doubt on the widely accepted notion of a positive relationship between education, economic development, and mobility. In such a context, I argue that the social mechanism at work is an institutionalized cultural-capital crisis experienced firsthand by istambays.

For those who were forced to leave school, especially the male, most-vulnerable youth respondents, their lack of required educational qualifications restricted their work choices to manual, contractual, and low-paying jobs. Their lack of formal training means an educational capital deficit that situates them along the margins of limited employment. On the other hand, a different level of institutionalized cultural-capital crisis that is more symbolically severe is experienced by those case study respondents who attained collegiate degrees—that is, the failure to convert the educational capital that their parents and families invested over a long period of time into a decent form of employment. This is the school-to-work transition problem that this institutionalized cultural-capital crisis generates.

The youth case studies indicated that there were some who were trapped in the process of converting this cultural good—the institutionalized cultural capital—which forced them to standby until the right time arrived. These educated youth already had tickets to board a life vehicle of their choice, but unfortunately, these tickets, in this highly regulated world, have to go through inspection. It is only when these tickets get stamped for clearance that they can start their employment journeys.

Social Mobility Crisis

Closely related to the institutionalized cultural-capital crisis is the aggregate of tensions that inactivity brings into the process of becoming socially mobile. This crisis further highlights the apparent absence of jobs in the

Philippines affecting a large number of young Filipinos, including the educationally qualified. In the case studies, this issue of unemployment has generated disappointment not only with youth respondents but also with mothers and teachers. Most of them felt the adverse effect of unemployment in the lives of their respective families. In the following interview excerpt, Coy vividly articulated how unemployment breeds inactivity. He illustrated how the lack of trabaho immobilized even the educated, like him, demonstrated how he became istambay, and expressed the frustrations that come with inactivity. His voice echoed what the reported national youth statistics actually meant on the ground.

> *Clarence* *So, are you fishing again?*
> *Coy* *Indeed! I said to myself, how come that I finished my studies but I am fishing again . . . While waiting (for a job), I will fish for my family . . . This is necessary . . . One needs to work hard even if you are educated . . . I need to work even as a fisher, I need to sacrifice for my family . . . Yes. Many finished education, and there are still more studying. Those who were not studying before were encouraged to go to school . . . They are now istambays.*
> *Clarence* *So, what about work?*
> *Coy* *Istambay. You see, look at me now, I have an education but I do not have a job. I have done everything to apply for a job, but I was never accepted. They (employers) would say, "Just wait for our call." . . . For now, what I like is to apply abroad because life here is difficult, even for those who finished education. It is really very challenging to get work. . . Sometimes, there's no hiring. Sometimes, they (employers) will just tell you to wait for their call. Of course, I expected that I will receive a call, but it is as though you are waiting for nothing . . . Of course, I feel sad.*
> *Clarence* *But how is it that you could still smile?*
> *Coy* *Yes, I am still happy . . . Even with this situation, probably, the right opportunity will come my way, and I will have a stable job. Maybe now is not my time, but it would come. . .*
> *Clarence* *Do you think that the government has something to do with your lack of work?*
> *Coy* *Hahaha . . . Yes, big time!*

The crisis of social mobility among the istambays centers on the factors that hinder their entry to employment. One of these, as reported in youth labor statistics (Ericta, 2003), is the defective and limited employment structure that cannot absorb new labor entrants into the economy. The lack of availability of jobs in a developing country like the Philippines has its greatest toll on the young people. Inactivity among the istambays is one of the impacts of this rising level of unemployment in the country. While the economic crisis made it difficult for those educated youth to find work, this further marginalizes the employment chances of fellow youth who were first disadvantaged educationally. This is like the process of stratification I observed in boarding a train, bus, jeepney, or boat in the Philippines. Usually, there are 'special trips,' in contrast to 'ordinary trips.' The former promises to be more comfortable, faster, and fully air-conditioned, while the latter is just plain with no fancy services except to reach the destination. All istambays, both educated and less educated, patiently wait in transport stations for their time to board. The difference, however, is that the educated are at least carrying their tickets. In contrast, the less educated need to find alternative ways to get on board. In the meantime, it does not matter whether the trip that these istambays take is special or ordinary, because all of them are standing by. Yet, they know that when the employment transport vehicle arrives, the educated istambays would be prioritized.

SPACES OF HOPE AND SHARED SOCIAL SUFFERINGS

Familial-Faith Dynamic

The web of crises that breeds inactivity in the lives of some Filipino youth generates varying levels of vulnerability. As observed in the lives of self-identified male istambays (Emong, Araw, Jepoy, Mon, Rex, and Coy), difficulties in labor integration have relative implications on their self-esteem not only due to gendered social expectations on Filipino males as providers but, more importantly, because of the workings of a familial-faith dynamic that is deeply embedded in the habitus of these respondents. I argue that this social mechanism allowed the istambays to remain relatively optimistic compared to the observed discouragement, alienation (Edelman et al., 2006; International Labour Organization, 2006), and social withdrawal (Furlong, 2008; Kaneko, 2006) of fellow inactive youth in some developed economies. Central to this process is the collective fulfillment of the family's aspiration rather than individual achievement. This is a site of transitional crises that is negotiated by istambays in varying degrees and strategies. However, the istambays' negotiations with inactivity are not mainly restricted by their reliance with family and religious support. Case study data suggest that equally important is the istambays' apparent disconnection from the state apparatus, which may be the reason why these respondents appear to know nothing about the youth state agencies or fail to recognize what assistance they could avail of, for instance, from the National Youth Commission (NYC) and the Technical Education and Skills Development Authority's (TESDA), which are lawfully mandated to develop sound policies and programs for their wellbeing. This is another site that istambays negotiate, suggesting how the system of governance, particularly in the Philippines, has failed to live up to their expectations (International Labour Organization, 2006, p. 34).

This familial-faith dynamic among Filipinos, as found in the life histories of youth respondents in the context of their varying istambay experiences, may be traced along the discourse of Filipino values. Early attempts (e.g., Bulatao, 1962; Hollnsteiner, 1964; Lynch, 1964) to identify the salient values of Filipino society opened up an interesting debate on the historical and social conditions that impact the construction and constitution of these claimed values. This debate has directed local researchers, for example, Jocano (1966), to argue that these values should not be seen as exclusive to Filipinos but rather shared, in varying degrees, by other societies. Another input to this debate is the historical inclusion of colonial experience and the project of nationhood into the analysis of values. Here, the indigenous studies of Philippine psychology (Enriquez, 1992) are most noted because they were able to show that the reported Filipino values (e.g., 'pakikisama' [getting along well with others], 'hiya' [a sense of shame or propriety], 'utang na loob' [internal debt of gratitude]) in earlier studies may be seen as only surface values. They claim that there are core values ([e.g., 'damdam' [feeling], 'kapwa' [a shared identity with others] and 'loob' [inner self]) that work as a fundamental mechanism in the practice of these identified surface values.

Despite the underlying differences in researching values in the Philippines, the general themes emerging from these studies are consistent. On the one hand is the collective orientation towards the *family*, which, despite facing external pressures (Raymundo & Cruz, 2004), has remained the seat of values, particularly in terms of support, nurturance, and protection in Philippine society. On the other hand is the Filipinos' persistent dealings with religion (mainly Catholic), which arguably impact the development of moral values (Social Weather Station, 2002) among Filipinos. Data from the World Values Surveys persistently show how Filipinos place higher value on religion than other countries (European and World Values Surveys Four-wave Integrated Data File, 1981–2004). In this study, the impact of familial and religious social fields is salient in the lives of youth respondents, especially during the istambay time, their time of waiting. I found how a family's situation impacts the positive disposition of istambay and how the concept of God is implicated in istambays' search for equal treatment and opportunities in life.

For youth respondents, the family is the primary source of support while the church provides the spiritual dimension on the observed practices of the culture of care among the families and communities in these case study sites. There were also instances, like in the cases of Rey and Rhea, that illustrated how the church assisted them financially even in their studies. This familial-faith dynamic emerged more prominently in times of crisis such as inactivity. Thus, despite the complex web of crises in the lives of istambays, the future aspirations of these respondents remain relatively optimistic. Such optimism is traced on how they placed the family at the core of their 'pangarap' (dreams), and 'kinabukasan' (future). This familial protection engendered a hopeful habitus reflecting, on the one hand, aspirations centered on improving the situation of their families, and on the other, faith that God would help them fulfill these dreams. Rey's response to my question about the best lesson he learned in life vividly captured this dynamic. He expressed:

> *The best lesson in life (I learned so far), let's see? It is faith and trust in God, as a human being, strong trust in God is necessary and of course, love, not only for oneself but for the whole family. One has to be responsible.*

In the Philippine context, this practice of the culture of care is captured by the local term 'pagmamalasakit,' which means an act of caring in times of need. When applied to understanding the istambay phenomenon, the root word of this term, 'sakit' (illness), becomes more meaningful. Against the backdrop of the worsening employment situation in the country, the cultural practice of pagmamalasakit among Filipino families functions as a tool for survival and necessity. Here, youth work remains at the private core of families nourished by the church, aptly reflected in positive religious dispositions towards life.

Thus, metaphorically, those istambays in the bus, train, and jeepney stations or fish ports may be feeling tired of waiting for their employment journeys to start, but they are not fully discouraged and withdrawn. As a matter of urgent need, they choose to stay and wait because they know that giving up will worsen the precarious economic situations of their families. To keep from leaving the stations, they remind themselves of the aspirations of a better future for their families, combined with a deep sense of prayer; they patiently wait to get on board any vehicle that would take them to an employment destination.

Disconnected Filipino Youth

Though they may be waiting for an employment opportunity, this does not mean that istambays and the other case study respondents are not mindful of the relationship between inactivity and the social world beyond their families and immediate communities. As observed in the earlier discussion of poverty of families, the state apparatus—the Philippine government, and its apparent mismanagement of the economy—is intricately configured into the stories of the respondents. The commentaries about the government indicate their disappointment and distrust with the state, implying a sense of disconnection from the Philippines as a nation. What might explain the sense of disillusion these istambays feel against the government, which has the structural power to assist them in times of need? Is it because no youth services are made available to them? Is it because these projects simply benefit the few? Or is it because these istambays fully know that these projects are caught in government corruption?

As a case in point, Jefferson, a youth focus-group participant in Manila, expressed his disgust with the government when asked about the possible solution to the youth unemployment problem in the Philippines. He emphatically expressed, "For me, I think the government is the solution . . . they need to fix our government. For now, you see, we should be ashamed of our government, it is too much!" This comment reflects the voice of a Filipino youth who was frustrated with the blatant corruption in the government but remained cognizant that the government has the machinery to fix the problem of unemployment in the country. This commentary indicated a feeling of frustration that may build up grievances (International Labour Organization, 2006) that in the future, may pose a danger to Philippine society.

Over the years, the government's failure to improve the labor conditions in the country (Wallace, 2008) appears to have alienated the young population from believing that they still have a good employment chance in the country. A clear manifestation of this process of disconnection is the Filipino youth's aspiration to work oversees, to work 'abroad' (Miranda, 2003). This disturbing observation constitutes the future aspirations of some study respondents, such as Gilda, Rey, Coy, and Siza, and some focus group youth participants. While the logic behind their intentions is noble, that is, to uplift the conditions of their families through overseas employment, it also raises a critical issue of the failure of the government to create accessible employment opportunity structures for the new labor entrants. This suggests how young Filipinos are systematically excluded from actively participating in the local labor market. Consequently, the process of disconnection becomes a push factor for these disadvantaged Filipino youth, like the istambays, to seek alternative work in the global economy, which promises better pay and stability—an emerging new global space of youth work and services in the global migration milieu needing novel approaches that are transnational and multi-cultural.

Indeed, the istambay phenomenon could be perceived as a waste of Filipino youth's potential that has been lost amidst the government's inefficiency and which has worsened the economic crisis in the Philippines. Consequently, this structural defect spawns an interesting view that disconnects the istambays from trusting the government, the state apparatus which has the power to make the employment routes accessible to them. These istambays' distrust of the government may have blinded them to seek solutions within the country; instead, for some, the inactivity experiences have forced them to look for an alternative elsewhere. This sense of disconnection may be likened to those istambay youth who may be waiting along with fellow inactive youth in bus, train, and jeepney stations or fish ports, but are open to the idea of traveling beyond by land or sea. These are the istambays who are looking up in the sky and aspire to take the airplane instead. This overseas trip would take them further away from the limited and problematic employment route and destination that the Philippine government has yet to stabilize.

Reversing Istambay Status

How is istambay status reversed? Where do the istambays locate their spaces of hope? In what ways does the phenomenon of istambay reproduce social sufferings in the Philippines? Responses to these questions raise three additional research insights, namely:

1. The problem of istambays in the Philippines may be reversed by: (a) creating education and employment opportunities, especially for those who are poor and economically weak; (b) strengthening the training employment strategies to better prepare these youth before entering the labor market; and (c) actual generation of jobs.
2. While there is distrust in the government's ability to provide employment, particularly by the young new labor entrants, the state remains a powerful apparatus in developing policies and implementing social programs that shall make education and employment routes accessible to these youth locally or abroad.
3. Failure to reverse the istambay status indicates the deepening crisis of youth marginalization in the country, highlighting the social reproduction of inequality in the Philippines, where youth inactivity plays a salient part in the family's intergenerational transmission of poverty.

The lack of trabaho (work) is central to istambay discourse. However, as I argued earlier, the concept of istambay is entangled in a complex web of crises impacting their transition towards gaining a legitimate status such as a being a worker. Key to better understanding the strategies of reversing istambay status is situating the discussion not exclusively on the lack of trabaho but rather along the education-employment nexus—that is, establishing the link between the varying dis/connection of these inactive Filipino youth's education and training with employment routes and (limited) occupational opportunities available in the country and abroad and determining the focal points of system deficiencies in order to identify mitigating measures, which might reverse inactivity.

Recently, an emerging area of youth work that the present Aquino regime implemented has focused on improving the Philippine Basic Education System by strengthening its curriculum and increasing the number of years from 10 to 12. The law is known as the Enhanced Basic Education Act of 2013 (Republic Act No. 10533, 2013), adapting the universal approach to basic education known as the 'K to 12 Program.' Following international standards, this law seeks to provide training for a new generation of Filipino high school students to gain more globally competitive skills that better prepare them for future employment; an alternative structural approach to making transitions from school to work in the Philippines less problematic. To what extent the K to 12 program would lessen the growing number of istambays in the future is something to look forward to, but for now, the disillusionment of some istambays remain.

As with the case study respondents, overseas employment appears to be one alternative solution to inactivity. Yet, working abroad is intricately related to the economic means of the family as well as the educational attainment of applicants. These two factors, economic and educational capital, are important in facilitating overseas employment. For instance, in the cases of Gilda, Rey, Coy, and Siza, their college degrees provided them a better chance of getting employed abroad. But equally important is having enough money to pay the application and employment placement fees. Thus, while overseas employment may be a promising alternative employment route for some educated istambays, it only functions well when the economic and social resources of families are well established.

Even locally, the process of finding a job requires the utilization of different forms of capital (Bourdieu, 1986). As narrated by case study youth respondents Camille and Rex and teacher Jing, the job application process requires not only personal determination and education but also money. According to them, in most instances, their mothers were the ones who 'found a way' to provide them allowance while looking for work. Having no money to process job applications lengthened their istambay status. When I asked the youth respondents about their views on what the government should do in order to moderate the problem of youth unemployment, particularly among istambays, their responses manifest the crucial yet undervalued connection between education and employment. According to these respondents, both systems of education and employment should be given equal attention, underscoring this study's observation that the deficiencies in these systems breed inactivity, particularly salient when the interrelationship of these systems is undermined. In the minds of these youths, it seems that the problem of istambay is reversible, and the solution is as simple as providing government support to education and jobs. However, in developing countries like the Philippines, these types of programs are often muddled and mixed up with the political practices that enable the persistence of varying forms of social inequalities in the country, which is a fascinating area of youth work and services that both the government and the civil society might pay more serious attention to and eventually reform.

Therefore, reversing istambay status is heavily dependent on, first, making necessary provisions for the education of youth and, second, creating employment opportunities. In this study, the families of youth respondents, despite poverty and lack of government support, have continued to invest in the education of their children. However, this investment yielded varying outcomes in the context of the istambay phenomenon; it appears that this educational capital is undervalued in the midst of economic crisis. When rates of unemployment for the general population remain high over the years, it takes the greatest toll on the youth. In such a context, the istambay phenomenon in the Philippines could be viewed as a manifestation of the deepening crisis of youth marginalization in the country. The extent of inactivity among these Filipino youth determines the consequences of their failures to transition into gaining legitimate status. That is, the longer the inactivity, the more severe the socioeconomic situations of their families. Istambays' precariousness is informed, shaped, and reproduced by the conditions of their own social positioning, which is only worsened by the lack of external support, such as government intervention. This process generates and reproduces the social sufferings of istambays and their families where more concrete directed youth work programs are needed.

CONCLUSION

This chapter endeavors to paint a story of Filipino istambays who, over the years, have been the subject of media attention but have remained under-researched and taken for granted by policymakers. By examining their life contexts and highlighting their varying levels of vulnerability, this research revealed that the core of their social suffering is entangled in a web of transition crises hindering them from acquiring legitimate statuses as workers, family providers, and socially involved Filipino citizens. External social forces such as economic crisis and the poverty of their families coerced them to become inactive, a process that disappointed some of them but did not totally discourage them from facing the everyday struggles in their lives. For those educationally advantaged, the failure to convert their accumulated institutionalized capital into some form of work further hindered their social mobility. While reversing istambay status is possible through overseas employment and continued training and education, these too are entrapped by the economic crisis of their families. When the state apparatus—the government—fails to provide assistance to fundamental needs such as the education and employment of young Filipino people, inactivity entrenches their marginalized position in Philippine society as well as the poverty of their respective families. However, the social suffering of these istambays is negotiated by a familial-faith dynamic that provides protection and inspiration, amidst the overwhelming web of crises, to aspire for a better life not for their own individual fulfillment but for uplifting the conditions of their families.

The social problematic of Filipino istambays illustrates how traditional indicators such as social class, gender, and educational attainment continue to differentiate the life trajectories of youth in the country. However, these indicators should be understood as deeply entangled in the macro structures of the Philippine political economy. The question of the hidden logic of economic structures (Bourdieu & Passeron, 1990/1977) continues to press on in Philippine society over disconcerting issues such as who controls labor resources and what production processes are constructed and formed that may be navigated by young Filipino workers.

Inactivity halts the growing-up process of these istambays in securing a legitimate space in Philippine society. They negotiate their inactivity status along with the gamut of factors that reflects the pervasiveness and persistence of various forms of inequality in the country. This is like watching a huge number of young people congregate in transport stations where istambays are lost in the crowd. It is not difficult to locate them because the voices of their social sufferings can be overheard in the halls of the station, trading stories about their disappointment and discouragement with fellow istambays while patiently waiting for the life vehicle of employment to arrive. Such conversation is data for youth workers and advocates to be fascinated about, to learn from, to critically analyze, and to develop strategies and approaches towards with regards to the general wellbeing of youth in marginalized situations, such as the Filipino istambays.

NOTES

1. This work was carried out with grant aid from the International Development Research Centre, Ottawa, Canada (www. idrc.ca); Commission on Higher Education (CHED), University of Santo Tomas (UST)—Philippine Higher Education Research Network (PHERNET) Program, known as CHED UST PHERNET Program; and the Research Center on Education, Culture and Social Issues (RCCESI), UST, Manila, Philippines. The author also acknowledges Mark Abenir, Keith Aaron Joven, Andrew Lacsina, and Janssen Martinez for their valuable comments on an earlier version of this paper.
2. A *jeepney*, or *jeep*, is a cheap, mass-based means of transportation that can be traced back to the Second World War. They remain one of the cheapest means of transportation in the country, and reflect, in some ways, the art, culture, life, and humor of the Philippine society.

REFERENCES

Aldaba, F.T., & Ang, A.P. (2010). *Youth, employment and migration: Key policy issues*. Unpublished report, International Labour Organisation & International Labor Studies, Manila.

Almario, V.S. (Ed.). (2001). *UP Diksiyonaryong Filipino*. Pasig City: Sentro ng Wikang Filipino, Sistemang Unibersidad ng Pilipinas & Anvil Publishing Inc.

Arnett, J.J. (2002). Adolescents in Western countries in the 21st century: Vast opportunities for all? In B.B. Brown, R.W. Larson & T.S. Saraswathi (Eds.), *The world's youth: Adolescence in eight regions of the globe* (pp. 307–343). Cambridge: Cambridge University Press.

Auyero, J. (2011). Patients of the state: An ethnographic account of poor people's waiting. *Latin American Research Review*, *46*(1), 5–29.

Bartolome, H. (1992). Istambay. *Mga Awit ni Heber: Banyuhay Compilation*. Manila: BMG Records.

Batan, C.M. (2010). *Istambay: A sociological analysis of youth inactivity in the Philippines*. Doctor of Philosophy in Sociology Dissertation, Dalhousie University, Halifax.

Batan, C.M. (2012). A conceptual exploration of the istambay phenomenon in the Philippines. *Philippine Sociological Review*, *60*, 101–130.

Bourdieu, P. (1977). *Outline of a theory of practice* (R. Nice, Trans.). Cambridge: Cambridge University Press.

Bourdieu, P. (1984). *Distinction: A social critique of the judgment of taste* (R. Nice, Trans.). Cambridge, MA: Harvard University Press.
Bourdieu, P. (1986). The forms of capital. In J. Richardson (Ed.), *Handbook of theory and research for the sociology of education* (pp. 241–258). Westport, CT: Greenwood Press.
Bourdieu, P., & Passeron, J.-C. (1990/1977). *Reproduction in education, society and culture* (R. Nice, Trans.). London: Sage Ltd.
Brown, F. (1980). *The transition of youth to adulthood: A bridge too long: A report to educators, sociologists, legislators, and youth policymaking bodies.* Boulder, CO: Westview Press.
Bulatao, J.S.J. (1962). Philippine values: The Manileños mainsprings. *Philippine Sociological Review, X*(1–2), 1–26.
Bynner, J., & Parsons, S. (2002). Social exclusion and the transition from school to work: The case of young people not in education, employment and training (NEET). *Journal of Vocational Behaviour, 60*, 289–309.
Cabreira, J.P. (1979). *Ang Tsimay at Ang Tambay.* Philippines: Movie Masters.
Camo, L. (1997). Kung Ikaw. On *Philippines: Sino Camo?* [Album]. Quezon City, Philippines: Star Records.
Canlas, M.E.L., & Pardalis, M.C.R. (2009). *Youth employment in the Philippines.* ILO Asia-Pacific Working Paper Series. Geneva: ILO.
Castillo, G.T. (1979). *Beyond Manila: Philippine rural problems in perspective.* Manila: Canada International Development and Research Centre.
Coles, B., Hutton, S., Bradshaw, J., Craig, G., Godfrey, C., & Johnson, J. (2002). *Literature review of the costs of being 'not in education, employment or training' at age 16–18* (Research report RR 347). York, UK: Department for Education and Skills, University of York.
Collins, R. (1979). *The credential society.* New York: Academic Press.
Côté, J.E. (2000). *Arrested adulthood: The changing nature of maturity and identity.* New York: New York University Press.
Coté, J.E., & Allahar, A.L. (1994). *Generation on hold: Coming of age in the late twentieth century.* Toronto: Stoddart.
de Dios, E.S., Diokno, B.E., Esguerra, E.F., Fabella, R.V., Gochoco-Bautista, M.S., Medalla, F.M., Monsod, S.C., . . . Tan, E.A. (2004). *The deepening crisis: The real score on deficits and public debt.* Quezon City: University of the Philippines (Diliman).
Edelman, P., Holzer, H.J., & Offner, P. (2006). *Reconnecting disadvantaged young men.* Washington, DC: Urban Institute Press.
Enchi (Writer). (2005). Dungagi ni! In G. Records (Producer). Philippines: Galaxy Records.
Enriquez, V.G. (1992). *From colonial to liberation psychology: The Philippine experience.* Diliman, Quezon City: University of the Philippines Press.
Ericta, C.N. (2003, May 15–17). *The Filipino youth: A statistical profile.* Paper presented at the Fifth National Social Science Congress, Philippine Social Science Center, Diliman, Quezon City, Philippines.
European and World Values Surveys Four-wave Integrated Data File. (1981–2004). *The European values study foundation and world values survey association.* Aggregate file producers: ASEP/JDS, Madrid, Spain/Tilburg University, Tilburg, the Netherlands. Aggregate File Distributors: ASEP/JDS and ZA, Cologne, Germany.
Franzén, E.M., & Kassman, A. (2005). Longer-term labour market consequences of economic inactivity during young adulthood: A Swedish national cohort study. *Journal of Youth Studies, 8*(4), 403–424.
Furlong, A. (2006). Not a very NEET solution: representing problematic labour market transitions among early school-leavers. *Work, Employment & Society, 20*(3), 553–569.

Furlong, A. (2008). The Japanese hikikomori phenomenon: Acute social withdrawal among young people. *The Sociological Review, 56*(2), 309–325.

Furlong, A., & Cartmel, F. (1997). *Young people and social change: Individualization and risk in late modernity*. Buckingham: Open University Press.

Galaway, B., & Hudson, J. (Eds.). (1996). *Youth in transition: Perspectives on research and policy*. Toronto: Thompson Educational Publishing.

Hogan, D.P., & Astone, N.M. (1986). The transition to adulthood. *Annual Review of Sociology, 12*, 109–30.

Hollnsteiner, M.R. (1964). Reciprocity in the low land Philippines. *Four Readings on Philippine Values*. Quezon City: Ateneo de Manila University Press.

International Labour Organization. (2006). *Global employment trends for youth*. Geneva: International Labour Office.

Jocano, F.L. (1966). Rethinking 'smooth interpersonal relations'. *Philippine Sociological Review, 14*(4), 282–291.

Jocano, F.L. (1969). Youth in a changing society: A case study from the Philippines. *Youth & Society, 1*(1), 73–89.

Kaneko, S. (2006). Japan's "socially withdrawn youths" and time constraints in Japanese society: Management and conceptualization of time in a support group for 'hikikomori'. *Time & Society, 15*(2–3), 233–249.

Kerckhoff, A.C. (1990). *Getting started: Transition to adulthood in Great Britain.* Boulder, CO: Westview Press.

Lehmann, W. (2007). *Choosing to labour? School-work transitions and social class.* Montreal: McGill-Queen's University Press.

Lynch, F. (1964). *Four readings on Philippine values.* Quezon City: Ateneo de Manila University Press.

Margold, J.A. (1995). Narratives of masculinity and transnational migration: Filipino workers in the Middle East. In A. Ong & M.G. Peletz (Eds.), *Bewitching women, pious men: Gender and body politics in Southeast Asia* (pp. 274–293). Berkeley: The University of California Press.

Mills, C.W. (1959). *The sociological imagination.* New York: Oxford University Press, Inc.

Miralao, V.A. (2004). *Filipino youth in special high schools: A survey of senior students at the Philippine science high school.* Philippine High School for the Arts and OB Montessori High School. Quezon City: Philippine Social Science Council: UNESCO National Commission of the Philippines—Social and Human Sciences Committee.

Miranda, F. (2003). *Leaving for good?* Retrieved from http://www.philstar.com/philstar/News200309162605.htm

Natividad, J.N. (Ed.). (2004). *Filipino youth in transition: A survey of urban high school senior students* (Vol. I). Quezon City: Philippine Social Science Council: UNESCO National Commission of the Philippines—Social and Human Sciences Committee.

Philippine National Youth Commission. (2005). *National framework for youth development (Philippine Medium-Term Youth Development Plan) 2005–2010.* Quezon City, Philippines: National Youth Commission.

Philippine National Youth Commission. (2012). *Philippine youth development plan, 2011–2016.* Quezon City: National Youth Commission.

Population Reference Bureau. (2013). *2013 data sheet. The world's youth.* New York: Population Reference Bureau.

Ralph, M. (2008). Killing time. *Social Text 97, 26*(4), 1–29.

Raymundo, C., & Cruz, G.T. (Eds.). (2004). *Youth sex and risk behaviors in the Philippines.* Diliman, Quezon City: Demographic Research and Development Foundation, Inc.; University of the Philippines Population Institute.

Republic Act No. 7796. (1994). Technical Educational and Skills Development Act of 1994.

Republic Act No. 8044. (1995). Youth in Nation Building Act of 1995.
Republic Act No. 10533. (2013). Enhanced Basic Education Act of 2013.
Santiago, P. (Director). (1963). *Istambay film*. Philippines: Joseph Ejercito Productions.
Social Weather Station. (2002). *SWS selected survey on religiosity SWS snapshot*. Quezon City: Social Weather Station.
Thiessen, V., & Looker, D. (1999a). Diverse directions: Young adults' multiple transitions. In W.R. Heinz (Ed.), *From education to work: Cross-national perspectives* (pp. 46–64). Cambridge: Cambridge University Press.
Thiessen, V., & Looker, D. (1999b). *Investing in youth: The Nova Scotia school-to-work transition project*. Nova Scotia: Human Resources Development Canada Minister of Public Works and Government Services Canada.
UNDESA. (2012). *Youth employment: Youth perspectives on the pursuit of decent work in changing times*. World Youth Report. New York: United Nations.
UNESCO. (2010). *Reaching the marginalized: Education for all global monitoring report 2010*. Oxford: UNESCO Publishing & Oxford University Press.
United Nations. (2007). *World Youth Report 2007: Young people's transition to adulthood: progress and challenges*. New York: United Nations.
Vicassans's Pilipino-English Dictionary (Abridged Edition). (2006). Manila: Anvil Publishing Inc.
Wallace, P. (2008, February). *Where to the Philippines?* Manila: The Wallace Business Forum.
West, M., & Newton, P. (1983). *The transition from school to work*. London: Croom Helm.
White, R., & Wyn, J. (2008). *Youth and society: Exploring the social dynamics of youth experience* (2nd ed.). Melbourne: Oxford University Press.
Williamson, H. (1997). Status zero youth and the "underclass": some considerations. In R. MacDonald (Ed.), *Youth the 'underclass' and social exclusion* (pp. 70–82). London: Routledge.
Williamson, H. (2004). *The Milltown boys revisited*. Oxford: Berg Publishers.
Willis, P. (1977). *Learning to labour: How working class kids get working class jobs*. New York: Columbia University Press.
Wyn, J., & White, R. (1997). *Rethinking youth*. London: Sage.
Xenos, P. (2001). *The national youth population of Asia: Long-term change in six countries* (East-West Center Working Papers: Population Series No. 108–2). Honolulu: East-West Center.

7 Youth Work in England

An Uncertain Future?

Helen Jones

England's youth workers have always tended to look back to a golden age when funding was available, there were apparently fewer restrictive regulations, and, presumably, the sun shone on well-resourced programs. The post-war period, when government funding was channeled into work with young people via local authorities and third-sector or voluntary organizations, provides the touchstone for reminiscence. For once, there appear to be firm grounds for nostalgia. Drastically reduced funding for all forms of work with young people provides the context for this chapter. Cuts in funding have served to reinforce and extend inequalities. The UK magazine *Children and Young People Now* published an article entitled "Youth sector on a 'knife-edge' as third of organizations at risk" (N.K., 2013). It presented a depressing overview of reductions in expenditure and a pessimistic prediction of the future. Shortly afterwards, Butler (2013) reported that over a two-year period, cuts to youth services averaged 27% and in some places amounted to 50% while a handful axed their entire youth budget. It is clear that youth services have been subject to drastic cuts accompanied by amalgamation with targeted and acute services for young people.

In addition, the very character of England's youth work is under threat. The profession was built on strong values and an ideological foundation. First, youth workers worked with young people who were there voluntarily: They might commit to a project, but they did so because they chose to. Second, youth workers worked with groups of young people. They valued 'association.' Third, youth work was essentially an educational enterprise. Informal education lay at its core. Over the last 20 years, these three values have been corrupted: Surveillance has tarnished voluntary engagement, individualization has replaced association, and welfarism has begun to take the place of informal education.

This chapter identifies the aspects of young people's lives that have been affected by different financial cuts and other policy changes. To provide examples, current youth work practitioners were asked to write about their experience of the sector. Jo Bambrough and Delia Toberty are experienced workers based in the northwest of England, employed by a local education authority's youth service. The service has undergone radical funding cuts and cultural change as many public services have been dismantled. Matthew Wilson and Gareth White entered the field more recently, working for another local authority and a housing association respectively. Kimberley White, Annette Wilson, and Alex Taylor are newly qualified workers based in Yorkshire. They all focused on the dimensions of their work that they feel are most significant to the overall theme of the chapter: how reductions are impacting youth work, youth, and (in)equality. Their words are used as symbolic examples of voices of practice as they adapt to a much-changed environment and a profession struggling to find a new place while surrounded by insecurity. Their input has been juxtaposed with the narrative and highlighted through the use of italics. These provide a powerful account that balances the environment of uncertainty with underlying vision and determination. Their writing was spontaneous: They were not interviewed but rather wrote about what matters most to them as practicing youth workers.

> *Statutory work is disappearing across all regions of the UK and is currently being viewed as a luxury. Young people are not a money generator, which makes such provision easier to axe. The illusion is that young people are more tech savvy and will engage with virtual youth work via tablets and iPhones. They don't need real youth workers or dedicated youth centers to go to.*

Clearly, youth work is only a part of young people's experience, and the devastating reductions to provision are just one element of their experience of public services. Nonetheless, it is not difficult to paint an unremittingly gloomy picture of how young people are affected by the current economic situation in England[1]. Perhaps it is not surprising that UNICEF (2007) found the UK's children and young people to be the unhappiest out of those living in 21 developed countries. Aspects contributing to this result included attitudes to education, personal wellbeing, home and family life, and general satisfaction with their lives. The OECD (2013) has found that young people are most likely to suffer from governmental austerity packages; they suffer most from cuts. They are also, in political terms, the most powerless.

> *Services for young people are currently facing some very uncertain times. The opportunities that are available to young people through voluntary engagement with youth workers is something we should hold onto dearly. Providing a space for people to engage with a range of opportunities and resources that open up new doors and empower them to make better-informed decisions and a stronger sense of identity within wider surroundings.*

In early 2013, almost 20% of 16- to 24-year-olds were 'NEET', the acronym for young people who are 'Not in Education, Employment, or Training' that has evolved into a noun in its own right, with politicians and professionals referring to 'NEETs,' often in disparaging tones. Young people's financial plight has been exacerbated by changes including the removal in 2011 of the Education Maintenance Allowance, which had been paid to 16- to 18-year-olds to encourage them to stay in education by providing them with a small weekly grant to help with fares and other overheads. The following year, young people opting to attend university found themselves paying vastly increased tuition fees, making higher education an increasingly costly option. Young people who were too young to vote in the 2010 election are paying the price of austerity.

THE 'BIG SOCIETY' PRETENSE

When David Cameron became the UK Prime Minister in 2010, the idea of the 'Big Society' was launched in parallel with the introduction of spending cuts. The electorate was told that massive cuts to public expenditure were vital to achieve what was termed 'balancing the books.' However the concept appeared to be a way to shift responsibility for provision, which had hitherto been part of the welfare state, onto volunteers. As Liz Such notes, "definition of the Big Society is elusive. It is perhaps best described by what it is not: it is not the State" (Such, 2012, p. 90). For right-wing politicians and supporters who favored the idea, the Big Society would revitalize civic society. They envisaged people being excited to take responsibility for the management of facilities and services: Volunteers would have the opportunity to staff museums, art galleries, sports centers, libraries, and youth clubs. Isolated people would be brought into their local communities, and a new sense of community would be created. Indeed, a few people have been excited to take roles in local facilities but for most, as Nicholls (2012) observed, the Big Society is:

> nothing other than a smokescreen for dismantling the public sector and the traditional public sphere of civil society and voluntary organizations and charities. It was an attempt to reintroduce self-help into social concerns and 'philanthro-capitalism', as they called it, instead of social giving. The welfare state is being replaced by a distorted form of self-help (p. 224).

The 'Big Society' needs to be located in its historical context. Across western Europe, welfare states were set up as part of post-war reconstruction following the Second World War. From the richest to the poorest, everybody had suffered during the war, and there was a sense that rebuilding should benefit all. Britain's welfare state was designed to ensure the end of what the system's architect, William Beveridge, referred to in his famous 1942 report as the 'five giants' of want, disease, ignorance, squalor, and idleness (Timmins, 1995). The list today might be poverty, poor health, poor education, bad housing, and unemployment. People would have a right to state services rather than having to beg for charity: free healthcare, free education, old age pensions, unemployment, and other benefits would be paid for through direct taxation and would be a right rather than a privilege. Direct taxation meant that people were paid in relation to their income. Provision would be consistent and fair across the nation. The state was trusted to provide the best for all its citizens. Professions developed to ensure the provision was made during an era of broad consensus, which is often characterized as founded on broadly egalitarian values.

During the 1950s, youth work became an aspect of state provision with paid workers. However, it never achieved the status of a statutory requirement; the provision of youth services by local government never became a legal obligation. At the time, some people were optimistic about the introduction of state-run youth work, although others saw worrying echoes of youth movements such as Germany's compulsory Hitler Youth and questioned whether paid work with young people should lay within the state's aegis. Subsequently, as youth work never achieved the status of being a statutory requirement, it joined services such as public libraries, sports centers, museums, and toilets as an obvious place to make financial cuts.

> *In 2014, youth work is being delivered from a variety of locations, including children's centers, libraries, and village halls. Work has morphed from a universal provision for all young people to a more streamlined, less responsive service. Delivery has been reduced, and buildings have closed. There's an increasing trend moving towards the use of shared buildings in order to cut down core costs . . . this is a move away from the 'youth center.' As such we are not able to guarantee that we can offer the same level of 'safe space' for young people as they no longer have an environment that is exclusive to them.*

Over the last few years many youth workers have lost their jobs with local authorities, although the situation across England varies considerably. Kerry Jenkins reported that 25% of England's youth services face cuts of between 21% and 30%, which is three times higher than the level of cuts faced by other council departments (Jenkins, 2013). Some authorities are consulting residents about priorities. For example, in Kirklees, a local authority area in the north of England, a survey found local residents strongly agreed that its youth services should provide services for as many young people as possible. 92% favored a focus on early investment that would help to prevent 'problems which may be costly later' such as teenage pregnancy and substance abuse (Kirklees Council, 2013). The apparent favor expressed by residents for 'universal' provision contradicts the view often taken by politicians and professionals.

> *Where you live has a massive impact upon your experience as a result of investment local cultures and economic factors. It usually determines*

> *what school you go to. The school that you attend may have a very different approach to a neighboring school in terms of curriculum and its response to its duty of care. [Formal agreements] have been initiated by the Youth Council and successfully introduced in [local] schools around sex and relationships education as well as anti-bullying strategies.*
>
> *You see local authorities only providing what is expected of them rather than being radical and progressive about youth work that [values] the diverse skills and knowledge of its practitioners. Overlooking the talent that is readily available . . . leads to people feeling undervalued, underappreciated and disillusioned.*
>
> *Some staff were 'assimilated' into a new role, often with no induction and no retraining. This clearly impacted on delivery work as staff feel adrift and under pressure until they adjusted to new ways of working. The staffing in our service was reduced by the equivalent of 130 full-time posts. . . We are currently seeing a higher staff turnover rate and an increasingly introspective workplace culture which feeds competitive working practices rather than a supportive team.*

Various culprits have been identified as responsible for the gradual undermining of the British welfare state before the recent onslaught. During the 1970s and 1980s, Margaret Thatcher and the Conservative Party promulgated an ideology which challenged the hitherto-accepted collectivism and began to privatize public services: The welfare state was caricatured as 'the nanny state,' knowing what was best for everyone, interfering with personal choice, and restricting individual freedom. The welfare state's destruction formed part of Thatcher's legacy and has continued under subsequent governments of all political persuasions. Gradually, 19th-century ideas differentiating between the 'deserving' and 'undeserving' poor were revived. Imogen Tyler sees this as part of the impact of the "arrival of the concept of the underclass in Britain in the 1980s, courtesy of the American political theorist Charles Murray [which] incited public consent for the decomposition of the welfare state" (Tyler, 2013, p. 187). Murray's ideas were promulgated through publication in the national newspaper *The Sunday Times* and soon achieved widespread acceptance. New prejudices against certain groups of people developed and inequalities were further entrenched. As unemployment grew in the twenty first century, unemployed young people (disparagingly re-characterized as 'chavs' and subsequently 'neets') were identified increasingly as undeserving. They are seldom in a position to challenge the characterization effectively.

DEFINING 'YOUTH WORK'

Within England's occupational field, there are heated debates about the differences between 'youth work,' 'youth and community work,' and 'work with young people.' However, to the majority of politicians and policymakers, as well as the population at large, these distinctions are bewildering and based on subtle, barely discernible differences. For many practitioners, 'youth work' and 'youth and community work' have a long and proud history (for example, the YMCA was created in London in 1844 and Scouting in 1907) now supported by degree-level qualifications that are validated for professional purposes by England's National Youth Agency (NYA). On the other hand, 'work with young people' does not require such advanced qualifications and does not attract professional rates of pay. Some people see the occupation 'work with young people' as epitomizing de-professionalization, although others see it as forming part of a range of occupations extending from voluntary work through to graduates in professional grade posts.

> *Youth work is not defined by an activity. Youth work is about empowerment and education. My methods have been youth work methods regardless of the setting.*
>
> *Youth work should start from where young people are, in relation to their own values, views and principles, as well as their own personal and social space and environment.*
>
> *[Youth work offers] an open door policy which delivers so much more than many people imagine. It could, through young people accessing provision and engaging with peers with such diverse experiences and perspectives. Unlike school and more formal structures, people are not thrown together and expected to perform in a particular way, rather they are welcomed and allowed to be. In a harsher society this can be the only positive and affirming experience some people have.*
>
> *Fundamentally the relationship between a young person and youth worker should be one of co-production.*

As indicated earlier, England's approach to traditional youth work is grounded in a strongly articulated value base with three particular key aspects: voluntary engagement, informal education, and the importance of association. Anti-discriminatory practice is its powerful foundation. Originally founded in 1904, the charity The Youth Association explains in its 2014–16 Strategy, "Our work is always most effective when it is voluntary: its power to grow mutual respect between young people and adults comes from the rights of both to walk away from the process. It must be a positive choice."

> *I feel strongly that youth work is based on the voluntary attendance of young people and should be need and want led, with those needs and wants decided upon by the young people. To impose activities on them at a time when they do not want or need them is counterproductive.*

Youth workers are proud of accepting and respecting young people on their own terms and in their own chosen context: In the past, young people's names were not necessarily gathered and other data were often scant. This meant it was often difficult to provide the sort of evidence sought by managers, councillors, and public bodies. In 2011, members of Parliament set out to understand youth work's impact: "what government gets for its investment in youth work, and what evidence there is for any positive impact from that investment" (Thomas, 2011, p. 18). The politicians struggled to find 'objective evidence' (House of Commons Education Committee), although they had been provided with an "extensive and comprehensive" range of documentation by the youth workers' trade union (Nicholls, 2012, p. 41).

Nicholls posits a radical vision of youth work as an "elaborate and sensitive" transformative practice which is 'uniquely placed to advance young people and their issues' (Nicholls, 2012, p. 40). Anodyne 'work with young people' does not share youth work's profoundly empowering intent. Coburn and Wallace (2011) believe that youth work offers "the best possibilities for social change and emancipatory practice" (p. 86). They propose that youth work is a "synthesis of personal development and social education" (ibid). As such, it is a radical activity that questions policy and challenges conformity. This radical dimension can place youth work in an uneasy position with authority.

> *We work towards positive change with young people and this must be at the center of all our work. To successfully combine the individual needs of people with the conflicting organizational behaviors, ensuring not to pathologize the behaviors of young people. Even if the change is small and gradual it can have a significant impact on combatting injustice.*
>
> *I have been able to use my skills as an informal educator to break down and analyze subject matters and present them in ways that have been relevant to young people. . . I have managed to achieve this by working not 'on' the young person but working 'with' them . . . in an attempt to empower and help them to develop a conscious awareness of their situation.*

Youth workers were once found mainly in youth clubs and community centers. They might work within their clubs and centers or on a detached basis, working with young people on street-corners and in parks. Nowadays they are more widely employed and may be found in a wide range of agencies. With skills in engaging successfully with young people who are sometimes characterized as 'hard to reach,' youth workers are employed by an increasingly wide range of organizations and institutions involved in education (both schools and colleges predominantly serving young people aged 16–19), housing, youth justice and health. In many of these contexts, they might work with individuals rather than groups. There is debate as to whether this constitutes pathologizing young people or utilizing youth workers' skills effectively.

The recognition that we cannot change the structures of society but that we can change how people interact and respond to the structures is vital: to allow people to develop the skills and resilience to advocate on their own behalf and on behalf of others.

Based on practice in Scotland, Coburn and Wallace (2011) posited a typology of models of practice for youth work within schools and identified seven variants. These include the delivery of alternative curricula, usually to young people at risk of permanent exclusion, supplementing the core curriculum with programs such as anti-bullying or 'lads as dads.' and 'a complementary model' in which youth workers provide input which is "linked to the smooth running of school, e.g. anger management programmes" (p. 49). This picture also applies in England. Courses in anger management and work with very young fathers are types of work undertaken by youth workers.

I have found myself advocating on behalf of young people on a regular basis when I feel the young person's voice is not being heard. I have used this one-to-one, professional method of advocacy as a tool to 'respect and promote the young people's rights to make their own decisions and choices' (citing NYA guidelines, 2001).

YOUNG PEOPLE AND TRANSITIONS

In England, the definition of youth has not remained consistent but is currently seen as individuals aged 13–19. The upper age is raised to 22 or 25 for work with young people with disabilities, although the support may be limited to young people remaining in full-time education. Many youth workers identify the age range 11–13 as a missed opportunity that should be regarded as a priority. Some services are considering further integration that might involve shifting the focus to 'work with families.'

The latest rumblings are that the service will work with young people from the age of 12 who have been identified as needing support. An early support service for young people, options are being considered around which agencies can be 'aligned' in this work. . . we're looking at being a key part of the 0–19 service for young people. . . This may mean merging with services we wouldn't ordinarily as youth workers align ourselves with.

There has been significant change within children and young people's services, which has seen the youth service becoming part of the bigger integrated youth support service . . . I have recognized a change in people. Workers are now being considered about their work and how much they are prepared to share.

England's school-leaving age is 16, but since September 2013, young people have had to spend another year participating in some form of education, training, or full-time employment (over 20 hours per week) alongside part-time education or training. The age rises to 18 in 2015. It seems that the raising of the compulsory 'participation age' and consequent postponement of a key youth transition has been accepted with apparently few challenges from young people themselves.

The decision to raise the age of participation in education was taken by the Labour government in 2007. and the policy was not changed when the Conservative-Liberal Democrat Coalition government was created soon after the 2010 election. The thinking behind the decision was presented as being in young people's best interests: Most young people decided to remain in education of their own volition, but those who left tended to be those who were 'more vulnerable and lower-achieving.' The government considered them to be the exact group which most needed to stay in education so they can achieve useful skills which will prepare them for life. Indeed, "the time has come to consider whether society is letting these young people down by allowing them to leave education and training for good at 16, knowing they are not adequately prepared for life" (DfES, 2007, p. 1). Politicians appeared to agree on the wisdom of the decision. The fact that there would be an obvious impact on the number of NEET young people was not widely discussed although the reduction is likely to be presented as a positive achievement. A few critics pointed out that some young people whose previous experience of education had not been positive might not be well served by another year following immediately on school. Some suggested that alternatives might include the opportunity to spend some time entirely away from educational institutions before returning to learning, but this has never formed part of politicians' plans.

Britain's national newspaper *The Independent* estimated that around 52,000 extra young people would be impacted by the changes (Garner, 2013c). After several months of this policy, it remains unclear how the system is to be policed. For example, what penalties will be implemented when young people have not succeeded in finding employment, training, or a place in education? At what point will this be ascertained? What action will be taken against young people who 'disappear'? The government believed that sanctions would not be required as young people 'have the opportunity to access the learning opportunity they want' (Garner, 2013b), and it was unclear whether the rules affecting school truancy would be employed. In addition, if a young person is working for an employer that then closes down, how will this be identified? For these reasons, Garner described the generation as 'guinea pigs' (Garner, 2013b).

The day before the autumn term began in most of England's schools and colleges in 2013, the government announced an additional change: Any young person who had not achieved a grade 'C' in the mathematics and/or English examinations taken the previous June would be required to continue to study the subjects (Garner, 2013c). How schools and colleges were going to re-timetable where necessary and recruit additional staff if required was not made clear. The emphasis on achieving grade 'C' in examinations, which are graded A-G, has to be set against the government's stated aim to end perceived grade inflation. Are young people being set up to fail?

Alongside increasing the age of participation, the government shifted responsibility for providing careers guidance to schools themselves. It appears that the quantity and quality of provision have decreased greatly. The Labour government (1997–2010) had set up the Connexions service to provide advice and guidance to individual young people on issues including careers. By the time of its abolition, it had gained widespread recognition: Young people were aware of the service. Without the careers-guidance workers employed by Connexions, many young people receive scant advice on future courses or careers. It has been suggested schools with sixth forms (years 12 and 13) tend to promote their own courses, which might not necessarily be in young people's best interests (Russell, 2013). Thus the situation for young people combines the legal rise in participation age, which defers a key transition to adulthood, with a shortage of professional guidance in taking vital career decisions. Youth workers increasingly are being tasked with fostering young people's development in the context of employment and education. This serves to undermine the traditional youth work relationship between workers and young people and forms part of the increased targeting of work with particular individuals.

> *We are measured on [. . .]:*
>
> - *Recorded outcomes (a form to show a set target and progress for a young person)*
> - *Accreditations (certificated learning that can help with employment and future learning)*
> - *Intended destinations (what a young person aims to do when they leave compulsory education)*
> - *NEET figures*
>
> *You can clearly see that we're to provide an extensive service with a clear focus on young people's engagement and transitions in relation to the labor market.*

SHIFTING INEQUALITIES

It is iniquitous to seek to construct a hierarchy of inequality or disadvantage, but there are documented groups and issues which merit particular concern. There have been shifts in the narrative of disadvantage. Cuts in public spending, the economic decline, and rise in unemployment have had a devastating impact on services for virtually all young people except for the most affluent who are less likely to use public services. Some cuts have eroded programs that were overtly intended to address inequality.

For example, Aim Higher was a scheme under the Labour government and ran from 2004–11. It aimed to encourage university applications from young people from non-traditional and disadvantaged backgrounds. Short courses, day schools, and visits were funded, but the program was scrapped soon after the 2010 election.

> *Concepts such as values and social impact are very rarely spoken of within the work environment and certainly not with . . . urgency, formality or frequency.*
>
> *As funding becomes harder to obtain . . . people chase funding streams that offer money for particular pieces of targeted work and the delivery of this work will be at the expense of work that is actually wanted and needed by young people. I hope that this is not a trend that becomes more established and that the actual purpose of youth work, to deliver work that is truly needs led and voluntarily taken part in, is not overlooked in the chase for funding.*
>
> *Our poverty campaign is running in an area of high socioeconomic deprivation, initiated by a small group of young women who came across statistics in the local press showing the high numbers of children and young people in their ward who are growing up below the poverty line. They have met with local food banks, run a food drive, put together curriculum resources and are learning currently how to make a film to make this more high profile.*

Nowadays, tiny voluntary initiatives provide models of good practice but can only meet a fraction of the unaddressed need. For example, two young women school teachers, Becca Dean and Charly Young, set up the Girls' Network to mentor girls aged 14–19. Their participants include the daughters of asylum seekers and refugees, but their initiative is tiny in comparison with Aim Higher, which was a national scheme (Murray, 2013). Girls' Network appears to reflect core youth work values yet was set up by teachers, working as volunteers.

> *Now more than ever, I feel disempowered in my position to really address the key issues and barriers facing young people. Working for a service that is not nearly sufficiently flexible and integrated as is necessary to meet the needs with which we are presented. Provision is very functional and outcome-driven and at present doesn't come with much security due to current government agendas and austerity measures.*

Gendered disadvantage cannot be examined without considering additional aspects such as race, culture, class, sexuality, and disability. For example, at a time when young women school students are achieving measurably better than young men in public examinations, the examinations are being changed (BBC, 2013). Research has shown that irrespective of class, culture, or disability, young women thrive when ongoing coursework grades are included as an element in final examination grades, while many young men prefer cramming for 'sudden death' exams at the end of the year. The government has decided to shift away from coursework (which arguably reflects the skills of drafting and redrafting that are required in the world outside school) towards final exams (which demonstrate the skill of memorizing material that is generally not retained thereafter). From 2014, girls will be systemically disadvantaged in public examinations, returning to the situation in which education has been designed and redesigned to advantage boys. Michèle Cohen has traced the history of boys' comparative underachievement and the shifts in narrative explaining why girls' demonstration of apparent achievement should not be linked with intelligence. Girls' superior performance was written off as superficial, and ways of measuring success have been reconsidered over several hundred years (Cohen, 1998). The changes to public examinations cannot be explained by austerity but rather echo current political ideological attitudes to education. The successes achieved by feminists during the 1970s are being eroded.

Meanwhile, politicians are expressing concerns about young men's educational outcomes. In particular, working-class young white men are increasingly established as a disadvantaged, unequal group that has been to some extent marginal to the rhetoric of equality. Far more boys than girls are excluded from school and end up in Pupil Referral Units where formal examinations might not be offered. David Jackson outlines how girls' underachievement was identified in the 1970s. Causes were analyzed and initiatives introduced, but changes that addressed girls' needs appear to have disadvantaged boys, and 20 years later the focus shifted to boys' disadvantage and educational failure (Jackson, 1998). A further 15 years had passed before government minister David Willetts observed, "I do worry about what looks like increasing underperformance by young men" (cited in Garner, 2013a). In response, Joan Smith wrote,

> Teenage boys from poor families tend not to value education, and their schools don't have the resources to challenge so many connected problems. They also have competing models of masculinity, linked to sexual performance, conspicuous consumption and violence. Ofsted (the government's Office for Standards in Education, Children's Services and Skills) has identified the problem succinctly as the lure of the three Fs: fighting, football and fucking. (Smith, 2013)

Increasingly, researchers and authors have examined the situation, but there are scant examples of effective projects addressing the situation. Furthermore, disadvantaged young straight white working-class men are the group most likely to be attracted to far-right-wing, often violent racist movements such as the English Defence League.

Hanbury, Lee, and Batsleer (2010) see gender stereotyping as underpinning the attention given by government. Young men "are seen as anti-social, involved in gun and knife crime . . . [they] misuse drugs and alcohol." while young women "need protection and [are] at risk of self-harm and pregnancy" (Hanbury et al., 2010, p. 117). Money focused on emancipatory gender-based youth work with young women has largely been abandoned, and emancipatory work with young men never started in the first place. Many youth workers reflect the reluctance of the wider general public to characterize themselves as feminists. Nonetheless, some women are seeking to re-invent feminist work with young women and rediscover gender-based radicalism. Janet Batsleer celebrates the work undertaken in England's northwest by the Feminist Webs initiative. She shows how its new wave of activism dates back to a 2005 initiative, Done Hair and Nails: Now What? (Batsleer, 2013). However, in many areas a limited agenda underpins much work with young women: sexual health and pregnancy, food and healthy eating, hair, nails, and beauty have eclipsed the adventurous work which opened up new opportunities and experiences. There is scant provision offering activities such as canoeing, rock climbing, and other outdoor pursuits.

More positively, social media has opened up new potential for young people to campaign and make a powerful impact themselves. For example, in February 2014, 17-year-old Fahma Mohamed spearheaded the fight against female genital mutilation. Her online petition secured 250,000 signatures in a fortnight and gained national recognition. Fahma and her friends met with the Secretary of State for Education and succeeded in their campaign to ensure information is sent to all schools before the summer holidays and to remind teachers of their responsibility to protect their pupils (Topping, 2014). Their work garnered widespread accolades, including from UN General Secretary Ban Ki-moon.

Little has changed in the three decades since I wrote an essay as part of my professional youth work qualification asking what anti-sexist work was being undertaken with boys and young men in single-gender groups as a counterpart to feminist work with young women. In 1983, I found virtually none. Yet, the White Ribbon Campaign (the UK branch of the global movement) is developing exciting work across the country. Men campaigning against male physical and emotional violence are working with groups of young men in a wide range of different contexts, including schools, youth clubs, and universities, with informal education as a central method. They cite research showing that 1 in 5 young men believe that women 'often provoke violence' (whiteribboncampaign, 2014). In many places this initiative is true to youth work's values: Young men participate voluntarily, they work in groups, and education lies at the core.

While White Ribbon focuses on men as potential perpetrators, workers also focus on victims. Bullying is an issue for many young people and in particular those who are lesbian, gay, bisexual, and transsexual, a situation noted by campaigning organization Stonewall (2013). Stonewall's (2007) research, The School Report, showed that "homophobic bullying is almost endemic in Britain's schools" (p. 2), and their 2009 publication The Teachers' Report found that, "primary and secondary school staff confirmed that homophobic bullying is the most frequent form of bullying after bullying because of weight" (Stonewall, 2009, p. 3). Yet in the population as a whole, as the Pew Research Center found, "the view that homosexuality should be accepted by society is prevalent in most of the European Union countries surveyed," with about three-quarters or more in Britain (76%) sharing this view (Pew Research Centre, 2013).

Youth workers in many cities and towns are involved in dedicated groups that offer opportunities for LGBTQ young people to meet in a safe environment. For example, Sheffield Fruitbowl runs a weekly group for school-age young people in the city center, staffed by qualified youth workers. The group was set up in 2003 by Sheffield's Centre for HIV and Sexual Health in recognition of the fact that groups for LGB young people tend to span a very wide age range, yet 13-year-olds may have little in common with 21-year-olds. On its website, Fruitbowl says, "if you are exploring your sexuality or gender identity and want to chat to somebody about it, then Fruitbowl is a good place to contact. The youth workers are all trained and have lots of experience of working with LGBT young people so probably have a good understanding of what you are going through" (Sheffield Fruitbowl, 2010).

LOOKING AHEAD

At the time of writing, individual programs undertaking innovative and exciting work with young people are so few and far between as to be entirely atypical. In a country which appears to have accepted the rhetoric of austerity as grounded in common-sense, hegemonic logic, voices raised against the language of ever-more drastic cuts to public expenditure are barely audible in the wider public sphere. For example, in May 2014, the Twitter feed from the passionately anti-cut ChooseYouth coalition boasted fewer than 2,000 followers. Nicholls is sure that local authority youth services constitute the first public service to be 'destroyed.' He argues that the reason for this is that the youth service "is the only public service built and sustained by young people themselves in a real 'big society' partnership and a service designed to give young people a voice and to develop critical thinking and collective action for change" (Nicholls, 2013). Thus, of course, it constitutes a potentially articulate and subversive force. What Thomas could refer to charitably as "long-term under investment" in 2011 (Thomas, 2011, p. 28) has transmogrified into savage cuts and, in places, total obliteration.

In some towns and cities, faith-based youth work has stepped forward as the sole provider of youth work following the removal of provision by local authorities. Many Christian churches are prepared to work with any young people who come forward, but others see their role as essentially working with young people of faith or potential faith: They are primarily missionary in nature. Many insist on employing only workers who profess their Christian faith. This presents a barrier for some workers and many young people. Similarly, some synagogues work with any young people while others restrict provision to people of Jewish faith. Islam and Sikhism are also developing their youth work dimension.

> *I always had a strong sense of social justice, something that I associate with the overtly religious upbringing I had. My family were far from perfect [but] they had their ideals.*

One group of workers is brave enough to work outside the state structure because of their profound belief in the value of youth work grounded in voluntary engagement, association, and informal education. London's Voice of Youth (VoY) was set up as a workers' co-operative with a strongly egalitarian approach to its work with young people aged 8–19. Workers are 'a mixture of new and experienced Youth Workers ranging from different backgrounds and experience,' and they 'make decisions together . . . try to work as equals . . . do not have bosses or managers, and . . . all paid the same rate.' (VoY, 2014). Sadly VoY seems to be unique: Comparable initiatives have not been found in other cities.

Some new jobs have been created within schools and other mainstream organizations because youth workers are often skilled at working with young people who are hostile to other professionals. A small number of new opportunities for youth work practice have emerged within different structures. For example, housing associations offer rental homes to people on low incomes and are responsible for some entire social housing estates (projects). Their tenants might find the very existence of groups of young people scary or intimidating. Youth workers, often working away from buildings on a detached basis, are able to build relationships with young people and, in some cases, to bring young people and older people together in inter-generational programs. Consequently, some housing associations have identified youth workers as the people best placed to engage with young people whose presence on the streets is seen as problematic by residents. However they have not grown to fill the vacuum left by the withdrawal of state resources.

> *I recognized at an early stage [with the housing association] that I had the capacity to have a huge influence on the young people I was working with. Recognizing this ability helped me realize that I was a role model for young people.*
>
> *There are many professionals desperately trying to improve outcomes for young people and while I still see significant benefits to the*

> *work we deliver, there is a vast untapped potential that the current climate simply isn't offering.*

In London, two hospitals have responded to the proliferation of gang-based knife crime by employing youth workers in Accident and Emergency Services. Youth workers focus on any young people who visit regularly due to being repeatedly assaulted or otherwise involved in violence. They offer follow-up support, advice, and counseling around issues such as anger management and also seek to make contact with young women who may be exploited by gangs. The Centre for Social Justice recommends youth workers being employed more widely in hospital settings (CSJ, 2014). This work is a new and exciting development, but whether it is extended to other cities remains to be seen. It is also depressing because it deals with the result rather than the cause: If youth workers were employed in sufficient numbers to run youth clubs or work on the streets, there might be a far lower level of gang-related violence.

The government has redirected funding from youth work into the National Citizens' Service (NCS), which provides a 3-week, full-time experience for 15- to 17-year-olds in England and Northern Ireland. Youth workers are involved in some of the most successful delivery agencies, measured by participant satisfaction, retention, and other measures. Young people typically stay for 1 week at an outdoor pursuits center then deliver a social-action program while living away from home in student accommodation. The social-action program was intended to contribute to the erstwhile Big Society. However, its impact is probably greater on participants, who develop transferable skills including leadership and independence, than on local communities. NCS caters to around 90,000 participants each year, but in England alone there are over 640,000 16-year-olds (ONS, 2013): Under 14% of young people participate in NCS. Many youth workers are skeptical about the scheme, often on the grounds that money has been taken from long-term universal work and channeled into short programs, but young people who have participated are often very positive.

Numerous commentators and pundits have written in excoriating terms about politicians' approach to the economic management of Britain and its impact on young people. In 2010, Patrick Butler predicted that the combined cuts to services and provision for young people would have a 'multiple impact' on their lives. He quoted Dara Farrell, aged 17, a member of the UK Youth Parliament[2] who said that "working-class young people will be affected . . . more than any other group. Politicians say 'we are all in this together', but young people are in it more than anybody else" (Butler, 2010). Also in 2010, an editorial in *The Observer* described cuts as 'a giant experiment using Britain as the laboratory and some of its poorest citizens as guinea pigs' (Observer, 2010). After cuts had begun to affect people in practice, Will Hutton (2013) wrote that, "A society that neglects its young on this scale, and puts such pressure on them is one that has lost its way"

(Hutton, 2013). The more politically aware predict riots, which in the past have often preceded an increase in funding for work with young people. Others have suggested that the perceived combination of capitalism and fatalism found in the majority of young people render overtly politically inspired riots unlikely.

The universalism aspect of state-provided youth provision is being eroded by the destruction of the youth service. In some cities, there is now no discernible youth service, although others remain comparatively buoyant. Different priorities in neighboring local authority areas have resulted in a fragmented picture across England. As noted earlier, the O.E.C.D. (2013) report showed that people who were already disadvantaged are being affected disproportionately by cuts to public spending: Young people are easily marginalized by politicians. It is impossible to generalize about the state of youth work since the government has delegated the responsibility of making cuts to local areas: It is not feasible to state the extent to which young people are affected on a national basis. More optimistically, youth workers' skills are sought by a widening range of organizations. In conclusion, the 'uncertain future' of youth work is spread inconsistently across the profession and across the nation, with hope rearing its head in some places.

NOTES

1. England, together with Scotland, Wales, and Northern Ireland, is known as the United Kingdom. Scotland's education system, including its youth work, developed entirely separately. Wales and Northern Ireland have developed separate training requirements and structures recently. This chapter concerns England.
2. The UK Youth Parliament provides the opportunity for young people (11–18 years old) who have been elected by their peers to discuss social topics and gain experience with debating and democracy.

REFERENCES

Batsleer, J. (2013). *Youth working with girls and women in community settings.* Farnham: Ashgate.

BBC. (2013). *GCSEs: Gove pledges 'challenging' exam changes.* Retrieved from www.bbc.co.uk/news/education-22841266

Butler, P. (2010). Teenagers could be among worst hit by spending cuts warn charities. *The Guardian.* Retrieved from http://www.theguardian.com/politics/2010/oct/21/teenagers-spending-cuts-warning

Butler, P. (2013). If only cuts to youth services were fantasy. *The Guardian.* Retrieved from http://www.theguardian.com/society/2013/apr/30/cuts-youth-services-fantasy

Cohen, M. (1998). A habit of healthy idleness: Boys' underachievement in historical perspective. In D. Epstein, J. Elwood, V. Hey, & J. Maw (Eds.), *Failing boys?* (pp. 19–34). Buckingham: Open University Press.

CSJ. (2014). *Girls and gangs*. London: Centre for Social Justice.
DfES. (2007). *Raising expectations: Staying in education and training post-16*. London: Department for Education and Skills.
Garner, R. (2013a). Exclusive: Treat white working-class boys like ethnic minority, Willetts tell universities. *The Independent*. Retrieved from http://www.independent.co.uk/news/education/education-news/exclusive-treat-white-workingclass-boys-like-ethnic-minority-willetts-tells-universities-8436087.html
Garner, R. (2013b). School's not out: fears for teenage 'guinea pigs' forced to stay in education. *The Independent*. Retrieved from http://www.independent.co.uk/news/education/education-news/schools-not-out-fears-for-teenage-guinea-pigs-forced-to-stay-in-education-8760016.html
Garner, R. (2013c). Pupils who 'fail' GCSE English or maths will be forced to stay on at school and resit their exams. *The Independent*. Retrieved from http://www.independent.co.uk/news/education/education-news/pupils-who-fail-gcse-english-or-maths-will-be-forced-to-stay-on-at-school-and-resit-their-exams-8793614.html
Hanbury, A., Lee, A., & Batsleer, J. (2010). Youth work with girls: a feminist perspective. In J. Batsleer & B. Davies (Eds.), *What is youth work?* (pp. 116–128). Exeter: Learning Matters.
House of Commons Education Committee. (2011). *Services for young people: 3rd report of session 2010–11*. London: Stationery Office.
Hutton, W. (2013). Blame austerity, not old people, for the plight of Britain's young. *The Observer*. Retrieved from http://www.theguardian.com/commentisfree/2013/jun/23/blame-austerity-old-plight-young-hutton
Jackson, D. (1998). Breaking out of the binary trap. In D. Epstein, J. Elwood, V. Hey, & J. Maw, (Eds.), *Failing boys?* (pp. 77–95). Buckingham: Open University Press.
Jenkins, K. (2013). Youth services are being savaged by government cuts. *False Economy*. Retrieved from http://www.falseeconomy.org.uk/blog/youth-services-in-crisis
Kirklees Council. (2013). *Feedback note—e-panel survey Spring 2013*. Retrieved from http://www2.kirklees.gov.uk/involve/publisheddoc.aspx?ref=i10na5li&e=402
Murray, J. (2013). Watching girls develop in confidence is amazing. *The Guardian*. Retrieved from http://www.theguardian.com/education/2013/sep/02/girls-mentoring-networking
Nicholls, D. (2012). *For youth workers and youth work*. Bristol: The Policy Press.
Nicholls, D. (2013). Manifesto for a new youth service. *The Guardian*. Retrieved from http://www.theguardian.com/society/2013/may/02/manifesto-youth-service
NK. (2013, 16 April). Youth sector on a "knife-edge" as third of organizations at risk. *Children and Young People Now*.
NYA. (2001). *Ethical conduct in youth work*. Leicester: National Youth Agency.
OECD. (2013). *Crisis squeezes income and puts pressure on inequality and poverty*. Retrieved from http://www.oecd.org/social/inequality.htm
ONS. (2013). Age by single year 2011. *Neighbourhood Statistics*. Retrieved from http://www.neighbourhoodstatistics.gov.uk
Pew Research Center. (2013). *The global divide on homosexuality*. Retrieved from http://www.pewglobal.org/2013/06/04/the-global-divide-on-homosexuality
Russell, V. (2013). MPs unhappy with switch of careers guidance to schools. *Public Finance*. Retrieved from www.publicfinance.co.uk/news/2013/01/mps-unhappy-with-switch-of-careers-guidance-to-schools
Sheffield Fruitbowl. (2010). *All about us*. Retrieved from http://www.sheffieldfruitbowl.org.uk
Smith, J. (2013). The government has gone to great lengths to restrict access to university. Where was Willetts's concern for the disadvantaged then? *The Independent*.

Retrieved from http://www.independent.co.uk/voices/comment/the-government-has-gone-to-great-lengths-to-restrict-access-to-university-where-was-willettss-concern-for-the-disadvantaged-then-8437166.html

Stonewall. (2007). *The school report*. London: Stonewall.

Stonewall. (2009). *The teachers' report*. London: Stonewall.

Stonewall. (2013). *Homophobic bullying*. Retrieved from www.stonewall.org.uk/at_school/education_for_all/youth_workers/4168.asp

Such, L. (2012). Little leisure in the big society. *Leisure Studies, 32*(1), 89–107.

Thomas, P. (2011). Proving our worth? Youth work, 'race' and evidence.' *Youth and Policy, 107*, 18–33.

Timmins, N. (1995). *The five giants—A biography of the welfare state*. London: Fontana Press.

Topping, A. (2014, 25 February). Michael Gove agrees to write to schools over female genital mutilation. *The Guardian*. Retrieved from http://www.theguardian.com/society/2014/feb/25/michael-gove-schools-female-genital-mutilation

Tyler, I. (2013). *Revolting subjects*. London: Zed Books.

UNICEF. (2007). *EFA global monitoring report: Strong foundations: Early childhood care and education*. Paris: U.N.E.S.C.O. Publishing.

Whiteribboncampaign. (2014). *Educate young people*. Retrieved from http://www.whiteribboncampaign.co.uk

VoY. (2014). *Our approach*. Retrieved from http://voice-of-youth.org

8 The Scouting Experience and Youth Development

Olga Oliveira Cunha and Pedro Duarte Silva

In scouting, we dare our youth to share our values, to live experiences, and to commit to improve themselves and society as a whole. Scouting acknowledges that our world is full of inequality. Through scouting, we promote equal opportunities in an educational and empowering environment using a tried and tested method of youth work practice. In this chapter, we explore the historical origins of scouting and its roots as a social experiment created to provide opportunities for young men, and then young women, to learn from experience within natural environments and to build character that emphasizes self-discipline, respect, "doing good," citizenship, participation, and selflessness. The 'Scouting Method and Law' are explained, and the specific context of scouting in Portugal addressed. Of particular interest are the incorporation of young women to scouting and more recent policy changes in which the European agenda of 'social inclusion' and scouting's response to the more recent economic crisis has been incorporated within the Portuguese context. We provide evidence of the continued rise in the popularity of scouting in Portugal as a specific form of youth work practice that has adapted to the changing political and social context while staying true to the original values and methodologies outlined by Robert Baden-Powell at the outset of the 20th century. As of this writing, there are approaching 60,000 Portuguese scouts supported by over 14,000 adult volunteers (youth workers). We identify factors that allow scouting to contribute to a dialogue about youth work practices that work against social inequalities and note how scouting can continue to contribute to intercultural and intergenerational learning for all those involved.

Further, as Smith (1997) notes, many of Baden-Powell's ideas about education—for example, learning by doing and using natural social groupings as a key element of practice methodology—still resonate today in many forms of youth work. Our goal here is to demonstrate that his teachings, and modern scouting in Portugal, still have much to offer young people in a rapidly changing social environment.

THE ORIGINS OF SCOUTING

> *First I had an idea. Then I saw an ideal. Now we have a Movement, and if some of you don't watch out we shall end up just an organization.*
>
> —Robert Baden-Powell

Robert Baden-Powell returned to England as a military hero after the conclusion of the Boer War and his lead role in the Siege of Mafeking. He used his military experience and connected this with much thinking of the time about social ills, young people, and education to formulate his originating ideas of the Scouting Method. His initial experience of uniformed youth work came through involvement with the Boy's Brigade, which was founded in 1883 in Glasgow, Scotland. He was also greatly influenced by the woodcraft movement and the ideas of Ernest Thompson Seton, who went on to create the Boy Scouts of America. Both men (Baden-Powell and Thompson Seton) were acknowledging some of the same social concerns about social order and how best to provide working-class men with both physical and moral strength. However, the repetitive drill aspects of the Boy's Brigade movement struck Powell as an unimaginative response to establishing character in young people (Smith, 1997).

In the formative years of creating his Scouting Method, Baden-Powell had been in contact with famous pedagogues and other authors to add to his practical experience gained through active participation with both the Boys' Brigade and the Young Men's Christian Association (YMCA). He was progressively convinced that the answer to 'the youth problem,' meaning national wellbeing, was to involve them in a value-based training program in which they had the opportunity to build character while playing in small groups, sharing ideals, and experiencing the challenges only nature can provide. Springhall (1977) identifies this as a common trait among the upper classes of the time that was driven by a deep belief in a form of muscular Christianity created through the rigors of an elite public (private) school education. He started to draft a handbook, not on educational theory or for teachers or educators, but a handbook directly written for boys, containing "tales of adventures, camp-craft and outdoor life, all of this bound with moral values" (Sica, 2007, p. 15).

Before the publication of this handbook, Baden-Powell wanted to test out his theories and practical methods in an experimental camp with real young men (Woolgar & La Riviere, 2005). In the summer of 1907, he created his experimental camp on the small Brownsea Island, a private island in the Poole Harbour in the south of England. When constituting the group to participate in this first experimental camp, Baden-Powell invited 20 boys from 13 to 16 years old. He was deliberate in the mix of social classes he chose to participate in this first scout camp. He wanted to see how upper-class public (private) schoolboys mixed with working-class young men. He used his own personal connections to recruit 10 boys from aristocratic or wealthy families. These 10 young men were from England's most distinguished public schools: Eton, Harrow, Cheltenham, Repton, Wellington, and Charterhouse. He recruited his working-class young men from locally existing Boys' Brigade troops in Poole and Bournemouth; some of these young men were living on the street at that time.

To this deliberately socially engineered group of young men, he applied what we call today the patrol system or patrol method: Scouts were organized in small groups (about four to eight scouts) because he considered this the natural way boys worked together. They all wore uniforms to minimize evident differences amongst them. The patrol was supposed to be kept intact under all circumstances, including working, tenting, learning, cooking, and all the outdoor experiences they would share together. The main idea was that a scout has his own identity within the group and would learn character while working in groups with others. Patrol leaders were to learn the skills needed to take responsibility for others in their patrol. Baden-Powell's own successful army career can also be seen echoed in these foundational structures.

This initial experimental camp was a real testing ground for his practical ideas about the Scout Method as a tool for the personal development of these initial 20 young men. The method was premised on seven equally relevant elements: Law & Promise, Symbolic Framework, Nature, Learning by Doing, the Patrol System, Personal Progression and Adult Support. These elements remain in place today in modern scouting. It can be seen that at the outset of scouting, the associational life of young men was to be the bedrock on which the structure and purpose of scouting was to be built. It was also evident in this experiment that Baden-Powell was interested in creating an experiential learning environment where all young men could develop as equals regardless of their class affiliations and regardless of their family's financial situation.

The outcome of the Brownsea camp was the publication *Scouting for Boys*, which was originally published in biweekly articles sold individually; the first issue was sold in January 1908. At the same time as these were being sold, Baden-Powell was organizing a national speaking tour under the auspices of the YMCA. Sales were brisk, and a full book was soon to follow, with numerous groups of young men approaching adults and asking to form these new scout groups (Springhall, 1977). From these humble beginnings, today scouting is a movement with around 32 million members across the globe. The website of the World Organization of the Scout Movement shows the global reach and huge diversity of socially conscious involvement scouts have across the world (http://scout.org), indicating that the popularity of Baden-Powell's original ideas has not abated and remains relevant today.

As Kerr (1932, cited in Smith, 1997) notes, this early huge interest in scouting also stimulated a desire to join from many middle-class girls who had self-organized into groups. The first big rally for boy scouts was in

London in September 1908 with some 10,000 people attending, including some of these self-organized girl scouts. Approaches from girl scouts lead Baden-Powell, in the second edition of *Scouting for Boys*, to make suggestions for a separate but equivalent movement for girls, which he termed Girl Guides. The scout headquarters published in November 1909 Baden-Powell's article "Scheme for Girl Guides." Agnes Baden-Powell, sister to Robert, was in charge of this new organization, which followed a similar but adapted framework for young women. "Girls must be partners and comrades rather than dolls" (Jeal, 1989). It was not until 1974 that the Portuguese national scouting organization, Corpo Nacional de Escutas (CNE) approved new statutes and regulations that allowed girls to finally be part of the association as full members. Indeed, today in Portuguese scouting, in all age ranges, girls outnumber boys. The demographic breakdown of scouts is detailed in another section of this chapter.

THE SCOUT LAW AND PROMISE

The Scout Law and Promise are the foundational and fundamental idea of scouting, gathering and presenting the core values of scouting, which are shared across the world scouting fraternity organized through the auspices of the World Organization of the Scout Movement. In CNE, the Scout Law is as follows:

- A Scout's honor is to be trusted.
- A Scout is loyal.
- A Scout's duty is to be useful and to help others.
- A Scout is a friend to all and a brother to every other Scout.
- A Scout is courteous.
- A Scout is a friend to animals and plants.
- A Scout is obedient.
- A Scout smiles and whistles under all difficulties.
- A Scout is thrifty and respects others' property.
- A Scout is clean in thought, word, and deed.

CNE has also established three principles: 1) a Scout is proud of his faith and guides his whole life with it; 2) a Scout is a son of Portugal and a good citizen; and 3) a Scout's duty starts at home. In these three principles, we can see aspects of the national character of Portugal and the significant influence of the Catholic Church on scouting. Along with the Scouting Law, these three principles are accepted when joining the scout association. Scouts are required to also commit to the Promise, originating from Baden-Powell himself:

> *"On my honour and with God's blessing I promise that I will do my best to:*
> *- do my duty to God, the Church and my Country;*

- help other people at all times;
- obey the Scout Law." (Scout.org 2015)

THE SCOUTING METHOD

A tool for personal development, the Scout Method derives directly from Baden-Powell's plan and is a system of progressive self-education based on equally relevant elements. Combined, these elements provide the opportunity for each scout to self-develop. They are: symbolic framework, nature, learning by doing, the Patrol System, personal progression, and adult support.

Symbolic Framework

Regardless of age range, the scouting experience is always based on a very strong symbolic framework, which makes it more coherent and consistent.

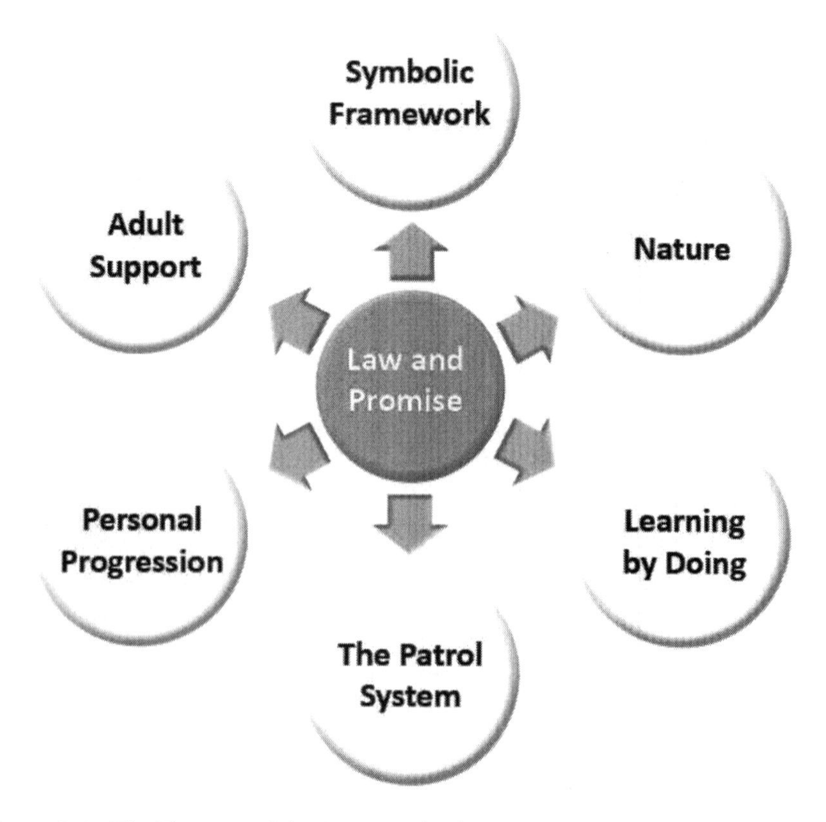

Figure 8.1 The Elements of the Scout Method

Each age range has its own imagery and lives it. This is an environment that surrounds each age range. and it is translated into their language and spirit. It is a story with heroes and symbols that induces a feeling of belonging to the group and facilitates the transmission of certain values:

- *The Jungle Book*, written by Rudyard Kipling (two volumes), provides the adventurous environment in which Cubs are meant to live their scouting experiences. *Lobitos* (Cub Scouts) are 6 to 10 years old.
- The imagery of Scouts is developed around the Scout himself—he is the one who goes further and discovers. *Exploradores* (Scouts) are 10 to 14 years old.
- Likewise, Pioneers also have imagery around the Pioneer himself—he is the one who establishes new ground, who builds and develops. *Pioneiros* (Pioneers) are 14 to 18 years old.
- Rovers do not have a formal permanent imagery as Rovers, being young adults, already feel their actions in their real daily lives. *Caminheiros* (Rovers) are 18 to 22 years old.
- CNE also has Sea Scouts, which use different terminology for the three older sections, respectively *Moços* (Lads), *Marinheiros* (Sailors), and *Companheiros* (Companions).

At the same time, each age group has and lives its own mystic, which are proposals for spiritual frameworks and experiences that intend to deepen the discovery of God and communion with the Church. The Symbolic Framework of the Educational Program of CNE is based on a four-step scheme that aims for a full human and Christian education that is solid and mature. These steps are sequential. Each one is developed in an age range and they complement each other, as they are connected and reach their full meaning when together. These provide a logical path to follow, creating an individual and communal growth itinerary that is suggested to each scout:

- Praise to the Creator: A Cub praises God-Creator, finding Him in all things that surround him [the Cub].
- Discovery of the Promised Land: A Scout accepts the Alliance that leads him to the discovery of the Promised Land.
- The Church under Construction: A Pioneer accepts his role in building the Church of Christ.
- Life in the New Self: A Rover lives in a Christian manner in all aspects of his life.

While on the suggested path, a scout should understand that his life has two dimensions, one that is supernatural and one that is natural, and that they relate to one another. First, Christ, Lord of Life, is not only about spiritual and mystic experiences of Man. Second, He is present in our day-to-day life and throughout all of whole human existence. He is, therefore, constantly present in the life of a scout. The specific history of the integration of scouting with the Catholic Church in Portugal is covered in another section of this chapter.

Nature

The crucial role of the natural environment is one of the most identifying elements of the Scout Method as an experiential method of informal learning. At the outset of scouting, Baden-Powell developed an integrative practice method based on exploring and living together with nature, using its resources, and benefiting from living outdoors. Since then, nature has always been a privileged space and environment for developing scouting activities. It allows young people to face their limits, enjoy natural resources, and learn to live a simple and healthy life outdoors. Within scouting, the outdoors (open fields and rivers and the sea, the latter having a particular interest for the nautical aspect of scouting) is the privileged environment for important scouting activities. Outdoors scout camps can be found around the globe, and each provides scout troops an environment in which to learn together. Safety procedures and specific ethical behaviors are always emphasized when using the natural environment, and each scout learns how to put these into practice in all of their activities relevant to their age grouping and level of maturity.

Learning by Doing

The goal of scouting is to help young people fully develop their abilities so that they become active and responsible members in the community. This development will progressively lead to more autonomy. In order for this to happen, young people cannot only listen to 'how it should be done' or see other people doing it. In order to learn, it is necessary to experiment, to feel, to be part of the situation. That is because learning is a dynamic and active process.

Activity, in a broad sense, is an essential element of scouting. In it, the young person finds challenges and obstacles that develop abilities and solidarity. They learn and grow up together. Experiential learning practices form the core of scouting activities.

Responding to aspirations of discovery and fulfillment, scouting activities are planned initiatives and actions that are developed by young people under adult supervision. The young people contemplate a sequence of diverse educational opportunities when choosing, planning, executing, and assessing the activity. As active agents when choosing the project scouts want to accomplish (motivated by their choices, peers, and healthy competition), young people also take part in preparing the activity. Therefore, they learn by doing; they understand the usefulness of what was learned (this motivates them to learn even more), they develop their abilities, and they discover skills and preferences that otherwise would not be known.

The project methodology is a well-structured experiential environment where engaged activity with others is the key learning process. It allows young people to actively and safely transform dreams and aspirations into actual enriching activities and experiences, which contribute to their personal development. Much of this methodology matches core aspects of other forms of youth work, providing youth development through structure, support, and activity. Project work, as planned communal activities, form the bedrock of practice on the ground (WOSM, 1998a). In general, a project is a set of related and specific actions that are planned and put into effect towards an ultimate goal. In this context, a scouting project is characterized as

- being a group challenge;
- having a clear goal and a set deadline;
- involving four main stages;
- being based on the Scout Method;
- incorporating many educational opportunities;
- taking individual interests, talents, abilities and needs into account; and,
- trying to commit each young person to reaching the common goal through personal effort.

In view of this, the educational value of the project methodology is based on

- developing the ability to dialogue and work in collaboration with others;
- assuring a genuine participation of young people in decisions that concern them and provide them with that 'training';
- developing responsibility;
- developing the sense of 'purpose' (motivator effect);
- allowing for the discovery and search for talents;
- allowing for training of many skills; and,
- creating habits of working 'with a project' (useful for contemporary life).

As can be seen by this experiential and group-project-based methodology, scout learning is about individual learning from within a strong group or community context (WOSM, 1998b). The values and outcomes of scouting can be seen here.

The Patrol System

This is a system in which the young people in a troop organize themselves in small groups with their own identity and life and with an internal leadership and organization. This system is one of the most important and distinct elements of scouting as educational pedagogy.

The patrol (or other designation the small group might have) is where young people, under the leadership of one of them, establish relationships and are called to fulfill many tasks promoting the common good. This motivates co-responsibility, which in turn enhances learning about democracy and solidarity as well as understanding the role of the leader and the importance of a good and balanced leadership for the development of the group.

The Patrol System is what makes scouting a true collaboration effort, a natural non-formal education method in which each young person, with his/her own specificities and personal interests, grows up with others and among others. It is where peers recognize themselves by living a common experience and putting the Scout Law into practice. It also helps young people let go of the egocentric perspective and allows them to get used to assigning tasks to themselves and to each other. This brings young people together for a common ideal while developing camaraderie, complicity, and friendship.

Meetings are also related to the Patrol System and to the way a section lives the project methodology. These meetings support the experience of living as a patrol and as a section.

Scouting mainly lives outdoors, in nature, but it does not ignore experiences in the headquarters, where each patrol has its own space, its corner, where their items and equipment are kept and where they meet and also cultivate and preserve their identity and memory as a group. This space where they meet is private for each patrol. It is where an important moment of growth happens. Therefore, it should be valued, as it fosters the sense of participating in a common experience based on dialogue and cooperation. It fosters organization and planning, critical thinking and assessment, and responsible self-management.

A crucial element for every section is the Patrol Leaders' meeting. It is a permanent organism that coordinates the section and its decisions and is supervised by the section's adult leader. The Patrol Leader is therefore fundamental not only to lead and coordinate patrols but also to represent each group in the section and in the Patrol Leaders' meeting. So, at its heart, scouting has a well-practiced system of representative democracy in which learning about decisions and accepting different roles are appropriately practiced.

Personal Progression

The development of each young person is the ultimate goal of scouting, and personal progression is how s/he accomplishes the educational goals according to each age range.

Personal progression is how we consciously involve each young person in his/her own development. It is the main tool, and it is based on a personal perspective by taking into account individual characteristics of each young person. This individualized path allows each Scout to reach his/her educational goals in the section (acquiring knowledge, skills, and attitudes), and it is a motivational element for the young person (being and doing better). It works as a guide in development, and it is an opportunity to increase skills and personal value or even to discover talents. Personal progression is more than a motivational tool: It also drives young people to acquire analytical and planning habits for their lives. Perhaps the best symbol of this in action is the important badge system, in which scouts are celebrated and rewarded with an ever-increasing number of badges that identify their personal progress within the system.

Adult Support

The aim of scouting is also to allow a young person to develop autonomy. The adult troop leader should, therefore, promote that autonomy. The relationship between the autonomy of a young person and the involvement of the adult should be gradually reduced and qualitatively differentiated throughout the educational progression of a young person through the age sections. The degree of 'free room' or 'freedom' and the type of companionship and complicity all depend on the age range. However, regardless of the age section, it is important that the adult is present and that young people know he/she is present, that he/she conveys safety, that he/she is there for whatever might happen, and that he/she is with them and walks alongside them in both good moments (motivating them) and in bad moments (directing them to better moments).

The adult leader should know how to get along with young people and almost be one of them. However, his/her role as an adult should never be mistaken. Balance is key to maintaining the educational relationship between young people and adults. At the same time, the adult leader is supposed to make sure safety rules are met in all initiatives and activities. Leaders should be particularly aware of risk behaviors and make good assessments of when and how unreasonable risks can be excluded from activities. The adult leader also has the primary responsibility to ensure the section works well and according to all aspects of the Scouting Method (CNE, 2013a).

THE ROLE OF THE CATHOLIC CHURCH IN PORTUGUESE SCOUTING

In Portugal, Corpo Nacional de Escutas (CNE) was founded under the patronage of the Archbishop of Braga, D. Manuel Vieira de Matos, on May 27, 1923, in Braga. The civil statutes were officially approved during the anticlerical times of the Portuguese First Republic. The Archbishop of Braga had participated in the previous year in the International Eucharistic

Congress in Rome and had returned very enthusiastic about the Italian boy scouts he saw there for the first time (Reis, 2007).

So, from the outset, CNE has always been a movement of the Roman Catholic Church, with canonical statutes approved by the Portuguese Episcopal Conference, constituting what the last revision of the Code of Canon Law calls a private association of the Christian faithful. Thus, scouting in Portugal arose from its religious connection and remains intimately tied to the Catholic Church. Local groups are parish-based and are quite often installed in the parish premises, with the vicar being inherently the group's spiritual chaplain. Regional organizations follow the ecclesiastical organization in dioceses, and bishops appoint the regional chaplain, who is a full member of the regional board; the same prerogative exists at the national level, with the Episcopal leadership appointing the national chaplain. Regional and national boards are democratically elected by universal suffrage, but candidates must be previously homologated either by the bishop or the Episcopal Conference. Roman Catholic teachings and practice are present in CNE ideals, youth programs, and in daily life. Adult leaders must be Roman Catholic believers and youngsters should be baptized or, at least, open to an initiation path. CNE is also a full member of the International Catholic Conference of Scouting (ICCS).

SOCIAL ISSUES IMPACTING PORTUGUESE SCOUTING

The inclusion of girls into what was historically a youth movement for boys and young men occurred in 1974. Indeed, the first election that took place in CNE was the vote to include girls in scouting. On April 25, 1974, this milestone in Portuguese history occurred when new statutes and regulations were approved allowing girls to finally be part of the association as full members.

A more recent concern for CNE has been the impact of the economic recession on families and young people. While the global recession of 2008 impacted many families, social inclusion and interclassism have always been integral to the soul and practice of CNE and can be seen clearly in the historical founding of scouting. Social inclusion is a dominant term in European countries and became a solid policy and practice issue for many organizations. For CNE, it was only in 2010 that a document stating the institutional and educational positioning of the association regarding social inclusion and defining guidelines for the association to act upon was drafted and approved (CNE, 2010a). With this document, the association, particularly in acute situations of social exclusion, is called upon to give extra effort to maintaining its offer of an educational space where all children and young people have a place to be, regardless of their family's financial situation. In this recent development in scouting, we can see the organization responding to the larger issues of social inequality and poverty caused by the impact of the recession and the subsequent consequences on families in Portugal.

Alongside this social inclusion document, other special additions were made by CNE in response to the changing social context in which scouting operates. In the content of these we can see scouting being a responsive and socially connected national organization that adapts and changes to match the needs of modern times. New documents were created covering the scouting response to young people with special education needs, reaffirming the importance of interculturality, and supporting a concern with the promotion and protection of the rights of children and young people at risk. These policy changes and additions, taken as a whole, clearly position CNE as a thoughtful adaptive institution concerned with maintaining core values and remaining an inclusive movement for all young people.

The social inclusion document clearly states that CNE does not accept, promote, or practice socially exclusive procedures or behaviors. Social exclusion is seen as a clear obstacle for full participation of all young people in Portuguese scouting. In the impact of social exclusion we can find opportunities for scouting to deliver on their core beliefs of service and respect for others. A concern for those less fortunate can be seen in response to its social inclusion policies. Scouting activities that serve those in need, particularly those living in poverty, provide relief to those struggling with the impacts of poverty. We believe scouting can play an important role in helping people suffering due to their life conditions. Scouting provides coaching and activities that encourage children and youngsters to help others and become active citizens aware of, and committed to, all people in their communities. These social inclusion guidelines also made scouting associations and scout leaders much more aware of their specific role in making additional efforts to provide educational spaces and opportunities for young people regardless of each family's financial situation.

The most recent change to scouting was piloted through 92 local groups between 2008 and 2009 and fully implemented across CNE in the autumn of 2010 (CNE, 2010b). This was a vast renewal of the youth program, which is also echoed in the new publication of the *Renewed Approach to Programme* approved and published by the World Organization of the Scout Movement (WOSM, 2000). This new youth program made changes to previous practices to enhance the community connections in the final educational objectives for each boy and girl. This enhanced the outcomes for a scout finishing his or her educational path in all six of the personal development areas (physical, emotional, character, spiritual, intellectual, and social).

THE RENEWED YOUTH PROGRAM

The renewed youth program was a response to recruitment and retention issues for scouting across the globe and driven by the need to update program practices while maintaining fidelity to the origins and values of scouting. Within the world of scouting, 'youth program' has a specific meaning which encompasses ". . . the totality of what young people do in Scouting (the activities), how it is done (the Scout method) and the reason why it is done (the purpose)" (WOSM, 2013, p. 3). This renewal was mainly focused in three of the elements of the Scout Method: Symbolic Framework, Personal Progression, and Adult Support. The changes in the Symbolic Framework were introduced to give more coherence to the whole concept, reinforce the identity of each age section, and restructure some sections' religious approaches, which included the updating of patrons, models, and symbols.

The deepest renewal was in the element of Personal Progression, with the implementation of a new progressive scheme replacing the previous one that had still retained some traces of a formal education approach in the personal evaluation. The new program was much more faithful to Baden-Powell's original proposal. Now personal progression is assessed in reference to the scouts' educational objectives and concentrates on the achieved knowledge, skills, and attitudes. These objectives are now decided and planned by young people themselves with guidance from leaders. The assessment of this personal progression is not tested in any traditional sense, but is noted as young people pass through a range of educational opportunities they encounter. The new program also allows for the additional possibility of external initiatives being acknowledged in the assessment process.

In this sense, we can see scouting adapting to the emerging knowledge of the time in which young people's involvement in decision-making became increasingly important. It also opened up the scouting model to assessable external activities being brought in to the mix.

Patrol Leaders and Patrol Leaders' meetings are crucial in this process, and they gained an enhanced role in this renewal. For the oldest age group, *Caminheiros*, a new proposal was created: *Desafio* (Challenge). It consists of a personal project of voluntary communitarian service that each *Caminheiro* in his/her last year must create and develop outside the unit for a minimum of three months, preferably in partnership with civil society organizations, the parish, or local government agencies. The notion of community service played an important role here and was enhanced by these changed requirements for the organization's oldest members.

Regarding Adult Support, the Adult Leader role was revisited with respect to the enhanced role of youngsters in their own personal development and in the planning and management of activities (CNE, 2013b). Here again we can see the youth development literature influencing the more 'adult-led' earlier versions of scout leadership guidance.

This renewed youth program will be evaluated nationwide for the first time in 2014. We believe these modernizations and adaptations to the changing national and global contexts stimulated the following important outputs:

- improved coherence in the pedagogical structure;
- implemented a more personalized approach;

- brought CNE educational methodology much closer to Baden-Powell's original style;
- reinforced the coordination of the personal progression with the project method;
- stimulated the adult-young people educational relationship;
- stimulated the scout life relationship to daily life; and,
- initiated the renewal of the leader's recruitment and updated training system.

SCOUTING AND THE ECONOMIC CRISIS

Supported in this recent renewal and educational updating, CNE is honoring and staying faithful to the successful characteristics of its first nine decades, yet is prepared to face today's challenges. The most unpredictable and worrying future challenge is the demographic breakdown due to a low fertility rate trend in Portuguese society. The total fertility rate in Portugal has been in decline for many years and in 2012 hit its lowest rate in 60 years—an average of 1.28 births per adult woman (World Bank, 2014). This strikes at the heart of Portuguese families, communities, and the future of scouting if so few children are being born to renew society. Many commentators connect this significant decline in birth rates to the economic crisis and meltdown that began in 2008 and resulted in severe austerity measures being implemented in Portugal.

Scouting's response to this crisis extended beyond the national borders and resulted in the European Scout Region publishing, in both English and French, *Scouting and the Financial and Economic Crisis* (Christou, 2009). This publication explored the impact of these adverse phenomena on scouting as well as the need for strategy to face challenges, avoid threats, and benefit from opportunities. This document was translated into Portuguese by CNE in 2010, and a smaller brochure was produced about the crisis and delivered to all local groups, bringing awareness and allowing groups to strategize about the future. *Como Responder a Inquietações Sócio-Económicas* (How to Answer to Socio-Economic Concerns) encouraged leaders to face these times of challenge with assertiveness, creativity, hope, and joy.

The scouting response to the economic crisis can be organized into two complementary and simultaneous approaches that touch on both social inclusion and the educational approach. Leaders are encouraged to pay detailed attention to families, since their financial or employment situations could be causes of members' absence or unexpected withdrawal from a scout troop. A list of concrete indicators to help leaders recognize impoverishment and new exclusion situations was presented. This was accompanied by attitude stances and practical suggestions to help leaders to face these newer situations. A key recommendation was to consider reducing the cost of scouting activities for participants in the light of the economic crisis and its impact on families.

The economic crisis is also viewed as presenting many educational opportunities. There were four focus areas in this aspect: to incentivize parsimony; promote creativity; stimulate fundraising activities; and educate for service (and in service). This brochure gave local leaders guidelines on how to face crisis, maintain children and youngsters in scouting, and pass on a message of hope and optimism. It is not possible to assess the impact of this response document, but it is important to note that despite this overwhelming crisis in the economy, CNE membership actually grew.

PARTICIPATION IN PORTUGUESE SCOUTING: GENDER AND AGE

CNE is widely present in all the national territory—the mainland and the Atlantic islands of Azores and Madeira—and has two extra-territorial groups in Macau (China) and Genève (Switzerland), and is organized into 20 regions corresponding to the 20 Portuguese Catholic dioceses. There are 1039 active local (parish) groups, including 26 in the process of constitution, mainly located in the urban and suburban areas and along the coast, which are the most populated regions of Portugal. According to the most recent census, participation in scouting is as follows:

In the last few decades, membership has increased irrespective of the demographic breakdown in terms of youth population that has had serious impact in Portugal, as already outlined. In fact, in 1981, 42.1% of the Portuguese population was under the age of 24, and 25.5% was under the age of 14. In 2001, only 30.3% of the population was under the age of 24 and 16% under the age of 14. In 2011, an even lower 25.7% of the population is under the age of 24, and only 14.9% are under 14 years old. These figures really show the impact of the birth rate decline. Against these significant decreases in our youth population, it can be seen that the scouting population of young people over the same time period has more than doubled, from 22,653 in 1981 to 59,184 in 2014 (CNE, nd; see Table 8.1). If we look at the age breakdown of our most recent membership numbers we can see that the dominant age range is young people between the ages of 10 and 14 years old (see Table 8.2). According to recent research, the average Scout Leader in CNE is a married man or woman between 22 and 40 years old with one or two children, employed, and with higher education (Sardinha & Cuhna, 2012).

Table 8.1 Total Participants in Portugal Scouts by Age and Gender

Young people		Adult leaders		Total participants
Male	Female	Male	Female	
28,079	31,105	8,177	6,004	
Total young people—59,184		Total adult volunteers—14,181		73,365

Table 8.2 Number of Youth Members by CNE Membership

CNE membership	Number of youth members				Number of groups
	Cub Scouts	Scouts	Pioneers	Rovers	
2014	17,307	20,072	14,663	7,142	1,039

Dealing with these exclusion/inclusion matters requires some discretion and care in order to respect and preserve the child, or youngster, as well as family privacy. It is also important for leaders to search for integrative solutions that provide help when needed and when it is most appropriate. This assistance must also be provided without encouraging dependency. The purpose of these interventions is to promote proactive and participative attitudes in the child and their family. Leaders are also encouraged to seek solutions at the smallest group level—team or tribe, before working on solutions that may involve the whole unit.

In CNE, we educate for (and through) service through which young people become self-fulfilled as individuals and play a constructive role in society. There are core values central to scouting which, in Portugal, are closely intertwined with the four cardinal virtues of the Catholic Church: temperance, justice, prudence, and fortitude (WOSM, 1998, 1998b, 1999). Our belief is that these virtues should always be encouraged and should be clearly enhanced by the current times of crisis. Some of our young people have real experiences of scarcity and poverty but this does not exclude them from experiencing the duties and benefits of solidarity and sharing. The creativity that shared experiences and faced challenges that each group/patrol/team/tribe encounter develops in each young person a much stronger esprit de corps.

While some of these values may seem at odds with elements of our modern culture, they provide scouts with solid training and values-based education that prepare them for the challenge and joys of the our modern world. Since 2012, scouts across the globe have contributed well over half a billion service projects to thousands of communities (http://scout.org/worldmap). Scouts also contribute to peace and reconciliation around the world:

> As you know, we live in a challenging world. The 21st century has not only brought with it technological and social revolutions, but it has also unveiled serious challenges for the human race. Numerous people around the world suffer daily from serious deprivations such as civil war, extreme poverty, hunger, social discrimination, lack of inter-generational and inter-cultural dialogue, and natural disasters. These challenges are driving people away from humanity's ultimate goal: **Peace.** (Teare, 2014, p. 1)

CONCLUSION

The scout approach to informal education through youth work is person-centered because it accepts each young person as a unique human being with his or her own personal background, experience, capacities, interests, and pace of development. It is also community-related because it promotes a sense of belonging in young people not only to their scout unit but also to their local, national, and international community and helps young people to adapt constructively to changes in society. Becoming a scout links a young person to other scouts in their local unit, surrounds them with supportive and concerned adults, and connects them to a truly international global community (Vallory, 2012).

Solidarity and hope are key values that should be sustained throughout the whole scouting experience, not just in times of crisis and great need. There is no sentimentalism in promoting progressive autonomy, self-esteem, character, and community building. Scouting always educates the self in relation to the other, which promotes, in line with the Gospel message, attention and service to others.

Excellent educational opportunities can be provided through building solidarity amongst members. Young people are also encouraged to seek out these community building actions on their own initiative. It is important that through these educational activities children and youngsters not only provide physical community work but also are provided with the opportunities to meet realities, understand ways to help others, and reflect on work being developed and its role in creating a better world.

Regarding its membership, both in absolute numbers and penetration rates, CNE is today, more than 90 years after its founding, the largest and most successful youth organization in Portugal. What were the reasons for this amazing success? According to Sousa (2013), the reasons for this success can be found in 13 lessons from the past nine decades:

- an adequate investment in children and youth education (being a precursor);
- a right focus in the crucial ages in terms of education;
- to be based on self-education and non-formal education;
- to have always been independent and free, regarding the State, political parties or ideologies;
- the Christian inspiration;
- the ecumenical spirit;
- to have a global perspective;
- to have always been able to adapt to the country historical and sociological changes
- an holistic view of the person, in its several dimensions (psychological, emotional, intellectual, volitional, spiritual, civic);
- to have always been an interclassist movement;

- the growing presence and role of female members;
- to have always been based in a sound intergenerational dialogue; and, finally;
- the constant challenge it constitutes, based in its experience and with its well-known flexibility, to the traditional formal educators.

We want to particularly emphasize that one of the historical success factors is attributed to the interclassist character of CNE. As Sousa (2013) said in his keynote address, "Education for Life in the 21st Century": "CNE is not an institution of class. It is an institution that integrates classes, which is a factor of integration in Portuguese society."

There is inequality in the world, and we are confronted with it in our daily life. Social exclusion, economic crises, and lack of opportunities are some of the difficulties that our youth as well as adults have to deal with. Since its beginning, scouting, through its organisation and activities, has supported the development of young people as active citizens and change agents to build a better world. It has been recognized as a real expression of active citizenship and a tool to engage young people, helping them to develop their personal skills and actively contribute to the development of society as a whole.

Scouting, with its non-formal education methods and focus on youth empowerment, enables young people to develop core competences in leadership and other life skills which empower them in their daily lives, promotes intercultural and intergenerational understanding, builds a strong sense of identity, and provides real experience in decision-making. Of great importance is that all scouts are given opportunities to become involved and take action in their local communities, helping them develop a sense of solidarity, a sense of community and, often, life-long habits of civic engagement. A sound and consistent concern about inequality, both *ad intra* and *ad extra* the movement, has been present in scouting since its very beginning. Scouting encourages young people to take action on these issues in their own lives and in our larger global community. Our longevity and success as a movement indicate that we still have much to offer as an effective and impactful member of the youth work family.

REFERENCES

Christou, M. (2009) *Scouting and the Financial and Economic Crisis.* Retrieved from: http://giftsforpeace.scout.org/en/novosti_i_publikacii/library/financial_management/s couting_and_the_financial_and_economic_crisis

Corpo Nacional de Escutas. (2010a). *Posicionamento Institucional e Pedagógico—Inclusão Social.* Lisboa: CNE.

Corpo Nacional de Escutas. (2010b). *Programa Educativo.* Lisboa: CNE.

Corpo Nacional de Escutas. (2013a). *Adultos no Escutismo.* Lisboa: CNE.

Corpo Nacional de Escutas. (2013b). *Sistema de Formação de Adultos no Escutismo.* Lisboa: CNE.

Jeal, T. (1989). *Baden-Powell*. London: Hutchinson.
Reis, J.V. (2007). *Corpo Nacional de Escutas—Uma história de factos (Subsídios)*. Lisboa: Corpo Nacional de Escutas.
Sardinha, B., & Cunha, O. (2012, October 25–27). *Corpo Nacional de Escutas—Caracterização do Voluntariado*. Paper presented at CRIARS 2012–2.° Congresso Ibero-Americano de Responsabilidade Social, Lisboa.
Scout.org (2015) Promise and Law. Retrieved from: http://scout.org/promiseandlaw
Sica, M. (2007). *Where it all began, Brownsea, August 1907, The First Experimental Scout Camp* (Centenary Edition). Roma: Fiordaliso.
Smith, M.K. (1997). Robert Baden-Powell as an educational innovator. *The encyclopedia of informal education*. Retrieved from http://infed.org/mobi/robert-baden-powell-as-an-educational-innovator/
Sousa, M.R. (2013, November 9–10). *Escutismo, Educar para a Vida no Século XXI*. Keynote speech presented at Congresso "Escutismo: Educar para a Vida no Século XXI" (transcription), Lisboa (unpublished).
Springhall, J. (1977). *Youth, empire and society. British youth movements 1883–1940*. Beckenham: Croom Helm.
Teare, S.A. (2014). *Better world: A thousand ways to make a difference*. Retrieved from http://scout.org/sites/default/files/library_files/BetterWorld_MoPMagazine_eWeb.pdf
Vallory, E. (2012). *World scouting. Education for global citizenship*. New York: Palgrave MacMillan.
Woolgar, B., & La Riviere, S. (2005). *Why Brownsea? The beginnings of Scouting. Brownsea* (Centenary Edition). UK: Brownsea Island Scout and Guide Management Committee.
World Bank. (2014). *Fertility rate (total births per woman)*. Retrieved from http://data.worldbank.org/indicator
WOSM. (1998a). *The essential characteristics of Scouting*. Geneva: World Scout Bureau.
WOSM. (1998b). *Scouting: An educational system*. Geneva: World Scout Bureau.
WOSM. (1999). *The mission of Scouting*. Geneva: World Scout Bureau.
WOSM (2000). Renewed Approach to Programme. Retrieved from: https://www.ppoe.at/scoutdocs/programme/programme_development.htm
WOSM. (2013). *The World Programme Policy*. Retrieved from http://scout.org/node/6135

9 Aotearoa New Zealand's Indigenous Youth Development Concepts Explored in Practice Today

Rod Baxter, Manu Caddie, and Graham Bidois Cameron

Aotearoa New Zealand was colonized by Europeans nearly 250 years ago, yet a unique treaty signed between Māori tribes and the British Crown in 1840 has been increasingly recognized in legislation and society as establishing a bi-cultural country. Youth work practice over the past 30 years has taken increasing cognizance of the treaty-based rights and responsibilities of both Indigenous peoples and people of the treaty. We have written this chapter in an effort to reflect the ethos of our bi-cultural work: We are three youth workers from three different cities in Te Ika-a-Maui (the North Island) of Aotearoa New Zealand. We are a mix of Māori, Tongan, and Pākehā (White or European) descent. We have aspired to collaborate and create cohesion between our varied perspectives, experiences, and voices. This chapter explores the influence of Indigenous rights and cultural competence in youth work modalities, including the development of a national Code of Ethics from the experience of youth workers in Aotearoa New Zealand. Ultimately, a number of practical Indigenous approaches are offered with the hope youth work practitioners might explore these in work with young people.

YOUTH DEVELOPMENT TRADITIONS IN MĀORI COMMUNITIES

Historically, adolescents (taiohi) in Māori communities participated in a range of developmental processes to prepare them for adulthood and mark the transition to roles of responsibility within their extended family and sub-tribe (Caddie & Cameron, 2013). These processes demonstrate ways of using power that promote respect and wellbeing and place relationship building at the center of the communal education process. Intergenerational transmission of knowledge and values were critical to the wellbeing of the tribe and involved passing on the skills and understanding that were essential to survival in terms of economic and social wellbeing. Elders were considered a vast repository of important information and their wisdom and knowledge essential to the teaching of practical and social skills, ethics, and esoteric knowledge (Hemara, 2000).

The development process was initiated before birth and carried on throughout childhood and adolescence. Children were active participants in political affairs and were encouraged to engage in community discussions and activities from an early age (Hemara, 2000).

At least three common strategies were employed to ensure adolescents developed in ways that were healthy and equipped the tribe with people who could protect and enhance the interests of the community (Caddie, 2011). We present these three Traditional Indigenous Approaches as an inter-related package named TIA! The imperative 'tia' in Māori means to steer and to paddle vigorously (hence the exclamation mark); these actions seem fitting in contemporary youth work and the metaphor needs little explaining. Furthermore, as a noun, 'tia' can be used to describe pegs, stakes, and pins, which in this context could reflect the stabilizing power of rediscovering Indigenous methods. The three TIA! are briefly defined as follows:

1. Pukengatanga: One of the most common and important strategies was one in which an elder (pūkenga) took a young person under his/her care and taught him/her directly as a mentor to feed them knowledge. The student would accompany the elder to community events and special occasions for the tribe. The child functioned as a link between generations that ensured survival of critical knowledge about connections between people, places, and the natural world (Stirling & Salmond, 1980).
2. Whare Wānanga: These are formal group structures and schools of learning established to pass on specialist skills and knowledge. Participants were often selected because they displayed innate talents and gifts in the particular interests of each whare wānanga. While this modality is named after a physical building (whare), learning did not necessarily happen indoors (Best, 2005; Royal, 2003).
3. Urungatanga: A third approach has been termed urunga, or 'education through exposure,' in which participants were not given formal instruction but were exposed to a situation and expected to work out what was going on and solve problems that arose. This type of education included areas as diverse as cultivation, childcare, and public occasions such as the structure of and roles within gatherings and funerals (Hemara, 2000).

These traditional systems were undermined by European colonization since the middle of 19th century. Intergenerational relationship traditions were usurped by the British education and social systems imposed on Māori. The legacy of this historical process continues today, and the Indigenous peoples continue to compete with both the influence of the state education system and the powerful multinational corporate interests that compete for the allegiance of young Māori. Youth workers in Aotearoa New Zealand must have an awareness of traditional customs and the historical events that have created contemporary society as a part of decolonizing and therefore restoring hope and opportunity to young people, especially Indigenous and minority communities.

HISTORICAL CONTEXT OF AOTEAROA NEW ZEALAND

Captain James Cook and the *Endeavour* left Aotearoa New Zealand after a series of encounters with Indigenous inhabitants, the Māori[1], in 1769. What was retained in Māori oral traditions was not the encroaching power and authority of the British empire but the restoration of genealogical connections between Aotearoa New Zealand and the South Pacific through Cook's interpreter, the revered elder Tupaea from Tahiti (Salmond, 2003).

This brief reflection on a first encounter emphasizes an important yet often downplayed reality of the history of Aotearoa New Zealand from 1769 to present day: Māori were, and remain, active participants, activists, negotiators, supporters, and interpreters of a response to colonization, and the slow task of decolonization since that time (see Danny Keenan's *Huia Histories of Māori: Ngā Tahūhū Kōrero*, a collection of essays from 16 Māori scholars exploring Aotearoa New Zealand history from an exclusively Māori worldview).

After Cook's visits, an increasing number of whalers, sealers, and flax gatherers from Australia, Britain, France, and North America worked the shores and eventually settled in Aotearoa New Zealand. By the turn of the 19th century, a significant trade was in place. This immigration and industry also opened Māori eyes to the wider world. At the time of the signing of Te Tiriti o Waitangi in 1840, Māori were prominent local entrepreneurs, having their own ships and trading companies and exporting and importing goods. The lingua franca was the Māori language; Māori chiefs regulated trade; Māori lore settled disputes.

The increasing immigration and contact brought unforeseen trials that Māori society struggled to assimilate and respond to: Venereal diseases arrived with Cook's crew and proliferated wherever Europeans visited; small pox, tuberculosis, influenza, measles, and other disease decimated tribes; the introduction of the musket led to an imbalance in inter-tribal warfare and increasing death and casualties; British immigrants' actions and attitude led to misunderstandings and lawlessness.

In the midst of this possibility, growth, challenge, and threat was the missionary influence. The key missionaries in this early contact period were the Christian Mission Society, the Roman Catholic mission, the Wesleyans, and the Presbyterians. It was not until the arrival of Henry Williams and William Williams in 1823 that Anglicanism made significant inroads into Māori communities. Both men were committed and intelligent missionaries who learned the Māori language, interpreted the Bible, and immersed themselves in local tribes, focusing on conversion to Christianity. As a result, significant number of Māori were baptized and educated and began to build an Indigenous mission.

The lawlessness of Kororareka, a small town in the Bay of Islands that was the heart of Aotearoa New Zealand trade, was the catalyst for the first official British involvement with the arrival of James Busby as British Resident in 1833. While he quickly disappointed local Māori with his inability to take any meaningful action to resolve the problems at Kororareka, he did facilitate the writing of the first statement of Māori sovereignty through the Declaration of Independence of New Zealand in 1835. In 1837, the New Zealand Company, a private British corporation speculating on land and immigration, began to purchase large tracts of land for the purposes of settling Aotearoa New Zealand. These purchases were completed with neither the real agreement of Māori, nor with any knowledge of the challenges of local geography, and by 1839 the company claimed to have purchased up to 20 million acres. The British Crown felt compelled to act.

Between February 4 and 6, 1840, William Hobson, representing the British Crown, negotiated a treaty at Waitangi with Māori. The enduring debate over the Treaty of Waitangi centers on the substantial differences between the Māori text and the English text. The large majority of Māori who signed the treaty signed the Māori version. The treaty has three articles:

Article One: in the English version, Māori chiefs cede absolute sovereignty to the Queen. In the Māori version, Māori chiefs cede governorship to the Queen;

Article Two: in the English version, the Queen agrees to the undisturbed and exclusive possession by the chiefs of the lands, estates, forests and fisheries and received the first right of refusal on land purchases. In the Māori version, the Queen agrees to the tino rangatiratanga (it is possible to define this as supremacy, sovereignty or self-determination) of the chiefs and the protection of their lands, settlements and tāonga (a general and wide ranging term for whatever one treasures);

Article Three: Māori are afforded the rights of British citizens. What is notable is that there was no discussion nor awareness that with those rights, Māori also agreed to be subject to British law and justice (Orange, 2011).

Suffice it to say, the ambiguous motivations and actions of the negotiators and translators of the Treaty of Waitangi have ensured it is an enduring source of conflict. Yet, this was also a unique moment in world history when an empire sought to reach a humanitarian agreement with an Indigenous people and avoid conflict. It was also underpinned by the gracious offer of Māori to create a pathway for continued immigration while protecting the Indigenous way of life.

Within a few years of 1840, the pressure to acquire land for settlement and the paternalistic and colonizing attitude of the British led to a pattern of unjust and illegal land purchases and war with local Māori, ending in confiscation of large tracts of land. War covered much of Aotearoa New Zealand, beginning in Northland, then moving to Taranaki, to the Waikato and King Country, to the Bay of Plenty, and eventually to the East Coast and the Whanganui and Horowhenua regions. Conflict was marked by atrocities against Māori, leading to their impoverishment, the foundation of the marked levels of poverty and failure in the Māori communities today. But it was not war that ultimately condemned Māori; it was a pattern of racist and destructive legislation that has continued to the modern day. In 1840, Māori were guardians of 66.4 million acres of land; by 1850, that had halved; by 1890, it was 11 million acres; and in 2011, it was a mere 3.6 million acres (Ministry for Culture and Heritage, 2013).

In all of those long years, Māori have never failed to be assertive and to reiterate the promises made under the Treaty of Waitangi. Māori have petitioned the British Crown, petitioned the Aotearoa New Zealand Parliament, taken action through the courts, used local media to highlight their cause, established their own media, established their own equivalent political institutions, taken up arms and fought against the Crown, established prophetic and non-violent movements, and protested injustice. Māori have passed the story of injustice from one generation to the next, coupled with a story of resilience. Māori are beaten and wounded, but unbowed. In the words of Rewi Maniapoto at the battle at Orakau in 1864: *Ka whawhai tonu mātou! Ake! Ake! Ake!* We will continue to fight forever!

A BRIEF HISTORY OF YOUTH WORK IN AOTEAROA NEW ZEALAND

While sophisticated Indigenous youth development practices supported healthy communities pre-colonization, the formal and organized structures of youth work began in the mid-1800s, much like other parts of the Western world. Aotearoa New Zealand followed trends in the UK and established organizations such as the YMCA, Scouts, and Boys' and Girls' Brigades, which were explicitly Christian, usually uniformed, and largely focused on discipline, boundaries, and a sense of citizenship (Harrington, 2011 cited in Ara Taiohi, 2011). One example of this is the young Scot, Sir George Troup, who in 1883 spent some time with a youth group in London en route to New Zealand (Troup, 1982). Benefiting from their services firsthand, Sir Troup was inspired to establish the Wellington Boys' and Girls' Institute, which is explored later in this chapter.

The faith-based focus of youth work continued for a solid century (and actually until the present day) and then saw the formation of the National Youth Council during the 1960s. The Council comprised adult leaders from established youth organizations and, over two decades, became interested in sociopolitical issues impacting young people (Hanna, 1995, cited in Martin, 2005). The preservation and advancement of Indigenous youth development practices, as well as bicultural youth work modalities, were certainly common topics (Hanna, 1995, cited in Martin, 2005), potentially for the first time on a national scale.

In the late 1970s and 1980s, central government became very interested in youth work, establishing a Ministry of Youth Affairs in 1989 (now known as the Ministry of Youth Development, or MYD). Arguably the greatest achievement of the Ministry is the publication of the Youth Development Strategy Aotearoa (YDSA) in 2002, which was written through extensive consultation with the youth sector from the late 1990s onwards (Ministry of Youth Affairs, 2002). This framework most often appears as a distillation of the YDSA's six principles:

1. *Youth development is shaped by the 'big picture.'* In Aotearoa New Zealand, youth workers are committed to (and must receive training about) our Treaty of Waitangi, aware of international obligations such as the United Nations Convention on the Rights of the Child, conscious of current values and belief systems, and concerned with social, cultural, political, and economic trends. An understanding of the aforementioned history and subsequent potential reconciliation is ideal for modern youth workers.
2. *Youth development is about young people being connected.* Youth workers do not work with young people in isolation. We have a firm focus on connectedness, which requires an awareness of young people's social domains. This means youth workers will form intentional connections with family and whānau, schools, churches, and community groups.
3. *Youth development is based on a consistent strengths-based approach.* Acutely averse to labels such as 'at-risk,' youth workers aspire to language and approaches that focus on young people's resilience, talents, gifts, assets, and protective factors. The essence of this is captured in a proverb by Sir Āpirana Ngata, which inspired the national framework for Taiohi Māori Development (Keelan, 2002):

   E tipu e rea mō ngā ra ō tōu ao
   Ko tō ringa ki ngā rākau ā te Pākehā
   Hei ara mō tō tinana
   Ko tō ngākau ki ngā taonga ā ō tīpuna Māori
   Hei tikitiki mo tō māhuna
   Ko tō wairua ki tō Atua, nāna nei ngā mea katoa

   Grow up and thrive for the days destined to you.
   Your hands to the tools of the Pakeha
   to provide physical sustenance,
   Your heart to the treasures of your Māori ancestors
   as a diadem for your brow,
   Your soul to your God, to whom all things belong

4. *Youth development happens through quality relationships.* Conversations amongst youth workers will inevitably cover the nature of their relationships with young people. This is celebrated in Lloyd Martin's book, *The Invisible Table*, a pioneer text for youth work in Aotearoa, which asserts that it is the place of relationships that defines youth work. Other professionals will build a relationship in order to effectively deliver a service. A youth worker will offer a service in order to build a relationship (Martin, 2002).
5. *Youth development is triggered when young people fully participate.* Engaging young people in decisions that affect them is at the heart of youth participation practice in Aotearoa. This principle indirectly acknowledges the exclusion of young people under the age of 18 years old from voting and begins to consider alternative pathways for youth workers to support youth citizenship and democracy. Many youth workers facilitate groups of young people with a specific participatory and/or community activism agenda, often acknowledging UN's Rights of the Child and sometimes supported by MYD through Youth Participation Advisors, resources, and funding for youth-led projects.
6. *Youth development needs good information.* Research about youth work may be limited in Aotearoa; however, youth workers will regularly evaluate practices and programs, freely share resources, and support each other through supervision and collegial networks.

There is a sequence to these principles: the first two describe the context in which young people develop, while the remaining four suggests how a youth development approach might operate. It is common practice for youth workers to discuss these principles and to attend training on the approach. The YDSA features in all national youth work qualifications.

When a national Code of Ethics for Youth Work in Aotearoa New Zealand was developed, the YDSA principles provided a structure for clauses. The sequence was intentionally altered to emphasize the unique role of the youth work relationship as primary. The concept of a code of ethics was originally tabled at a significant youth work conference in the town of Ngaruawahia in 1995. This conversation prompted a localized code in the southern city of Christchurch two years later, and the pioneers of this initiative led youth workers nationally to form the National Youth Workers Network Aotearoa (NYWNA). An early notable achievement of the network was a comprehensive survey of the youth work sector, titled *Real Work* (Martin, 2005). The national network united the youth work identity and rapidly advanced an agenda concerned with raising standards, ethical practice, professionalization, qualifications, and ultimately celebrating young people in society.

The YDSA is now over 10 years old. Initiatives like the NYWNA were an attempt to implement the principles in the practice of youth workers nationally through partnering with central government. One by one, these initiatives have failed or fallen short of expectation. Yet the YDSA has not failed;

indeed, it has been central to the development of strong and nationally consistent youth work in Aotearoa. We contend that TIA! offers a framework that explains the success of youth work despite the failure of formal government efforts. TIA! is always localized and contextual; we can move from a fixation on the failure to secure consistent institutional and governmental support for youth work to celebrating the successful efforts in local contexts by youth workers that are congruent with the YDSA.

With the recent emergence of increased youth work qualifications, it seems that specialist-training providers are leading the way for the sector's current and future development. Of these, the Praxis network shines; it is a network of educators who remain actively engaged in youth work practice. In recent years Praxis has expanded, humbly, not only around Aotearoa New Zealand but also into Australia and throughout several Pacific nations. Praxis is known as Ola Fou[2] in the Pacific Islands and is rapidly developing a consortium of regional youth work leaders, many of whom gathered in Wellington, New Zealand, in late 2013 for the first ever Pacific/Oceania/Australasia youth work conference. Praxis is also responsible for the publication of Aotearoa's two most significant youth work texts, *The Invisible Table* (Martin, 2002) and *Small Stories* (Martin & Martin, 2012). Ultimately, youth work in Aotearoa New Zealand is led by the sector and has not been captured by government, academic, or business interests. We hope to see the sector continue to lead the development of our profession, and this must include an increased fluency with Indigenous youth work approaches. Most Aotearoa New Zealand youth workers are familiar with the holistic developmental lens offered by Professor Mason Durie (1998), and this work is furthered by people like Teorongonui Josie Keelan, who has used Māori mythology to understand youth development (Keelan, 2014). Likewise, TIA! brings past wisdom into current and future youth work practice.

TIA! TRADITIONAL INDIGENOUS APPROACHES IN ACTION

In this section we demonstrate the localized and contextual approaches of TIA! with a handful of practical youth work stories. These contemporary examples bounce between urban and rural environments and various cultural populations and are supported by both Māori and Pākehā youth workers. While our framing of TIA! as a model is new, the awareness of these approaches has been increasing since the publication of the first Code of Ethics for Youth Work in Aotearoa New Zealand (NYWNA, 2008). The Code offered more than a set of ethical clauses; it has also provided context and prompted conversation around these practice standards.

Pukengatanga

While Pukengatanga happens through an intentional, long-term mentoring relationship, the ways in which these develop are often more about being open to possibility and working with youth who self-identify than selecting those whom one thinks will succeed. These first two examples demonstrate both a personal journey through generations at a youth center and a highly structured mentoring program to address the personal impacts of colonization in youth's lives.

Example 1: The significant loss of land through the mid-20th century triggered a rapid and government-planned movement of Māori populations to urban centers. In this setting, traditional family roles were undermined, leading to a breakdown in the family unit, a rise in sole-parent families, and a loss of fathers as role models. Merivale, in the city of Tauranga, is one such urban community. In 2008 in Merivale, two 16-year-old Māori youth (from sole-parent homes with significant levels of poverty) joined the local youth group at the Merivale Community Centre. Both had ended any formal and regular schooling at age 14 and had connection to neither their tribe nor their language at that time. They were keen attendees of the youth group and quickly took leadership roles among their peers. Over five years, the two were regularly mentored by three older men who were employees of the community center. The two youth moved from being attendees, to volunteer workers, to support workers. They are now learners of the Māori language, comfortable in Māori cultural contexts, and proud of their tribal connections. They both completed diplomas in Community and Youth Studies through Praxis in 2012 and are now the lead Youth Workers at the Merivale Community Centre. One of the youths has applied to a New Zealand university to pursue his interest in engineering.

Example 2: The mentoring program 'Challenge for Change' was developed by a group of community members and handed to the Wellington Boys' and Girls' Institute (BGI) to co-ordinate. BGI initially recruits, trains, and selects a mentor for a young person 9–13 years of age and begins with a highly structured 20-week program combining group events and one-on-one intentional relationships. The mentoring partnerships meet twice weekly to work through a therapeutic journal and have fun. What follows is an additional six months (to reach a year) and then, ideally, a connection to one of BGI's other youth groups. BGI has seen a number of young people stay committed, volunteer as peer leaders and, eventually, become mentors themselves after they turned 18.

Whare Wānanga

Whare Wānanga are organized environments for learning and development. Māori youth who grow up in an urban setting and are disconnected from traditional tribal settings and connections are often fascinated by an opportunity to re-establish those connections and, in the process, start the journey of forming their own identity. These two examples again feature Merivale and Wellington and show how a progression from Pukengatanga to Whare Wānanga can lead to more specific curricula and content that interests young people.

Example 3: 'Kia Mōhiotia' was an intensive program run by the Merivale Community Centre in 2011 for 20 young people aged 11 to 16 years who had been identified by local police and state agencies as at risk of offending behavior. A whare wānanga approach to youth work was done in five one-week-long wānanga that focused on building a sense of identity and socialization. Each wānanga was based at traditional places of learning to which some or all of the young people had genealogical connections, but where they had never been. The week included an Adventure Based Learning component and independent living skills. Over the year, the youth explored their genealogy as a way of developing their own narrative about who they were. The Kia Mōhiotia wānanga were led by the social workers and youth workers of the community center, and other workers from the police, state agencies, and other community providers attended as part of normalizing relationships between these youth and the workers. The youth who were part of the wānanga attended regularly, and the state agencies noted a drop in their offending behavior over the period of the program.

Example 4: BGI facilitates a street-art program of weekly workshops with local legal graffiti artists that culminate in school holiday murals. A large number of youth have become involved, more than expected. The 'whare' (physical spaces) exist beyond typical classrooms and are often located in dirty alleys and public lanes. The group established protocol based on students' expectations of BGI, the projects, the group, the facilitators, and themselves personally. Strong relationships are felt when young people trust youth workers enough to share what words/names they tag. Young people are accepting responsibility for previous crimes and are open to being held accountable for their behavior. Youth workers have even been able to introduce former 'taggers' to the owners of buildings they have defaced. The warmth, humility, and grace of adults in authority seem to be more surprising and powerful to youth in efforts to prevent recidivism. Regular celebrations after completing a project are crucial milestones to publicly honor the boys in front of their families and dignitaries. Youth workers used Facebook via mobile phones to post photos online, keeping parents and other friends informed and documenting progress along the journey. The aim is to substitute destructive behavior with constructive community activity. The core task is shifting towards a group/collective focus rather than an egocentric individualism. When two boys had a fight, a youth worker asked, "What do you think we're trying to do here?" One boy replied, "We're trying to build a family."

Urungatanga

Young people achieve new levels of responsibility through regular participation in particular practices and knowledge (Caddie, 2011). As noted earlier, urunga can be translated as 'education through exposure.' Urungatanga enables extended learning and development through exposure to community values/practices. Many of the communities that Indigenous or minority young people live in have poor reputations in their cities and towns and are associated with high levels of crime, poor parenting, high levels of violence, gangs, and youth behavior. In many instances, these reputations are not supported by evidence and are founded in a racist fear of Māori and Pacific Island communities (Kirton, 1997; Spoonley, Pearson & MacPherson, 1996; Walker, 1990). While Pukengatanga and Whare Wānanga address the direct needs of youth in relationships, it is Urungatanga that broadens the focus, providing an opportunity to demonstrate the positive values of a community not just to local youth, but also to the wider city or town.

Example 5: The Merivale Community Centre has run an annual festival to celebrate positive local community values with organization, implementation, and evaluation led by local youth. With support from workers at the center and other local community leaders, the Merivale Festival is a half-day event run with health and community stalls, children's activities, food stalls, and a stage for local and national music acts. It has had a regular attendance of 2,000 to 2,500 people. This is a positive news event for Merivale, fronted by young people who are often slated in the same media with assumptions about their lifestyle. The Merivale Festival has proven a good event to increase the support, involvement, and goodwill of local community leaders, politicians, and trusts in resourcing and running other activities for young people.

Example 6: The Link crew at BGI meet weekly after school to develop leadership skills, organize events, and create youth-led projects such as an 'Insiders Guide' to the city that promotes free/cheap and alcohol-free things to do for anyone of any age. Link also volunteer at the aforementioned Challenge for Change camp, role modeling pro-social peers and giving a sense of unity/cohesion to the organization as a whole. The role of Link leaders at the camp thrusts young people into situations they have never faced before, often in the outdoors with a measured level of risk, where they are responsible for the safety and wellbeing of younger peers as well as adult volunteers. Link was formerly described as an 'action research' and 'youth participation' initiative; however, recent members have expressed a preference for identifying the focus as 'leadership and community service,' suggesting new levels of meaning, ownership, control, and connectedness (Wierenga, 2003).

TIA! is a holistic, sequential approach, rediscovering pre-colonial Indigenous concepts of education and youth development in contemporary youth work. Each of the examples above are from varied contexts with a combination of formal, trained youth workers, community-led development workers, social workers, untrained volunteers from the host community, and others working to the principles of YDSA yet often without a formal awareness of those principles. TIA! resolves the problem of how to categorize and explain youth development in communities and environments that are seemingly unrelated (Ministry of Youth Development, 2009).

TIA! INFLUENCES

TIA! is a synthesis of theory and action. There are currently models of practice that have contributed to our thinking on how to construct TIA! in such a way as to capture what is happening and to allow space for what could occur. The following Maia model demonstrates this aptly, synthesizing local and international Indigenous thinking in modern youth work practice.

Maia

Te Ora Hou Aotearoa is a national network of faith-based Māori youth and community development organizations established in the 1970s. While it had its genesis in Māori expressions of evangelical Christianity, the member organizations of Te Ora Hou have developed a much broader theology and praxis that has been influenced by Indigenous development theories and the shifting political landscape for Māori over the past 40 years.

A model of practice being implemented by Te Ora Hou is known as Maia. It is adapted from two independent conceptual structures for understanding Indigenous peoples' health and development (described below) and Te Mauri o Te Ora Hou—a set of distinctives that the network has identified as being core to the essence of the organization since its inception.

The Circle of Courage

The first conceptual framework influencing Maia is the Circle of Courage (see Figure 9.1) attributed to Lakota Sioux traditions of the Medicine Wheel. It is a model of positive youth development emphasizing four archetypal growth needs: Belonging, Mastery, Independence and Generosity (Brendtro, Brokenleg & van Bockern, 2002). These traditional values are consistent with the findings of Stanley Coopersmith (1981), who identified four foundations for self-worth consistent with First Nation philosophies of child-rearing, the heritage of early pioneers in education and youth work, and contemporary resilience research. Since its initial introduction in 1990, the Circle of Courage has been applied worldwide in schools, treatment settings, and family and youth development programs, including spawning the Reclaiming Youth movement. Te Ora Hou and others have adapted these four foundations using concepts from Te Āo Māori (the Māori worldview):

Whakapūmau Whānau—Building Whānau Capacity

Professor Mason Durie's 'Whakapūmau Whānau' (Durie, 2006) is the other major framework of the Maia model. It emphasizes progressive advancement rather than the management of adversity, and the focus is on functional capacities. The model includes six indicators of a healthy family: the capacity to care; the capacity for long term planning; the capacity to

Figure 9.1 Circle of Courage

empower; the capacity for consensus; the capacity to endorse Māori culture, knowledge, and values; and the capacity for guardianship.

Integration and Application

The Circle of Courage and Whakapūmau Whānau have been combined into Maia[3] to provide a holistic framework for Māori youth development in the context of their family and neighborhood and/or sub-tribe (see Figure 9.2). Family members inevitably get involved in supporting community service activities, which increases community cohesion and the attendant sense of belonging. Educational and employment success and responsibility-taking are also encouraged in the initiatives aligned with the Maia model.

Recent experience suggests that young people and their family are demonstrating a holistic integrity in their lives. They are externalizing expressions of generosity and benevolence that were inherent in traditional ways

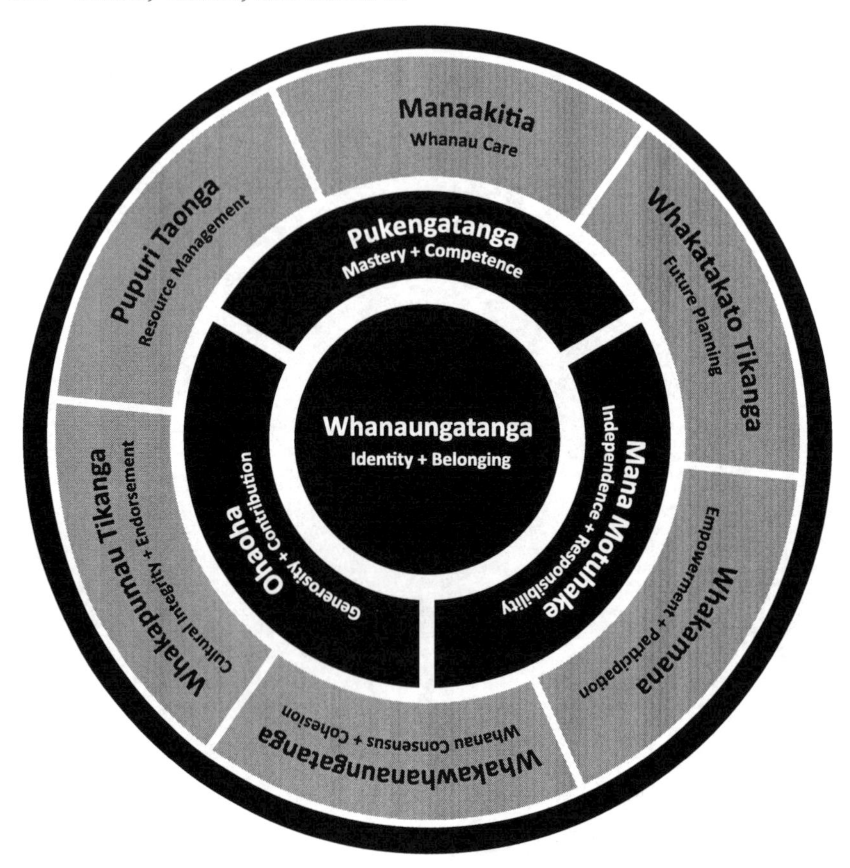

Figure 9.2 A Holistic Framework for Māori Youth Development

of relating to wider society and can be identified in the earliest historical accounts noted at the start of this chapter. Young people are initiating acts of service such as cleaning up vandalism and caring for older members of their family, where previously their expression of rebellion against dominant cultural values was limited to causing the vandalism or dislocating themselves from their extended family in preference of a limited set of peer group associations.

The pithy rhetoric of 'young people are our future' lacks the complexity to describe the Aotearoa New Zealand experience. Young people are bifocal, fascinated by a historical richness that can inform future opportunity. TIA! offers just such a structure, and the fruits of this approach can be demonstrated in a current BGI project.

BGI decided to renovate the inner-city youth and community center and welcomed active participation from young people and local Māori advisors. A young Māori architect, Ihaia, with personal connections to BGI staff suggested installing a tall carving in the central atrium. This 'pouto-komanawa' (a post that represents the heart of the building and community) was to embody BGI's 130+ year history. TIA! readily describes the inter-relationship of mentoring, formal learning environments, and involving young people in their wider communities evident in the development this special carving:

- Pukengatanga: A reputable local carver, Ihaia Puketapu, was employed to lead the project. In addition to his knowledge and skills with traditional Māori carving, Ihaia also works in a secure statutory youth residence. BGI opened an invitation to young people, especially Indigenous young people with genealogical connections to the local area, to spend time learning carving techniques from Ihaia. These relationships have developed very organically, and a group of protégés emerged, supported by Ihaia's humble mentoring and tutoring. The overt task was to carve a tall tree while additional intentional developments occurred with young people during the process.
- Whare Wānanga: Ihaia adapted traditional learning sequences for master carvers into accessible programs for young people. Throughout a series of regular workshops, young carvers created smaller artworks while conversations explored wider Māori beliefs, ultimately strengthening the final product. Learning also needed to explore BGI's history, which was again led by young people. BGI acknowledges that although the historical narrative was not originally Māori per se, it aspires to become bi-cultural in modern practice.
- Urungatanga: When the totara tree was felled to become the actual carving, young people were thrust suddenly into positions of great responsibility in the eyes of the local tribal and youth development communities outside of BGI. Under Ihaia's tutelage, young people were welcomed to carve the wood. When mistakes were made, these were accepted and embraced as part of the unique character of the pouto-komanawa. The original architect who conceived the idea returned with additional participants, and the task needed to be concluded collectively, regardless of age, culture, or expertise; inclusive partnerships were the highest priority.

CONCLUSION

This chapter has introduced TIA! (Traditional Indigenous Approaches) with the hope that conversation about these practices may extend globally to benefit young people locally. TIA! is a synergy of concepts and models we have seen working in diverse organizational contexts, a distillation of our learning from current youth work practice. We noted that TIA! is informed by several youth development frameworks and models that are currently in practice throughout Aotearoa New Zealand, including the Youth Development Strategy Aotearoa (YDSA) and Maia, with a firm grounding in the Code of Ethics for Youth Work.

Colonization, the disruption of economic, social, and community foundations, and the broad levels of violence in our history and contemporary experience, have left an indelible mark on our national character. Our young people have reaped the cost in their struggle to find meaning in disconnected lives. We argue for a return to wisdom that has not arisen from within the economic and social systems that drove the British empire to these shores. Some would call that ancient wisdom, but a linear view of time disrupts our relationships with our ancestors. It is the right wisdom at this time when we seek to shed the colonized person in each of us. It is our path for decolonization of the self, the family, the community, and our society.

We are learning that it is possible to rediscover ancient or Indigenous practices and apply or translate into contemporary contexts with young people and families. Both elders and young people are required, in overtly intentional and intergenerational relationships, to sustain and develop practices that sustain the health of communities and their cultures. Youth workers are positioned in this work as enablers and facilitators, requiring skills of inquiry and creative reflection. Understanding historical harm and injustice often motivates youth workers and young people alike in shared attempts at restoration.

Māori are generous people, and as we offer our interpretations of these traditional approaches, we welcome conversation with other cultures and societies about the relevance and resonance with similar concepts in other post-colonial contexts. We are acutely aware these ideas have other names in other languages and will resonate with youth workers in different ways in different parts of the world. In this vein, it seems fitting to conclude with another whakataukī (also in our Code of Ethics):

> Nāku te rourou, nāu te rourou, ka ora ai te iwi.
> With your food basket, and my food basket, we will feed the people.

NOTES

1. For ease of understanding, the authors are using the term 'Māori' to refer to the Indigenous people of Aotearoa New Zealand. However, at this point we must acknowledge that the term was not used for self-identification by the Indigenous people at the time of these encounters and is today a generic term that denotes an identity as a nation in an Indigenous society whose primary identity continues to be local and tribal.
2. http://www.praxispacific.org/olafoupasifika
3. For further information about Maia, please refer to www.teorahou.co.nz

REFERENCES

Ara Taiohi. (2011). *Code of Ethics for Youth Work in Aotearoa New Zealand* (2nd ed.). Wellington, New Zealand: Ara Taiohi. Retrieved from http://arataiohi.org.nz/Code

Best, E. (2005). *The Whare Kohanga and its lore.* Wellington, New Zealand: Te Papa Press.

Brendtro, L.K., Brokenleg M., & van Bockern, S. (2002). *Reclaiming youth at risk: Our hope for the future.* Bloomington, IN: Solution Tree Press.

Caddie, M. (2011). *Hei Tikitiki: Māori rites of passage & youth development.* Wellington, New Zealand: Te Ora Hou Aotearoa.

Caddie, M., & Cameron, G. (2013). Mana Ngākau: Community compassion: Māori and Pasifika 'volunteer' work. In L. George & T. Brown Pulu (Eds.), *O.H.F. Te Momo* (pp. 138–160). Auckland, New Zealand: Massey University.

Coopersmith, S. (1981). *The antecedents of self-esteem.* Palo Alto, CA: Consulting Psychologists Press.

Durie, M. (1998). *Whaiora: Māori health development.* Wellington, New Zealand: Oxford University Press.

Durie, M. (2006). *Measuring Maori wellbeing.* Guest Lecture, NZ Treasury. Retrieved from http://www.treasury.govt.nz/publications/media-speeches/guestlectures/pdfs/tgls-durie.pdf

Hemara, W. (2000). *Māori pedagogies: A view of the literature.* Wellington, New Zealand: NZ Council for Educational Research.

Keelan, T.J. (2002). *E Tipu E Rea: A framework for Taiohi Māori youth development.* Wellington, New Zealand: Ministry of Youth Affairs.

Keelan, T.J. (2014). *Ngā Reanga Youth Development: Māori Styles.* Auckland, New Zealand: ePress.

Kirton, J.D. (1997). *Paakeha/Tauiwi: Seeing the unseen: Critical analysis of links between discourse, identity, 'blindness' and encultured racism.* Kirikiriroa/Hamilton: Waikato Antiracism Coalition.

Martin, L. (2002). *The invisible table: Perspectives in youth and youthwork in New Zealand.* Palmerston North: Dunmore Press.

Martin, L. (2005). *Real work: A report from the national research project on the state of youth work in Aotearoa.* Wellington: National Youth Workers Network. Retrieved from http://arataiohi.org.nz/sites/default/files/Real% 20Work%20 %20 youth%20 work%20in%20Aotearoa_0.pdf

Martin, L., & Martin, A. (2012). *Small stories: Reflections on the practice of youth development.* Lennox, South Dakota: Circle of Courage Publications.

Ministry for Culture and Heritage. (2013). *Māori land loss, 1860–2000.* Retrieved from http://www.nzhistory.net.nz/media/interactive/maori-land-1860–2000

Ministry of Youth Affairs. (2002). *Youth development strategy Aotearoa.* Wellington: Ministry of Youth Affairs. Retrieved from http://www.myd.govt.nz/resources-and-reports/publications/youth-development-strategy-aotearoa.html

Ministry of Youth Development. (2009). *Structured youth development programmes: A review of evidence.* Wellington: Ministry of Youth Development. Retrieved from http://www.youthpolicy.org/national/New_Zealand_2009_Youth_Programme_Review.pdf

National Youth Workers Network Aotearoa. (2008). *Code of ethics for youth work in Aotearoa New Zealand.* Wellington, New Zealand: National Youth Workers Network Aotearoa.

Orange, C. (2011). *The treaty of Waitangi* (2nd ed.). Wellington, New Zealand: Bridget William Books.

Royal, C. T. A. (Ed.). (2003). *The woven universe: Selected writings of Rev. Maori Marsden*. Otaki, New Zealand: The Estate of the Rev. Maori Marsden.
Salmond, A. (2003). *Trial of the Cannibal Dog: The remarkable story of Captain Cook's encounters in the South Seas*. USA: Yale University Press.
Spoonley, P., Pearson, D. G., & MacPherson, C. (1996). *Nga Patai: Racism and ethnic relations in Aotearoa New Zealand*. Palmerston North: Dunmore Press.
Stirling, E., & Salmond, A. (1980). *Eruera: The teachings of a Maori elder*. Wellington, New Zealand: Oxford University Press.
Troup, G. (1982). *George Troup: Architect and engineer*. Palmerston North: Dunmore Press.
Walker, R. (1990). *Ka Whawhai tonu mātou: Struggle without end*. New Zealand: Penguin.
Wierenga, A. (2003). *Sharing a new story: Young people in decision-making*. Melbourne: The Foundation for Young Australians.

Section III

Social Progress Through Youth Work: Radical and Democratic Possibilities

10 Democratizing Urban Spaces

A Social Justice Approach to Youth Work

Susan Matloff-Nieves, Dana Fusco, Joy Connolly, and Monami Maulik

> Democracy increasingly appears damaged, if not fatally wounded, as those who are young, poor, immigrants, or people of color are excluded from the operations of power, the realm of politics, and crucial social provisions. (Giroux, 2006, p. 238)

The result of this 'damaged' democracy is further stratification of a social/class system that polarizes and oppresses (some of) its citizens. Engaging youth in social justice work then is inseparable from building democratic spaces in urban communities and as such has broad social and educational goals. New York City has a particular history with community organizing, and youth engagement in social justice in particular, that is as rich and diverse as it is controversial. We looked at six current efforts to engage young people in social justice in the dynamic context of this history and the shifting social context in order to better understand how youth workers conceptualize the inequities facing urban youth today and how those conceptualizations translate into methods for engaging young people in social justice work. In this chapter, a collaborative of thinking, discussing, reflecting, researching, and writing, we share our reflections from the past, our findings from the present, and our hopes for the future.

First, why social justice? "The right to remake ourselves by creating a qualitatively different kind of urban sociality is one of the most precious of all human rights" (Harvey, 2003, p. 939). That right, we believe, can and should be extended to young people at every possible corner of political, intellectual, and economic life. In fact, we take as starting points two basic premises: 1) young people can and should be part of solutions for transforming their environments, particularly when those environments are oppressive and unjust; and 2) engaging young people in naming and altering unjust and oppressive conditions is necessary for the healthy development of young people as well as for democratizing urban spaces and building healthy communities. Today, some argue that the sociopolitical aims of youth social justice are falling by the wayside due to newer individualistic epistemologies. 'Youth development,' for instance, emerging as an adult-defined approach to youth engagement, focuses on the growth of individual young people without necessarily fostering the growth of the urban communities from which they come (Ginwright & Cammarota, 2002). While youth development and positive youth development (PYD) have done much in raising awareness of the negative impacts of a narrow focus on youth problems, pathologies, and preventions, the PYD approach "runs the risk of dismissing serious social, economic, and political influences in the lives of urban youth" (Ginwright & Cammarota, 2002, p. 84).

Then, one way to view social justice work with young people is as an engagement strategy that provides a context for development at the individual level (Dworkin, Larson & Hansen, 2003; Shernoff & Vandell, 2008). Through social justice work, young people develop organizing skills in the context of a community, harness their frustration towards positive change, manage negative emotion away from its internalized harmful effect, and learn communication and negotiation skills (Mthethwa-Sommers, 2012; Sutton, Kemp, Gutierrez & Saegert, 2006). A second way to view social justice work is as a strategy for transforming societal inequities and affected communities (Ginwright, 2011; Ginwright & Cammarota, 2002). A third way is to view social justice work as bridging individual (youth service/youth development) and systemic change (youth organizing/youth activism) (Austria, 2006). Lastly, youth engagement has been defined along a continuum on which youth organizing represents the most engaged strategy because young people are examining and impacting the social, economic, and political systems that challenge their capacity to engage democratically (LISTEN, Inc., 2000).

Consistent among these different categories is the expressed belief that young people are entitled to be active agents of change in their lives. Engaging young people in experiences whereby they lead the change they want to see/be in the world is powerful, and there are many great examples of programs that provide young people with that space, including those studied here. The space that gets co-created when adults work alongside young people in learning, in healing, and in the struggle for social justice is transformative for all and particularly critical for young people who have been marginalized by dehumanizing social, political, and economic structures, laws, and policies (Fusco, 2014). However, caution is also warranted. There are examples of social movements that engage young people in fighting for causes defined and led by adults. These efforts use young people instrumentally towards a predetermined adult agenda (Austria, 2006). While participation in social causes may promote youth voice and leadership, limited is the role of agency for designing one's life and way of being in the world, personally and communally. A transformative relational practice with young people requires a balancing of adult and youth vision and authentic voice. Young people must be heard as well as seen at the table. We entered this research with the assumption that examining the processes of youth engagement in social justice work would be critical to understanding youth work's potency for triggering change at the individual and community level.

We expected to find that in practice youth organizations do not fit neatly within one or another category but rather move in, through, and between categories depending on a dynamic context. Youth development, activism, and other engagement strategies fluctuate, and organizations calibrate the balance between them according to varying conditions.

BRIEF HISTORY OF SOCIAL JUSTICE WORK WITH YOUTH

The involvement of young people in transformative social justice efforts has a long and rich history. Young people have actively opposed inequality for decades. In the urban centers, youth organizing surged in response to issues that impacted their lives. As far back as the turn of the 20th century, teenage workers were active in the efforts to unionize and improve sweatshops, acting as leaders of strikes against sweatshops in which they worked. Subsequent organizing efforts grew out of specific neighborhood and local conditions and were developed by and within adult-run organizations (Sherwood & Dressner, 2004). During the 1960s and 1970s, children and teens were central to the Civil Rights struggle in organizing against the war in Vietnam and in the emerging women's and environmental movements (Sherwood & Dressner, 2004; Warren, Mira & Nikuniwe, 2008).

It wasn't until the 1990s that there was an emergence and significant growth of youth-led organizing (Delgado & Staples, 2008). The trend corresponded with the definition of 'youth' as a political interest group (Hosang, 2003) as well as a surge in funding for campaign-driven youth organizing and the creation of intermediaries to support youth campaigning (Ishihara, 2007). In New York City, 20 new youth organizing groups were founded in 1995 alone (Ishihara, 2007). Many of the founders were young people of color from low-income urban neighborhoods and were often immigrants addressing social injustices affecting their own communities. Some traditional youth organizations, such as UPROSE in Brooklyn, shifted from delivery of youth services to community organizing with young people in response to neighborhood conditions such as environmental injustice. At the same time, youth development organizations were integrating youth organizing into their practice (Cahill, 1997). The nature and intensity of organizing was to some extent determined by resources; funders influenced both strategies and issues as outcome measurements shifted toward measurement of campaign results.

In New York City, youth organizing found cultural inspiration and expression in hip-hop and a chance to reclaim and envision the culture, spaces, and images that had been wrestled from their control (Ishihara, 2007). Hip-hop and other forms of music, visual arts, and spoken work have always provided an outlet for expression and grounded youth in a common culture that articulated their pain and anger at societal injustices. These art forms continue to be incorporated into youth programming in many organizations with the specific goal of promoting youth engagement in social justice (Baszile, 2009; Seidel, 2011).

The integration of youth development and youth organizing built on theoretical frameworks developed within adult-run community organizations. The tension between individual development and campaign-driven organizing reflects the merging of diverse theoretical frameworks. Saul Alinsky, in *Reveille for Radicals* (published in 1946) and *Rules for Radicals* (published in 1971), created a methodology for building community power through a succession of collective actions on specific and immediate issues. By bringing together community residents to conduct dramatic and systematic campaigns against a specific target, organizers fostered collective power to correct unjust conditions and foster democracy in the here and now. This campaign-driven strategic methodology created a powerful framework for community empowerment; however, it lacked a focus on the development of leaders. The goal was tactical unity for immediate victories rather than development of an ideology or sustainability of a movement that included young people.

Conversely, Marxist theoretician Antonio Gramsci (see *Prison Notebooks*, written from1929 to 1935 during the rise of Fascism in Italy) posited the concept of cultural hegemony in which the status quo is embraced and maintained even by those whose interests and wellbeing it opposes because of a framework of thought that is broadly held. Gramsci believed that learning to think critically, whether in schools or in workers' circles, would ultimately lead to a more just state as people developed the tools to question the hegemony of the state and the social relations that dominant ideas fostered. Such writings embraced notions similar to those later espoused by critical pedagogues such as Frantz Fanon (French Caribbean) and Paulo Freire (South America). Freire's model of popular education, first appearing in *Pedagogy of the Oppressed* in 1968, was also embraced by many youth organizers for its alignment with educational development to foster critical thinking and analysis by creating methodologies for people to assess their lives and communities and develop actions based upon their analyses. Organizers adapting Freire's writings to their practice emphasized the development of critical consciousness as a first step in organizing, beginning with the lived experiences of community members. His framework included a moral imperative to address inequality: "therefore we need to intervene not only pedagogically but also ethically" (Freire, 2010, p. 20). Organizers informed by Gramsci and Freire placed individual consciousness-raising at the center of their social justice work.

The divergence in these theoretical frameworks (Alinsky's instrumental approach versus the opening up of consciousness by Gramsci and Freire) informed the dialectical tension between developing group power and fostering individual leadership. One way that youth organizers have attempted to bridge this gap is by forming collaborative efforts to address common citywide and national issues while maintaining space in their local organizations for the youth to grow at their own pace. The collective strategy provided a citywide voice and wider arena for youth to be heard and exercise skills while providing the safety of collective solidarity so that no one organization or individual could be singled out for repercussions. These tensions are addressed explicitly and implicitly by the six youth organizations that participated in this study.

METHODOLOGY

The purpose of this research was to examine the processes of youth engagement within organizations that focus on social justice work with young people. The research set out to examine how adults who partner with young people conceptualize the inequities facing urban youth today and how those conceptions translate into practice (e.g., into methods for engaging and supporting young people to promote social justice). We wanted to understand the key inequities staff identified as critical in the lives of urban youth today and how young people are engaged in understanding and responding to such inequities (what processes are used). Specifically, we posed three broad research questions:

1. What are the key inequities youth workers identify as critical in the lives of urban youth ('Key Inequities')?
2. How do youth workers engage young people in understanding and responding to such inequities ('Key Processes')?
3. Why do youth workers believe it is important to engage youth in social justice ('Key Rationales')?

Programs were recruited via email first and then by phone. The programs selected were those that we knew had a long history (15 years or more) of engaging young people in social justice issues. We conducted in-depth interviews with lead staff from selected social justice programs in the Northeast of the United States. Interviews were used as the main method of data collection because they afford complex and rich information that comes from supporting the interviewee to reflect and think critically about the questions being asked (Marshall & Rossman, 2010). All interviews were audio recorded and later transcribed. The data provide a rich, contextualized, and phenomenological perspective on issues of inequality as experienced by those who work to address its impact. Each of the authors were involved in researching the organizations through interviews, analyzing and interpreting the data, and writing. Two of the authors, Susan Matloff-Nieves and Monami Maulik, also served as interviewees as they both are also directors of programs that were included in the research. All research 'subjects' were invited to collaborate in the analysis and writing of the chapter. In an iterative process, data from the interviews were sent back to the participants for member checking (Guba & Lincoln, 1994). Further all participants read and commented on the first and second drafts of this paper and noted where the authors' interpretations were consistent or inconsistent with their own. Mostly, members worked to ensure that their organizations were accurately represented, rendering descriptions authentic to the voiced practice of those included.

The six organizations that were included in the research are significantly different from each other, but all have a commitment to engaging youth in social justice work. Three engage in youth organizing. One provides support to local organizations that do organizing. One is an educational organization and one a social service organization, both of which have a core commitment to social justice. Some of the organizations are neighborhood based, some citywide. One has a specific population focus. All operate in more than one site. The domains in which they work include policies, institutions (family, community, school), and identity and relationships. The issues they choose to address emerge from the young people and thus vary: education, environmental issues, neighborhood issues, safety, criminalization of youth, and inadequate public resources. All collaborate with other organizations (in some cases, with each other) and/or in coalitions. Each organization has a theory of change, which articulates the ways in which participation by young people enables them to speak in their own voice and act upon the world impacting their own development and the development of their communities.

THE PROGRAMS

DRUM—Desis Rising Up and Moving was founded in 2000 to build the power of South Asian low-wage immigrant workers, youth, and families in New York City to win economic and educational justice as well as civil and immigrant rights. The youth of DRUM are low-income, South Asian young people, ages 13–21, who attend public schools. There are approximately 400 youth members, with 100 youth active in DRUM's total membership of 2,400. One of DRUM's programs is YouthPower!, a youth-led program that builds the leadership and power of low-income Desi youth in New York City to win educational and immigrant justice. These youth meet and mobilize weekly to work on a number of campaigns directly related to the issues they've identified as important to their own lives and their communities.

Global Kids (GK) was founded in 1989 with a mission to prepare youth from underserved communities to become global citizens and community leaders. GK is an educational organization that reaches its mission through engaged, interactive global learning and youth development. The youth of GK are predominantly 14–18 years old. The programs run out of public middle schools and high schools throughout the city as well as out of the main GK office, allowing GK to work with up to 800 young people on a weekly basis (900 if GK programs in Washington, DC, are included). The youth are ethnically diverse and vary from neighborhood to neighborhood, representing the ethnic boundaries of the city.

Project Reach (PR) is a youth- and adult-run, multi-racial, multi-gender, grassroots, anti-discrimination youth organizing center with a clear mission and commitment to challenging the destruction of, between, and among New York City's most marginalized youth communities. As a program of the Chinese American Planning Council originally founded to address gang activity among Chinese youth in Manhattan's Chinatown, Project Reach now brings together Black, Latino, Asian, Native, Arab, and White youth who would otherwise never meet and engages them in citywide trainings, activities, and out-of-the-city retreats. The approach to social justice is promoting consciousness of oppression among youth and providing the tools for them to look critically at how oppression affects them as well as how they may be instruments of oppressive behavior towards others. Its well-established Social Justice Boot Camp and OUTRIGHT Consortium include over 35 schools, immigrant organizations, and outer-borough LGBT centers and programs citywide.

Queens Community House (QCH) was founded in the settlement tradition in the mid-1970s. Currently in 22 sites throughout Queens in NYC, it is dedicated to providing individuals and families with the tools to enrich their lives and build healthy communities through a network of programs and opportunities for the diverse residents of Queens. Embedded in its programs are several social justice models in which youth identify and address community and global problems: Access for Young Women engages girls (ages 13 to 18) in organizing a conference on gender equity; Youth Food Justice (ages 11 to 18) promotes critical thinking and data analysis, leadership development, and community organizing tools; a Youth Community Planning Collaborative involves middle school age youth; and a youth organizing initiative revolving around LGBTQ safety and respect in schools (formerly Yo to Yo) is primarily driven by high school students.

Sistas and Brothas United (SBU) is a youth program of the Northwest Bronx Community and Clergy Coalition. It is one of the more established youth organizing projects in NYC. SBU's mission is to develop the leadership of youth in the Northwest Bronx community. SBU leaders fight for educational justice, more jobs for youth and community residents, and more community-based resources. The core membership consists of 80 youth who are involved in the leadership of the organization and training of other youth. The membership is mostly Black and Latino youth, and the catchment area is the Bronx, specifically the northwest area and three schools. SBU focuses on two aspects of youth justice to promote safe and supportive school communities: restorative justice and college access. All staff are former program participants.

Youth In Action (YIA) is a youth-led nonprofit organization based in Providence, Rhode Island, and started by teenagers in 1997. Since its inception, youth have played key leadership roles at every level of the organization, making up the majority of the Board of Directors and running all of its community programs. For the past 16 years, more than 1,500 youth members (primarily young people of color from immigrant families) have changed the landscape of Providence by reaching more than 14,000 of their peers with health education and violence prevention programming, youth-produced media, multi-cultural events, community renovation projects, and school improvement initiatives. Over the years, YIA has grown from a small grassroots organization into one nationally recognized as a positive force for developing youth agency and community collaboration.

FINDINGS

Naming the Work

Before addressing the main research questions, a secondary finding emerged in relation to what each organization names their work. It is important to note that, while we have chosen to call the work 'social justice work with young people,' we had hoped for a simpler phraseology to emerge. In fact, the issue of linguistic representation only became more complex as the study progressed. Some terms used by the organizations in this study included: youth work, youth development, youth organizing, youth activism, youth engagement, social justice with young people, civic engagement, youth empowerment, youth leadership, and global education. The language varied not only across organizations but also within them, with participants noting language that they use 'in house' versus with external audiences as well as shifting descriptions depending on the intended external audience.

> *We see ourselves as youth workers who engage the young people we work with in youth development, leadership, and to some extent activism (although we're not official youth organizers, our work overlaps with that community). Helping youth to learn about social justice issues and to solve problems in their community with that in mind is also a big part of what we do. We never use civic engagement because it just seems too general to be an appropriate description of what we do.*
>
> *Off the top of my head I think the language we would prefer to use is Youth Empowerment, Anti-Adultist/Anti-Ageist, Anti-Discrimination/Social Justice Training, Youth Rights, Organizing Readiness, Youth and Adult Partnership. . . . . definitely NOT Youth Development (which I feel is adult-controlled and conceived).*
>
> *I have to admit that we are careless with language. Our department is called "Youth Services." I have tended to use "Youth Development" . . . particularly to distinguish our work in the Dept of Ed context. We also freely use "youth work" when we talk to each other. The social justice work we tend to call "leadership development."*

The complexity of verbal definition reflects the complicated nature of practice: organizations employ more than one practice and description of practice, depending on occasion and audience. Models that outline youth work categorically might then misrepresent the true on-the-ground approaches of youth organizations.

Key Inequalities

> The city has emerged in recent years as an indispensable concept for many for the struggles for social justice we are all engaged in—it's a place where theory meets practice, where the neighborhood organizes against global capitalism, where unequal divisions based on race and class can be mapped out block by block and contested, where the micropolitics of gender and sexual orientation are subject to metropolitan rearticulation, where every corner is a potential site of resistance and every vacant lot a commons to be reclaimed, and, most importantly, a place where all our diverse struggles and strategies have a chance of coming together into something greater. (Call for Participation, The City from Below, 2009, cited in Lipman, 2011, p. 1)

In urban communities, like Baltimore, where this "call for participation" was issued, youth experience patterns of institutional failures in their everyday lives in schools, employment, housing, healthcare and elsewhere. In these urban spaces, the web of inhospitable conditions for youth, particularly youth of color, creates a formidable task for personal and social change. The data from our study consistently point to the fact that not one but all of youth's embodied spaces and everyday contexts (home, school, streets/neighborhoods) are stressed and under-resourced. Socioeconomic obstacles were a key inequality faced by the young people and were considered by participants to be 'the overriding inequality.' Through all the racial and cultural and gender identity issues, class continues to be the 'one common denominator.'

> *The economy is still terrible for low-income kids of color, especially our young people feel that a lot, especially our young people in the Bronx. Many of them, their parents are recent immigrants or second generation immigrations so our young people have to take on a lot of responsibility, whether taking a job to help support the family, or translate for the family, watching little ones or whatever the case may be, so there's all these things that young people have to do to support their families.*

Public education was identified as one of the key areas where the impact of class/social economics is palpably unjust. This was not surprising to the authors, as research attests that public schools in low-income communities typically receive the fewest financial resources, are assigned the least experienced teachers, and have the worst physical facilities (Alexander, 2010; Biddle, 2014; Darling-Hammond, 1996; JBHE, 1998/99). The New York City educational system is the most segregated in the United States, according to a recent UCLA Civil Rights Project report: Whereas 65% of students overall graduate high school in four years, that percentage is only 37% for Black and Hispanic males (Orfield & Frankenberg, 2014).

> *. . . in the context of school it's a depletion of anything that would be considered a school. So resources for basic materials: we still have really old books you know, really old books, really torn books, not a lot of school supplies; teachers who have to go into their pockets to buy basic tools. A lack of technology, a lack of sports, a lack of teachers who are capable of teaching certain subjects, and so like the Math and Sciences, sometimes not even people who are certified to teach those subjects, in place of like trying to hold things down. Never mind advanced placement courses, and other things that people would consider a quality education. So the lack of infrastructure, for what most Americans would call a quality education, in many of our schools, down to the physical plant like buildings falling apart.*

Political and fiscal pressures are putting heavy demands on urban public education to take austerity measures. The current crisis is both historically driven and exacerbated by the growing testing movement. Sizable numbers of urban youth have been found below state or national standards, and test-driven education reduces the opportunities for enrichment enjoyed by wealthier peers. Punitive strategies to raise achievement and accountability have been forwarded at all levels of government without taking into account systemic political and economic disadvantages in urban public education systems (Lipman, 2011). Moreover, these policies have contributed to rising dropout rates, suspension rates, and the criminalization of youth in schools (Giroux, 2008; Pownall, 2013). The transformation from 'community policing' to 'military policing' began during the Reagan Administration with the passage of the Military Cooperation with Law Enforcement Act, which provided local, state, and federal police increased access for drug interdiction (Alexander, 2010). Since the 1980s, drug arrests have skyrocketed as law enforcement teams swept through urban housing projects, patrolled freeways, and instituted "Stop and Frisk" programs on urban streets. The Advancement Project reported that black boys are three times more likely than white boys to be suspended (Advancement Project, 2011). Nationally, African-American youth are nearly five times more likely to be confined than their white peers; Latino and American Indian youth are between two and three times more likely to be confined (Annie E. Casey Foundation, 2013). The process of criminalization is linked to racial, gender, or sexual orientation stigmatizing and was identified as one of the key inequalities.

> *Our students often talk to us about social emotional supports in the school, there's not a lot of that. LGBTQ safe spaces for young people. There's not a lot of that. A lot of police and young people interactions, not positive interactions, young people being harassed by NYPD and that's not just in the neighborhoods that like in the schools because it's all NYPD that oversees the school safety agents so that's all NYPD to us and the young people talk a lot about that.*

Oppressive conditions in schools and in neighborhoods seem to invite policies that further exploit this fragile ecology, blaming youth for being unemployed, underachieved, and overly aggressive—all without any attempt to unearth the root cause(s) or discounting those causes as irrelevant. Rather than addressing real issues, such as the overcrowding in schools, that might lead to frustration and teen-on-teen aggression, policies like zero-tolerance are uncritically accepted as the only way to manage 'unruly' kids and neighborhoods.

Alone, any one of these factors would be enough to generate madness. Each brings with it a plethora of obstacles, struggles, and despair. However, what really stands out among the interviews is that these factors do not operate in silos. These lived inequities form a complex web, a nexus of issues that cut across other issues. Having been packed together in such a dense and tangled mess, they leave many working for change to wonder where to begin. Due to an unwavering commitment on the part of the adults and young people working together, these youth workers persist through the tangle, sometimes opting for finding the one dangling loose end that offers hope; sometimes opting to simply start anew.

> *We all know its messed up but there's not a real sense that anything can be done within the system that exists. It's so broken, It's so falling apart; it's so under-resourced in many ways, and also expensive at the same time, you know, where do you even go to try to unwind, untangle this big mess?*

Key Processes of Engagement

Differences in organizational size, mission, funding, and structure, as well as the concerns of youth participants, influence the specifics of each organization's approach and the scale to which they can accomplish their goals. Through honest discussion with young people and analysis of social issues, some concerns emerge that might lead youth to action. In some cases, even those in which the organizations may not have a mechanism for promoting participation in collective action, the young people themselves seek out opportunities. As an example, a youth leader at QCH organized a citywide youth action on the city's pending budget. The organization provided computers, space, contacts, and guidance. Specific youth development approaches may fall along a continuum ranging from focusing on consciousness and community building to taking action on toxic policies. Education and social service organizations have advocated for the Dream Act (financial aid for undocumented youth), climate justice, educational issues, language access for immigrants, and other youth-identified concerns. However, funders or some professional organizers may not recognize what these organizations do as youth organizing because of the narrowness of the definitions. Funding requirements for youth organizing concern winnable policy outcomes achieved within a particular time frame informed by the Alinsky model. Further, professionalization of organizing sometimes overlooks the longitudinal work by youth organizations that prepare young people for leadership. The culture of campaign-driven organizing undervalues the importance of leadership development and community building due to the challenge of documenting short-term measurable outcomes.

With such differences in the backdrop, our research identified several common processes essential to engaging youth in social justice. First, young people are engaged in ways that challenge standard ageist principles that privilege adults' capacity to lead over their own. In the context of working with young people, space is created for young people to engage in authentic conversations about their lived experiences in all of their complexity. Beginning with identifying issues of concern to them, time is spent focusing attention on those issues, unpacking them, and illuminating the injustices that surround them (as well as taking personal responsibility when applicable). Contextual framing of issues affords opportunity for critique and transformation of the conditions surrounding youth (the hegemony), and in particular, for addressing youth inequities by inviting young people to become allies in their own transformation and that of the world.

> *(The issues) primarily emerge from young people having discussions about things that bother them whether things in their schools, or their neighborhoods, things come up over time and then things turn into critical questions that we're trying to grapple with and then those usually end up turning into program areas, particularly when we think that we can secure funding around the ideas or secure partnerships to support the work. We tend to build momentum around things that come up again and again.*
>
> *In terms of what the process is I would say we're trying to do a few things: One, we're trying to build their awareness about the issues that are going on in the world and also build self-awareness about themselves and their leadership and their capability. Then we're trying to get them to analyze these issues; analyze their own personal development and where they are, what they want to aspire to and become, and the third piece is to take action. Whether it's action on the issues they care about or action to kind of help them develop.*

Youth workers were unilaterally clear that skill building was a necessary prerequisite to taking collective action. Youth need to work on developing a range of skills—planning, research, data analysis, public speaking, and especially workshop and meeting facilitation skills. They have to learn to navigate the obstacles created by inequality, including recognizing how daily experiences of inequalities have 'shut them down.' These include avoiding self-destructive behaviors (drinking and drug abuse), refraining from violence while developing strong verbal communication skills and emotional self-discipline, and making good decisions (about choices of friends, future plans for higher education, etc.). In a group setting, critical reflection of lived experiences helps move issues from the personal to the shared experience, from the micro to the macro factors that shape those experiences. Here, the pedagogy is often conversation supplemented with specific activities that help unpack bias and raise awareness. Sometimes the lessons are explicit, such as studying the history of oppression or reviewing current policies and legislation that are having the "felt impact" (Freire, 1993). Young people may also be supported to gather data, for instance, statistics on educational funding formulas that illuminate the underlying causes of their felt experiences and that indicate avenues of future action. Responding effectively requires awareness, critical thinking, and a cohesive analysis of power and oppression. Awareness of injustice is not about searching for ways in which one is a victim of oppression but understanding how one's own behavior and beliefs also might perpetuate injustice.

> *I think the beauty of the boat exercise is that it allows any given community of people to discover, or rediscover what discrimination is all about. Because you don't sit there and say "Well, what is discrimination" because when you say that everyone will be afraid that you will point a finger and say "well, you're a racist" or whatever. What we do is present a scenario and we say "you're not one of those people but there are 14 people on a roof who need to be saved but you don't have space for them all and have to make choices about who to save and why" and right from the very beginning they start to realize that you have to judge or not judge in order to make a decision. And it's always wonderful when somebody says, "do we have to discriminate in order to solve this problem?"*

There are very few spaces for young people to be heard in a way that matters in the world. Within the context of working on critical issues, youth have a social context that legitimizes their voice and their concerns about unemployment, education, the environment, the foods they eat, bullying, and transportation, to name a few mentioned in our interviews. Once issues have been identified, adults invite youth to envision solutions. Voice leads to identification of issues; identification leads to envisioning of solutions.

> *The youth kept saying to us over the years 'we wish our schools were more like Youth In Action because we'd be better students and more prepared for the future.' They were also feeling bad that other young people don't have the opportunity to learn about their history, culture, and community like they do here. They wanted to change that reality, so that's why our youth started providing professional development to urban teachers in RI. We're also working with the local department of education and an organization called the Business Innovation Factory to create a student-designed school in RI, which will be created based on what some of our most marginalized students say they need as learners. Youth here are really excited about bringing it to life.*
>
> *Do you feel like this is a problem? If you had an ideal school, what would it look like? What are the things you want? Why do you think we don't have them, how do you think we can get them?*
>
> *The kids there are part of a campaign to get young people officially made representatives on the community boards which do community planning decisions in New York . . . the age limit is 18 and they want to lower it to 16 so that youth can have input on community planning issues and that is significant to them because it includes park utilization.*

A key to engagement is the engagingly collaborative nature of the adult/youth relationship, which empowers youth as authorities while supporting them concretely towards actions and facilitating connections between and among youth organizations to foster change.

Key Rationales

Youth workers engage in social justice from a commitment to individual young people and an optimistic belief that social conditions are malleable and can be changed. Many had engaged with social justice work as young people themselves or were drawn to this approach after working with youth in this manner. All had a passionate commitment to the personal development of young people as well as a desire to change the toxic conditions that harm them. An appreciation of the complexity of young people's lives and the tangle of distinct but intertwined injustices informed their approach. They balance their commitment to the personal transformation of individual youth with the urgent need for policy change. This two-pronged approach holds the potential for promoting deep societal transformation.

In common with other youth programs, social justice work helps young people to envision and pursue a future. The six profiled groups seek to open opportunities for youth through higher education and employment and give them the skills and analysis to break cycles of poverty. However, unique to social justice work are the tools for institutional change. The leadership skills that youth develop as community advocates are applicable to the barriers they face in college and community settings. This understanding of community and the need for organizational advocacy is distinctive from programs that solely support academic outcomes and college access. The youth trained in advocacy understand systems and have the confidence to navigate the complexity of higher education institutions.

> *They leave with a clear path for higher education, with resources for higher education that they have chosen well, in terms of. . . schools that provide enough financial aid and resources for young people of color pursuing higher ed but they also know how to navigate their community; they know how to understand the things that go on in their community but also how they might be able to leverage change in a specific environment. . .*

The tools of Freirean consciousness-raising enable youth to step outside of the toxic conditions and analyze and how these affect them They question the cultural hegemony of racism, classism, sexism, homophobia, and xenophobia that informs them they are worthless and uneducable. Developed as Gramscian intellectuals, they question the hegemony, step outside its confines, and begin to change it.

> *There is a second part of it which is the critical and transformative moment when the intellectual consciousness merges with not just practical skills but also the internal realization of internalized oppression (undoing it) especially with low income women and young people of color and they realize that they have something to say that they should not ashamed of who they are racially, economically and in society and they can act on it. Doesn't happen because of us and doesn't happen to everyone but when it does it is powerful. It can take 2 years and there is an "aha" moment when it all comes together for some people.*

Self-awareness helps achieve a positive sense of self and social and cultural identity (Ginwright & Cammarota, 2002) and can bring youth to that 'aha' moment. Social justice work with youth fosters self-awareness so that young people can understand "*what it is that's holding them back, what is it about their practices that hold them back, we want them to talk about their own oppression, not to make them feel bad but to understand why it's happening and how to recognize it when it's happening so that we can start to begin to break a lot of that.*" In the context of understanding oppression, and through the intense interrogation of the systems that perpetuate injustice, young people are freed from the constant self-deprecation that comes from internalizing hatred. They begin to heal.

> *We not only had to raise young people's awareness about discrimination but also figure out a way to have them embrace power in a way that gave them greater control and gave them greater say in the future*

> *of their own education and the future of their own participation in society.*

As with adults, young people come into social justice work as whole people. As such, they exhibit both strengths and issues. Effective social justice work with youth will take this into account by maintaining structures of adult support and by ensuring the adults working with youth are prepared for personal as well as strategic setbacks. The organization has to have a framework for supporting youth through their transformation into leaders even in spite of obstacles or persistence of destructive and self-destructive behaviors. Even as they lead community and citywide actions, youth may experience depression, arrest, or other setbacks, and staff must be ready to provide support and guidance.

Besides self-awareness and support to overcome challenges, engagement in social justice fosters skills development in a way that feels urgent and relevant to young people, particularly to those who are marginalized and disengaged from school. A number of providers quoted youth asking why they were not learning the same critical content in school. In the realm of urban public education, youth organizing creates a "counter-narrative to failure" in education (Warren et al., 2008). Through their activism, young people, particularly low-income youth of color, rewrite both the story of their own trajectory through the educational system and the perception of their danger to the educational system. For young people who are seen as uneducable due to their race, class, sexual identity, ethnicity, citizenship status, and communication style, transforming their role into professional change agents has a powerful impact. Youth organizing is attractive to those who were alienated by their experiences with educational systems and who found a sense of belonging in gangs as a youth-driven support; they engage as leaders and find a meaning and purpose to gaining the skills of analysis and critical thinking. They discover a sense of purpose and put their own learning at the center of their education.

> *When [our organization] started, the most active young people were gang members and what most people would deem at risk youth. I myself did not go to school, was a truant, terrible in school, horrible grades, was always in trouble . . . We see that a lot with our young people. . .*

At the same time, education officials may shift their perception of the capacity of urban youth through encountering them in meetings and activities. Concerned officials see youth organizers as a source of information about the systems that they manage and where these need improving from the perspective of students whom the schools are failing (Shah & Mediratta, 2008). Young people, drawn from the ranks of those who were not exemplary students and trained in restorative justice work become resources to their schools; at some of the same campuses where students may have been arrested or suspended, the trained youth mediators are engaged as resources by the faculty.

The result of their work is tangible. Young people have affected change in the actual policies that impact the quality of their lives. In both Providence and New York City, youth campaigned for and won city funding for public transportation to and from school, without which their families would face crushing expenses. Aggressive policing has been actively opposed, with youth and adult allies pushing back against specific practices and winning. Young people have turned garbage-strewn lots into clean, well-equipped playgrounds and green spaces, have worked with adults to open new schools and contributed to their design, and have successfully fought the opening of waste-transfer stations and power plants in their neighborhoods. Each of these victories results in the improvement in their daily lives as well as a sense of hope and empowerment to take on the next struggle. Ultimately, the integration of these methodologies creates lasting social change through the transformation of individuals into leaders for social justice with a common moral imperative to change and the skills and tools to do so. The integration of personal development and development of tools for action creates a generation of young people able to bring about lasting changes.

> *If individuals walk away with a dramatically transformed understanding—that in itself has a ripple effect on the rest of society.*
>
> *We want them to be progressive social justice activists engaged for their lifetime whatever work they go into.*
>
> *These are the young people who in schools it was like "arrest them, suspend them and get them out of the building." It took the community based organization to invest that time into them and now they're doing all these amazing different things.*

A positive dynamic reinforces young people's talent and value both externally and internally.

Whether channeling youth voice into the larger policy debate or putting it at the center of organizational decision-making, young people's voices shape the institutions that frame their lives. Social justice work provides a context and support for them to experience themselves as responsible and active shapers of institutions and guides them towards an understanding of how to use power in a way that is responsible. Their understanding of leadership becomes more nuanced and developed, as one executive director noted: "there should be space for many different kinds of leaders. And leadership doesn't have to look like this one person."

The direct one-to-one work is an example of classic organizing and levels the playing field for youth who may not have regular access to technology (as is the case for poor youth). Organizing is by nature optimistic and assumes that our efforts will result in changes that are positive. The changes may be external (policy changes, creation of new institutions) or they may be in the ability of young people to thrive under adverse and denigrating conditions when they recognize that the conditions are obstacles and reject the internalization of negative stereotypes.

> *With everything becoming virtual as well, Facebook activism, Twitter and this, we feel like there's a role for all of that and social media but it can't replace, especially for poor communities that don't have a lot of access to that. The computers, the Internet, all that, it really comes down to the door to door, person to person, and there's language, there's multiple languages, there's trust issues so nothing replaces the human contact and the consciousness that comes out of 30 people or 50 people sitting in this room and seeing each other and understanding it's not just them, it's not their fault, there are structural things in place and that we can actually impact it together. That is really the value of the organizing. That is builds leaders, that's what empowers people.*
>
> *If we can chip away at an ideology that marginalizes youth voice, we've done something.*

CONCLUSION

The youth organizations interviewed engage in social justice work with young people through a continuum of youth development programming, consciousness-raising, and direct-action campaigns. We found through the interviews a spectrum of activity that incorporates not one or another, but often all. By seeing the fullness of engagement and eliminating the either/or dichotomies, we open the door to embracing social change as a practice that can be integrated into all youth work practices. The legacy and history of collective organizing is seen side by side with organizing for more individualistic purposes: youth engagement serves as a means to an organizational end or efforts with a goal of fostering individual youth success without shifting social, economic, educational, or political conditions (Marwell, 2007). We believe that the deepest societal transformation with the greatest promise of sustainability will result from work that develops young people into capable and confident leaders by working collaboratively with them in the complex social context of interconnecting social injustices.

The growing shift towards 'youth development' in the United States can be understood within political and economic conditions that privilege individual accomplishments over collective ones. Foundation support for organizations engaged in social justice youth work has seen a rapid decline, and much of the support that still exists has shifted focus to more academic and youth development outcomes (Sukarieh & Tannock, 2011). Social justice advocates, organizers, and educators demonstrate an ethic of care (Mthethwa-Sommers, 2012) and unwavering commitment to young people and to helping reshape an oppressive, power thirsty, and driven, competitive world. A broader neoliberal context contributes to this shifting of funding mechanisms as well. Neoliberal ideologies hold that the state must actively build markets as well as promote market-supporting behaviors. Apple (2006) states, "The message of such [neoliberal] policies is what might best be called 'arithmetical particularism,' in which the unattached individual—as a consumer—is deraced, declassed, and degendered" (p. 32). Organizations committed to social justice are able to work between the lines by developing individual consciousness and the skills of community organizing. As evidenced in the differential naming of the work for internal and external audiences, the variety of practices may be described as adapting to these external demands while maintaining the integrity of focus on social justice work. All of the interviewees gave examples of skills development valued in the current funding context: critical thinking, applying academic skills to social problems, or using a social justice framework to effectively address individual challenges. Youth development should go hand in hand with social justice work.

The distinguishing characteristic of youth social justice work, regardless of its setting, is a focus on the long-term development of the young person, an approach to consciousness-raising that illuminates social conditions through examination and sharing of young people's lives and developing their intellectual (not academic) gifts. By illuminating their issues and helping them to frame their personal issues as social and political, and by nurturing the development of the skills that they need to take action effectively in public domains, youth organizations of all types promote social justice and develop young people who are able to take action on the conditions that limit them and their communities. Youth are empowered to speak up for themselves in multiple settings and to be citizens rather than consumers. The young person's vision of who they want to be and how to get there is realized. By developing democratic tools and awareness of the complexity of oppression, youth begin to create a more just society. They do this within their own youth organization, particularly when they are engaged in running these. They create new institutions such as small schools shaped by their own vision. They break down ageist stereotypes of youth and deepen their collective policy impact through collaborations and partnerships with adult-run entities. The experiences are themselves transformative, empowering marginalized youth to see their ideas taken seriously and experience the power of collective activism and cooperative community development.

We began our investigation by wondering whether youth activism was a dying practice. By deepening our understanding of social change and by examining the theories of social change that inform social justice work with youth, we found the practice to be not only alive and well but thriving within organizations that are not identified as youth organizing programs. Even as funding for youth organizing has diminished, the practices that lead to deep social transformation are maintained in a diversity of youth programs. The diversity of organizations that we examined demonstrates that there is a possibility of promoting social justice work with youth in all types of organizations. The organizations that we interviewed operate along a continuum of individual consciousness-raising to strategic campaigning. By seeing this as a continuum rather than an exclusive dichotomy, the breadth of models for deep social change is diversified while recognizing a common set of concerns and practices that are closely aligned with quality youth work. In sum, our research illuminates spaces where the lived experiences and counter narratives of youth converge, where youth deconstruct existing assertions and then envision and enact collective responses to social change. We think we have uncovered nothing more or less than the power of youth democratizing urban spaces.

REFERENCES

Advancement Project. (2011). *Telling it like it is: Youth speak out on the school-to-prison pipeline*. Retrieved from http://www.advancementproject.org/resources/entry/telling-it-like-it-is-youth-speak-out-on-the-school-to-prison-pipeline

Alexander, M. (2010). *The new Jim Crow: Mass incarceration in the age of colorblindness*. New York, NY: The New Press.

Annie E. Casey Foundation. (2013). *Kids Count Data snapshots: Reducing youth incarceration in the United States*. Retrieved from http://www.aecf.org/m/resourcedoc/AECF-DataSnapshot/Youth Incarceration-2013.pdf

Apple, M. W. (2006). *Educating the right way: Markets, standards, God and inequality*. New York, NY: Routledge Falmer.

Austria, R. S. (2006). Toward a movement: Uniting organizers and direct service provides in a movement for juvenile justice reform. *Afterschool Matters, 5*, 30–40.

Biddle, B. J. (2014). *The unacknowledged disaster: Youth poverty and educational failure in America*. Rotterdam: Sense Publishers.

Cahill, M. (1997). Youth development and community development: Promises and challenges of convergence. Unpublished report, Youth Development Institute of the Fund for the City of New York, New York.

Darling-Hammond, L. (1996). The right to learn and the advancement of teaching: Research, policy, and practice for democratic education. *Educational Researcher, 25*, 5–17.

Delgado, M., & Staples, L. (2008). *Youth-led community organizing: Theory and action*. Oxford: Oxford University Press.

Dworkin, J. B., Larson, R., & Hansen, D. (2003). Adolescents' accounts of growth experiences in youth activities. *Journal of Youth and Adolescence, 32*, 17–26.

Freire, P. (2010). *Pedagogy of the oppressed* (30th anniversary ed.). New York: The Continuum International Publishing Group.

Fusco, D. (2014). The social architecture of youth work practice. In B. Belton, *'Cadjan-Kiduhu': Global perspectives on youth work* (pp. 47–60). Rotterdam: Sense Publishers.

Ginwright, S. (2011, Spring). Hope, healing, and care: Pushing the boundaries of civic engagement for African American youth. *Liberal Education*, 34–39.

Ginwright, S., & Cammarota, J. (2002). New terrain in youth development: The promise of a social justice approach. *Social Justice, 29*, 82–95.

Giroux, H. (2006). *America on the edge: Henry Giroux on politics, culture, and education*. London: Palgrave Macmillan.

Giroux, H. (2008). Education and the crisis of youth: Schooling and the promise of democracy. *The Education Forum, 73*, 8–18.
Guba, E.G., & Lincoln, Y.S. (1994). Competing paradigms in qualitative research. In N.K. Denzin & Y.S. Lincoln (Eds.), *Handbook of qualitative research* (pp. 105–117). Thousand Oaks, CA: Sage.
Harvey, D. (2003). The right to the city. *International Journal of Urban and Regional Research, 27*, 939–941.
Hosang, D. (2003). *Youth and community organizing today* (Occasional Paper Series on Youth Organizing, no. 2.). Washington, DC: Funders Collaborative on Youth Organizing.
Ishihara, K. (2007). *Urban transformations: Youth organizing in Boston, New York City, Philadelphia, and Washington, DC* (Occasional paper series on youth organizing, no. 9.). Washington, DC: Funders' Collaborative on Youth Organizing.
JBHE. (1998/99, Winter). The persisting myth that Black and White schools are equally funded. *The Journal of Blacks in Higher Education, 22*, 17–18.
Lipman, P. (2011). *The new political economy of urban education: Neoliberalism, race, and the right to the city*. New York: Routledge.
LISTEN, Inc. (2000). *An emerging model for working with youth* (Occasional paper series on youth organizing, No. 1). Washington, DC: Funders Collaborative on Youth Organizing.
Marshall, C., & Rossman, G. B. (2010). *Designing qualitative research* (5th ed.). New York: Sage publications.
Marwell, N. (2007) *Bargaining for Brooklyn: Community organizations in the entrepreneurial city*. Chicago, IL: The University of Chicago Press.
Mthethwa-Sommers, S. (2012). Pedagogical possibilities: Lessons from social justice educators. *Journal of Transformative Education, 10*, 219–235.
Orfield, G., & Frankenberg, E. (2014). *Brown at 60: Great progress, a long retreat and an uncertain future*. The Civil Rights Project at the University of California, Los Angeles. Retrieved from www.crp@ucla.edu/research/k-12-education/integration-and-diversity/brown-at-60-great-progress-a-long-retreat-and-an-uncertain-future
Pownall, S. (2013). *A, B, C, D, STTPP: How school discipline feeds the school-to-prison pipeline*. New York Civil Liberties Union (NYCLU). Retrieved from http://www.nyclu.org/publications/report-b-c-d-stpp-how-school-discipline-feeds-school-prison-pipeline-2013
Seidel, S. (2011). *Hip hop genius: Remixing high school education*. Maryland: Rowman & Littlefield Education.
Shah, S., & Mediratta, K. (2008). Negotiating reform: Young people's leadership in the educational arena. In S. Deschenes, M. McLaughlin, & A. Newman (Eds.), *New directions for youth development: Community organizing and youth advocacy* (pp. 43–60). San Francisco, CA: Jossey-Bass.
Shernoff, D. J., & Vandell, D. L. (2008). Youth engagement and quality of experience in afterschool programs. *Afterschool Matters, 9*, 1–11.
Sherwood, K., & Dressner, J. (2004). *Youth organizing: A new generation of social activism*. Philadelphia: Public/Private Ventures.
Sukarieh, M., & Tannock, S. (2011). The positivity imperative: a critical look at the 'new' youth development movement. *Journal of Youth Studies, 14*, 675–691.
Sutton, S. E., Kemp, S., Gutierrez, L., & Saegert, S. (2006). *Urban youth programs in America: A study of youth, community, and social justice conducted for the Ford Foundation*. Washington, DC: CEEDS for Change.
Warren, M. R., Mira, M., & Nikundiwe, T. (2008). Youth organizing: From youth development to school reform. *New Directions for Youth Development, 117*, 27–42.

11 Between Radical Possibilities and Modest Reforms

The Precarious Position of Adult Allies in Youth Movements for Racial Justice

Hava Rachel Gordon

Over the last few decades, neoliberal education reforms have taken hold of public education systems across the world. These reforms include the privatization and deregulation of the public school system (Saltman, 2007), the dismantling of democratically elected school boards in favor of mayoral control over public schooling (Shaker & Heilman, 2004), and the promotion of market-based systems of school choice that tend to advantage middle-class families (Ball, 2003; Robertson & Lauder, 2001). The neoliberal education reform movement champions a vision of individual advancement over public and communal wellbeing (Harvey, 2005) and is characterized by the use of market and corporate language in discussing educational problems and solutions (Saltman, 2000). Neoliberal reform rhetoric emphasizes saving low-income students of color from substandard education and closing the achievement gap while consistently deemphasizing the role that systematic racism plays in creating this gap in the first place (Noguera & Akom, 2000). On a macro level, this education movement has become a central piece of urban gentrification and corporate-led globalization (Klein, 2007; Lipman, 2004, 2008; Lipman & Haines, 2007).

Youth of color in urban school systems face a host of racial injustices in their everyday experiences of schooling. These injustices include disproportionate zero-tolerance discipline policies that push kids out of school and into the prison pipeline (Tuzzolo & Hewitt, 2007); school cultures characterized by low academic expectations; a paucity of school funding, which leaves students without functioning bathrooms, textbooks, and other basic necessities (Kozol, 1992); public school curricula geared towards standardized testing instead of college admissions requirements; abrupt school closures and 'turnarounds' characteristic of urban education reform which disrupt students' access to neighborhood schools; the racial politics of school choice and lack of transportation to city schools; the lack of healthy food choices in public schools; education reform experimentation in low-income neighborhoods; and barriers to college entry for undocumented students. Low-income youth of color respond to these educational and racial injustices in a variety of ways. When neighborhood schools are shut and transformed into charters, for example, or when new standardized testing schemes are implemented that delay advancement through the educational system, students join other community members and teachers in mass protests and walkouts. At other times, students—especially in cities anchored in rich social movement traditions—resist these inequities by joining funded nonprofit organizations that aim to organize youth into collective and long-term educational justice campaigns. As Kwon (2013) notes, these organizations can be embedded in a neoliberal logic that encourages 'at risk' youth to become empowered, self-directed, responsible citizens, what Kwon (2013) terms "affirmative governmentality," in ways that both enable and constrain young people's ability to make social change.

THE ROLE OF YOUTH-COMMUNITY COLLECTIVES

What has been understudied in this critical literature on education reform is the extent to which low-income community collectives, particularly the Black, Latino, and immigrant youth who become objectified in educational policy discussions, are able to mobilize youth voice in order to bring racial justice issues to the forefront of neoliberal education policy. In Lipman's research on education reform and urban gentrification in Chicago, low-income African-American communities are routinely denigrated, dismissed, and distorted in white elites' remaking of the city school system (Lipman, 2004, 2008; Lipman & Haines, 2007). In this picture, communities of color are virtually shut out of education reform processes. However, in many places local education reformers do make efforts to form at least token community alliances, especially with community-based nonprofit organizations. Given the community outrage over school closures, mayoral takeovers of elected school boards, and educational reform experimentation in mostly low-income Black and Latino neighborhoods (see the NAACP 2010 report which criticizes the Obama Administration's school-reform experimentation in communities of color and the lack of sufficient community participation in school-reform decisions), reformers often use civil rights rhetoric (Miner, 2004) and seek alliances with community organizations in order to bring a much needed legitimacy to the implementation of contentious reforms. Importantly, these relationships can also be powerful venues for community voice to impact what would otherwise be elite education reform policymaking, especially if these voices demand racial justice. How do community collectives compel educational elites to wrestle with both decades-old racial injustices in the school system and renewed racial inequities triggered by neoliberal education reform processes? What are their tactics? What explains their successes and setbacks? And to what extent can low-income youth activists of color steer the course of reform in their cities? The key to exploring these questions is to understand the pivotal role that youth workers (specifically, young adult organizers who are in their early to mid20s) play in community-based nonprofit organizations.

Nonprofit organizations provide powerful leverage for teenagers to coalesce around various racial-justice campaigns that transcend their particular neighborhoods and schools. As they do this, the youth gain social visibility, voice, and political clout that they would not otherwise have without this nonprofit community anchor. As staff organizers, youth workers play a vital role in the political socialization of low-income teens of color. In this chapter, I will detail the role that these youth workers play in facilitating the political power of low-income youth of color. I argue that the political education and mentoring these young adult allies do with teenage activists is crucial in bringing youth voice into adult-dominated education policy discussions. I also detail the stress of youth workers in formalized nonprofits to both develop youth leaders and help these leaders project a collective youth presence that is respectable and ultimately palatable to adults in power so that they can maintain legitimacy in educational politics. As paid staff in community nonprofits, these youth workers are also under pressure to respond to foundation funding mandates and demands for deliverables. They are interfaces to funding bodies and are ultimately responsible for demonstrating youth leadership 'success' to funders. In trying to satisfy these mandates, and in trying to establish youth voice as a permanent fixture in education reform discussions, youth workers in nonprofit organizations often find themselves having to moderate both their own activism and curb youth radicalism. In so doing, youth workers reluctantly blunt youth activist power and create dissonance between youth activists' worldviews and their actual collective political impact in the public sphere.

METHODOLOGY

This chapter will examine the multifaceted and sometimes contradictory role that young adult allies play in mentoring teenage activists in these racial justice organizations. This data are drawn from ethnographic research that follows the tactics of four community educational and social justice groups (three of which include at least some youth activist focus) as they attempt to shape school reform in one mid-size city in the United States.

In this particular city, almost half of all high school students do not graduate. Nearly two-thirds (72%) of the students in this city's district qualify for free or reduced lunch. White students make up 20% of the city's student population across the 162 schools in the district. In conjunction with urban revitalization efforts, various local school reformers have stepped into the fray to help re-design public education in this city. This convergence of educational entrepreneurs has made a dramatic impact on the city school system, namely in the closing and transforming of struggling neighborhood schools in communities of color. Out of these sometimes disastrous experiments have arisen informal networks of mostly Black and Latino community members who have been organizing to oppose neighborhood school closures like these, as well as what they perceive to be other gentrification projects in their own neighborhood and other low-income neighborhoods around the city. This study involves participatory action research (PAR) with one of these informal networks.

There are also formalized community nonprofit organizations in this city that advocate for racial justice and youth voice in education reform. This study features three of these organizations. Some of these formal nonprofits, including those that house citywide youth activist campaigns, are visible and respected by elite reformers. These organizations periodically align with reformers and include collectives of low-income Latino parent and youth activists who have their own agendas for racial justice in the school system. Two of these groups have existed long before the reform movement descended upon this city and have grown out of previous racial justice struggles emerging in the 1960s.

In total, this project included 73 in-depth interviews with reformers and activists from these four groups ranging from 1 to 3 hours each, three focus groups, and participant-observation data over a span of 5 years (2008–2013). Ethnographic activities have included attending and participating in rallies, protests, demonstrations, neighborhood association meetings, school-reform events, school board meetings, house parties, and community organizing meetings. To protect confidentiality, all names that appear in this study are pseudonyms.

The teen activists and the youth workers who mentor them have organized around issues as diverse as dismantling zero-tolerance discipline policies, increasing student funding, expanding school transportation, promoting college readiness, bringing in youth and community voice in teacher evaluation processes, and fighting for educational justice in tandem with comprehensive immigration reform. Like the self-identified reformers in this study, these youth activists and workers view this moment of education reform as an unusual opportunity to make changes to a public school system long plagued by racial, class, and age inequalities.

YOUTH WORKERS AND RADICAL POSSIBILITIES

Turning Political Education into Political Empowerment

Youth activist organizations are not simply instrumental places where students mobilize for action for a specific campaign. They are often powerful alternative spaces for consciousness-raising where students gain a political education that is relevant to their lives. This political education can often serve as a potent antidote to the internalized hopelessness that substandard schooling practices can foster among low-income and poor students of color (Gordon, 2007, 2010). Youth workers, those young adults who most often come from students' own communities and can relate to them but who are outside of their school systems and have access to alternative knowledge, tools, and social networks, are charged with this political education. 24-year-old Berto consciously positions his organizing work as oppositional to the disempowering experience that youth receive in under-resourced schools:

> *They [the youth] are who's going to be born the next leaders. . . they need to be given the tools necessary to do that. The leadership, the critical thinking skills, that is so important. Not being conformist, and not thinking, "oh let's just do the easy thing and just show up to class." Students are told that. "Just show up and you'll pass." That's what I did. I showed up and I passed. But it's not enough to show up and pass. Because outside of these walls, you don't just show up to the real world and pass. There's real, real struggles out there and there's real oppression. There's real attacks on our community. You don't just show up. You have to fight.*

Organizing low-income youth of color and cultivating a political education that enables youth to become engaged, outraged critical thinkers and activists is a struggle in schools where the low-income students who haven't been pushed out of the school system survive because they have learned to keep their criticisms silent and to not displease adults (Fine, 1991). As 21-year-old youth worker Carlos explains:

> *Well, like I said all the troublemakers are out! They already got them out. So the ones who would voice it are not there anymore. And I think, because that's how they made it to senior year, because they follow all the rules. That's how come they make it.*

Youth workers who do outreach with these high school students try to interrupt this process, catching students *before* their criticisms of schooling crystallize into a decision to leave school, or into a disempowering silence that gets them through until graduation. Student activists often link the alternative education they receive in politicized youth nonprofits to their own sense of political power. As 18-year-old youth activist Shanti remembers:

> *They [youth organizers] invited us to a meeting, and from then on I stayed ever since. It was a really safe place for outside of school, where we learned about things that weren't being talked to us at school. We learned about all the social systems, different institutions and their role. They were really up front about racism and classism and oppression, different forms of oppression. So we learned a lot that we weren't learning in school. And that's what kept me coming back.*

This political education is not just about expanding students' horizons and learning abstract political history. It is also about working with youth to undo the internalized oppressions among them that contribute to racial and ethnic tensions rather than solidarity. For example, in student organizing retreats in one youth nonprofit, youth organizers teach student activists about labor movement history and the ways in which Black workers have been pitted against poor white workers in order to foil class solidarity and cross-racial alliances. This political education is geared towards helping students understand how internalized oppression and racial stereotypes are often propagated by people in power to divide and conquer. As 23- year-old Rayanne observes:

> *It sort of elevates their thinking into realizing that they're being taught to think that way about themselves and about other people so that they don't have power. Because if they had power, what would the world look like? . . . So the job of an organizer is to look at the whole picture and help them see this systemic picture of what's happening.*

Youth organizers foster leadership skills amongst the most marginalized youth populations. 20-year-old Lisa, who organizes youth to participate in school-reform policy discussions, explains how this political development is directly opposed to the more standard kind of 'leadership' development of more privileged youth in school settings:

> *So when we talk about emerging leaders, it's not the honor roll, and it's not student government. Emerging leaders are not the traditional leaders. You can't have a student tell you how to engage them unless those students have experienced being disengaged.*

As Lisa points out, low-income youth of color are uniquely positioned to be 'experts' of sorts in school-reform policy discussions, even if they are tokenized. Their stamp of approval carries weight—as they are the ultimate objects of school reform. The struggle for youth, then, and the task for the youth workers who mentor them, is to transform youth from two-dimensional objects of school reform into active subjects who take control of these education discussions and turn them into dialogues about racial justice.

Turning Political Empowerment into Political Power

Young adult youth workers cultivate 'emerging leaders' through sustained and carefully structured political education workshops, retreats, and programs. They also equip student activists with concrete skills that most youth will never learn in school: how to speak to adults in power; how to identify allies, conditional allies, and targets in a given campaign; how to speak to the press, and how to plan events. Students move from a generalized political outrage about the everyday unjust conditions of their lives to possessing the skills to operationalize this outrage. They learn how to envision an outcome and solution, map out a strategy, set campaign benchmarks, and figure out their division of labor. As Angela Ards (1999) pointed out in her seminal article "Rhyme and Resist," youth expression enabled by politically charged youth cultures like hip-hop hold enormous potential for social change, but expression might not necessarily be enough to move the needle. Steering public policy often necessitates a more organized campaign as well. Youth workers provide the organizational skills and resources required to do this. This means moving youth beyond 'voice' and expression and making sure that youth access domains of power where elite adults craft policy. Youth workers must walk a careful line in terms of helping students develop these skills, as they must assess a complex political landscape without taking over student voice and autonomy. 24-year-old Antonio explains the careful process by which he helps to transform youth political analysis and outrage into an organized social movement campaign:

> *What we do is we provide an analysis of what the conditions are. Politics or whatever it is, the players. What's the power analysis? What's the outcome you want from this meeting? What should be our talking points? And then students put their own stories behind it, and that's where the prep is. We provide them with what they need to know, and they execute in their own way.*

This power analysis in particular—the process of identifying potential allies, possible coalition partners, and potential targets—is key to strengthening the value of student voice in spaces dominated by adults. Cassie, a 17-year-old student involved in a youth organization focused on integrating youth concerns into educational reform policy, explains her strategy to keep showing up at key meetings and forge alliances with specific policymakers. Her organization's demand that students have a real voice in teacher evaluation processes began to gain traction in state-level policy discussions about school reform. Locating the political power of her voice in the alliances she strategically made with adults in power, she notes:

> *So, like if I wouldn't have had those few allies, easily my comments would have been thrown out the window. And the allies would not have been there had we not showed up in force over and over. So it's really a bunch of leg work, a bunch of little things that make it so that our voices matter.*

Of course, youth are not always able to garner enough respect from powerful adults in a given institutional domain or successfully forge alliances with adults who will legitimize their voice to other adults. It is in these times when youth organizers will accompany youth to negotiate with adults in order to interrupt ageist power dynamics (Gordon, 2007). For example, youth organizer Hannah joined students for a tense meeting between themselves and the principal of their high school about the suspension and expulsion rates of Black and Latino students in the school. In a mostly student-led meeting, Black and Latino youth expressed their disappointment with the principal's reliance on suspension and expulsion, having seen many of their friends bear the brunt of these policies and having even experienced these policies themselves. The principal became defensive, calling on specific students in the meeting to speak up if they had ever felt attacked or harassed by the school's discipline procedures. Knowing that the principal deliberately skipped over students in the room who he had suspended in the last few months, youth organizer Hannah wrested control of the meeting from the principal and interrupted: "Wait a minute, wait a minute, Jason or Tanisha; do you want to tell your story?" In this moment, Hannah created an opening for these two students to tell their stories and regain control of the meeting.

These are key instances when youth organizers step in to swing ageist power dynamics back towards students in contentious settings. However, as much as they can, youth organizers work with students so that their own voices and experiences are foregrounded in educational policy meetings, community meetings, press conferences, and even rallies, walkouts, and street theater. Here, the focus is not on getting students to simply tell their stories or express their opinions: Youth work in this context means actively maximizing students' chances of *being heard* and *respected* by adults in power. Youth workers help students think critically about their own experiences of zero-tolerance school discipline policies, substandard education, and racial profiling in schools, and link them to their campaign talking points in powerful testimonials. This requires several hours of preparing, practicing, and polishing, since these youth don't often speak to (white) adults in power. For example, in preparation for an accountability meeting a week away, youth organizers Berto and Rayanne had students take turns walking to the front of the room to share their seven-minute testimonials and demands that they had carefully worked on, their words read off of notecards and their voices shaking. At the end, during a round of applause, several of these students would often look down or put their face into their hands, embarrassed about tripping over words or a mistake they had made in the delivery. Berto would ask the students what they thought was the most positive thing about what they had prepared and how they delivered it, and what could be improved. Did the students make eye contact with the audience? Did the students remember to emphasize their demand at the end? Did the students articulate the very important talking point about racial disparities in referrals to law enforcement? Did the students tell their story from the heart? Then Berto solicited feedback from other students watching from chairs around the room. Through this process, youth workers prompt students to identify their own areas for improvement and take ownership over their prepared statements while also helping them to develop the confidence and entitlement to speak to wealthier, more politically powerful adults. After addressing these adults at several meetings, 18-year-old Jacquelyn discusses her own transformation from being intimidated to speak to feeling entitled to speak:

> *At first I thought about feeling intimidated, but then I was like, this issue is more important than my intimidation and allowing myself to feel powerless. Like, I knew I had the power to do this. And so it kind of—it overtook my intimidation. I went on and I was just like, "You know what? These students are going through this every day." So it is my duty to tell them that there is somebody out there speaking for them. . ..So I was like, "forget the fact that you're a politician or you're a teacher, or you're a principal. Like you're another person, you're a human.*

In this way, youth workers prepare students to enter political conversations in which actual youth voices are often absent and young people's needs and experiences are objectified, marginalized, and distorted in policy discussions. Through power mapping, political analysis, campaign-development, preparation, and leadership development, youth workers facilitate young activists' presence in these policy discussions. Many of these teenage activists, who themselves pivot between high-level policy discussions and their own school-based organizing, marvel at their more regular presence at these meetings and the growing respect they are accorded from high-profile adults. As Cassie reflects:

> *Just like the first meeting we went to, to where the adults weren't so much interested in what we had to say. Now, to like the last meeting, they asked us "What do you think?" or "How do you feel on this topic?" Like, it was huge change. It felt good to know that like we changed their opinions on student voice. Like they easily didn't really know much about student voice, they didn't care . . . To now, where they are asking us what we think. So that was a huge change. And I think that's what it is. We just don't go away!*

This sustained youth presence in policy circles differs from the more limited political possibilities for youth political impact offered by structures like adult-sanctioned youth councils (Taft & Gordon, 2013). In structures like youth councils, there are few mechanisms in place to enable youth voice to penetrate the actual processes of policymaking. In the case of a community-based nonprofit, it is the youth workers who provide the crucial political education to foment critical thinking about social inequalities and expose youth to lessons about social movement histories in order to craft new social movement aims, organizing tactics, and campaign strategies. It is also the youth workers who make sure that this political education translates into effective, sustained, and respected youth presence in adult-dominated spaces. The work that these youth organizers do, then, holds enormous potential to bring the radical possibilities that youth activism generates to a political terrain normally dominated by adults. Unfortunately and ironically, it is also this sustained youth presence, this 'seat at the table' that youth workers work so hard to ensure, that begins to exert a repressive force on the radical possibilities of youth organizing.

YOUTH WORKERS AND MODEST REFORMS

Cultivating Valuable Partners: Cooperation over Political Outrage

The more that youth activists refuse to go away, the more likely they are to gain a seat at the table with powerful adults and hold them accountable to their word. However, the longer that youth are 'at the table' and the more respect they gain from adults—as youth representing formal nonprofit organizations—the more that these relationships of accountability can turn into constraining relationships of cooperation. This can happen especially in cases when elite education reformers seek partnerships with community-based organizations in order to demonstrate to a broader audience that their target reforms resonate with the communities affected. As Carlos notes, one of the hardest things about being a youth organizer is knowing how to respond to a 'target' that slowly turns into a 'partner':

> *We sometimes struggle a lot with how aggressive to be. What tactics to use. So kind of like deciding what tone to take. Should we straight up call them out and just say, "You haven't done anything, how dare you, you should be ashamed of yourself!" Or should we say, "You're doing some good things, but you know, this little progress is not enough. Let's work together to close that gap."*
>
> *And I think it all depends on the time place and conditions. When you have [a target] that is moving in the right direction that is pro-change, sometimes in organizing you shouldn't be so "anti" with those people in power. Because in the end, to move things into power, sometimes you have to work with them. And in organizing sometimes that's really hard to see. When you don't know how aggressive or how mean you should be towards your target.*

Youth workers are charged with making these complicated calls and then encouraging youth activists to adapt to their read of 'place and conditions.' This can be a source of dissonance for the youth activists involved. Many times throughout the school year, youth outrage—first and foremost stemming from their own experiences but also stemming from the political education they receive in the nonprofit context—prepared students for more direct, radical demands and action than the youth organizers were willing to support. For example, students who were working on a statewide school-discipline policy wanted to demand that police officers be removed from city schools completely. In several organizing meetings, youth organizers had to lead students through a discussion about why that would be a good goal but wouldn't be politically possible at that very moment. Hannah struggled with this: "It's hard to go back to them and try to explain that right now, this is not possible. Our power is not that high, we're not strong enough yet. We can't make those sorts of demands. Or we could, but know that it might fail." This message of constraint at times conflicts with youth organizers' messages of radical possibility communicated through their political education and leadership training. Over time, some youth organizers notice that teen activists become more complacent, and they notice themselves becoming more complacent too. As one youth organizer in another nonprofit admits:

> *I mean I think it's because we've been honest with students every step of the process of like, why these compromises need to be made, but maybe it has made them a little bit more complacent about it as opposed to like just slapping it all on them at the end. Sometimes when we realize that it's okay to not always do what the students want, like it like is a way for us to relax into like being complacent. I don't think any of us really are yet, but maybe we are becoming that way.*

As translators of both political possibility and adaptation to constraining conditions, youth organizers find themselves in a bind that exhausts them and periodically makes them feel like they are betraying the very youth they work with.

The Costs of Maintaining a Seat at the Table

The pressures to keep youth at the table with elites through the course of long-term campaigns can steer youth movement away from radical possibilities and towards the kinds of modest reforms that are carefully crafted not to alienate elites. In one sense, bringing youth voice 'to the table' is what organizing is all about, as Rayanne observes:

> *We should be working alongside teachers, alongside principals, alongside educators to find solutions together. Because I think that's what organizing is about. To bring in all the decision makers, all the players, all the people that have a say and that play a role in shaping our education. And together coming up with solutions.*

But this organizing approach does not always leave room for youth activists or youth workers to express political outrage and dissent. One 25-year-old organizer remembers: "When I first came on board I was saying 'Why isn't this city on fire? Why aren't people burning up garbage cans and throwing them in the streets saying we are not moving until the graduation at [local high school] goes from 30% to 80%, to 90%?' That's a frustrating thing to think about." Over time, this organizer learned that a tactic like this would probably sever fragile relationships with adults in power who could be important campaign allies. Another organizer, James, expresses his ongoing frustration with targets-turned-allies who do not follow through on their promises: "So you get frustrated with different outcomes with whatever they're doing. But at the same time they're so nice to you and they want to work with you to address it. So that is difficult." In one organization, youth activists helped to co-write a report on racial disparities in academic achievement rates, and they were going to target specific education officials with this report. In a meeting, youth organizers and youth activists grappled with how aggressively to word the report, since this document was one public mechanism to hold adults in power accountable. Yet the report could not be so aggressive that it would alienate those very same adults. Several youth activists in the room favored the use of the word 'demands' to push elites to more aggressively tackle racial disparities in education practices. A youth organizer asked students how they would feel about framing these as 'recommendations,' as 'demands' might damage the relationship they were trying to build with high-profile education movers and shakers. After a protracted debate, students and the youth organizers agreed that 'a call-to' was a good way to phrase their messaging in order to assertively (but not aggressively) hold education elites to their word. As Hannah reflected afterwards: "We could have made this report scathing, but now it's like, very nice. It all depends on where we are in that relationship [with elites]. Ah, it's hard."

As a result, the "backstage" (Goffman 1959) radical speak, so carefully cultivated by youth workers, dissipates as it drifts towards the "frontstage," where youth directly confront adults in power over educational injustices in policy forums. As one youth activist, Gabriel, notes, this can mean tamping down his own political outrage and political analysis in a roomful of education reformers. Depending on the players in the room, it can also mean framing issues less collectively and systemically and couching them in more individualistic and aspirational terms:

> *When I speak to those legislators, I make it all about "caring more about school" and not being so angry about the mistreatment. You definitely have to let them know, "This is going on in my life right now. And it's keeping me from school." Like "I want to graduate, I want to go to college. I don't want to have a criminal record when I'm in high school 'cause I care about my future and I want to go and get my diploma and be ready to get my college degree without anybody questioning me about something stupid that happened in high school."*

> *So you do have to link that, because it also gives more of an emotional feeling. Like not just saying, "Oh, kids are being criminalized in school." You know?*

Another youth activist explained his discussions "backstage" with other youth, and how these differ from the discourses they use "frontstage" when speaking about educational and racial justice directly to politicians:

> *We're all like "politicians are being idiots right now, they need to get this together." But you can't really say that to a white politician. You can't say, "Oh, it's B.S. how you're treating Black people, it's B.S. how you're treating Hispanics, it's B.S. how you're treating Asian people," you know? You have to give them little pictures and charts and everything.*

As another youth activist from a different organization explains:

> *We're not radical, but we're like all for the racial equality and gender equality and everything. So of course we all want to be like the Malcolm X type or Martin Luther King or Caesar Chavez type people. Like in our discussions with each other. But we can't be like, extremely radical with them, because then they would take that as, "Oh, you're totally against our government."*

Although still powerful, the distance between students' critical worldviews and their actual 'calls-to' exerts a repressive pressure on youth movement and creates tensions within youth organizations.

Youth Organizers as Grant Enforcers

Part of youth organizers' read of 'time, place, and conditions'—their own political analysis of the scope of possibility—must take into account the constraints of funded campaigns. In the neoliberal nonprofit, youth organizers are rarely the grant writers for the funded organization. And yet, it is youth organizers who must mediate between what youth activists want to accomplish as a collective—and what they are supposed to deliver with their grant funding. Exasperated, Antonio admitted: "Sometimes I honestly think that we have allies or enemies based on grants. And like, we need to be allies with people because of a grant or we can't be too opposed to something because of a grant." These grant restrictions can be a source of major stress for paid staff organizers in youth-action nonprofits, and often take youth organizers away from their most treasured task of leadership development and mentorship. In fact, the constraints of grant deliverables often privilege quantitative benchmarks over the more amorphous and qualitative process of political education and leadership development (Kwon, 2013). For example, to fulfill the conditions of one grant, Lisa is charged with a specific kind of skill development for a full 50% of the youth she works with. She must show that she successfully developed this skill over the course of one year:

> *So, these are impossible goals and they're not like—it's not the way I want to think about my youth, in these numbers. I mean in a way it's good to have a number, because it challenges me to like do the house visits and actually make sure I'm meeting with my youth. But I don't want to like see them that way, as like, "I need to develop you for a grant."*

As Carlos remembers: "For a few months that was our only job, was to meet these deliverables. Everything else was put on the back burner. And that's not why I became an organizer."

As youth workers themselves struggle with the contradictions of youth organizing within the neoliberal confines of the funded nonprofit structure, they constantly assess whether or not the benefits outweigh the costs. They bask in the success of facilitating youth voice into the adult domains of educational policy usually dominated by elites. They bring authentic community concerns to the table, and at times they successfully compel these elites to actively wrestle with age, race, ethnic, linguistic, and class inequalities that might have otherwise gone unaddressed in school-reform discussions. However, in the moments when paid youth workers are pulled more towards grant deliverables and further from what their mentees want to take on, they must contend with this dissonance between their base and their grantors. These funding pressures create tensions within youth organizations. Like the pressures to maintain a respectable youth voice in policy discussions, funding pressures also threaten to destabilize the powerful relationships between youth workers and the teens they mentor.

CONCLUSION

Youth organizers, especially those in the funded nonprofit context, play a vital role in helping to translate low-income teens' everyday experiences of racial and educational injustices into political outrage, political consciousness, and political efficacy. These youth workers help to connect teen activists to a legacy of multiracial social justice activism, which is instrumental in combating the internalized hopelessness fostered by racial violence, segregation, under-resourced and punitive schooling systems, and poverty. Connecting youth to these histories also teach youth about what can be won, what kind of political victories are possible, and the long timeframe for social justice goals to come to fruition. This long-term view of social movement history (which these youth do not learn in schools) equips students with the resolve, long-term perspective, and patience necessary to sustain long-term campaigns and endure periodic setbacks.

When necessary, these youth workers act as 'faces' for an especially de-valued student population when elite adults are reluctant to listen to youth. Youth workers pry open spaces for youth voice in adult conversations where educational policy (whether at the school or legislative level) is crafted. At other times, these workers give young people the coaching and tools to speak to adults in power face-to-face by themselves, and to effectively mobilize a student base. Because of these youth organizers, youth of color transform school-reform discussions among elites and counter disempowering educational environments at the grassroots. They speak for themselves, share their own stories, and make their own calls for racial justice in what would otherwise be 'colorblind' neoliberal education policymaking.

The larger neoliberal context, however, which structures the institutionalized nonprofit, charges youth workers with other conflicting responsibilities vis-à-vis teenage activists that places on their shoulders an emotional, political, and work burden which wears them out. This in itself can endanger youth organizing, since stable mentorship is key to youth activist successes in these adult domains. The job of the youth organizer is to raise the political consciousness of marginalized youth, facilitate discussions about the political possibilities for radical change, give youth the tools to craft campaigns, and open spaces for their voices amongst adults. But the job of the youth organizer is to also bring disparate actors together in cooperation with one another across the long haul of a campaign. These educational and policy elites are often eager to have the cooperation of organizations based in low-income communities of color, as these partnerships bring legitimacy to contentious education reforms. At the same time, there is very little tolerance for youth radicalism in these circles, and the respect that youth of color receive at the table is fragile and can be revoked. For the sake of maintaining youth voice in educational policy, youth workers curb youth radicalism and channel youth outrage into less threatening modes of dissent as a campaign moves forward. The nonprofit organization's reliance on grants further complicates the relationship between marginalized youth and adults in power, and youth organizers must be the arbiter between the two. Between the grant pressures and the fragile respect given to youth of color by mostly white adults in power, youth organizers reluctantly find themselves steering radical youth aims into modest calls for action.

As Eliasoph notes in her work *Avoiding Politics* (1998), political apathy is actively constructed. In her ethnographic research, she found that political discussions flare in backstage conversations while people learn to silence these in more public, frontstage conversations. This silencing threatens the very essence of democracy. In the context of youth organizing, this silencing is actively, albeit reluctantly, facilitated by youth organizers: the very people who also help to usher youth activism into the public (adult) sphere of policymaking. While massive youth protests and walkouts related to racial injustices in education are routinely ignored, belittled, or minimized by mainstream media and education reform elites, youth workers in the nonprofit sector help bring visibility and presence to some of these youth concerns. However, these community concerns and demands become distorted as they make their way into education policy. What does it mean that in the context of the neoliberal state (Kwon, 2013), nonprofit youth workers become the very instruments of social-movement repression that they so revile? What are the costs of widening the gap between youth activist visions and their actual impact on public policy? What radical possibilities are lost in the space between the backstage discussions about racial justice and the frontstage calls for action? The strain on youth workers and the youth activists they mentor—the stress of continually weighing radical possibilities for change against the specter of more winnable modest reforms—is one manifestation of the ways in which the neoliberal context distorts youth voice as it fights its way into public policy.

REFERENCES

Ards, A. (1999, July 26). Rhyme and resist: Organizing the hip-hop generation. *The Nation*, 11–20.

Ball, S.J. (2003). *Class strategies and the education market: The middle classes and social advantage*. New York: Routledge Falmer.

Gordon, H.R. (2007). Allies within and without: How adolescent activists conceptualize ageism and navigate adult power in youth social movements. *Journal of Contemporary Ethnography, 36*(6), 631–668.

Gordon, H.R. (2010). *We fight to win: Inequality and the politics of youth activism*. New Brunswick: Rutgers University Press.

Eliasoph, N. (1998). *Avoiding politics: How Americans produce apathy in everyday life*. Cambridge: Cambridge University Press.

Fine, M. (1991). *Framing dropouts: Notes on the politics of an urban public high school*. Albany: State University of New York.

Goffman, E. (1959). *The presentation of self in everyday life*. New York: Doubleday.

Harvey, D. (2005). *A brief history of neoliberalism*. Oxford: Oxford University Press.

Klein, N. (2007). *The shock doctrine: The rise of disaster capitalism*. New York: Metropolitan Books.

Kozol, J. (1992). *Savage inequalities: Children in America's schools*. New York: Harper Perennial.

Kwon, S. A. (2013). *Uncivil youth: Race, activism, and affirmative governmentality*. Durham: Duke University Press.

Lipman, P. (2004). *High stakes education: Inequality, globalization, and urban school reform*. New York: Routledge.

Lipman, P. (2008). The cultural politics of mixed income schools and housing: A racialized discourse of displacement, exclusion, and control. *Anthropology and Education Quarterly, 40*(3), 215–236.

Lipman, P., & Haines, N. (2007). From accountability to privatization and African American exclusion: Chicago's 'Renaissance' 2010. *Educational Policy, 21*(3), 471–502.

Miner, B. (2004, Spring). Distorting the civil rights legacy. *Rethinking schools*, 17–20.

Noguera, P. A., & Akom, A. (2000, June 25). Disparities demystified. *The Nation*, 29–31.

Robertson, S., Lauder, H. (2001). Restructuring the education/social class relation: A class choice? In R. Phillips & J. Furlong (Eds.), *Education reform and the state: Twenty-five years of politics, policy, and practice* (pp. 222–236). New York: Routledge Falmer.

Saltman, K.J. (2000). *Collateral damage: Corporatizing public schools—a threat to democracy*. Lanham: Rowman and Littlefield.

Saltman, K. J. (2007, Spring). Schooling in disaster capitalism: How the political right is using disaster to privatize public schooling. *Teacher Education Quarterly*, 131–156.

Shaker, P., & Heilman, E. (2004). The new common sense of education: Advocacy research versus academic authority. *Teachers College Record, 106*(7), 1444–1470.

Taft, J.K., & Gordon, H.R. (2013). Youth activists, youth councils, and constrained democracy. *Education, Citizenship and Social Justice, 8*(1), 87–100.

Tuzzolo, E., & Hewitt, D. T. (2007). Rebuilding inequity: The re-emergence of the school-to-prison pipeline in New Orleans. *The High School Journal, 90*(2), 59–68.

12 Co-Creating a Culture of Participation Through a Youth Council

Brian Hubbard

In an adult-centric society, there are few opportunities that allow for youth participation and engagement in structural decision-making (Roholt, Baizerman & Hildreth, 2013). Youth are rarely invited into established structures of decision-making, and they are rarely trained to participate in decision-making to benefit themselves, their programs, and their communities (Bradford & Cullen, 2012; Sabo-Flores, 2008). As a result, youth are often seen as apathetic and lacking engagement (Roholt, Baizerman & Hildreth, 2013). I have seen firsthand the benefits of working with and alongside youth to support their involvement in improving the services that affect them and their communities. It is that experience that allows me to be comfortable claiming the need to involve youth and adults in the ongoing process of decision-making to create the programs, organizations, agencies, and systems that are designed to serve them.

Paradoxically, well-intentioned attempts by adults to create decision-making positions for young people, such as placing them on boards of directors or charging them with leadership of projects, have often failed because young people and adults were not adequately prepared to work together (Percy-Smith, 2007). This is often due to the lack of opportunities that invite and support a culture of participation in agencies for youth to become involved with adults in real decision-making. In response, funders and policymakers are requesting that youth agencies begin to build a culture of participation that involves young people in decision-making processes (Williams, Ferguson & Yohalem, 2013). The belief underscoring these expectations is that when an agency supports and invites a culture of participation it gives a voice to young people, builds social capital, and generates and applies knowledge in improving services, programs, political structures, and community contexts while simultaneously extending rights of citizenship (Kirby, Lanyon, Cronin & Sinclair, 2003; Percy-Smith, 2007).

With that in mind, to create conditions for young people to become actively involved in decision-making, I created a youth council within my work at the Conservation Corps. The Conservation Corps is a nonprofit organization in the state of Minnesota that provides hands-on environmental stewardship and service-learning opportunities to youth and young adults while accomplishing energy conservation, natural resource management, and emergency response work. The Conservation Corps is an AmeriCorps program, which is part of a national service movement that addresses challenges in our nation's communities through the dedicated service of its youth participants and its AmeriCorps members. Conservation Corps youth participants, ages 15–18, and AmeriCorps members, ages 18–25, enroll in the programs to give back to their communities while gaining a strong foundation of marketable skills for careers in natural resources. Activities include managing natural resources in parks and public lands and participating in daily training and education. The Conservation Corps Youth Council is made up of youth participant alumni, AmeriCorps member alumni, and program staff of the Conservation Corps.

Much has been written about the impact of youth councils and youth participation (Bradford & Cullen, 2012; Jeffs & Smith, 2012). In my career as an educator, I have been met with frustrations with institutional barriers that work against opportunities where youth councils and youth participation can affect real decision-making powers between youth and adults. Specifically, this can be found in two different elements of youth development approaches. The first is attributed to adult-assigned projects for youth participation. The second type is designed for youth participation to consult on projects or programs that are designed to serve them. I question the effectiveness of these two types of youth participation and the effect they are having on the lives of young people and public services. There is a need to develop skills to create conditions that envision shared power between youth and adults at all levels of decision-making.

In this chapter, I will illustrate an approach to working with and on behalf of a youth council that works to build a culture of participation within the organization together with youth and adults. This vision and goal is to continue to provide access to and create inclusive environments for young people throughout the organization and amongst partner agencies. I will demonstrate and recognize respective roles and responsibilities of youth and adults while placing special emphasis on involving youth that are traditionally under-resourced and underrepresented. I believe this approach can help develop solutions for common problems that affect our organizations and communities. I will describe this approach, which involves youth ages 15–18, youth workers, and program staff from the Conservation Corps, and how it was built on democratic principles, specifically to enhance a culture of participation between youth and adults in the agency. I will describe how youth council projects create an opportunity for youth and adults to work together to integrate youth into decision-making roles and to create new conditions for youth to influence decision-making processes. I conclude with identifying a program model of youth participation and describe the underlying skill sets for facilitating this process, as well as further opportunities for engaging young people.

DEFINING DEMOCRATIC PRINCIPLES IN PARTICIPATION

Participation between youth and adults is a multi-layered concept, with the same term often used to describe very different processes. Participation can be considered along the following dimensions: level of participation; focus of decision-making; content of decision-making; nature of participation activity; frequency and duration of participation; children and young people involved (Kirby et al., 2003). Furthermore, participation might be seen as a necessary prerequisite for youth development, a strategy for community development, a democratic ideal for grooming young citizenry, or a political act for challenging hegemonic and oppressive structures (Fusco & Heathfield, 2015).

A culture of participation thrives when youth and adults are invited and choose to participate in the creation of democratic spaces that they define together. The aim is to maximize abilities for youth and adults to work together to stretch capacities, to reach beyond previous knowledge and enhance self-concept upon achievement and sense of satisfaction (Checkoway & Richards-Schuster, 2004). The Council began by creating two parallel methods together with youth and adults in the agency. The first was through an invitation to develop a program model for the Council together with youth and adults in the agency. The second was to invite participation in projects meaningful to youth and adults in the agency as well as their communities. The Conservation Corps Youth Council is based on the principles of collaboration and cooperation. This is done through working together with Conservation Corps Youth Council members, youth workers, and program staff to co-create pathways for decision-making within the organization. We engage our alumni in the everyday work of the Conservation Corps Youth Council, such as developing the program model, writing, media, evaluation, planning, problem solving, and continuing to participate in environmental restoration projects to support the mission and values of the Conservation Corps. This process of participation, I believe, is more authentic than what more commonly occurs, e.g., when adults need input to make programmatic decisions on young people's behalf, they have youth fill out questionnaires or surveys. Adults analyze this data and use it as the basis of identifying outcomes, designing programs, and generating reports. Youth have not been invited to contribute their voice and perspective, to be strategic partners together with adults, or engage in critical analysis of issues. Youth and adults have not been working together in meaningful ways in producing knowledge to identify outcomes and design and evaluate programs.

My personal philosophy of participation in youth work is based on democratic principles rooted in the pre-history of the youth development field, the foundation laid by pragmatic educator and philosopher John Dewey. Dewey emphasizes the fundamental value of democratic principles that supports a culture of participation together with experiential and service learning. This ideology stems from his book *The Good Activity* in which he says, "To foster conditions that widen the horizons of others and give them command of their own powers, so that they can find their own powers, so that they can find their own happiness, in their own fashion, is the way of 'social' action" (Dewey, 1922). The culture of participation that I am engaged in articulates this "social" action that John Dewey describes between youth and adults and the process in which together they develop their leadership capacities by engaging in real world leadership contexts as decision makers. Together, youth and adults in the Conservation Corps Youth Council meet the historical and theoretical influences described in the field of practice in which youth and adults simultaneously exercise and develop their leadership capacities to produce shared outcomes and valuable knowledge.

THE CONSERVATION CORPS

Youth participants in the Conservation Corps are 15–18 years old and can be employed in two natural resource management programs with the Conservation Corps. The first program opportunity is the Summer Youth Corps program, which brings together urban and rural youth in the summer months of June through August at a residential camp. Summer Youth Corps participants are from diverse backgrounds: 40% from communities of color, equal numbers of males and females, equal urban and rural participants, 15%–20% of whom are deaf or hard of hearing, and 70% from low-income households. All youth apply to the Conservation Corps and are selected by staff for one of two sessions, each four weeks in length during the summer months. Service projects improve water quality, preserve biodiversity, and enhance outdoor recreation; 95% of service projects are performed in rural communities with urban and rural participants. The Conservation Corps hires sign language interpreters to lead crews that include youth who are deaf.

The second youth program with the Conservation Corps is the Youth Outdoors program, which is an afterschool employment opportunity in the fall and spring that is based at different community recreation centers in Minneapolis and Saint Paul. Urban youth participants aged15–18 complete natural resource management projects in or near the metropolitan areas. Work projects in natural resource management include building structures, invasive species management, planting trees, and watershed management. All of the participants in Youth Outdoors are youth from households with incomes at or below 80% of the City of Saint Paul's area median income of $48,235 (http://www.mncompass.org/profiles/acs1/st-paul). Currently, about 82% of program participants are African American and 18 percent are Asian. The Youth Outdoors and Summer Youth Corps programs help bring diverse community groups together that are historically underrepresented in conservation efforts and related jobs.

The Conservation Corps Youth Council: The Beginnings

The Conservation Corps Youth Council was designed and implemented together with youth alumni 15–18 years old, youth workers, and program staff from both of the Conservation Corps youth programs, Youth Outdoors and Summer Youth Corps. The youth workers are AmeriCorps members that lead Conservation Corps youth participants in natural resource management after school and during the summer. The Conservation Corps Youth Council is one of the strategies established by the organization to engage our youth alumni in ongoing service-learning opportunities. I presented the idea of starting a youth council to my supervisor because I believed it would be a positive addition to the agency goal of collaborating with youth. I was asked to write a proposal that would define what the Conservation Corps Youth Council would accomplish and how it could be supported within the organization before I started the project. I used this planning time as an opportunity to engage youth and youth worker alumni, together with current youth participants in the Conservation Corps, to build a program model and establish guidelines of the Conservation Corps Youth Council. I held several meetings with program staff and organizational leaders in the initial stages of the Conservation Corps Youth Council to garner support for the effort. Once organizational leaders were on board, youth alumni were invited to participate in the formation of the Conservation Corps Youth Council structure, develop guidelines for the Council, and determine how it would interact with the larger organization. About 200 youth alumni were contacted to participate in the formation of the Conservation Corps Youth Council by email, phone, and social media. A total of 12 youth alumni responded to the initial request and attended the first meeting.

There are a total of seven active members in the Conservation Corps Youth Council from diverse locations in Minnesota. The members receive no paid stipend for their participation. Our meetings are conducted in person, by conference call, or online to incorporate youth who do not have access to transportation or do not live in the area where the meetings are conducted. Two participants are deaf and three are English Language Learners (ELL). Deaf youth and English Language Learners face issues with accessibility, respect, equality, and chances for opportunities in their everyday lives (Hehir & Wilkens, 2008). The Conservation Corps Youth Council strives to empower, educate, and inspire deaf and ELL youth to work together on projects that are important to them, the organization, and their communities.

The Conservation Corps Youth Council promotes youth as active resources as a means to produce useful knowledge, skills, and abilities through organizing their own research and environmental-based projects.

The following sections will describe projects from the Conservation Corps Youth Council that demonstrate how to build a culture of participation together with a youth council. The projects work to bridge knowledge gaps between youth and adults and look to reduce disparities of the diverse communities of youth from low-income households, English Language Learners, and the deaf population to further opportunities with education and employment.

SAMPLE PROJECTS

The Conservation Corps Youth Council is committed to youth voice. Therefore, youth are invited to participate in all the stages of planning and decision-making, beginning with the guidelines of the council itself. The Conservation Corps Youth Council members created the guidelines during three meetings that engaged in activities designed to form meaning from the needs of the group as well as individual youth council participants. The group uses these as a guide to promote democratic approaches to choosing projects, agenda making, group consensus, strategic planning, and communication.

An example of using the guidelines for strategic-planning purposes was when Council members identified what the fundamental skills, areas of knowledge, and experiences were needed for youth and adult participants to play meaningful and powerful roles in planning, design, and implementation of the youth council. For example, one important aspect was identified by Eh Eh, a 16-year-old male participant, who pointed to the need for developmental capacities within the group. He stated, "As a group, we all have different backgrounds and experiences, and at the same time, we share an experience of being a youth alumni. It is important for youth to be open to sharing these experiences." He points to the aspiration of an ideal method of the Conservation Corps Youth Council—to create opportunities and to maximize youth participants' ability to speak about the issues that concern them in ways that are most comfortable and supportive. This ideology is supported by Lev Vygotsky, an educator who identified the Zone of Proximal Development (ZPD), which bridges the gap between what is known and what can be known. Vygotsky (1978) describes the ZPD as "the distance between the actual development level as determined by independent problem solving and the level of potential development as determined under adult guidance or with peer collaboration with more capable peers" (p. 86). I believe the Council members and program staff work together to create guidelines that identify the technical and social skills needed to support new conditions that foster relationships between youth and adults in the agency.

Another example of using the guidelines for strategic- planning purposes would be the Conservation Corps Youth Council members being trained in volunteer management at the beginning of their experiences as a youth participant in the Summer Youth Corps and Youth Outdoors programs. They led volunteers on several projects throughout the year. Local cities, parks departments, and community groups have the ability to reach lots of potential volunteers, but they often have limited capacity to manage large volunteer groups on site. The Conservation Corps youth participants were able to fill a critical role in managing volunteers by providing instruction and project supervision. For example, in Saint Paul, Conservation Corps youth participants manage more than 1,000 volunteers involved with the city's annual Spring Park Cleanup. Discussions within the Conservation Corps Youth Council focused on wanting to be a part of the process to plan and implement a Spring Park Cleanup event. After discussion of their previous roles in the event, they saw opportunities to push beyond being volunteer coordinators on the day of the event that would enable them to gain skills they were not invited to practice previously with the parks department. By planning and implementing, they determined that they would be more likely to invite their friends and family to the cleanup project. They identified that this was a way to act as community leaders, which enables their shared vision for their neighborhoods. As a result, the Conservation Corps Youth Council members and program staff planned and implemented a Spring Park Cleanup to benefit the Mississippi River watershed in Saint Paul, Minnesota. Council members invited youth program alumni, friends, and family of the Conservation Corps to attend the trash cleanup. Conservation Corps Youth Council members mapped routes for several groups to do trash cleanup in different neighborhoods. Council members surveyed the neighborhoods to identify high-need areas for the trash cleanup. A late spring snowstorm cancelled the annual Spring Parks Cleanup event that typically engages more than 1,000 volunteers in different parks across Saint Paul. The Conservation Corps Youth Council decided to move their event to the following weekend as a result of the storm. On the day before their planned event, another late season snowstorm left about two inches of snow on the ground. As an example of their confidence in managing an event, I was unable to attend the project to help with logistics due to a death in my family, but I had confidence in their ability to manage an event. The Conservation Corps Youth Council members proceeded with the project and successfully led volunteers in trash cleanup and educational activities.

The Conservation Corps Youth Council values the empowerment processes experienced by youth and adults to identify issues and understand problems together. To accomplish this, the Conservation Corps Youth Council found that there were several steps needed to partner with and invite youth in decision-making processes within the organization. First, the Conservation Corps Youth Council members created an interview protocol with current youth program participants, youth workers, staff members, and the board of directors that focused on their perceptions and experiences of what happens before, during and after a Conservation Corps youth program. From this process, members provide an additional platform to better understand more clearly how these specific groups in the organization think the programs work to achieve its goals and objectives. For example, Council members interview youth program participants on their first day of the program, during the program, in the final closing week, and one month after their participation. Once the interviews are completed, members analyze and prepare data for presentation to the larger community—youth workers, program staff, and the board of directors. As a result of the interviews and presentations of data, this project has increased reflective dialogue within the Conservation Corps youth programs. Conservation Corps Youth Council members have presented their findings at board of directors and staff meetings. Staff and board members have the opportunity to hear and ask questions related to data gathered by Council members from their interviews with Conservation Corps youth participants.

To support the involvement of the Conservation Corps Youth Council members in meetings, facilitators found it was necessary to train adults and Council members before, during, and after meetings. For example, before the meetings it was necessary for each group to be prompted with questions they would discuss at the meeting. During the meetings, facilitators helped the groups focus on the interview protocol developed by Council members that focused on their perceptions of what it is like to be a young person in the youth programs. This activity was the impetus for additional meetings to support creating a program model for the Conservation Corps Youth Council together with Council members, program staff, and Board of Directors.

AN EMERGING MODEL

Throughout the beginning stages of the development of the Council, we learned how critical it is to foster relationships between youth and adults that can effect systematic changes in structural decision-making within the agency and its partners. The Council deemed it important to sustain this effort to create conditions that foster relationships between youth and adults in the agency. The Council found that this was one of their functional purposes as a group—to be clear about their aims and goals. The Council's aims contributed to learning new social skills that were not deemed possible or even desired before the Council was formed. A challenge to this work was communicating this effort to the program staff, youth workers, board of directors, and other stakeholders. To combat this challenge, the Council decided to focus on creating a model that would serve as a communications tool for what they hope to accomplish in their present and future work. The emerging model was created in a series of activities with Council members and program staff. This was accomplished by first reviewing the interview data that Council members received from previous interviews with program participants. This data was reviewed and analyzed to look for common themes in what youth participants were saying about their experiences with the Conservation Corps youth programs. After this review, themes were then shared with the participants as part of the interviews by email and other personal communications. The participants of the interviews were asked to share feedback on the themes that were developed by the Council. Next, the Council participated in a mapping activity that focused on finding descriptive words from the themes that symbolized best practices of their work between youth and adults in the agency. These words were then placed into several core themes in the program model. To further the Council members and program staff knowledge of what program models were, they were invited to research this concept. This was done either through their direct participation in a youth program they were connected with or through an online search of youth program models. During the next meeting, the Council and program staff came together to share what they found. After this presentation of existing program models, everyone was invited to develop their own program models based on best practices for the Conservation Corps Youth Council.

After reviewing the activities and program models, the Council chose to adapt an existing model that was produced to support individual students to be successful in mathematics and science (Jolly, Campbell & Perlman, 2004). The model the Council adapted aims to foster a collaborative approach to participation that includes youth and adults in intergenerational relationships that build on analytical and critical thinking skills (see Figure 12.1). Five programmatic elements are most important for the Conservation Corps Youth Council. The Conservation Corps Youth Council Program Model below illustrates how these elements interact.

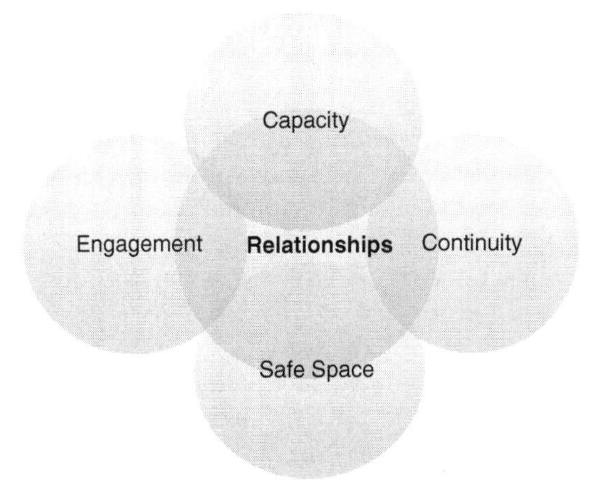

Figure 12.1 Conservation Corps Youth Council Program Model[1]

The middle circle, Relationships, is where all four elements intersect. This identifies that there are four equal parts to nurturing relationships by achieving:

- engagement—what draws the youth and adult participant to work together;
- continuity—pathway or system that offers resources necessary for advancement and collaboration;
- capacity—fundamental knowledge needed to advance to more rigorous or advanced levels;
- safe spaces—physical and emotional environment.

An attention to relationship building between youth and adults, as well as among youth participants, is a central component to the success of the Conservation Corps Youth Council. By starting with relationships, which is perhaps the most important element of all, young people are able to feel safe, be engaged, have the capacity to become more involved, and experience the continuity to further their own development.

Opportunities Through a Culture of Participation

Through creating an organizational culture of youth participation, the following guidelines are simultaneously created and utilized together by youth and adults in the agency. The development of the Conservation Corps Youth Council Program Model assisted in defining the following guidelines by Council members and staff in the agency.

- Youth and adults work together: Youth Council activities in collaboration with youth and adults. Young people in the youth council make decisions on how activities are done for youth alumni and supporting youth participants in partnership with program staff.
- Promoting understanding and respecting differences: Because the council is diverse, there are multiple opportunities for young people from different cultural backgrounds to be together in a safe environment, share experiences and develop understanding of each other.
- Open to youth alumni: The Conservation Corps Youth Council is a leadership opportunity for Conservation Corps youth program alumni that are 15 to 18 years old.
- Participation and inclusion: Every youth member gets a chance to express their voice, views and participation in the program.
- Develop skills and experiences: Engaging in fun activities offers new experiences, providing opportunities that they would not have normally had.
- Reflections: Reflect and evaluate experiences that have they have been involved in from team-building activities to planning service-learning

projects. They reflect on what they did and what worked, and what they would do differently next time around.

- Continuation of the Conservation Corps Youth Council and youth programs: The Conservation Corps Youth Council supports the continuation of the council and youth programs by helping in outreach efforts, producing supporting materials, and providing funding.
- Create together: The Conservation Corps Youth Council believes it is important for young people to actively participate in collaborative processes by implementing research, evaluation, and planning of youth programs together with program staff.
- Celebration: The focus of the Conservation Corps Youth Council is the importance of celebrating accomplishments and sharing what they have learned while providing opportunities for participants, peers, and families to express this pride.

Skill Sets to Foster a Culture of Participation

The breadth and depth of the skills needed to facilitate this process with diverse communities speaks to the need for organizational commitments and resources. These are needed to support the recruitment and on-going professional development of staff and the training of youth and adults in decision-making processes. One of the hardest parts of the facilitation of the Conservation Corps Youth Council is the development of adults—including me. That is, we have a lot to learn, such as often difficult lessons on how to be a good adult partner and facilitator when collaborate with people to effect systematic changes in the organizations and institutions that affect our lives.

I believe there are two skill sets of facilitators of these processes that highlight the beneficial aspects of co-creating a culture of participation through a youth council. The first skill set; it is necessary to maximize impact within the organization by including all stakeholders. As a facilitator and advocate, I believe it is necessary for a youth council to be seen as critical to the immediate wellbeing of the organization, communities, and institutions, not just the youth council members involved. This skill set looks to create an atmosphere to make sure youth voice is heard and acted upon appropriately from youth councils within the institution or organization.

I believe this skill set engages in reflective dialogue, both with youth and amongst program staff. The reflective dialogue can be a difficult process for the facilitator. For example, young people advocating for something program staff may not want can establish a difficult challenge to both staff and the facilitator. As a facilitator, it is important to work together with youth and program staff to develop a capacity to respond effectively to a youth council and make it a productive part of a continuous improvement process within the agency or institution.

To do this, it is necessary to begin with co-constructing the democratic spaces and conditions between youth and adults in a youth council. This must be done together with all stakeholders, including the council members, the council members' peers and families, program staff, and organizational leaders. Through this process I have learned we must define co-construction of the principles and guidelines as an integral and basic right of the council members when creating a youth council. This will be most beneficial when youth and adults work together and are valued for their participation in helping with identifying best management practices, problems or issues, and how to best utilize and support a youth council.

The second skill set identifies the importance of advocating and allowing time to write and reflect about the work with and on behalf of youth. I have found it beneficial to do this while also including Conservation Corps Youth Council members in my writing process. This has shined light on their experiences and held me accountable to be truthful to myself and utilize them as a sounding board of our work together. Furthermore, through the process of writing and reflection, I have been able to capture dialogue, create intentional projects, and increase my own self-awareness of work with and on behalf youth. This process stretches my capacity to reach beyond previous knowledge and enhances my understanding of building a culture of participation together through our achievements and sense of satisfaction. I believe that when this process is actively engaged it pushes beyond individual learning and development and focuses on changing surroundings or environments for youth and adults to work in partnership to collectively address issues.

This skill set requests facilitation of group dialogue between youth and adults. As a facilitator of this process, it is necessary to acknowledge the different skills and knowledge of Council members and staff. We found that Council members and staff differed in their relationship with experiences about a specific issue or topic. As a result, it is important that the group establishes ground rules on best management practices of group dialogue. This helps to make sure all participants are invited to speak regardless of their knowledge of the topic. In addition, we found that it was important to engage in trainings to assist Council members and staff to provide appropriate feedback and recommendations. By establishing ground rules on group dialogue and engagement of trainings we increased the opportunities for Council members and staff to work together. This attention to balancing the conversation affects how shared decision-making generates a process of cognitive, social, and emotional interchange between all stakeholders.

These two key skill sets suggest that when youth and adults work together they are more likely to succeed when a 'third party' provides coaching and support to both adults and youth. This will require significant work, and it is necessary to stay committed to young people. The problems, issues, and challenges facing youth agencies, institutions, and our communities are becoming more global and complex. This suggests the need for youth and adults to work together to be a platform for joint action and crucial discussions on common issues and problems that affect them and our communities.

To strengthen our efforts towards developing and sustaining this work, we must look to young people as allies. As allies, we can empower and partner together to advance and increase the intentionality of our work. When young people are viewed as part of the solution, we encourage positive behavior of both youth and adults.

CONCLUSION

The Conservation Corps Youth Council is a model that is lived through the efforts to create meaningful conditions that foster a culture of participation between youth and adults. The active participation of youth in this agency contributes to an inclusive society that values social learning. By removing institutional barriers that keep youth from actively participating in their own lives and communities, we can seek social justice and democratic conditions that foster a better world where authentic, respectful, and understanding relationships can be built between youth and adults, providing a platform for crucial discussions and joint action. An example of these democratic values is contributed by Fusco and Heathfield (2015): True democracy demands equal representation and voice among all citizens across age, gender, race, class, sexual preference, religion, and political affiliation. It does not presume equality but rather assumes that there is dominant power that has no interest in shifting the status quo. Democracy's role, then, is to antagonize such power relations in order to ensure decision-making remains representative (Fusco & Heathfield, 2015). Adults are the gatekeepers to government, school, housing, food, and news media. Through our positions, we hold the capacity to disconnect and deny young people access to ways of being civically engaged. Every community member, educator, planner, community decision maker, and community advocacy group has the ability to partner with and invite youth participation in authentic projects and issues meaningful to them and to others. There is an ongoing need to provide access and to create inclusive environments for young people rather than blocking them from participation in their/our community.

NOTE

1. Adapted from Jolly, E., Campbell, P., & Perlman, L. (2004). *Engagement, capacity and continuity: A trilogy for student success*. Retrieved from http://www.campbell-kibler.com

REFERENCES

Bradford, S., & Cullen, F. (2012). *Research and research methods for youth practitioners*. New York, NY: Routledge.

Checkoway, B., & Richards-Schuster, K. (2004). Youth participation in evaluation and research as a way of lifting new voices. *Children, Youth and Environments, 14*(2), 84–98. Retrieved from http://www.colorado.edu/journals/cye/

Dewey, J. (1922). *Human nature and conduct*. New York, NY: The Modern Library.
Fusco, D., & Heathfield, M. (2015). *Modeling democracy: Is youth participation enough? Italian Journal of Sociology of Education, 7*(1), 12–31.
Hehir, T., & Wilkens (2008). Deaf education and bridging social capitol: A theoretical approach. *American Annals of the Deaf, 153*(3), 275–284.
Jeffs, T., & Smith, M. (2012). *Youth work practice*. New York, NY: Palgrave Macmillan.
Jolly, E., Campbell, P., & Perlman, L. (2004). *Engagement, capacity and continuity: A trilogy for student success*. Retrieved from http://www.campbell-kibler.com
Kirby, P., Lanyon, C., Cronin, K., & Sinclair, R. (2003). *Building a culture of participation: Involving children and young people in policy, service planning, delivery and evaluation*. Retrieved from http://www.gyerekesely.hu/childpoverty/docs/involving_children_report.pdf
Percy-Smith, B. (2007). You think you know? You have no idea: youth participation in health policy development. *Health Education Research, 22*(6), 879–894.
Roholt, R. V., Baizerman, M., & Hildreth, R. W. (2013). Introduction: A big surprise?. In M. Baizerman, R. W. Hildreth, & R. V. Roholt (Eds.), *Civic youth work: Co-creating democratic youth spaces* (pp. 1–9). Chicago, IL: Lyceum Books.
Sabo-Flores, K. (2008). *Youth participatory evaluation: Strategies for engaging young people*. San Francisco, CA: Jossey—Bass.
Vygotsky, L. S. (1978). *Mind and society: The development of higher mental processes*. Cambridge, MA: Harvard University Press.
Williams, A., Ferguson, D., & Yohalem, N. (2013). *Youth organizing for educational change*. Retrieved from http://forumfyi.org/files/Youth_Organizing_for_Education_0.pdf

13 Indigenous Youth and Higher Education

The Role of Shipibo Youth Organizations in the Peruvian Amazon Region

Oscar Espinosa

The Shipibo, or officially 'Shipibo-Konibo,' is the third-largest Indigenous people living in the Peruvian Amazon region. The traditional territory of the Shipibo people includes a large portion of the Ucayali basin, which is formed by the Ucayali river and its tributaries. The last national census, in 2007 calculated the Shipibo population at around 23,000 persons, although it could be a larger population, reaching up to 30,000. According to the same official census, 42% of the Shipibo population are children and teenagers under the age of 14; approximately 18%–25% live in the urban areas of Pucallpa and Yarinacocha (Tournon, 2002); and most of these are young people.

The Shipibo people have been in contact with Western society since the 16th century when the first Spanish conquistadores arrived to the Ucayali basin (Myers 1974; Salinas Loyola, 1557), but most especially through the contact with Catholic missionaries since the 17th century. This long-standing relationship has enabled the Shipibo people to creatively adapt themselves to Western civilization and, since the 20th century, also to life in the city, although at the same time they have maintained their own cultural traits and traditions both in rural and urban areas. Particularly important are the creation of urban Shipibo communities in different Peruvian cities, such as Tingo Maria, Pucallpa, and Lima, as spaces where they can reproduce some aspects of their communal life.

The experience of youth is relatively new for most Indigenous peoples in the Amazon region (see Virtanen, 2007 for a review). Until a few decades ago, children became adults after initiation rituals at puberty. As soon as a girl or a boy was able to biologically reproduce, and after giving proof that they were capable of obtaining the necessary food to survive, they were ready to become parents. Thus, a new social group of 'youth'—composed mainly of teenagers and young people in their early 20s—appeared in Indigenous communities along with Western culture, school, and modern urban life. In some cases, the phenomenon is so new that neither the young people nor their parents know how to deal with this life period. In many places throughout the Amazon region, the number of suicides or sudden violent episodes between teenagers and adults could be a sign of this maladjustment.

Particularly relevant is the attraction of Indigenous communities to education. As in other societies, many Indigenous families believe that education secures their path to progress. According to Roperto Noningo Sesén (2001), most parents in Amazonian Indigenous communities repeat constantly "I don't want my children to be frustrated like myself. . ." He adds that this phrase, repeated almost like a mantra, has had an enduring influence among Indigenous children and teenagers who now believe in the importance of working hard in order to succeed in their studies. Therefore, the majority of families in the Amazon region try to secure for their children at least the completion of primary school and, if possible, secondary school (high school). According to Patricia Ames (2002), in Shipibo communities located in the Upper Ucayali basin, primary school appears to be the minimum desired by all parents.

Secondary school often implies a special effort in time, money, and dedication for both parents and children. Nowadays, practically all Indigenous communities in the Amazon region have a local primary school. The Peruvian government requires the existence of at least 25 children in the community to open a primary school with one bilingual teacher. However, this is not the case for secondary school. Only large communities can ensure a significant number of students, and therefore most families have to send their children away to another community to continue studying. Unlike urban settings, the distance between the community where the home of the family is located and the community where the high school is located could be several hours by boat, so families need to pay for food and lodging in order to continue studying. Nonetheless, the number of Indigenous families making this special effort to secure the education for their children has grown through time.

It is important to mention that the separation of the children from their homes does not only imply an economic or emotional cost for the families but also has an important impact on the cultural and moral education of the children. In many Indigenous societies in the Amazon region, the early hours of the morning (usually between 4 and 5 a.m.) is a crucial moment in family life: They talk together, tell ancient stories, decide upon important family matters, and learn about the world and how to behave with others. Afterwards, during the day, the younger siblings stay near the house, supervised by older siblings or other close relatives. Later on, the boys accompany their fathers and the girls their mothers on their trips to the river, fields, or forest, learning how to fish, hunt, and cultivate the land while talking with their parents and learning about their culture, the animals, the trees, and how to cure oneself—learning about everything possible, both the trivial and the profound. It is also important to note that, traditionally, Indigenous children in the Amazon are not expected to work for the family. They may help out with simple chores, but they do not work. Moreover, children in the Amazon traditionally have been raised under a great liberty. Amazonian peoples encourage their children's autonomy, and it is very rare to see

Indigenous parents intervening in their kids' affairs and even more rare to punish them.

The great majority of the Indigenous youth in the Amazon region are therefore in close contact with educational institutions and, in growing numbers each year, with city life. However, both formal education and city life are ambiguous for Indigenous peoples. They offer tools for defending themselves in a hostile and racist society but at the same time endanger some basic traits of their traditional culture, especially the use of their own language and, in the Shipibo case, the knowledge about plants and spiritual life, which are crucial aspects of their way of life.

The urban setting, with its everyday contact with *mestizo* culture, demands from young Indigenous people strong adaptive skills that ultimately intensify the process of losing their Indigenous language, customs, and values. Modern life and education are not a free ride. If they want to succeed in their education and be socially accepted, they will probably have to lose something in return. This process of cultural negotiation, however, cannot be explained by acculturation, as was suggested in the anthropological studies of the past century. Social and anthropological theories of the last decades have shown us that interactions between dominant and Indigenous societies are more complex: there is a powerful cultural domination, but there are also Indigenous agency, resistance, and negotiation.

CHALLENGES FACED BY SHIPIBO YOUNG MEN AND WOMEN NOWADAYS

Access to Higher Education

As mentioned before, the majority of Shipibo families have satisfied their expectation of having their children finishing primary school. The obvious next step is to have them completing their secondary school (high school), and to continue, if possible, their studies at a higher education institution. There are different reasons behind the desire for pursuing higher education studies. One of the most important ones is to gain a better social place within Peruvian society. Most Indigenous parents, and also young people, believe that through higher education they may avoid discrimination and gain enough money to enable them to have access to new objects and services linked to modern life. At the same time, the new knowledge and capabilities obtained through higher education can help them become more efficient leaders or members of their communities and Indigenous societies and thus depend less on the professional services offered by non-Indigenous people. This is clearly the case of those persons who pursue careers in law, the medical sciences, agricultural and environmental sciences, etc.

In the last decade, the number of Indigenous young people completing secondary studies who wish to continue studying has grown exponentially, and for the first time in the history of the Peruvian Amazon region there are a significant number of Indigenous young people from this region studying in universities and in other higher education institutions. According to the 1993 national census, approximately 3,000 Indigenous persons from the Peruvian Amazon (of 229,497 registered in this census) had access to at least one year of higher education studies, representing approximately 1.5% of the total Indigenous population from the Amazon region registered in this census. In the 2007 national census, this number grew to more than 9,000 persons, representing approximately 2.7% of the total Indigenous population. However, it is important to indicate that both censuses only registered information from rural communities, leaving out a large portion of Indigenous persons who had access to higher education and who were living in a city in those years. The lack of evidence in this case is crucial due to the fact that usually the persons who have access to higher education tend to live in a city.

If we consider only the number of Indigenous persons finishing their higher education studies, or if we only consider the number of those finishing university studies, the number will decrease significantly because the majority only have access to technical schools or to teacher education programs. There are many reasons to explain this fact. For the Indigenous youth, to pursue courses of study for technical careers or to become teachers has a series of advantages: they are cheaper; it takes less time to finish them (two or three years as opposed to the traditional five for undergraduate studies at a university); they require less academic effort; and, eventually, the knowledge they acquire may be put into use easily either in an urban or rural milieu, thus enabling them to obtain employment quickly. Another advantage lies in the fact that there are technical institutes in smaller cities, closer to the rural communities. There are also a few Indigenous communities who are proud to have a technical institute, among them the Shipibo community of Caco Macaya in the Upper Ucayali River. In larger cities, Indigenous young people can have access to a wide variety of these institutes. Nonetheless, these advantages do not imply that all students finish their careers, although the number of those who abandon at mid-career is considerably lower than those studying at a university. In effect, a study done at the beginning of the 21st century (Espinosa, 2007) showed that out of a group of Shipibo students who received scholarships for Higher Education programs, thirty graduated from Technical Institutes while only twelve completed their coursework in Universities.

One of the main obstacles for Indigenous teenagers is their educational background. For those coming from rural areas, the poor quality of education received in their communities constitutes a major setback. Although the Indigenous peoples in Peru continuously demand Indigenous bilingual teachers for their schools, local authorities from the Ministry of Education still favor *mestizo* teachers. Moreover, these authorities send the worst teachers or the newest and youngest ones to these communities, and most of the time they are not prepared to teach in a bilingual and intercultural setting. By the end of their education, most Indigenous teenagers finishing secondary school in the Amazon are not only unprepared for higher education and life in the city but also for life in their own communities because they have wasted valuable hours during their socialization process in classrooms while losing important opportunities to learn from their parents, grandparents, and their environment. In the case of those who have studied at a secondary school in a city, their chances improve a little due to the fact that they will be competing with other young people who studied in similar schools. However, if they obtain a scholarship to study in Lima or in more prestigious universities, they become handicapped again.

On the other side of the relationship, most universities are not prepared for receiving, accommodating, or tutoring Indigenous students. The lack of special programs or offices for Indigenous students is also a problem in those universities located in the Amazon region. The majority do not include an intercultural perspective in their study plans, and this is also true for the two intercultural universities that are currently active in the Amazon region.

Indigenous young people wishing to continue their studies in higher education institutions encounter a wide variety of academic, economic, social, and cultural challenges and obstacles. According to Noningo (2001), some of the reasons why Indigenous students abandon their studies are: the education is not related to the Amazonian reality, thus not preparing the students to become professionals engaged with their own milieu; there are very few chances for obtaining a job; and finally, there is a lack of social and emotional support that eventually contribute to cultural identity crisis and a lack of communication with their own parents and their own people.

Everywhere, higher education studies require some basic level of academic knowledge and capabilities. However, the majority of Indigenous students from the Amazon region have had a deficient basic education that leaves them without a proficient use of Spanish language. Moreover, although most of them have received a bilingual education, they are not proficient in either Spanish or their own language. This lack of proficiency does not refer only to written expression but sometimes also to the oral use of the language. Thus, the Indigenous students at higher education institutions have a hard time understanding the classes or required readings. A similar problem is faced in math classes. A few years ago, I personally observed the great capability of Shipibo students for learning math and working with numbers, even with complex formulas and equations. However, the main obstacle they face is their proficiency in Spanish does not allow them to properly understand math problems verbally formulated. The problem was not with the numbers but with the language. In addition to the lack of proficiency in Spanish, Indigenous students—like most other Peruvian students from rural or urban poor backgrounds—lack adequate knowledge and skills needed for higher education.

In order to improve their basic education, Indigenous parents send their children to a nearby city to study in high school. This practice is becoming more common in the Amazon region. Studies in an urban high school do not guarantee access to higher education institutions, but at least Indigenous students become more proficient in the Spanish language. A bonus advantage of living in a city is that children will also learn the ways of urban life sooner and thus avoid the experience of future culture shock.

Racism and Emotional Challenges

Unlike academic or economic challenges, social and cultural obstacles are less visible, but are often the main reason why Indigenous students drop out of higher education programs. According to Noningo (2001), for Indigenous students, higher education in the city is often accompanied by the experience of suffering racist discrimination and the experience of culture shock. Most authorities, professors, and students at the higher education institutions are not familiar with the social and cultural background of the Indigenous students from the Amazon region. This is also true for the institutions located at the Amazon region. This attitude is often justified by arguing that Indigenous students should be treated in the same way as other students because all of them 'are equal.' However, this argument may hide a more subtle form of racism: By referring to an abstract discourse on equality, it justifies the situation of unequal access to higher education and takes away the responsibility for the establishment of culturally adequate policies and practices.

In some cases, there is no attempt to hide explicit discrimination, even at the intercultural universities such as the Universidad Nacional Intercultural de la Amazonia (UNIA; the Intercultural National University of the Amazon), located in the city of Pucallpa. In the year 2010, the Indigenous students from this university went on a long strike protesting racism and discrimination against them (Sarfaty, 2011). The majority of Indigenous students feel marginalized within their own higher education institutions. There are different ways in which racism and discrimination is perceived. At San Marcos University, some Indigenous students mentioned that they were not chosen by the other students to form study groups. In other cases, the non-Indigenous students mock the heavy accent with which they speak. Indigenous students are often referred to with offensive words or receive offensive nicknames.

This situation occurs not only in the capital city of Lima but also in the regional city of Pucallpa, where a fifth of the Shipibo population live. For decades, the *mestizo* population of Pucallpa has regarded the Shipibo—who contemptuously are called *chama*—as people who are inferior, savage, ignorant, and incapable of learning and who should only aspire to work in the city as servants or in menial positions. Sarfaty (2011) has shown, in the case of UNIA and in the city of Pucallpa, how racism is still very active nowadays and how the Indigenous students are victims of discrimination.

The final outcome of these discriminatory practices is low self-esteem among Indigenous students and consequent shyness, insecurity, and a sentiment of inferiority. Sometimes it also leads to cases of depression and, eventually, abandonment of their studies. The majority of Indigenous students often express their fear of being discriminated against, and thus some try to hide their origins, to deny their ethnic identity, and to become ashamed of their own cultural background and families.

The experience of being discriminated against is perceived by the Indigenous students as probably one of the most important difficulties of living in an urban setting far away from home and family. For those Indigenous students who have also traveled to cities outside the Amazon region, the emotional impact and culture shock is more profound. They need to deal not only with new customs and a new social surrounding but also with different weather and meals. The rate of abandonment and dropping out is higher among Indigenous students living far away from the Amazon region, in cities like Lima or Cusco.

In a survey I conducted in 2002 among Shipibo teenagers living in Pucallpa and Yarinacocha, when asked what they disliked most about life in the city, the majority answered 'parties.' I was surprised by the answer. My first thought was that I was facing a group of religious fanatics who rejected having fun for moral reasons. However, when I interviewed them individually, they assured me that they were normal, healthy teenagers who enjoyed partying. The problem was attending *mestizo* parties in the city, where they did not know the cultural codes for romance or behaving adequately, making going to parties a stressful situation.

Economic Difficulties and Lack of Job Offers

Another set of challenges faced by Indigenous students is related to the lack of economic means while studying. Even in the case of public institutions, students are always in need of money: Besides housing and boarding expenses, they need to buy books or photocopy articles; they need notebooks and school materials; they need access to Internet, transportation, etc. For the majority of Indigenous students, the economic support received from their parents is usually very modest. In some cases, their families send some money or food, especially if these students live in a city located nearby in the Amazon. Therefore, the most common way to solve their economic needs has been to work while studying. However, it is not easy for Indigenous students to find either academic-related jobs or well-paid jobs that would enable them to continue their studies easily. Usually they have access to time-consuming jobs with low salaries, which forces them to advance slowly in their studies and sometimes to abandon them temporarily or definitely.

In other cases, the Indigenous students have tried to obtain scholarships. Until recently, most Indigenous students do not have the know-how or the social capital needed to have direct access to scholarship programs, so they depend on the initiatives and contacts established by Indigenous organizations or non-governmental organizations (NGOs) related to their communities, as will be discussed later. However, in 2013 this situation started to change with the establishment of a new program from the Peruvian government to provide scholarships for students classified as 'very poor.'

HELPING SHIPIBO YOUTH FACE THESE CHALLENGES

Through time there have been a wide variety of persons and institutions working with Shipibo young men and women, especially those living in the cities of Pucallpa and Lima. Among these are not only state offices but also different programs carried by NGOs, churches or religious congregations, and, of course, the Shipibo Indigenous organizations.

Official State Programs

In Peru, the only official public policies for Indigenous students are part of a recent initiative regarding the access of 'poor' students to higher education institutions. This program is called Beca 18 (Scholarship 18), and it helps students finishing high school who have already been accepted into a higher education institution to receive economic aid. This scholarship covers both university fees as well as a monthly allowance for meals, boarding, and other expenses. The other requirement is that the students or their families have been included in the database of the Ministry of Development and Social Inclusion as 'poor families.' The first year in which this program was implemented was 2013, so there is little experience and still some problems in its application, especially regarding the criteria for selecting who should be considered 'poor.'

The Indigenous students from the Amazon region could apply to this scholarship through two different channels: through the regular program as members of Indigenous communities or through the special program for those who want to become bilingual teachers. In both cases, there is a limited list of higher education institutions where they can apply, and there is also a limited list of career possibilities offered by these institutions.

In 2014, there were only four universities in Peru accepting Indigenous students from this scholarship program: three are located in the capital city of Lima (Cayetano Heredia, San Ignacio de Loyola, and Universidad Científica del Sur) and one located in the city of Chachapoyas (Universidad Mario Peláez Bazán), which is located in an Andean area near the Amazon region. All four of them are private universities. Regarding the programs offered to Indigenous students, there are serious limitations. For example, at the

Cayetano Heredia University, the most prestigious private university in the field of the medical sciences, Indigenous students can apply to the following programs: health administration, nursing, psychology, or nutrition; they cannot apply to study medicine or odontology. In a similar vein, the other universities offer a few programs that the universities see fit for the Indigenous students.

Public national universities enroll Indigenous students only in cases when they pass the exams prepared by each university. As mentioned before, most Indigenous students are not prepared to compete with urban mestizo students due to bad primary and secondary schooling. There have been, however, some exceptions, and a few public universities have had special programs for Indigenous students. This was the case at the University of San Marcos, the oldest and most prestigious public university in Peru. San Marcos offered a special channel of admission for Indigenous students between the years 1999 and 2012. This initiative allowed Indigenous students from the Amazon region to compete against other Indigenous students rather than mestizo students. However, as in the case with the Beca 18 program, the space available for Indigenous students depended on each department. Thus, in the linguistics department there were 15 spaces for Indigenous students, while there were none in law or medicine. Moreover, although the university offered free lunch and some spaces at the university residence halls for the Indigenous students, there were problems due to the low grades obtained by them. At San Marcos, if students want to have access to the dining room or to the residence halls, they need an average of 15 over 20 points (or roughly a grade of C). When the university authorities realized that practically all the Indigenous students were obtaining lower grades than those required for board and food support, a specialized office was created to solve this situation.

Civil Society: Religious Associations, Churches, and NGOs

Besides the official programs, there are different institutions in civil society interested in aiding Indigenous students to succeed in entering or completing their studies at higher education institutions. These institutions are usually religious associations or NGOs. There are a few of these institutions working with Shipibo students during the last decade. One of the most successful programs is the one offered by the Centro Antropológico de Antropología y Aplicación Práctica (CAAAP) in Pucallpa. CAAAP is a Catholic NGO, and since the late 1990s has offered a program that consists mainly in remedial courses and tutoring for Indigenous students who want to pursue higher education studies. Another interesting case is the Nopoki program in Atalaya. Nopoki is an initiative of the Catholic Bishop of San Ramón for Indigenous students in those communities in the vicinity of Atalaya, and it functions as a decentralized program of the Catholic University Sedes Sapientiae of Lima. There are also more specific initiatives in which different

NGOs, such as Warmayllu, support some intercultural activities developed at UNIA in Pucallpa.[1]

It is important to add that there are also international NGOs, religious associations, and higher education institutions which offer different kinds of scholarships for Indigenous students. And, finally, in the last decade some international oil companies have begun offering some scholarships for Indigenous students. However, in this last case, sometimes the Indigenous communities view these scholarships as bribes offered by these enterprises to convince them to accept their activities within their territory.

Indigenous Organizations

The local, regional, and national Indigenous organizations from the Peruvian Amazon region have been very active in demanding access to higher education and State support for their Indigenous students. Since the 1980s, some of these organizations have obtained scholarships and have signed agreements with different universities and higher education institutes for this purpose. A notorious case is that of the Asociación Interétnica de Desarrollo de la Selva Peruana (AIDESEP; the Inter-Ethnic Association for the Development of the Peruvian Jungle), the most important national Indigenous organization from the Peruvian Amazon region. Since its origins in 1980, AIDESEP's Educational Program has made important efforts for securing scholarships for Indigenous students. The Scandinavian countries have been particularly generous supporting AIDESEP with higher education scholarships. Between the years 1983 and 1987, and again between 1991 and 1995, AIDESEP obtained scholarships for 61 Indigenous students to study at different universities in Lima (Chirinos & Leyva, 2004). However, almost half of these students could not finish their studies. This high dropout rate led many funding institutions and NGOs to stop aiding AIDESEP with scholarships. The economic factor was the main reason for dropping out. On different occasions, some of the students supported by AIDESEP told me that this economic aid was not enough. The money they received only covered the tuition fees and boarding expenses, so they had to work for their food and other expenses. But there were also other reasons that impeded their studies, especially academic problems, lack of tutors and advisors, and the general social and cultural challenges explained before.

Other Indigenous organizations have also struggled supporting Indigenous students access to higher education institutions. For the Shipibo students, the role of the Federación de Comunidades Nativas del Ucayali (FECONAU; Federation of Native Communities of Ucayali) has been very important. FECONAU was created in 1981, and for many decades was the most important Shipibo organization, representing approximately 130 Shipibo communities located along the Ucayali river.[2] From 1982 to 1983, FECONAU obtained almost 20 scholarships for Shipibo students. However, in a similar manner to what happened with the AIDESEP scholarships, the high rate of dropouts led to a difficulty in obtaining more scholarships, until the creation of COCEBESH, which will be discussed later. FECONAU tried to solve the lack of funding by directly negotiating with the universities and higher education institutions for a place for Shipibo students. Thus, FECONAU established different agreements with the Switzerland Technological Institute of Pucallpa, the National University of Ucayali (UNU), the National Agrarian University of Tingo María(UNAS), and with the National University "Enrique Guzmán y Valle" (UNE).

Shipibo Youth Associations

Despite all the initiatives mentioned above, the most interesting work with Shipibo Indigenous students has been done and is being done by other Shipibo young people. As described elsewhere (Espinosa, 2012), since the 1970s, Shipibo students have organized themselves in ethnic youth associations in order to be recognized as Indigenous students and to find common solutions to the problems they faced as Indigenous students in the city. The distance from their families and communities, in addition to the new life in the city, was perceived by the young students as a perilous situation that endangered their cultural identity. In effect, these young men and women faced the challenge of acquiring the skills and knowledge specific to modern Western culture while at the same time maintaining and recreating their own traditions and culture. Therefore, an important dimension prioritized by these youth associations was the promotion of activities oriented toward the diffusion and valorization of their cultural heritage.

These associations also were designed to express the general needs, rights, and demands of Indigenous students. In this sense, they are not only groups for emotional support or mutual aid, but also an instance of representation through which the Shipibo students channel and express their claims. Moreover, the establishment of these organizations coincided in those years with a general political climate that favored this type of activism. The Shipibo youngsters had the opportunity to become involved with other social struggles taking place in the city, including those of marginal urban dwellers, teachers and student unions, and diverse political parties active in the region. For these young Shipibo people, the discovery of the importance of their cultural heritage and the experience of political activism were part of the same process of becoming 'Indigenous subjects' or, in other words, of acquiring an 'ethnic consciousness.' Moreover, all these experiences provided them with a valuable training in leadership and political skills.

There is a large list of Shipibo youth associations to help them cope with the challenges of higher education: the Consejo de Estudiantes Nativos del Ucayali (CENU; Native Student Council of Ucayali); the Consejo de Estudiantes Shipibos Universitarios (CESHU; Shipibo University Students Council); the Association of Shipibo Students in Lima (ADESHIL); the Asociación Cultural Shipibo-Lima (Shipibo Cultural Association); and, also in Lima, although not exclusively for Shipibo students, the Asociación Indígena de Estudiantes Universitarios de la Amazonía Peruana (AAUPI; Association of Indigenous University Students from the Peruvian Amazon), whose current president (2012–2014) is a Shipibo student at La Cantuta National University.

But among all the different Shipibo youth associations that have been created since the 1970s, there is one in particular that I want to highlight: the Comité Central de Becas para Shipibos (COCEBESH; Central Committee for Shipibo Scholarships). Unlike other Shipibo youth associations, COCEBESH was directly created in 1990 as an answer to the academic, economic, and cultural challenges brought about by the experience of higher education that the Shipibo youth needed to address. Its main purpose was to search for scholarships for higher education studies. But the other objective of this association was to aid the best Shipibo students to satisfactorily conclude their studies. Thus, the members of COCEBESH contacted different institutions that might provide them with economic funds for financing the scholarships, and they managed the money received; at the same time, they established a system to follow and supervise the studies of the beneficiaries of these scholarships.

The persons in charge of this task were the other beneficiaries. In other words, they organized a system by which students followed up with and supervised other students: everyone supervised a colleague, and everyone was supervised by a colleague. They met as a group regularly, and besides supervising one another, the group offered space where they found emotional and moral support as well as help with their academic chores. Finally, the group of students belonging to COCEBESH interviewed the younger students in order to select those who would receive a new scholarship. The reason behind this practice was to ensure that the new applicants, and future members of COCEBESH, would be able to succeed in their studies. Moreover, they did not accept a new student until an older one had finished studying or dropped out. If the latter occurred, then the money that the dropout student was receiving went directly to the new member.

During the years that COCEBESH was active, from 1990 to 2005, more than 15 students graduated with good or excellent grades from the university, and more than 30 successfully graduated from Technical Institutes. This record is, so far, the best achieved by any program supporting Indigenous students in the Peruvian Amazon region.

CONCLUSION

The Indigenous youth in the Amazon region are facing new challenges brought by education and city life. The young Shipibo people want to access university and higher education institutions; however, this is not an easy task. They face different academic, economic, and cultural challenges. There have not been, until recently, state policies or programs to support the Indigenous students in Peru, and those being implemented at the moment need to be evaluated. Apparently, these may not be culturally adequate due to the lack of an intercultural perspective. The same could be said about the different programs and initiatives developed in the last decades by Peruvian universities and higher education institutions. At the same time, civil society associations such as NGOs and Indigenous organizations have been more proactive and more preoccupied by the challenges faced by Indigenous students. However, they have not been able to adequately support them either. The most successful institutions have been those organized by the Indigenous youth themselves. The different Shipibo youth associations created since the 1970s constitute an interesting example of what Indigenous young people can do for themselves and for other Indigenous students. The experience of COCEBESH results are particularly relevant, and although it does not exist anymore, it could be a model to follow in the future.

NOTES

1. There are also similar experiences in other parts of the Peruvian Amazon region. Examples include the Waymaku Center of the Catholic Church, which aids and supports Awajun and Wampis Indigenous students living and studying in the city of Jaén; the CAAAP programs in the cities of Satipo and La Merced, which support Ashaninka youth; and others.
2. At the beginning of the 21st century, FECONAU was practically replaced by ORAU, AIDESEP'S regional organization in the Ucayali, as the main political organization in the region. However, FECOANU still exists, although much more geographically reduced and with lesser political impact.

REFERENCES

Ames, P. (2002). *Para ser iguales, para ser distintos. Educación, escritura y poder en el Perú.* Lima: Instituto de Estudios Peruanos.

Chirinos, R. A., & Leyva, M. Z. (2004). *Educación indígena en el Perú.* Informe elaborado para el Programa Observatorio de la Educación Superior del Instituto Internacional de la UNESCO para la Educación Superior en América Latina y el Caribe. Caracas: IESALC/UNESCO. Retrieved from http://www.iesalc.unesco.org.ve

Espinosa, O. (2007). *Para vivir mejor: Los indígenas amazónicos y su acceso a la educación superior en el Perú.* Fundación Equitas, Foro ISEES, Nr. 1.

Espinosa, O. (2012). To be Shipibo nowadays: The Shipibo-Konibo youth organizations as strategy for dealing with cultural change in the Peruvian Amazon Region. *Journal of Latin American and Caribbean Studies, 17*(3), 451–471.

Myers, T. P. (1974). Spanish contacts and social change on the Ucayali river, Peru. *Ethnohistory, 21*(2), 135–157.

Noningo, S. R. (2001). Juventud Indígena. *en Voz Indígena 1*(1), 26–28.

Salinas Loyola, J. de. (1557/1965). Descubrimientos, conquistas y poblaciones de Juan de Salinas Loyola. In M. Jimenez de la Espada (Eds.), *Relaciones Geográficas de Indias* (Vol. III, pp. 195–232). Madrid: Biblioteca de Autores Españoles.

Sarfaty, S. (2011). *La experiencia de ser estudiante universitario e indígena amazónico: Prácticas discriminatorias al interior de la Universidad Nacional Intercultural de la Amazonía (UNIA)*. Tesis de Licenciatura en Antropología, PUCP.

Tournon, J. (2002). *La Merma mágica. Vida e Historia de los Shipibo-Conibo del Ucayali*. Lima: CAAAP.

Virtanen, P. K. (2007). *Changing lived worlds of contemporary Amazonian Native young people*. Manchineri Youths in the Reserve and the City, Brazil-Acre. Doctoral dissertation, University of Helsinki.

14 Working for Justice in Chicago Public Schools

Judy Gall and Michael Heathfield

> We are seated in a very modern conference room in downtown Chicago on a January evening when the temperature is bumping around zero degrees Fahrenheit. There are over 200 people packed into the room and not enough chairs for all to sit. The room is also full of warmth, passion, articulacy and humor alongside some very thoughtful planning to bring these key stakeholders together. There are community organizers, public school officials, union officials, nonprofit staff and executive directors, lawyers, policy and advocacy group representatives, a sprinkling of higher education people, foundation executives and at least one police officer. Our purpose is to share, connect and strategize across the many interests and systems we are all connected to. (Field notes, M.H., January 28, 2014)

This might seem a good broad and encompassing meeting in which charting a collective path forward for restorative justice work in Chicago was the key goal. Indeed, it was. We were witnessing the culmination of 15 years of work within Chicago Public Schools (CPS) to introduce the principles and practices of restorative justice to mitigate the devastating and disproportionate effects of the school-to-prison pipeline on Chicago's young people of color. Yet, this was not the most hopeful and energizing feature of this meeting. It was the fact that at least half of the participants were young people and they were presenting, organizing, and managing the event. They were sharing the realities of their experiences within the school and criminal justice systems that often deliver injustice in their lives. They were acting on their shared commitment to build communities in which justice and equality were at the heart of human relationships.

The unchanged imperative for the many people involved in Chicago's important restorative justice work has been to ensure CPS provides safe, secure, and successful education for *all* of its students and that in its disciplinary procedures there is equity and social justice. This is a case study of incremental successes and of building an increasing community of practitioners and supporters and a demonstration of both the personal and organizational characteristics required to exert change in large systems that are central to the lives of young people. Often, these large systems espouse a commitment to the successful future of all young people while also struggling with embedded practices that defeat that noble purpose. This is not a story of good guys and bad guys but a story that demonstrates the complexity of change for social justice. It does, however, require presenting an accurate picture of inequality at work for some Chicago young people. Many adults working in the nonprofit world are driven by a calling to change unequal opportunities and outcomes for young people; this narrative explores a very specific context for this global commonality.

In this chapter we present a case study of a north side Chicago nonprofit agency called Alternatives, Inc. that has been working for over 15 years with CPS to establish restorative justice within the school system. A mixed methodology was used in the research for this chapter. A series of lengthy conversational interviews with the long-term executive director of Alternatives, Inc. (Judy Gall) provided the foundational data on which this study is built. Observation and participation at a large-scale citywide event as well as numerous shorter conversations with restorative justice practitioners (including four Alternatives, Inc. restorative justice staff) and CPS students from across the city provided additional field notes. Additionally, a document review of key records kept by the agency provided both supporting quantitative and qualitative data (Alternatives, Inc., 2010, 2011). Through these mixed data, we reflect on this long-term work within the third-largest public school system in America. We provide a historical narrative to this evolving work and present data to quantify systemic injustices and youth-led remedies. We also present the lessons learned, qualitative voices of impact, and the challenges and pitfalls encountered, and we strategize about the requirements for the work to ramp up for expanded future successes.

FORTY YEARS OF ALTERNATIVES

Alternatives, Inc., a multidimensional youth work agency on the north side of Chicago, was established in 1971 as a direct response to the drug and alcohol use of neighborhood young people. In the early 1970s, it offered a print shop and a coffee shop as two social enterprises to provide skill-building and employment opportunities to young people. Over time, it has continually adapted to the changing neighborhood context, the pertinent issues of local young people and the broader social, political, and policy context in which all of its work is grounded. During the 1980s, it was the lead youth agency in Illinois offering transitional services and targeted programming for the burgeoning Southeast Asian refugee youth and their families settling on the northeast side of Chicago.

Partnerships and collaborations have always been a central aspect of Alternatives' work, and through strategic relationships in the 1990s, it worked with over 3,000 of Chicago's young people through such initiatives as afterschool programming, gender-specific programming, school reform efforts, violence prevention, and community advocacy. Throughout this expanding influence, it has maintained a solid focus on youth participation as a central aspect of youth work for social justice. Despite the consistent scrabble for funding, challenge of managing a patchwork of income sources, changing funder demands, and complexity of sustaining human resources, it remains a somewhat unusual community agency that continues to maintain a dual focus on the provision of both clinical services and youth work.

In the late 1990s, Alternatives embarked on its pioneering work of embedding restorative justice principles and practices within the CPS system. This work began at one high school when youth worker Pat Zamora became increasingly frustrated that many of the young people she was working with were consistently getting suspended for minor infractions of the discipline code, thus making it impossible for those who needed it the most to attend school-based youth programming.

> *... suspension kept them out of class and isolated them from the school, putting them further behind.*

From that one seed planted by a youth worker in one school in 1996, Alternatives has, to date, provided training and technical assistance to over 2,000 CPS students, teachers, and administrators in over 60 schools within the CPS system. The peer mediation, peer jury, and circle work initiated at Nicholas Senn High School was an unusual place to start this work. Senn is the most diverse public high school in Illinois, with its student body representing 55 countries and speaking 44 different languages, and with 39% of students being born outside of the U.S. (Johnson, 2011; Senn, 2014). As of 2014, Alternatives' restorative justice work is happening in 11 CPS high schools and nine elementary schools across the city, with the majority of schools being on the south side of Chicago, the predominant home of the city's African American communities. This case study of the work of one small nonprofit agency must first be located within the larger systemic backdrop in which the work resides. It may seem a large and unconnected leap for the reader to move from what happens when there are everyday conflicts in high school to a review of what has occurred in the U.S. criminal justice system over the past three decades. However, if you are a young African American male living in one of Chicago's poorer neighborhoods, this is much less of a leap. Indeed, for too many young men this initial high school stumble is a fall that can have lifelong consequences. There have been some very pervasive inequities in the U.S. criminal justice system over the past 30 years.

CRIMINAL, WITHOUT MUCH JUSTICE

The criminal justice system has been dominated for decades by an approach defined as largely retributive. It is easy to represent retributive justice as a direct contrast to the principles and practices of restorative justice, although one of the leading thinkers in the field cautions against this simplistic binary approach (Zehr, 2002). The recent history of this dominant retributive approach, and its attendant expense, has given American exceptionalism a whole other meaning. The 1980s saw a large political shift in criminal justice policy and began a range of discriminatory policies in which equity and justice played little part. The failed "War on Drugs," "Zero Tolerance," "Three strikes and you're out," and "Tough on Crime" federal and state policies led to an explosion of incarceration for low-level crimes and huge increases in the American prison population. The explosion was primarily at the expense of African American men who were predominantly incarcerated for minor drug offenses with hugely disproportionate sentences. In the 30-year period since 1980, the American prison population increased 240% (Schmitt, Warner & Gupta, 2010). This inequality is only now being addressed in the national political domain, while the American love affair with incarceration remains problematic.

In 2013, America had some 2.3 million inmates in federal, state and local prisons, generating the highest per capita incarceration rate in the world. We have just 5% of the world's population but a staggering 25% of the world's prison population. Our 2013 incarceration rate of 716 per 100,000 (International Centre for Prison Studies, 2013) is 5 times that of England, 8 times that of Germany and 12 times that of Japan (Prison Path, 2013). Despite this, it should also be noted that the U.S. prison population has actually been 'in decline' for the past four years (Glaze & Herberman, 2012).

The accounting of these statistics at the individual, family, and community level is often difficult to measure, but the economic consequences offer the most obvious option. In 2008, the Center for Economic Policy research estimated that America spent $75 billion on corrections, of which the largest proportion covered incarceration (Schmitt et al., 2010). However, the national dialogue seems to be shifting to an accounting that captures more than just monetary value, something U.S. Attorney General Eric Holder confirmed when he noted that it was difficult to account for the "the human and moral costs" of mass incarceration (Sullum, 2013). Really, the evidence is in: Mass incarceration does not work. It destroys families and communities and steals future productive lives. It leaves too many African American men with stunted future options, excluded from democratic processes, and struggling to rebuild relationships of hope and potential.

With regard to juvenile justice, there are also ways to register this carnage, and some comparative costs are informative. In 2013, Illinois paid about $90,000 to lock up a youth in juvenile prison for a year and only $6,119 to fund public K-12 education (Chiyouthjustice, 2013). In the CPS budget for 2014, $56,303,794 is itemized for school security personnel. Additionally, the central budget allocates $47,652,163 to fund safety and security across the whole system. So CPS will spend over a hundred million dollars on safety and security in one school year. In the same budget, it proposes to spend $24,428,202 for psychological service personnel (Project NIA, 2013). The disproportionate impact of mass incarceration with regard to race and ethnicity are equally explicit. Young men of color are massively overrepresented in the American prison population. Keeping young people of color out of the ravenous prison system is clearly a key aspect of the pursuit of social justice. 84% of all arrests of young people under 16 years old are of working-class young men of color. There is a body of research on disproportionate minority representation in our criminal justice system (for example, American Sociological Association, 2007; Mauer & King, 2007) that also includes the specific impact on young people when decision-making involves race (Higgins, Ricketts, Griffith & Jirard, 2013). A useful discussion forum for the broader aspects of global restorative justice work can be found at the Restorative Justice Online Blog (restorativejustice.org, 2014).

It strikes us as perverse that our public education system serves as one of the generators of crisis in young men's lives, setting them on the destructive path into this criminal injustice system. When young people are suspended, excluded, or removed from school, they are forced into a risk terrain that can have serious consequences. If this issue is connected with the ever-increasing policing within school buildings and school grounds (Justice Policy Institute, 2011), it is easy to see how an institution charged with learning and the endowment of future capacity can turn into an unsafe, risk-ridden, promise-stealing space that has to be negotiated with great care for many young men of color. For many young people, dropping out of high school is frequently the end result of a range of school-based infractions, suspensions, and exclusions. School dropout rates, therefore, signal a range of personal and systemic missed opportunities for positive change within schools and for young people themselves.

CHICAGO PUBLIC SCHOOLS

Data from CPS itself outlines the contours of this risk terrain for young men with some clarity. They also indicate that *some* schools in struggling neighborhoods can thrive and deliver on important educational outcomes for young people. Like many other urban American large school systems, there is the broad sweep of discrimination that also plays out in very differential ways in specific contexts. This differentiation also has prejudicial impacts on other specific groups of young people, such as those with learning disabilities, LGBTQ young people, and young people with mental health issues (Health and Human Development, 2010; Ross & Zimmerman, 2014; stopbullying.gov, 2014), but these impacts are outside the scope of this chapter. In public education, especially for young men of color, this means all too frequently sending them into what is known as the 'school to prison pipeline.'

In the 2012–2013 academic year, CPS was responsible for a total of 681 schools, of which 106 were high schools. In this total count there were also

96 charter school campuses, a contentious issue for many Chicagoans. The City of Chicago has actively supported the national movement to establish charter schools under the espoused framework of increasing parental choice and improving student outcomes. The charter school movement parallels academies in the U.K. and the development of independent public schools in Australia. All are similar political responses to the challenge of providing quality public high school education for all young people. In 2013, CPS chose to close 50 public schools, the largest single closing of schools in U.S. history; the bulk of these schools were on Chicago's south and west sides and thus disproportionately impacted communities of color. Like many large U.S. cities, and despite some neighborhood "globalization" (Logan & Zhang, 2011), Chicago still has many persistently segregated neighborhoods. In general, north side neighborhoods are dominated by white residents, south side neighborhoods by African Americans, and west side neighborhoods by Hispanic residents.

CPS in 2012 had a $5.11 billion operating budget and was responsible for some 404,151 students, 87% of whom were from low-income families. In this same year the CPS student racial and ethnic breakdown included: 41.6% African American, 44.1% Latino, 8.8% White, 3.4% Asian/Pacific Islander, and 0.4% Native American. A national trend is mirrored in Chicago, with the Latino population superseding the African American population as the largest minority group. CPS reported a citywide attendance rate of 91.4% for 2011–2012 (CPS, 2014a). In August 2013, CPS announced a record-high graduation rate of 65%, noting this was a 3% increase from the previous school year and presented a hugely different picture of system success in the education of the city's low-income young people. In 2003, the CPS graduation rate was only 44%, so clearly significant improvements have occurred over the past decade (CPS, 2014b). Graduating high school is a key indicator of personal and social success, thus the failure to graduate can also be a key predictor for a very different life trajectory. The failure to complete high school, as captured through dropout rates, becomes an important proxy for this important life transition for all young people.

> On virtually every measure of economic well-being and career attainment—from personal earnings to job satisfaction to the share employed full time—young college graduates are outperforming their peers with less education. And when today's young adults are compared with previous generations, the disparity in economic outcomes between college graduates and those with a high school diploma or less formal schooling has never been greater in the modern era. (Pew Research Center, 2014)

Data on dropout rates across CPS high school administrative clusters in 2012 show that there are huge disparities in dropout rates that transcend both geography and whether a high school remains at the heart of the

CPS system or is run under the leadership of other providers. North- and northwest-side schools post the lowest average dropout rates, closely followed by charter and contract schools. However, the variation between different schools within one administrative cluster can be vast, leading to a CPS system-average range of 12.76% to 71.97% dropout rates (CPS, 2014c).

There are two major points to make from these data. First, the huge disparity of performance within each cluster of schools leads us to infer that it is clearly possible for schools facing similar social and cultural circumstances to have wildly different dropout, and therefore success, rates. There is already excellent Chicago research that provides a detailed and evocative analysis of what it really requires for schools to succeed in impoverished environments (Bryk, Sebring, Allensworth, Luppescu & Easton, 2010). There is also strong international comparative research that explores what it takes to improve student outcomes in impoverished urban school environments (Hargreaves & Fullan, 2012). Second, and most importantly for the focus of this chapter, these patterns, when overlaid on the neighborhood geography of Chicago, are a good mirror of the racial and ethnic segregation patterns that are so evident in the city. Young people of color make up the dominant populations of the school clusters with the highest dropout rates. The communities of the north and northwest of the city are home to most of the minority white population of the city—45% of the city's population (U.S. Census Bureau, 2014). As noted, Nicholas Senn High School is very much an anomaly. Class, race, ethnicity, and educational opportunity, or the lack of it, for some Chicago young people matters intensely and is intimately tied to neighborhood. There is also evidence to suggest the CPS picture, despite the overall improved graduation rate, is not improving educational success for African American young people (de la Torre et al., 2013). It is perhaps also important to state for the benefit of our international audience, Chicago is not too dissimilar from many U.S. urban education systems (see Matloff-Nieves, Fusco, Connolly, and Maulik in this volume for a related discussion of New York City). Keeping young people of color from some neighborhoods out of danger has occurred in parallel with the huge increase in the policing of school systems.

Policing Schools

A similarity Chicago shares with many U.S. urban and suburban school systems is a moral panic about school safety accompanied by the increasing presence of police monitoring and activity on school premises and in school grounds (Patterson & Kaba, 2011). The nine-figure budget for security and safety in CPS schools delivers some unsettling results provided by the Chicago Police Department. The following data apply to the 2011 school year and show that 2,546 juveniles were arrested *on CPS properties*. It should also be noted that these arrest data only cover the first 103 instructional days of a 170-day academic year. Within this limited data set, 70% of those arrests were for young people between the ages of 15 and 17, 72% of whom were male and 75% African American (Kaba, 2013). The full academic year number of school-based arrests of young people is reported as 4,287, and this represents a 23% decrease in arrests since 2010 (Project NIA, 2013). Most of these arrests are for misdemeanor offenses (84%), and indeed the involvement of police in these altercations is frequently the decision of school officials at the time of the incident. Adult choices are made here, and young lives are changed at this exact point of conflict. CPS leadership has begun to seriously address this issue and is working in a range of ways to reduce the level of both arrests and all school-based infractions. It appears that the national political move away from retributive justice resonates through to recent City of Chicago policy and practice shifts. Indeed, in February 2014, the Attorney General and the Department of Education issued guidance and a warning to school districts that they may be opening themselves up to Civil Rights litigation if they did not address the disproportionate impacts of suspensions and expulsions (ED.gov, 2014). Within CPS, there is a renewed focus on youth development and a range of positive supports that seek to address some causes of student challenges and intervene before a crisis point is reached. The policy is framed as a new holistic approach to school safety. Mayor Emanuel identifies this significant shift in approach to justice with young people:

> It is our responsibility to keep our students safe and secure and focused on their learning while in the classroom. CPS's proactive strategy, implemented last year, intervenes on the front-end to prevent, protect, and teach children, putting a premium on support not punishment. (CPS, 2012)

It seems as if the whole CPS system is arching firmly into more restorative responses to conflict and the de-criminalization of young people. A central plank of this shift is providing young people themselves with the tools necessary to resolve conflict and build future-enhancing skills in their lives. For students, school staff, teachers, and security personnel, this shift involves developing a new mindset about human relationships and learning the specific skills to make this operational, especially at times of crisis. These injustices have generated a range of positive, creative responses from young people themselves, the busy downtown meeting that prefaces this chapter being one example. It is important, therefore, to ensure that we never only categorize young people as victims of systemic injustice, as many respond with action. A group of lesbian, gay, bisexual, transgender, and queer (LGBTQ) youth became action researchers, storytellers, and trainers, creating a multimedia project promoting alternatives to calling the police (Brewster & Hereth, 2013).

Another group of young people, representing the Juvenile Justice Council of the Mikva Challenge (a nonprofit working with underserved high school youth building civic leaders, policy makers and activists), created a new web app suitable for computers or smartphones that allows young people to see if they qualify to expunge their criminal records and then connects them with pro bono lawyers to assist in the process. The app is called Expunge.io (Mikva Challenge, 2014). At Michele Clark High School in Chicago's west side Austin neighborhood, student jurors trained by Alternatives, Inc. kept hearing how social media was impacting students, and they hypothesized that many negative situations and issues were occurring on Facebook and leading to fights in school. This group of students used an action research approach to discover more about this issue and investigate if their suspicions were correct. They designed a survey that was completed by over 100 students, and in analyzing the data they found many students were using Facebook for long periods each day and that social media postings did indeed lead to conflicts in school. Using these findings, this group of young people created a video and curriculum for teachers to stimulate dialogue in class about care and respect when using Facebook. Planting and feeding the seed of agency for justice within young people can reap unknown benefits.

RESTORATIVE JUSTICE

> Restorative justice is not a new practice, as it is rooted in the philosophies of many early indigenous societies that were non-hierarchically structured. Due to the strong collectivist paradigms of such societies, incidents were resolved without formal justice systems. (Adler & ICIRR, 2011, p. 4)

Restorative justice advocates offer differing definitions and are somewhat resistant to a one-size-fits-all definition of the philosophy and practices. Howard Zehr, a key figure in the North American movement, emphasizes the three pillars of restorative justice. These are the focus on harms and needs, obligations, and engagement (Zehr, 2002). The philosophy of restorative justice provides an alternative framework through which to view wrongdoing, to shift the offender-victim dynamic, and to seek collective agreements between a wider range of stakeholders when harm is done. In the North American context, the philosophy and practices came to prominence in the 1970s in communities with a strong Mennonite presence. These early practitioners acknowledge a debt to the native peoples of North American and New Zealand, where these practices are deeply embedded in Indigenous cultures (Zehr, 2002). Central to the philosophy is the interconnectedness of human relationships as both the territory of wrongdoing and the turf in which these wrongs should be put right. Crime is viewed as primarily a violation of people and their interpersonal relationships. This concept has a long historical and religious pedigree across diverse continents.

In the North American context it has gained the largest sphere of influence through implementation in school systems. In these more recent iterations, there are driving concerns with conflict transformation and peace building; indeed, these two concepts appear in many different interpretations across the field, and many programmatic and practice interventions reverberate these key concepts in a range of formulations. Title (2011), in *Teaching Peace*, explores the experience of one community through her multifocal lens of relationships, respect, responsibility, repair, and reintegration. Many of these themes should resonate with community practitioners and those invested in changing juvenile justice systems.

The most common practices associated with restorative justice in the U.S. context are talking circles, restorative conversations, peer conferences (frequently referred to as peer mediation), and conflict and healing circles. All of these may have slightly different contextualized meanings and operational distinctions but rest firmly within Zehr's three pillars of restorative justice. We will now look specifically at how Alternative Inc. delivers restorative justice programs within CPS and the important outcomes of using these approaches.

Alternatives' Practice for Restorative Justice

The bedrock of the work is to establish a restorative school culture in which specific practices can thrive and sustain themselves for the long term. There are five important keys to framing the culture to be established within a school environment (Alternatives, 2013). The school and all participating stakeholders must

1. intentionally build trusting and respectful relationships between staff and students;
2. understand the importance of both individual and collective healing;
3. seek to find and acknowledge the root causes of conflicts;
4. invite those who caused harm to creative positive solutions to repair it; and
5. use a dialogue-based process to resolve conflict.

These cultural requirements rest on a foundation of the values of dignity, respect, trust, and compassion and in practice require that any intervention is youth driven, individualized, and holistic. In the school environment, and among individual student participants, the purpose is to build capacities for successful implementation of restorative justice. Alternatives, Inc. provides interactive, experiential training for school students and school staff for them to understand the key tenets of this philosophical shift and to practice the subsequent skills required to deliver solutions to conflict that meet these philosophical requirements. Training can take place at the beginning of the school year with regular follow-up sessions during the semester. There is also a special summer camp providing another opportunity to train students from across the city in a concentrated and fun environment. Again, the practical implementation strategies may vary from school to school and can be highly contextualized; however, the cultural requirements, value basem and core restorative practices remain consistent.

Training for CPS students covers ages 12 through 17 and has strong correlations to key concepts in the U.S. youth development literature such as self-efficacy, social and emotional learning, critical thinking, youth-adult partnerships, and leadership development. Once trained, students are ready to use their new knowledge and skills. For example, students at Senn High School termed Peace Ambassadors are the primary actors for peer conferences, talking, healing, and conflict circles. The peer conferences take place during any of the seven lunch breaks that run through the school day. The school discipline office generally refers cases, and two Peace Ambassadors conduct the session in a private room, normally with two referred students. An adult advisor is present during the conference session. This could be an Alternatives staff member but is more often a trained schoolteacher or administrator.

Peace Ambassadors check to see if there are any cases before they go to lunch, and they usually eat their lunch while the referred students fill out their paperwork, which consists of an Alternatives intake form, the Oath of Confidentiality, and a pre-hearing survey. Each peer conference follows a structured process with clear guidance and rules about roles, behaviors, and responsibilities. The heart of the process is listening, respect, and problem-solving. The referred students (the disputants) are supported in coming up with an agreement about how the issue will be resolved and the harm accounted for. This agreement has to be signed by the referred students, each receiving a copy. A copy is also delivered to the school discipline office. If time allows, all involved in the process also complete reflection sheets. One Peace Ambassador is appointed with follow-up duties and will actively check-in with referred students a few weeks after the process to see if any further problems have arisen since the peer conference. This is a role that the adult advisor can also play. Larger conferences can occur after school and can be expected to last considerably longer; these are more likely to involve school deans and the specific referring teacher for the conflict to be addressed.

Restorative justice practices are used within a specific framework of student behaviors and written disciplinary codes. Within the CPS Student Code of Conduct, there are six levels of infractions of increasing seriousness. Table 14.1 summarizes the pertinent content from CPS's 68-page code (CPS, 2014d). The first three groups of infractions are those that come under the purview of peer conferences—a point that is noted in the published code. For these first three levels of infractions, one of the dominant punishments, before the advent of peer conferences, would be time-limited suspension from school.

Table 14.1 Summary of Chicago Public School Student Code of Conduct

Group one	Inappropriate behaviors: leaving class without permission, failing to attend without a valid excuse, persistent tardiness, and excessive noise in the hall or building.
Group two	Disruptive behaviors: initiating or participating in unacceptable minor physical actions, leaving school without permission, posting unauthorized written materials on school grounds, and failing to provide proper identification.
Group three	Seriously disruptive behaviors: gambling, fighting, forgery, overt display of gang affiliation, and bullying behaviors.
Group four	Very seriously disruptive behaviors: assault, vandalism, battery, theft, and false activation of a fire alarm that does not cause evacuation of the building.
Group five	Most seriously disruptive behaviors: gang activity, aggravated assault, inappropriate sexual contact, and false activation of a fire alarm that causes the evacuation of the building or causes emergency services to be notified.
Group six	Illegal and most seriously disruptive behaviors: use, possession, or concealment of a firearm; arson; bomb threat; and sale, distribution, or intent, to sell or distribute alcohol, illegal drugs, narcotics, controlled substances, 'look-alikes' of such substances, contraband.

Capturing the Impact of Restorative Justice in CPS

There has yet to be any systematic research conducted by CPS, Alternatives, Inc., or any other institution into the range of impacts brought about by embedded restorative justice practices in CPS schools. This is an important point we will return to in our conclusion. There have been a number of partial attempts, selected results of which we present here. These data give a strong sense of impact but do not meet the rigor of 'evidence-based practice' now more likely to be demanded by foundation, federal, state, and city funders. Key stakeholders are fully aware of the important need for research into impacts. Indeed, in the spring of 2007, CPS contracted with researchers at DePaul University and Northwestern University to do a preliminary evaluation of the program. Unfortunately, after this initial investigation, CPS priorities moved elsewhere and funds were not allocated for a more comprehensive study.

An unpublished report covering a three-year span of activity (2004–2007) records 2,541 cases heard by peer juries across the city. These cases resulted in 2,394 (94%) student agreements, of which 1,819 were completed. Completed agreements represent a 76% success rate for peer-jury interventions that diverted prospective suspension days for students committing infractions of the student code of conduct (Alternatives, 2007). Just like the Chicago

Police Department data on school arrests presented earlier, these data only present a partial picture that makes the full impact impossible to assess. Not all schools working with peer juries submitted reports and not all reports were complete. Thus, we could assume that the statistics reported above are an underestimate of the impact of peer-jury activity over those three academic years in CPS. With the same caveat, these researchers report that 1,026 suspension days were avoided for Chicago students during this three-year period. They also report that during the 2010–2011 academic year 87% of peer jury cases ended in a formal agreement. From these incomplete data snapshots, we surmise that peer juries have likely resulted in around 90% of students referred making a formal, restorative agreement with each other and their school to account for the harms they have created by their behavior.

Another data source, the High HOPES Campaign (Healing over the Punishment of Expulsions and Suspensions), a collaborative of seven Chicago community-based organizations committed to changing CPS practices, provides informative data on one CPS high school that gained national infamy in 2009 with the taped beating death of 16-year old Derrion Albert outside Fenger High School on the city's south side. The fallout from this horrific incident included Fenger appointing a new dean of students with significant restorative justice experience. During the following school year, 306 Fenger students received restorative justice services and 1,103 suspension days were prevented. Cases of misconduct dropped by 59% during this same school year, while arrests declined by 69% (High HOPES Campaign, 2012). The use of restorative practices when school systems are in crisis mode is an issue we will return to in our conclusion. However, this data snapshot infers considerable change within one high-profile school context.

Every year, as part of their evaluation strategy and reporting requirements for CPS, Alternatives staff reflect with student jurors and mediators—or Peace Ambassadors as they are now called. A range of methods can be used to collect data from those involved in restorative justice practices, including interviews, surveys, and focus groups, to capture young people's thoughts on their experiences. Student voices captured through this mixed methodology speak of a range of impacts that cover such things as individual skills, their familial relationships and larger scale social influences. These voices speak with clarity about growth that resides firmly within the youth work domain and consistently illustrate common aspects of important learning for youth participants:

> *"I learned that everyone has problems and it helps if you talk it out."*

> *"I learned respect: how to stay calm and not get mad at everything, to stay positive."*

> *"I learned not to judge people. I also took the cases as if it were me sitting there thinking about my own actions."*

> *"I've learned how to be a better person and understand that there are always two sides to a story."*

Students also commented on expanded leadership skills:

> *"I learned to be a better leader and to be responsible for my actions."*

> *"I am more aware of my actions; I have been leading by example."*

> *"I liked how peer jury will not only help you become a leader but also a role model to other students."*

They report also being aware of how their new skills have a broader impact beyond their peer-jury duties.

> *"I have become a problem solver because of what I learned and do in peer jury. I help many of my friends and family and help talk to them about the problems."*

> *"It allows me to resolve conflicts within my own household peacefully."*

There is also evidence of more holistic change that directly relates to identity and agency for young people involved in this process. For some it is a personal turnaround, and for others it has much broader communal reach.

> *"Peer Jury changed me. I used to be bad, but now I am good. So I want to spread the knowledge. I learned to with other people."*

> *"Because I wanted to change how our school is and change how people think."*

CONCLUSION

A youth worker with a keen eye for injustice and a supportive non-profit executive director alongside endless persistence in the face of huge bureaucracies—consistent mostly in their upheaval and change—can have far-reaching impacts. These impacts register at the level of both individual capacity in young people and city and statewide policy changes. Thus, the impact of restorative justice work has changed the punitive context for thousands of young people and the systemic imposition of restricted opportunities and outcomes. Restorative justice is not a new idea; indeed, it reconnects young people to Indigenous solutions and a renewed sense of agency through community. There is an inherently strong match between the restorative justice mindset, subsequent practices, and youth work. All see human relationships as central, and all value process at least equally with outcome. All are experiential practices undergirded by key values of respect, dialogue, collaboration, participation, and the resolution of agreed needs. All understand successful and sustained change can only be derived from within young people themselves and with their full engagement and leadership. Good restorative justice work with young people is good youth work.

In this case study, a collation of data sources and a mix of research methodologies had to be used to paint a partial picture of the impact of restorative justice practices in CPS delivered by Alternatives, Inc. From the sources provided here, it is clear that restorative justice can have a meaningful impact on individual lives and school cultures and within the policy domain in a very large school system. However, there is a great need for sustained and authoritative research that gives this specific field of practice a solid evidence base on which larger scale decisions can be made about how education and policing resources can be expended in the service of building restorative justice communities amongst young people, within schools, and across neighborhoods. The restorative justice field in Chicago is a jigsaw puzzle composed of numerous organizations working on related goals with diverse and complex funding and differing levels of expertise and impact. The diversity of this picture must not change in the future, but research on this complexity must begin at a larger scale. As the patchwork of data sources used in this chapter attests, there is no simple or unified access to common data that can serve the purpose of building a stronger evidence base for sustained citywide funding. This should be addressed across the city in a way that celebrates and sustains the diversity of contributions to the cause but that allows core data systems to be utilized for stronger outcome impact to be collated. Coherent, systemic evidence is a benchmark requirement and will continue to be so as government social-cause resources continue to come under increasing political pressure for 'proof.'

The youth work precedent has now been set in Chicago with large-scale research from the University of Chicago's Crime Lab using a randomized clinical trial to assess the impact of the Becoming a Man (BAM) program run by Youth Guidance Inc. (University of Chicago, 2012). This program works specifically in schools with 'at-risk' African American males, providing a blend of educational enrichments and in-school and afterschool programming alongside counseling and mentoring for violence prevention. Using data from nearly 2,500 young men in 18 schools, the research provided solid evidence that tutoring and intensive support for social and emotional learning in young men had hugely significant impacts on their outcomes. During the program year, there was a 40% reduction in violent crimes compared to the control group, graduation rates were increased by roughly 10%, and failing school grades were reduced by 37%. Suffice it to say that President Obama has visited the BAM program, and the BAM participants have made the trip to the Whitehouse. Mayor Emanuel has provided for 2013 an additional $2,000,000 for the program, tripling the original $1,000,000 budget for BAM's Sports Edition. Clearly there is more than evidence at play here, but if city and federal politics require optics about action and investment in reducing youth violence and crime, there are opportunities for restorative justice that have not yet yielded similar results. Restorative justice work in Chicago needs a solid research base on which all can build together on this great potential.

Large education systems are never free of political imperatives while they seek change and improvement in their performance. An unintended consequence of the rightful quest for better and more equitable educational outcomes for young people is the constant revolving door of programs that rise and fall in their popularity. Schools, teachers, and principals are bombarded with the latest idea attached to yet more data and reporting requirements. This is beautifully captured in what Hargreaves and Fullan (2012) call the "holiday tree effect," in which the newest, shiniest bauble is placed at the front of the tree while older ones are relegated to the back. This is not helpful when sustained and systemic development, over time, is required to reap solid results.

It is beyond doubt that politicians and education administrators in the city of Chicago are equally driven by the urge to improve educational outcomes for Chicago's young people. Over the past 15 years, CPS has undergone numerous systemic changes throughout all of its operations. It is a very large city bureaucracy that is consistent only in its political ownership. In this same time period, under only two mayors, it has had at least eight different leaders.

Commitment to restorative justice may now be codified in CPS's Student Code of Conduct, but this requires a consistent commitment and enactment across the system by leadership.

> Although the Illinois Juvenile code and Chicago Public Schools code of conduct specifically mention balanced and restorative justice, there appears to be little infrastructure and funding to ensure restorative approaches reach their full potential. (Adler & ICIRR, 2011, p. 16)

Alternatives, Inc. has sustained its restorative justice work with CPS for approaching two decades, and that persistence is what is required to embed and enhance the foundation laid by many different players over that time. As Judy Gall noted in an early conversation in the planning of this chapter, "You have to be really committed to be in the muck there with them (CPS) for the long-haul." This has been a process of expertise building through ever-changing funding circumstances and through the shifting focus and filters of new CPS and school administrators. School principals and teachers are rightly wary of how data can be used, especially those that indicate key challenges they face in educating working-class young people. Their careers, their schools, and the public perceptions of their performance have been highly politicized over the past two decades, and beyond doubt teachers remain professionals who have been subjected to the "discourse of derision"

(Wallis, 1993). This understandable protection is difficult to counterbalance and requires sustained trusting relationships between teachers, administrators, and nonprofit providers of much needed services to support and strengthen school impacts. A change in school principal can begin to shift the culture of a school rapidly, and years of careful work can be lost in newer driving imperatives. For the adults involved in public school education in Chicago, recent history supports their understandable wariness in handling citywide imperatives.

The Fenger High School example used earlier in this chapter also highlights a complex tension embedded at the heart of restorative justice work. Inherently, it is both crisis driven *and* about slower cultural changes in how people relate to each other. The primary use in CPS is to resolve conflicts, thus it is called to action when there is student/student or student/teacher conflict. However, it is not a quick-fix remedy, concerned with the imposition of behavioral solutions, nor is it a policing strategy. It requires all those involved in conflict to spend time with each other to go below the surface of complex human interactions and use empathy to gain a depth of understanding from which mutual solutions can emerge. Restorative justice work is not an off-the-shelf remedy nor is it a matter of sending key school staff on one-off training events. Both these strategies offer politically popular options when school systems come to be judged in mass public-media outlets that thrive on conflict, violence, and simplistic messaging of complex issues.

Resolve is needed and a deep faith must be sustained in the rightness of this approach when some may be driven by shorter-term, instrumental goals. Approaching school conflicts restoratively should be a culturally embedded preventative context providing huge change potential, especially when combined with other successful strategies that mitigate the interwoven impacts of poverty in neighborhoods, families, systems, and vital human relationships. While schools should not be in the business of sustaining the school-to-prison pipeline, neighborhoods should not be providing collapsing drainage systems that dispose of so many people without regard to the consequences to families and futures.

In the U.S. context, there is also a dominant aspect of the culture pertinent to youth justice and youth crime that is relatively unexplored. Indeed, it has been largely unexplored within this chapter, while hiding in plain sight. There seems very little critical analysis that is gendered beyond the obvious statement about the domination of young men in these data. We find it difficult to find much discussion of the specific forms of young masculinity at play here. Indeed, there appears to be a de-gendering in analysis of violence in much that is published about school violence, youth crime, and juvenile justice. There is much in the popular discourse about gun violence, school violence, and youth crime without much reflection and analysis of why these are predominantly the behaviors of men. Nor is there much reflection in popular discourse on how certain masculinities may be sustained and supported uncritically in the broader culture in which young men are raised, learn to survive and thrive, or not.

While it may appear inherent in the aforementioned "Becoming a Man" program—indeed, one of the six core values is "Respect for Womanhood"—publicly available materials do not really indicate a feminist analysis of why young men, in particular and predominantly, respond to challenges in externally violent ways. In this program, young men are also taught positive anger expression, anger management coping, and effective skills for expressing anger. We would support more exploration of why some young men reach for guns as a response to challenges in their lives. They live in the same neighborhoods where some young men do not reach for guns. Very few young women in the same circumstances reach for guns as a solution to the challenges they face. Young men are hugely disproportionately over-represented in this choice of external expression of anger, frustration, and payback for perceived slight to themselves, their friends, or their turf and territory. So it is young men who dominate school suspensions and incarceration rates and who are lone gunmen involved in high profile shooting sprees in the U.S. context. These mass acts of violence always appear to trigger a time-limited debate about gun control but never one about the correlations between masculinity and violence.

Restorative justice advocates and practitioners have shown persistence, creativity, and 'grit' before this latest bauble recently joined the U.S. youth development lexicon. Restorative justice advocates, allies, and practitioners must continue to maintain the primacy and the quality of localized relationships—indeed, building and sustaining community in its most elemental sense. However, there is a larger need to coordinate and cooperate, above and beyond current relationships, in the hope of achieving larger change goals. It appears that, in the U.S. context, the national political will is shifting towards more equitable solutions for young people involved in community and school conflicts. In the end, of course, one must follow the money. At federal, state, and city levels and through private and public foundations, consistent resources must be applied to restorative justice approaches and redirected from hugely expensive and failed punishment and incarceration strategies. This may indeed be finally happening at the Federal level with the announcement of a new $200,000,000 initiative called "My Brother's Keeper," which establishes an interagency taskforce to improve the opportunities and outcomes for boys and young men of color (The White House, 2014). In intent, this initiative seeks to build on the ground-level and grassroots work that has been happening for many years, like the sustained work described in this chapter.

So let us return to that bursting conference room in freezing downtown Chicago. The 100 or so young people in this room had made it downtown to speak with passion about something that was very important to their lives and their futures. They had not actually been in school for two full days—the weather had been so bad that CPS had canceled all school for two consecutive days. And yet, here they were, planning their future actions and asking adult allies to accompany them on this journey for justice. They should continue to demand nothing less from us adults who proscribe much of their world.

REFERENCES

Adler School Institute on Public Safety and Social Justice; Illinois Coalition for Immigrant and Refugee Rights (ICIRR). (2011). *White paper on restorative justice: A primer and exploration of practice across two North American cities.* Retrieved from: http://www.restorativejustice.org/RJOB/adlerandillinois

Alternatives, Inc. (2010). *Alternatives restorative justice program description and Chicago Public Schools peer jury 2009–2010.* Alternatives Inc. annual report. Chicago, IL: Author.

Alternatives, Inc. (2011). *A preliminary brief on the impact of restorative justice in Chicago Public Schools. Alternatives Inc. initial study report.* Chicago, IL: Author.

Alternatives, Inc. (2013). *Overview of restorative justice practices.* Chicago, IL: Author.

American Sociological Association. (2007). *Race, ethnicity and the criminal justice system.* Retrieved from http://www.asanet.org/images/press/docs/pdf/ASARaceCrime.pdf

Brewster, S., & Hereth, J. (2013). Chain reaction: A youth-driven, multimedia storytelling project promoting alternatives to calling the police. *Journal of Curriculum Theorizing, 29*(2), 26–34.

Bryk, A. S., Sebring, P. B., Allensworth, E., Luppescu, S., & Easton, J. Q. (2010). *Organizing schools for improvement lessons from Chicago.* Chicago: The University of Chicago Press.

Chiyouthjustice. (2013). *2013 in blogging.* Annual Report. Retrieved from: http://chiyouthjustice.wordpress.com/2013/annual-report/

CPS. (2012, December 17). *New CPS safety measures show promising results in creating safer and positive learning environments across the district.* Press Release. Retrieved from: http://www.cps.edu/News/Press_Releases/Pages/12_17–2012_PR1.aspx

CPS. (2014a). *About CPS at-a-glance.* Retrieved from http://www.cps.edu/About_CPS/At-a-glance/Pages/Stats_and_facts.aspx

CPS. (2014b). *About CPS—spotlight.* Retrieved from http://www.cps.edu/Spotlight/Pages/spotlight465.aspx

CPS. (2014c). *About CPS—graduation results.* Retrieved from http://www.cps.edu/Results.aspx?k=graduation%20rates

CPS. (2014d). *Student code of conduct—English.* Retrieved from http://www.cps.edu/Documents/Resources/StudentCodeOfConduct/English_StudentCodeofConduct.pdf

ED.gov. (2014). *U.S. Departments of Education and Justice release school discipline guidance package to enhance school climate and improve school discipline policies/practices.* Retrieved from http://www.ed.gov/news/press-releases/us-departments-education-and-justice-release-school-discipline-guidance-package-

Glaze, L. E., & Herberman, E. J. (2012). *Correctional populations in the United States, 2012.* Washington, DC: U.S. Department of Justice, Office of Justice Programs, Bureau of Justice Statistics.

Hargreaves, A., & Fullan, M. (2012). *Professional Capital.* New York, NY: Teachers College Press.

Health and Human Development. (2010). *The link between mental health and school expulsions.* Retrieved from: http://www.hhd.org/resources/story/link-between-mental-health-and-school-expulsions.

Higgins, G. E., Ricketts, M. L., Griffith, J. D., & Jirard, S. A. (2013). Race and juvenile incarceration: A propensity score matching examination. *American Journal of Criminal Justice, 38*(1), 1–12.

High HOPES Campaign. (2012). *Community renewal society: High HOPES campaign.* Retrieved from http://www.communityrenewalsociety.org/newsroom/high-hopes-campaign

International Centre for Prison Studies. (2013). *World prison brief, 2013.* Retrieved from http://www.prisonstudies.org/world-prison-brief

Johnson, S. R. (2011, May 25). Senn High School celebrates diversity at International Festival. *Chicago Tribune.* Retrieved from http://articles.chicagotribune.com/2011–05–25/news/ct-x-c-senn-international-school-20110525_1_international-festival-diversity-dances

Justice Policy Institute. (2011). *Education under arrest: The case against police in schools.* Retrieved from http://www.justicepolicy.org/uploads/justicepolicy/documents/educationunderarrest_fullreport.pdf

Kaba, M. (2013). *Arresting justice: Juvenile arrests in Chicago, 2011 and 2012.* Retrieved from http://chiyouthjustice.files.wordpress.com/2013/08/cpd-juvenile-arrest-stats-2011–2012.pdf

Logan, J. R., & Zhang, W. (2011). *Global neighborhoods: New evidence from Census 2010.* Retrieved from http://www.s4.brown.edu/us2010/Data/Report/global-final2.pdf

Mauer, M., & King, R. S. (2007). *Uneven justice: State rates of incarceration by race and ethnicity.* Washington, DC: The Sentencing Project.

Mikva Challenge. (2014). *What tools, policies, and practices do youth need to positively transition from corrections to community?* (Mikva Challenge Juvenile Justice Council, Summer 13). Retrieved from http://www.mikvachallenge.org/policymaking/

Patterson, C., & Kaba, M. (2011). *Arresting justice: A report about juvenile arrests in Chicago 2009 & 2010.* Chicago, IL: First Defense Legal Aid and Project NIA.

Pew Research Center. (2014). *The rising cost of not going to college.* Retrieved from http://www.pewsocialtrends.org/2014/02/11/the-rising-cost-of-not-going-to-college.

Prison Path. (2013). *In the United States prison statistics infographic: The largest population of inmates, prisons & solitary confinement.* Retrieved from http://www.prisonpath.com/incarceration-rates-prison-statistics-2013-infographic/

Project NIA. (2013, September). *From policy to standard practice: Restorative justice in Chicago public schools, 2012.* September Fact Sheet. Retrieved from http://www.dignityinschools.org/sites/default/files/FromPolicyToStandardPractice.pdf

Restorativejustice.org. (2014). *Restorative justice online.* Retrieved from http://www.restorativejustice.org

Ross, R. K., & Zimmerman, K. H. (2014, February 16). Real discipline in school. *New York Times*, A19. (New York Edition).

Schmitt, J., Warner, K., & Gupta, S. (2010). *The high budgetary cost of incarceration.* Washington, DC: Center for Economic and Policy Research.

Senn. (2014). *Senn High School homepage.* Retrieved from http://sennhs.org/apps/pages/index.jsp?uREC_ID=167284&type=d&pREC_ID=343573

Stopbullying.gov. (2014). *Who is at risk?* Retrieved from http://www.stopbullying.gov/at-risk/index.html

Sullum, J. (2013, November 22). *Eric Holder condemns mass incarceration (again).* Retrieved from http://www.forbes.com/sites/jacobsullum/2013/11/22/eric-holder-condemns-mass-incarceration-again/

Title. (2011). *Teaching peace.* Allen, TX: Del Hayes Press.

de la Torre, M., Allensworth, E., Jagesic, S., Sebastian, J., Salmonowicz, M., Myers, C., & Gerdeman, R.D. (2013). *Turning around low-performing schools in Chicago*. Chicago, IL: The University of Chicago Consortium on Chicago School Research.

U.S. Census Bureau. (2014). *State and county quick facts*. Retrieved from http://quickfacts.census.gov/qfd/states/17000.html.

University of Chicago. (2012). *BAM-Sports edition*. Retrieved from http://crimelab.uchicago.edu/sites/crimelab.uchicago.edu/files/uploads/BAM_FINAL%20Research%20and%20Policy%20Brief_20120711.pdf

Wallis, M. (1993) Discourse of derision: The role of the mass media within the education policy process. *Journal of Education Policy, 8*(4), 321–337.

The White House. (2014, February 27). *Fact sheet: Opportunity for all: President Obama launches my brother's keeper initiative to build ladders of opportunity for boys and young men of color*. Office of the Press Secretary. Retrieved from http://www.whitehouse.gov/the-press-office/2014/02/27/fact-sheet-opportunity-all-president-obama-launches-my-brother-s-keeper-

Zehr, H. (2002). *The little book of restorative justice*. Intercourse, PA: Good Books.

15 A Decade of Youth Civic Engagement in Morocco and Jordan

Loubna H. Skalli

Since their inception in early 2011, the youth-led democratic movements in the Middle East and North Africa (MENA) have confirmed the multiple challenges youth face in their societies. Young men and women (29 years and under) have been experiencing severe forms of exclusion from the political, economic, and social spheres of action and production. For nearly a decade now, youth work has focused on 'reconciling' youth to their societies and institutions by providing civic education programs as a strategy for strengthening youth's sense of belonging and re-engaging them with their communities.

This chapter focuses on youth civic education as a strategy for promoting positive youth development in two countries from the MENA region: Morocco and Jordan. These two countries have been playing the leading role in supporting youth civic education throughout the Arab world since Morocco's King Mohamed VI and Jordan's King Hussein II ascended their respective thrones in 1999. The two kingdoms' reform-oriented policies have encouraged the creation of centers, programs, and initiatives for civic education by a wide range of local, national, and international actors. Given the diversity of actors who intervene in the civic education of youth and the particular interest motivating each actor, civic education has grown to encompass a constellation of meanings ranging from youth engagement and political participation to empowerment, leadership, community development, and capacity building.

Given this diversity of actors and motivations, and the broader environment within which civic education has been 'rediscovered,' civics has become a coveted and contested space for reaching, educating, and engaging youth. However, despite the claims to inclusive citizenship that many actors make, civic education has remained a project riddled with tensions and contradictions that undermine any effort to unsettle the very structures that produce and perpetuate exclusive forms of citizenship. In the first section of the paper, I discuss the motivations driving various international actors to invest in civic education as a panacea for meeting youth's needs and rights. I specifically focus on the 'at-risk youth' category constructed and targeted by most actors to demonstrate how principles of positive youth development often collide with preoccupations with international security and political stability. In the second section, I focus on two leading civic engagement centers, one in Morocco and the other in Jordan, to examine the components of the civic education they promote and the scope of knowledge, skills, and competences they seek to build. The last section of the paper discusses the challenges these centers and services meet given the broader political and social contexts within which they operate. Drawing on interviews with youth, youth workers, and various actors in the youth sector, I reflect on youth's perceptions of and reactions to the services they are receiving.

YOUTH CIVICS: A COMPLEX SET OF MOTIVES

The turn to civic education for engaging youth in MENA is the product of a specific context and conjuncture that over the last decade has highlighted certain dimensions of youth identities while undermining others. What has been highlighted is a series of perceived deficits and vulnerabilities from which youth are seen to suffer even when the language of 'assets' and 'agents of change' is applied to the young population. What has often been undermined and overlooked, at least for decades leading to the so-called Arab Spring, are the conditions that prevent young people from exercising their economic, political, social, and cultural citizenship (Skalli, 2013). Numerous surveys conducted among youth have emphasized the unprecedented levels of political apathy, disengagement, and depoliticization among youth across the MENA region (Economist, 2007; Khatayba, 2009). In Morocco and Jordan, the young generation is perceived to suffer from a deficit in democratic knowledge and understanding of the basic roles and duties of the citizen. What makes this apathy alarming to both national and international actors is youth's disinterest in secular formal politics—a development that is systematically equated with young people's increasing vulnerability to recruitment to extremism, Jihadism, and global terrorism. In other words, it is neither youth's perceived political apathy nor their distance from secular political structures that constitute a concern for national or international actors. Rather, it is the security dimension of this 'apathy' that has renewed interest in both youth and their levels of political knowledge and participations.

This logic has been developing since the rise of Islamist movements in 1980s and the growing fear of the 'youth bulge' in MENA (see Anthony Cordesman's 1998 explanation of youth bulge in terms of "the population time bomb" in "Demographics and the coming youth explosion in the Gulf"; http://web.macam.ac.il/~arnon/Int-ME/Population/demograp.pdf). However, the tragic 9/11 attacks on New York City and Washington, DC, further convinced the international policy community that the proportionately large youth Muslim population is a serious security threat that needs to be contained (Skalli, 2013). A few months after 9/11, political scientist Samuel Huntington underscored the security dimension of the 'youth bulge' by stating that Islam was no more violent than any other religion; rather, he believed the key factor is the demographic fact that those who commit homicide are males between the ages of 16 and 30 (quoted in Steinberger, 2001). These observations were later confirmed by the writings of Graham Fuller, the former Vice Chairman of the National Intelligence Council at the CIA and senior political scientist on the Middle East at the Washington-based RAND Corporation. As he put it: "It is youth that often translates broader social problems into an explosive and radicalizing mixture" (Fuller, 2003, p. 12).

Thus, the international investment in the civic education of Middle Eastern youth is a project deeply shaped by the realities and anxieties of the post- 9/11 security environment that has imbued the training of youth in civics with a sense of both political urgency and expediency. It is important to underline that the youth who are targeted are primarily males from low socioeconomic backgrounds and peri-urban areas including industrial zones, poor neighborhoods, and slums as well as underfunded schools. The youth targeted with civic education are defined as 'vulnerable' or 'at-risk' of radicalization. Young women are targeted as well—not because they are perceived as a security threat but for their potential to modernize societies and pacify the threatening impulses of the 'angry' young men (Hendrixson, 2003; Skalli, 2014).

When the U.S. Agency for International Development (USAID) discusses the importance of civic education in Morocco among the countries it serves in MENA, it underscores both the class and geographic location of the targeted population:

> Marginalized youth at risk of disaffection are a growing cohort of youth 15–24 within the larger urban and peri-urban communities. This population's risk of engagement in extremist organizations is of considerable concern to USAID-Morocco and a number of USAID Offices and Bureaus in Washington and the MENA region . . . it is youth who are often protagonists in conflict . . . Providing civic education is one of the right tools in the right hands to do the right thing in order to better respond to the needs and aspirations of marginalized youth at risk of disaffection. (Equip3, 2007, pp. 4–6)

However, irrespective of gender, class, and age differences, the young population in MENA had been declared lacking in democratic knowledge, (self-) discipline, and political consciousness. Thus, efforts to reach youth with civic education before they turned terrorists meshed well with the post-9/11 Western democracy promotion agenda (Wittes & Youngs, 2009; Youngs, 2006). In 2003, for instance, a grant from the U.S. State Department's Middle East Partnership Initiative (MEPI) contributed to the creation of

Arab Civitas, a regional civic education network seeking to promote civic awareness among young people in 13 countries in MENA. Run by the Los Angeles-based Center for Civic Education (CEE) and funded by the U.S. Agency for International Development (USAID), Arab Civitas operates through partnerships with national ministries of education, local private and public schools, Arab educators, and non-governmental organizations. In addition, the U.S. government has been targeting young Middle Easterners through numerous other governmental and quasi-governmental organizations, including the National Endowment for Democracy, the National Democratic Institute, and the International Republican Institute.

Across the Atlantic, the European Union has also been investing in its young southern Mediterranean neighbors since 1995. Investment in youth was articulated within the European Neighborhood Policy, initially called the Barcelona process (Youngs, 2006). Civic education has generally been subsumed under the Youth Med-Programs and the activities of Salto-institute and increasingly complemented by the Egypt-based Anna Lindh Foundation (European Commission, 2009). EU's investment in the civic education of Middle Eastern youth is also supported by numerous European-based foundations (Friedrich Neumann, Friedrich Ebert), national development agencies, and countries' diplomatic services. Unlike the U.S., however, EU's selection of their targeted population for civic education is rarely identified openly as 'vulnerable' or 'at-risk.' This type of education was rather elitist given the socioeconomic status of the selected youth targeted as agents of change with a 'multiplier effect.' As Pace and Schumacher (2004) rightly observed, "in spite of its underlying all-inclusive character, too often" the EU-funded Youth Programs "turned out to be a *domaine réservé* of co-opted, privileged, non-religious actors in the southern Mediterranean" (p. 124). Participants in EU's programs are generally well-educated, middle-class young men and women who speak multiple languages. They are carefully selected by the EU as 'ambassadors' of peace that will relay the principles of tolerance to their peers. My interviews with many of these young ambassadors have confirmed their familiarity with European- and/or American-style education and their secular and middle-class upbringing.

The relative investment of MENA regimes in civic education was initially triggered by the international pressures to democratize and enhance citizen participation. Morocco and Jordan are considered the success stories in terms of government buy-in to pro-Western democracy and the project of educating youth in civics. However, the security dimension of this investment became the overriding motivation, especially when homegrown terrorism became a reality after the 2003 Casablanca (Morocco) terrorist attacks and the 2005 Amman (Jordan) bombings.

As allies in the Western war on terror, youth civics meshes well with these two countries' overall reform projects and investment in human capital for modernizing their countries. The promotion of civic education to counter youth's risky or extremist behavior can be found in numerous speeches by national leaders and government representatives from both countries. In Morocco, for instance, King Mohamed VI supported and financed numerous projects for youth civics soon after the Casablanca attacks left more than 40 victims dead. As he put it, "All these initiatives have been launched to disrupt the different manifestations of incivility, fanaticism, extremism and ostracism of all those, regardless of their ideological leanings and social motivations, within our country or elsewhere" (Ministere de la Justice, 2012, p. 203). In 2003, he supported the creation of the New National Youth Policy (NPNJ) with the professed goals of stimulating youth's spirit of creativity, engagement, and participation. Multiple departments of government were called on to execute the vision and programs of the NPNJ. The Ministry of Youth and Sport (MYS) was encouraged to review and revitalize the country so that young people could be taught tolerance and democratic values. A new National Institute of Youth and Democracy was also created in 2007 to advance the political education and democratic participation of the young and increase their civic engagement (personal interview with State Secretary of Youth and Sports, 2009).

In Jordan, King Hussein moved on to build youth councils, youth programs, and youth initiatives as soon as he inherited the throne. In his 2000 throne-opening speech, he promised his 60% of young population that "the government will also articulate a clear policy for the development of youth services. This policy will be predicated on scientific bases that consolidate the youth's sense of belonging and instill in them the values of professional, social, voluntary and creative work . . ." (http://kingabdullah.jo/index.php/en_US/quotes/view/page/2/cid/25.html). When the terror attacks hit Amman, the security component was made visible, as confirmed by the title of the July 2005 presentation by the Jordanian Minister of Education, Khaled Touqan, "Civic Education in Jordan: Developing Active Citizens to Advance Peace and Stability." The same year, Jordan also launched the 2005–2009 National Youth Strategy prepared by the Higher Council for Youth (HCY). The strategy is meant to encourage youth's participation in the country's comprehensive development. Taking stock of what has been accomplished within the first six years of the King's leadership, the HCY president celebrated the creation of 22 youth centers and seven youth houses, including the creation of the national scout team, youth parliaments, football stadiums, and multi-purpose sports halls. The new strategy was targeting the creation of 12 youth clubs established in the country with the coordination of universities, community colleges, and schools.

In addition to national strategies promoting civic education and international interest in youth, young people themselves became important actors in educating themselves and each other in how to be socially and politically active. With the help, support, and funding of various international donors and organizations, young people in both Jordan and Morocco have been encouraged to train each other and create spaces for discussing responsible citizenship. In Morocco and in Jordan, the funds came from USAID and the

U.S. State Department Middle East Partnership Initiative. The motivations of young social entrepreneurs, as discussed below, ranged from political investment in empowering their peers to the far more pragmatic project of self-employment and self-promotion in a sector that was attracting considerable funding. What is important to underline here is that civics has developed into a site that is structured by and expressive of power struggles among different political actors. The different motivations outlined above have produced a thriving industry around 'civic education' and 'engagement'—an industry that has had many contenders, agendas, and channels.

WHAT DO WE TEACH WHEN WE TEACH CIVIC EDUCATION?

The creation of Arab Civitas and the partnerships that have formed around and through this initiative provide context for describing what is meant by civic education and how it is delivered to the young with authoritarian regimes. Arab Civitas is not limited to Moroccan or Jordanian youth exclusively. However, the two leading centers are based in Morocco and Jordan. Understanding the larger context within which Arab Civitas was created sheds light on the goals of the centers as well as what is being or not being taught when we talk about civics. The regional network known as Arab Civitas was created in 2003 when USAID Washington funded a conference on "Civic Education in the Arab World" at the Dead Sea, Jordan, 2003.

The meeting brought together civic educators from a number of Arab countries who pledged to support a regional network that would promote civic awareness among MENA citizens, especially the youth. The initial small network of countries (Egypt, Jordan, and the West Bank and Gaza) soon expanded to include Morocco, Lebanon, Yemen, Tunisia, Algeria, Bahrain, Egypt, Saudi Arabia, Qatar, Oman, Kuwait, and the UAE. With its regional office set in Amman, Jordan, the network organized the first training workshop in 2004 (Cairo, Egypt) and the second in 2005 (Casablanca, Morocco). The organization of the conferences as well as the training materials for the center have been largely shaped and influenced by the Center for Civic Education (CCE), the California-based nonprofit educational corporation that has been active in the field of international civic education since 1996. The CCE has established its international reputation largely through its work in Eastern European countries to promote civic awareness in these countries during their post-Soviet transition. CCE's two flagship programs, Project Citizen and, have been reproduced around the world, and form the pillars of the many centers and training programs across MENA.

Project Citizen (PC) focuses on the middle-school-level extra-curricular program in which student teams follow a five-step process to identify and research a school or community issue, evaluate solutions, and prepare and implement an action plan to resolve the issue. The Foundations for Democracy (FOD) program targets primary school students (K-12) with interactive reading and discussion activities based on four elements of democratic behavior—justice, responsibility, authority, and privacy. Thus, while the first seeks to help young people "monitor and influence public policy," the latter "promotes civic competence and responsibility" among youth (MEPI, 2005). The teaching of CCE modules are also taken to some university-level students and other school clubs with the funding from USAID and its implementing partners, the United Nation Democracy Program and the many other international actors discussed in the first section of the paper. As outlined by Richard Nuccio, Director of Civitas International Programs at the Center for Civic Education, in his 2007 opening speech in Casablanca, "The Role of the National System of Education in Promoting Civic Behavior," there are four aspects of the curriculum.

> The Authority curriculum helps students (1) distinguish between authority and power, (2) examine different sources of authority, (3) use reasonable criteria for selecting people for positions of authority and for evaluating rules and laws, (4) analyze the benefits and costs of authority, and (5) evaluate, take, and defend positions on the proper scope and limits of authority;
>
> the Privacy curriculum helps students (1) understand the importance of privacy in a free society, (2) analyze the benefits and costs of privacy, and (3) evaluate, take, and defend positions on the proper scope and limits of privacy;
>
> the Responsibility curriculum helps students (1) understand the importance of responsibility in a free society, (2) analyze the benefits and costs of responsibility, (3) evaluate, take, and defend positions on how conflicts among competing responsibilities should be resolved, and (4) evaluate, take, and defend positions on personal responsibility; and
>
> the Justice curriculum helps students (1) understand and apply the basic principles of justice set forth in fundamental documents of democratic political and legal systems, (2) evaluate, take, and defend positions on the fair distribution of the benefits and burdens of society, on fair responses to remedy wrongs and injuries, and on fair procedures for gathering information and making decisions. (Nuccio, 2007)

It is within this overarching framework that one Center for Civic Education was created in Morocco and another one in Jordan with almost identical objectives, approaches, partnerships, and activities. The Moroccan Center for Civic Education was created in 2004 as an independent NGO with the mission to train and educate younger generations to "become responsible, effective and active citizens committed to democratic principles" (http://www.civicmorocco.org). Within one year of its creation, the Center was boasting the reach of its programs and presence in five out of 16 regions of Morocco. Such a presence is supported by the Moroccan Ministry of Education, The Higher Council for Education, numerous other governmental and non-governmental organizations, and the CIVITAS International network.

The Center provides several training workshops in various cities for teachers, supervisors, university students, and others who lead Arab Civitas programs in Moroccan classrooms. The Center also plays a leading role in organizing and hosting international conferences on the subject. In 2008, it helped organize the Twelfth World Congress on Civic Education, entitled "Sustaining Civic Education: Achievements and Challenges," where educators representing more than 65 countries and 30 U.S. states met in Casablanca and Ifrane to share the 'best practices' in securing the sustained commitment of educators, policymakers, and civil society to civic education programs around the world. In this, as in other meetings before and after it, the discussions take place under the High Patronage of His Majesty Mohammed VI King of Morocco.

Likewise, the Jordanian Center for Civic Education Studies (JCCES) was established one year prior to the Moroccan one with exactly the same objectives, allies, and partnerships. In addition to targeting young Jordanians, the Center also work with national NGOs, national media, schoolteachers, administrators, and universities to spread the teaching of civic education, rights, and responsibilities. The goals are typically carried out through the development of civic education and human rights curriculum materials, the organization of workshops and teacher-training seminars, and the establishment of a local trainers' network. In all of this, CCE's two flagship programs play the central role in both defining what civic education is and how it should be taught.

Like its Moroccan counterpart, the center diversifies its sources of funding and partnerships to sustain its work. Between October 2008 and November 2010, the Jordanian Center partnered with World Learning to implement their two-year USD 400,000 project The Student Civic Action: Engaging and Empowering Emerging Leaders in Universities in Jordan (UNJOREL).[1] The project worked to develop the capacity of young Jordanians (18–25 years old) in universities and NGOs to become youth leaders and build on their sociopolitical awareness and energy to help community development and to build active and democratic citizenship. For its training of teachers and university students, JCCES partnered with Konrad Adenaur Stiftung in Amman to conduct civic education and human rights workshops for educators in private and public schools and an introductory civic education workshop for students coming from different universities in Jordan. Between 2006 and 2008, the JCCES worked with the CCE to develop a software-based version of the Project Citizen civic education curriculum in Arabic and English for The Jordanian Ministry of Education Discovery schools.

The e-enabled program introduces 16 localized and developed e-lessons, covering Project Citizen curricular materials in both Arabic and English for the Jordanian students.

1. A citizen of the state
2. Intro to project citizen

3. What is public policy
4. Introducing concerns in the community
5. Information Gathering
6. Presenting information
7. Criteria for problem selection
8. Selecting a problem for project citizen
9. Developing a class portfolio
10. Group tasks in portfolio
11. Group networking
12. Portfolio Evaluation
13. Objective of presentation
14. Reflecting on the learning experience
15. Presenting a project citizen portfolio
16. The importance of participation in project citizen

The two centers stand today as the leading regional hubs for civic engagement that bring together national and international actors to deliver youth services ranging from the training of trainers to building youth's knowledge, skills, and competences. The curriculum components and the design of the training workshops all point to the considerable benefits of civic education on the formation of young citizens, as underscored by generations of scholars on the topic. Civic education is expected to enhance young people's knowledge about rights and responsibilities, build their competence and confidence to exercise them, foster a sense of belonging to the community and nation, and create motivation for them to be more engaged. In many ways, the gains from civic education fall under the broader umbrella of Positive Youth Development (Benson, Scales, Hamilton & Sesma, 2006), which emphasizes six types of youth assets: competence (enhancing social skills), confidence (self-esteem), connection (building social network and supportive relationship), character, caring, and contribution in reducing psychosocial risk and increasing wellbeing.

In the case of Morocco and Jordan, there are no measures for assessing whether these important goals are achieved despite numerous claims to success made by the centers' founders over the years. To date, there still are no rigorous, independent, or systematic evaluations of the projects developed or implemented by the Jordanian or Moroccan centers. What is available and made public (including information on their own websites and media coverage) speaks of youth empowerment and an increased sense of confidence, belonging, and ownership. The evidence of any impact is thus mostly anecdotal and is based on unquestioned assumptions including the linearity of the process of education. The logic here is that what is taught to young people will impact their behavior according to the objectives of the teaching. The systematic input/output logic is not only difficult to ascertain, given the complexity of determining any causality, but is also problematic. It denies the young actors their agency in interpreting and acting on this information within the contexts and constraints of their everyday lives. The logic also places civic education outside of the social, cultural, political, and economic context in which the centers are created, the programs designed and implemented, and the young people targeted.

The last section of this paper focuses precisely on these larger contexts and the voices of the trainers and young people themselves to underline the series of tensions and contradictions in which civic education is caught, particularly within authoritarian regimes. Drawing on interviews with youth, youth workers, and various actors in the youth sector in Jordan and Morocco, I reflect on some of the lessons learned from Jordan and Morocco.

PROMISES AND PITFALLS OF YOUTH CIVIC EDUCATION

The Jordanian and Moroccan centers for civic education provide an interesting basis for discussing the promises and limitations of civic education, especially when we contextualize the actors and their motivations for approaching youth. Whether the claim for promoting youth civic education is to produce 'active citizenship,' 'inclusive citizenship,' or 'responsible citizenship,' imparting civic knowledge entails fostering specific values and norms according to specific priorities and interests. This process is fundamentally political. As such, the success of the initiatives and programs targeting youth is variable and dependent on the priorities of those promoting them. The tensions and contradictions, therefore, emerge not only from the multiplicity of actors and agendas but also and mostly from the gap between the rhetoric and practice of civics—between what the projects promise to do and what the constraining realities allow them to achieve.

In the context of Morocco and Jordan, despite the pro-reform and pro-youth agendas of the Monarchs, civic education is defined as successful when it remains 'under the tutelage' of the political leadership and urban elite. That is, civic education is expected to empower the youth population, but only if such an empowerment does not disturb or disrupt the existing political arrangements and power structures. The project of civic education/participation is expected to simultaneously sharpen *as well as* constrain youth's political consciousness and their creative civic energies. Given the historical and political moment in which civic education was rediscovered, the project has become rather a tool for monitoring, pacifying, and countering the 'at-risk' behavior of youth and neutralizing their forms of dissent politics.

This politicization and securitization of civic education has produced an interesting cynical attitude among some young people themselves. To the question of why work on civic education, the founder of one of the main youth organizations I interviewed in 2009 in Casablanca responded: "Civic education and youth empowerment? This is where the money is. It is as simple as that. It is the law of supply and demand. Donors demand it and I can supply it." For other youth who did not use civic education as an income generating activity, their participation in training and workshop provided "a break from the daily routine. We are unemployed after all and all we have is time," as some expressed in their interviews. There is no denial, many confirmed, that they are learning a great deal from the training and the civic clubs, but they also like these because they "provide us with travel opportunities, free food, entertainment, and a space to meet and connect with other youth."

For many national and international promoters of civic education, success is measured in numbers: the number of workshops, young people who attend them, and civic classes and clubs. For others, impact is measured by how many young people cast a vote in local or national elections, no matter what or who they are voting for. For an interviewed USAID representative in Morocco, civic education has produced a "new, dynamic outlook on citizenship within the younger generation, which will likely translate into increased voter turnout in elections and possibly the choice of a career in politics among certain PC graduates." Many governments in MENA encourage civic education as long as it produces uncritically loyal citizens who know rights in the absolute but do not claim them from their political elite. This is why many of the young I interviewed did not see education increasing their trust in their local and national leadership or producing a motivation to participate in what many called 'dirty politics.'

In addition, contradiction in the teaching of civic education also arises when we take into consideration the characteristics of the learning environment in which it takes place and the pedagogical tools employed. In environments where teaching is knowledge-centered rather than learner-centered and where teachers are the ultimate producers of knowledge that students are expected to dutifully consume, there are minimal opportunities for developing critical, independent-thinking, and confident young citizens (Ksikes, 2005). Interviews with young people who participated in civics programs highlighted their frustration with the inconsistency between the rights-oriented curriculum and the repressive environments in which they are taught (including schools). Others complained about the sense of possibility the education creates and the limited opportunities they have for exercising it. Introducing new democratic values in fundamentally undemocratic structures and systems of learning, as one teacher confessed, "is akin to pouring a new drink in old bottles and expecting the drink to transform the shape of the bottle." For a young woman, civic education through the CCE modules has "complicated" her life. By this she means "now that I know my rights and have better understanding of the principles of democracy, I find it extremely hard to put up with so much corruption and repression around me. But I know I will use this knowledge." These statements were made only a few years before youth power rose up in MENA to demand justice and dignity.

Assessments of the civics curricula in various MENA contexts have confirmed the heavy orientation of the curriculum towards state institutions, formal political structures, and traditional paradigms of citizenship. Despite many documented innovative initiatives in the content and pedagogy of civics classes, there remains a visible omission of contemporary and controversial issues from the civic curriculum and the exclusion of information most relevant to students' immediate realities (Ksikes, 2005). Failure to engage youth in more current issues and more participative forms of learning about civic behavior seem to reinforce rather than diminish the distance between theory and practice.

CONCLUSION

In this chapter, I used Morocco and Jordan as cases for discussing how youth 'civics' is a political site of competing, colliding, and occasionally complementary interests. Various groups of stakeholders have been and still are implicated in this process: the state, supranational agencies, international NGOs, local partners, the political elite, and civil society organizations including youth groups.

The MENA region is undergoing considerable political, social, and cultural change, some of which is driven by its young people. Providing civic education is one of the foundations for promoting and institutionalizing the culture of rights, justice, and engagement. The global security context and the national authoritarian environments within which youth have been taught and trained in civics undermine the promises of this vital tool of acquiring political knowledge and skills. But, as the Arab uprisings and revolutions have demonstrated, despite all efforts to control how young people acquire and use civic knowledge, young people create alternative spaces for peer education, mobilization, and action. Thus, the belief entertained by many political leaders that civic education can simultaneously empower and contain young people is not only ill-founded but also counterproductive.

NOTE

1. For a detailed description of the objectives of UNJOREL, see the report produced in March 2011 by the UN Democracy Fund.

REFERENCES

Benson, P. L., Scales, P. C., Hamilton, S. F., & Sesma, A. (2006). *Positive youth development so far: Core hypotheses and their implications for policy and research*. Retrieved from http://www.isbe.net/learningsupports/climate/pdfs/positive-youth-dev.pdf

Economist. (2007). *Enquête Unicef-Fnuap «Jeunes en action» Au seuil du «conflit des générations»* (N. 2663). Retrieved from http://www.leconomiste.com/ . . . /enquete-unicef

EQUIP3. (2007). *Morocco cross-sectoral youth assessment report*. Retrieved from www.csy.edc.org/pdf/Morocco_Appendices.pdf

European Commission. (2009). *Euromed youth policies in intercultural dialogue*. Strasbourg. Retrieved from www.media-diversity.org/ . . . /index.php? . . . euro-med-youth-policies-in-int

Fuller, G. (2003). *The youth factor: The new demographics of the Middle East and the implications for U.S. policy* (Analysis paper 3). Saban Center for Middle East Policy, Brookings Institution.

Hendrixson, A. (2003). *The youth bulge: Defining the next generation of young men as a threat to the future* (Publication of the Population and Development Program, N. 19). 27–30.

Khatayba, Y.D. (2009). Obstacles to youth's participation in political parties (Text in Arabic). *Jordanian Journal of Social Sciences, 2*(3), 318–333.

Ksikes, D. (2005, May). Comment l'Education nationale forme de mauvais citoyens. *TelQuel* Retrieved from http://www.telquel-online.com/190/couverture_190_1.shtml

MEPI. (2005). *The Middle East partnership initiative: An overview*. Retrieved from www.fas.org/sgp/crs/ . . . /RS21457.pdf

Ministere de la Justice. (2012). *La «Justice» dans les Discours et les Messages de Sa Majesté le Roi Mohammed VI de 1999 à 2011*. Rabat, Morocco.

Nuccio, R.A. (2007). *Promoting civic behavior through civic education*. Kingdom of Morocco, High Council of Education, Rabat, Morocco. Retrieved from www.civiced.org/pdfs/PromotingCivicBehavior.pdf

Pace, M., & Tobias, S. (2004). Culture and community in the Euro-Mediterranean partnership: A roundtable on the third basket. *Mediterranean Politics, 9*(1), 122–126.

Skalli, L.H. (2013). Youth, media and the politics of change in North Africa. *Journal of Culture and Communication in the Middle East, 6*, 3.

Skalli, L. H. (2015). The *Girl Effect* in the Middle East: The insecurity of coloniality. *Alternatives: Global, Local, Political, 39*, 2.

Steinberger, M. (2001, October 21). So, are civilizations at war? Interview with Samuel P. Huntington. *Observer*. Retrieved from: http://www.theguardian.com/world/2001/oct/21/afghanistan.religion2

Youngs, R. (2006). *Europe and the Middle East: In the Shadow of September 11*. Boulder, CO: Lynne Rienner Publisher.

Wittes, T. C., & Youngs, R. (2009). *Europe, the United States, and Middle Eastern democracy: Repairing the breach* (Analysis Paper 18). The Saban Center for Middle East Policy at the Brookings Institution.

16 Paternalism in Educating and Developing Our Youth

The Perpetuation of Inequality

Marcus Pope

In simplistic terms, paternalism is a practice that involves an individual or institution serving in a relatively privileged capacity and making decisions that are purportedly for the good of the 'less fortunate.' Duflo (2012) defines paternalism as "the practice of providing a set of 'basic needs' for people (the set may vary), typically without consulting them on what their needs actually are" (p. 2). Paternalism consistently diminishes—and often disregards—the input of subordinate individuals when decisions are made on how resources are to be deployed to meet their needs. As such, it is a manifestation of a complex system of power, privilege, and wealth that implicitly seeks to maintain the status quo. Paternalism is distinct from overt racial oppression, operating as what one scholar has referred to as a more rational, durable, and legally justifiable form of oppression (Baker, 2001). Although paternalism is less overt than historical practices of discrimination, such practices ultimately perpetuate inequality. In fact, the paternalistic practices that are pervasive in youth development, philanthropy, government, and nonprofit social and educational services are often viewed as gracious and in some instances heroic efforts to improve the plight of those 'in need.' For example, consider youth leadership programs that are led exclusively by adults and aim to teach youth to conform to adult ideals. Or, high-profile efforts led by government bodies, philanthropies, or nonprofits to solve issues among marginalized populations that fail to involve those most impacted by the issue. Both examples embody, reinforce, and even perpetuate the problem they are attempting to address. Rather than excluding service recipients from the decision-making process, which often leads to privileged groups being the primary beneficiaries of resources allocated to support the less fortunate, I am proposing strategies that strive to eradicate paternalism and the adverse consequences it produces for youth impacted by inequality.

In the sections that follow, I use my rich professional experience as a youth worker, director of youth programming, and someone who currently works in a youth-focused philanthropic organization to offer the concept of paternalism as an explanation for inequality and as a concept to seriously consider as we seek to resolve the growing disparities that exist. I will provide critical background on the use of paternalism in the scholarly literature to crystallize the term's relevancy in the discussion of inequality in youth development, provide evidence related to the need for a sense of urgency to address paternalism, and offer practical strategies to mitigate its effects. The discussion will focus primarily on the field of youth development and others that impact youth such as the nonprofit sector, philanthropy, and K-12 and higher education.

THE DEMOGRAPHIC REALITY

The social mobility and welfare of young people representing communities of color are serious issues of concern within the United States. Population shifts over the past several decades are playing a major role in this growing concern. In 1960, whites comprised 85% of the nation's population, while blacks constituted 11%, and Hispanics and Asians comprised 3.5% and 0.6%, respectively (Taylor & Cohn, 2012). When considering more recent statistics, America's white population decreased to 63% in 2011, while the black population stayed relatively unchanged at 12%. Growth among the Hispanic and Asian populations was exponential, with the Asian population share at 9%, more than 8 times its population share in 1960; Hispanics more than quadrupled their share to 17% during that same time period (Taylor & Cohn, 2012). Further projections indicate that the U.S. will be a 'majority minority' nation by 2050, with whites representing less than half of the nation's total population and Hispanics representing approximately 30% (Taylor & Cohn, 2012).

Of equal importance is the demographic shift in the age of the American population. In several states, retired adults will outnumber school children within the next five to 10 years. In 1960, adults 65 and over represented 12% of the nation's population. The U.S. Administration on Aging (2005) projects that this population will comprise 22% in 2020 and more than 25% by 2050. With the graying of our nation comes an increased responsibility for young people—in particular, young people of color who represent the majority of the projected population growth—to become skilled decision-makers and productive citizens equipped to contribute to the sustainability of a healthy democracy.

Given the demographic reality, a sense of urgency is needed in addressing the disparities and inequality that currently exist in the United States. Significant disparities exist between white youth and those of other racial groups in outcomes across several areas, including health, education, and employment. For example, Native American and Latino youth scored below national averages on 11 out of 12 indicators of life chances on the most recent *Race for Results Survey* (The Annie E. Casey Foundation, 2014). Similarly, African American youth also scored below national averages in 10 of 12 categories. Conversely, white youth and Asian/Pacific Islander youth as a whole scored above average for each measure. In addition, African American, Latino, and Native American youth are also disproportionately enmeshed in government-run systems, including child welfare and juvenile justice. To address these issues, several strategies are being tested, validated, and replicated by government systems and nonprofits; yet grave disparities still exist—even as we promote evidence-based, data-informed, and research-based strategies. What is conspicuously absent in our efforts to eradicate inequality is the role, capacity, and self-determination of the less fortunate in devising, implementing, and evaluating strategies to address their own needs.

PATERNALISM DEFINED

Few have examined the concept of paternalism specifically as it relates to youth development. I am defining paternalism as the systematic practice on the part of individuals, organizations, and institutions in positions of authority restricting the autonomy, self-determination, and voice of those subordinate to them in the subordinates' supposed best interest. This exclusion is both deliberate and subtle as it plays out in the institutionalized practices of philanthropic organizations, government agencies, nonprofit organizations, school systems, and other actors that carry out and resource services targeting disadvantaged youth. Programs and services that implicitly and intentionally operationalize paternalism are diverse in nature. They can include positive youth development activities; formal education; youth intervention programming; formal K-12 education; and child welfare, juvenile justice, and other human services designed to address the various needs of youth and the community. Consistent is that paternalism is a cause and consequence of the inequality such programs and systems are working diligently to address. Systemic paternalism is beyond the individual in that it operates within the very fabric of our institutions. Yet it plays out on the individual level through the practices of individuals and the mindset of those who work directly with youth. I use the following story to highlight paternalism and how scenarios that do not align with paternalistic practices can cause confusion in the workplace.

> *Fresh from the University of Minnesota, and armed with an undergraduate degree with a focus on youth studies, I secured a job at a local adolescent shelter. My employment was a true joy and learning experience. Aside from the financial incentives of employment and building a resume as a young professional, it was an opportunity to give back and to have a positive impact on younger African American males who were experiencing life challenges. Many of the residents were African American, and a majority came from my local community. For the most part, they attended the same schools I attended, frequented the same community*

> *centers, and experienced similar life situations. My colleagues were also wonderful. We too shared some commonalities. However, it took time and relationship building to identify our shared interests and characteristics. My colleagues were largely white, the majority attended a local Christian College, and they exclusively grew up in communities that were clearly distinct from the communities the shelter residents grew up in. They were good colleagues and great human beings. Our relationship as colleagues was likely their first opportunity to consistently engage with someone with my background—an African American male from the inner city—as a peer or as an equal. One interaction with a co-worker exposed this reality and has stuck with me for over a decade. While observing me interacting with the residents, one of my colleagues chuckled and said to me, "You are just like them," referring to the residents as "them."*

When confronted with this moment, I looked at my colleague and smiled in response. I was proud of my identification with the residents and my ability to connect with them in authentic ways. As a shelter care worker, I employed different strategies to get compliance when necessary, though most of the time compliance was not necessary because we were engaged in shared experiences that consumed the moment at hand. My colleague was right. In a lot of ways, I was "just like them." When driving offsite to various activities, we often had consensus related to the radio station of choice; we could talk about our community in ways that foreigners did not understand; and I could 'talk trash' at the onsite basketball court in a way that would make them think they were playing hoops in their own neighborhood.

In retrospect, my colleague meant no harm or disrespect by her comment. However, the story exposes the harsh reality of the current system and exposes the implicit notion that I was out of place in my role at the adolescent shelter. All social norms and expectations positioned me on the other end of the service-delivery spectrum. Despite my degree and requisite experience, my similarity and identification with the social and cultural realities of the consumer of services was abnormal and potentially a cause for concern. This was especially true if I failed to be strategic about how to navigate my shared profile and lived experience with the residents. The volatility of the situation was especially evident during my early days on the job when I was mistaken for a resident by a cook who tried to reprimand me for actions inconsistent with how a resident should behave.

At the center of the discussion in the complex and disturbing dynamic of paternalism in 'help-giving' for disadvantaged youth is the argument that people "just like them," or those most impacted by the disparities in our communities, should be a part of developing, implementing, and allocating resources to address their needs. Two overarching problems with the paternalistic model are that services tend to be adult-driven rather than youth (or client)-driven, and services are largely designed by the majority culture with a consumer base that is largely made up of minority ethnic and racial groups. In both cases, the people who are being served have little or no voice in the conceptualization, design, or delivery of services that are supposed to have a positive impact on them.

Too often, those most impacted are relegated to the passive role of service recipient, while those most disconnected from the realities of inequality are resourced to solve the problems of others whose realities they do not fully understand. This troubling dynamic of paternalism in youth development results in poor outcomes for youth and families and ultimately perpetuates inequality.

HISTORICAL ROOTS OF PATERNALISM

The concept of paternalism is not new to the literature and has a rich history in philosophy, social psychology, medicine, legal scholarship, and the social welfare discourse. Its roots can be found in philosophy that links the relationship between the employer as patron and his workers to that of a father and his children who were considered inferior and under-developed. As delineated in Plato's *Republic* (1992, trans.), Plato believed in absolute power and viewed the role of the state and the king as protectors of citizens from themselves and immoral behavior. In this role, the king operated as a father to his citizens. Aristotle believed in a natural hierarchy and that individuals should be subject to a higher authority. Although Plato and Aristotle's views differed slightly, they both agreed on the roles of citizens as subordinates and their need to be guided toward virtue (Kleinig, 1983).

For critics of this theory, the biggest flaw is that paternalism overrides an individual's agency on the grounds that those in power presume to know better than those in need (Banerjee & Duflo, 2011). This belief can be particularly harmful. One good reason to reject paternalism is that public officials acting in some remote government office do not in fact know better whether an activity is detrimental to our enduring self (Klein, 1994). John Stuart Mill, one of the first contemporary philosophers to address paternalism, argues that conformity by coercion is only acceptable if the individual's actions cause harm or could potentially harm other people (Mill, 1859). Although Mill does not use the language of paternalism, in his 1895 publication entitled *On Liberty*, he clearly provides an argument against paternalism in promoting "social liberty" (Sankowski, 1985).

One could argue that the most extensive scholarly debate related to paternalism has occurred within the medical field. Although medical paternalism has many facets, the notion that the doctor knows best and can make unilateral decisions in the best interest of the patient is no longer considered best practice. Physicians have grown to view the values and desires of the patient as central to quality care. Some scholars have termed this transition "modern paternalism" (Weiss, 1985). He describes the evolution of medicine from paternalism to modern paternalism: "A more homogenous culture in the past allowed physicians to assume that they shared values with their patients, but in a pluralistic society, the patients' views can never be assumed. Today's physician must ascertain the values and interests of the patient. Omission of this step is a betrayal of the fundamental principles underlying modern paternalism" (Weiss, 1985, p. 186).

The move away from paternalism within medicine and in other areas was highly influenced by the era of the 1960s, as civil rights and civil liberties rose to the forefront of our nation's consciousness. During this era, the rights and self-determination of people of color, prisoners, children, the mentally ill, those under the care of state, and other groups we currently view as protected classes became the subject of critical debate (Reamer, 1983). The 1960s and 1970s also represented greater application of the concept of paternalism to the social service arena, with research findings showing greater paternalistic attitudes among those working in social services and, in particular, veteran employees in social service agencies (Stone, 1977).

The contemporary debate concerning paternalism involves numerous issues, including criminal legislation against the use of recreational drugs, regulation of food choices, and abortion as well as other topics in the area of social policy. Recently, a group known as Incite! has challenged the ability of the nonprofit organizations to achieve social change. Although the group does not specifically cite paternalism, the basic premise of the group's argument is that the conditions placed on government and corporate funding limit the ability of nonprofits to truly achieve a social change agenda. They argue for social change organizations to adopt other fundraising strategies that allow for greater autonomy in pursuing social change agendas (Incite! Women of color against violence, 2007).

Other scholars have examined the issues of paternalism as it relates to poverty programs. In their book *Disciplining the Poor: Neoliberal Paternalism and the Persistent Power of Race* Soss, Fording, and Schram (2011) use data from the last four decades to show how poverty governance in the post-Civil War era has become increasingly paternalistic; in particular, the authors show the pervasive and systemic nature of paternalism and how it plays out at the federal, state, and county levels.

APPLYING PATERNALISM IN YOUTH DEVELOPMENT

Factoring in the concept of paternalism moves the conversation beyond discussions regarding who is targeted for intervention or services (service recipient) to a more substantive conversation about who is driving decision-making and who are the primary beneficiaries of resources deployed to address youth inequality. Much work has been done on how to address disparities and eliminate racial inequality in education, the nonprofit sector, and philanthropy. Some of this work indirectly addresses paternalism, while other efforts completely fail to address how paternalism impacts and perpetuates inequality. For example, within K-12 education, there have been efforts to disaggregate data to identify youth who are struggling and hold districts accountable for closing gaps (Education Trust, 2009). In addition, there have been strong efforts to look at comprehensive school reform (Borman, Hewes, Overman & Brown, 2003) and collective impact strategies (Kania & Kramer, 2011) that advance educational outcomes. We have also debated the efficacy of neighborhood schools versus school choice options that embrace busing, charter schools, vouchers, and other alternatives that create a competitive marketplace for parents to exercise choice in education (Epple & Romano, 2003). Evidence-based practices have also been emphasized to ensure strategies are proven to be effective. Within government and philanthropy, we have seen increasing efforts to focus resources on targeting underserved communities and zip codes with the highest levels of violence and poverty and where residents are most in need. All of these efforts have merit. However, these efforts alone fail to address paternalism and, therefore, are insufficient in moving the needle as it relates to inequality.

Addressing paternalism within youth development forces programs and systems to consider key questions such as: who is being served; who is being paid to provide services; who is designing intervention strategies; and what perspectives are dominating the discussion and strategies used to address the needs of youth in community. More attention and research should be devoted to fully answer these key questions. However, when we examine national workforce trends related to the number of people of color who are working in key sectors that are critical to youth development, disparities are quite apparent. According to a Center for American Progress brief, people of color comprised 36% of the workforce as of June 2012 (Burns, Barton & Kerby, 2012). Yet these individuals are absent from key positions of influence. For example, blacks, Latinos, and Asians comprise just 4.4% of Fortune 500 CEOs who often are at the center of key decisions related to corporate philanthropy (Covert, 2013). People of color are also underrepresented in the nonprofit sector, which is a primary service provider of underserved communities of color. Burns et al. (2012) report that 82% of employees in the nonprofit sector are white, and 18% are people of color. In both scenarios, there is an obvious need for more engagement of people of color in decision-making that impacts their lives. We must increase the voice and participation of those most impacted by the problem as key decision-makers. They must also be the primary beneficiaries of the resources deployed to address the inequality. This means that resources distributed must not only allow for services to address inequality but also be intentionally distributed to allow the demographic group that is impacted by the problem to lead and staff the organizations and/or informal systems receiving funding to solve youth and community issues.

This perspective addresses two fundamental flaws in how the system is currently structured. The first flaw in the current system of paternalism is that the majority of resources used to address inequality are, for the most part, immediately transferred to organizations and eventually individuals that most likely do not represent the demographic most impacted by inequality. This reality undermines the purpose, goals, and objectives of the resources that should be used to promote a more equitable agenda. The second flaw in the current system of paternalism is the inherent conflict of interest that exists when one group is charged to solve the issues of another group representing a distinct racial/ethnic, socioeconomic, or cultural group.

MY LOCAL CONTEXT AS A CASE STUDY

In Minnesota, there is growing recognition that the prosperity of the state is dependent on the ability to generate equitable opportunities and outcomes for communities of color (Tran & Treuhaft, 2014). Consistent with the national demographic landscape, Minnesota's population is becoming more diverse. By 2012, the percentage of people of color had increased from 1.2% in 1960 to nearly one quarter (24.5%) of the metropolitan area's total population, and this increase is expected to continue (Minnesota Compass, 2014e). A report from the Minnesota Demographic Center estimates that the state's black, Hispanic, and Asian populations will double between 2009 and 2040 (Minnesota Department of Administration, 2009). In addition, the state is home to the largest Somali population in the nation and also has sizable populations of immigrants from other African countries such as Liberia, Nigeria, and Ghana. Population trends among Minnesota's young people also show changes in racial and ethnic makeup. Though white youth still make up the majority of Minnesota's population under the age of 20, that share has dropped from 82% in 1990 to 72% in 2012 (Minnesota Compass, 2014f). Projections indicate that by 2030, white youth will comprise less than 45% of the state's youth population (Metropolitan Council, 2014). Furthermore, students of color are expected to comprise more and more of the school population, with an anticipated 31% growth from 2012 through 2017 and 24% growth for the following five years, from 2017 through 2022 (Minnesota Department of Education, 2013). However, as of 2012, teachers of racial and ethnic groups were on the decline for Native Americans (-13%) and African Americans (-4%) (Minnesota Department of Education, 2013).

Disparities in Outcomes Among Minnesota's Growing Populace

With this changing demographic comes concern about how this will impact the overall well-being of young people. Traditionally, outcomes among Minnesota's minority youth are troubling. Research shows significant inconsistencies when comparing outcomes and quality-of-life measures of white youth with non-white youth in a number of areas, including health, education, income, and systems involvement. For example, Native American youth are 6 times more likely and African American youth are 4 times more likely than their white counterparts to be the subject of child-protection assessments or investigations (Minnesota Department of Human Services, 2010).

One the most worrisome trends centers on the gap in academic achievement. Education inequity is among the most chronic social justice issues that young people face (Youth Leadership Institute, 2009). Over the past eight years, black, Hispanic, and Native American students have continued to lag behind their white peers. In 2013, only 28.6% of Native American students, 29.4% of black students, and 33.5% of Hispanic students were meeting or exceeding standards for eighth-grade math achievement, whereas 65.7% of white students met or exceeded achievement standards (Minnesota Compass, 2014h). Reading scores for third-grade students indicate that 36.7% of students of color met or exceeded achievement standards, compared to 65.8% of white students (Minnesota Compass, 2014i). There are also stark differences by race in the four-year graduation rates among the state's high school youth. Minnesota Compass (2014d) reports that in 2013, more than three-fourths of Asians (77.7%) and whites (84%) graduated from high school on time. Conversely, just over half of blacks (57%) and Hispanics (58.3%), and less than half of Native Americans (48.7%) accomplished the same feat. Statistics on poverty and homelessness follow similar trends (Minnesota Compass, 2014g).

Paternalism as a Factor in Poor Outcomes

Paternalism cannot and should not be blamed entirely for poor outcomes among youth, but the lack of participation of people of color in Minnesota's labor force and the resulting disconnection from implementing solutions to the complex problems facing our growing population representing communities of color is striking. Consider the following: In 2012, Minnesota ranked second highest for its white-Southeast Asian employment gap and white-Native American employment gap (Minnesota Compass, 2014a, 2014b). Similarly, the state had the third-highest white-African American employment gap (Minnesota Compass, 2014c). A report issued by the National Urban League (2014) indicates that Minneapolis' black-white unemployment gap is among the highest, ranking at number 74 out of the 77 cities included in the analysis. In addition, the Hispanic-white unemployment gap is among the worst, ranking 74 out of 83 among metropolitan cities included in the study (National Urban League, 2014).

Another analysis on racial employment disparities in greater Ramsey County reported a significant employment gap in the Twin Cities' 13-county greater metropolitan area: Native-born blacks, with an unemployment rate of 20.6%, were three times more likely to be unemployed than whites (Ramsey County Workforce Investment Board, 2011). Adding to the stress of inadequate income, such disparities have also been connected to other problems, such as K-12 education success, high dropout rates, underdeveloped workforce and professional skills, and low rates of entrepreneurism.

Minnesota Council on Foundations (2011) conducted a survey of city officials in elected positions to measure racial, ethnic, and gender diversity. With a response rate of nearly 80%, the results point to a significant disparity in representation of color. The council reported that although 40% of Minneapolis residents were people of color, approximately 72% of the elected officials were white.

The racial breakdown of Minnesota's classroom teachers has consistently been an issue of concern in the population center of Minnesota. An article examining teacher diversity in two of the state's largest school districts (Minneapolis and Saint Paul) showed that although 76% of Saint Paul Public Schools students were non-white only 15% of teachers are of color (Reagan, 2013).

EVIDENCE OF PATERNALISM IN MY WORK AND LOCAL CONTEXT

The organization for which I work, Youthprise, was established by The McKnight Foundation with a mission to champion learning beyond the classroom so all Minnesota youth thrive. Youthprise strategically combines funding, capacity building, policy advocacy, research, and modeling youth engagement under one roof. This unique combination creates efficiencies, accelerates implementation, and maximizes impact. Youthprise invests directly in and seeks to align efforts across city, regional, and state systems that impact youth. A central tenet of our work is a commitment to racial equity and working to address the disparities faced by youth of color and other disconnected youth.

As a grantmaker that requires prospective grantees to submit youth participant, staff, and board demographic data, the findings are striking. Data collected from 101 organizations primarily serving the Twin Cities regions in 2012 showed that 23% of program participants were white/Caucasian, and the remaining 73% represented the black/African American, Hispanic or Latino, Asian/Asian American/Hawaiian or Other Pacific Islander, multiracial, or American Indian/Alaskan Native populations. Despite this strong emphasis on serving populations representing ethnic and racial minorities, staff and board composition shows a completely different trend. Among the same organizations, 72% of staff and 66% of board members were reported as white/Caucasian. This dynamic is reflective of paternalism, in which those who are most connected to the problem are systematically excluded from opportunities to solve their own problems.

Data regarding the philanthropy sector reveal similar concerns regarding the inclusion of people of color. In 2011, the Minnesota Council on Foundations (MNCOF) released *Working Towards Diversity IV*, which includes an analysis of a study on diversity in the philanthropy sector statewide. The study revealed disparities in several areas. Hispanics, Asians/Asian Americans, and persons identifying as "other" or multiracial were disproportionally underrepresented in leadership roles, including chief executives, board members/chairs, and executive staff (MNCOF, 2011). Less than half of the grantmakers in the study had formal board and/or staff diversity and inclusivity policies, and only one-fourth had such polices for executive staff (MNCOF, 2011). Further, the study found that board membership among African Americans and Native Americans/ Alaskan Natives has acutely declined during the five years preceding the analysis; Asians, Asian Americans, and Pacific Islanders have also experienced a diminishing presence in board membership during that time (MNCOF, 2011).

Although general staff composition for grantmakers was more diverse than board composition and executive leadership, there is a marked difference in the racial and ethnic makeup of grantmakers as a whole and the populations they serve. Of the grantmakers that mentioned targeted populations in their mission statements, 22.5% specified racial or ethnic populations and 45% specified economically disadvantaged groups (which generally have significant representation from racial and ethnic minorities) as at least one of their target beneficiaries (MNCOF, 2011). Yet, non-white individuals represented only 13.4% of Minnesota's grantmaking staff overall (MNCOF, 2011).

STRATEGIES TO ADDRESS PATERNALISM

The systemic nature of paternalism makes it difficult to totally eradicate it from programs and systems striving to promote the healthy development of youth. There is much documentation of how public systems designed to help children and families have functioned in ways that have denied opportunity to people of color—and even worked to push them down the ladder. Throughout much of our history, laws severely restricted access to jobs, health care, and education. Even today, despite great progress, opportunities are not equitably distributed to all Americans (Annie E. Casey Foundation, 2014). Despite this reality, there are steps that can be taken to mitigate the effects of paternalism and move toward progressive change.

A critical first step in addressing the structural issues apparent in government agencies, school districts, nonprofits, philanthropic organizations, and other organizations whose missions are dedicated to the needs of youth and the less fortunate is requesting that these entities voluntarily collect and report data on the demographic characteristics of their populations served versus the demographics of their employees, contracted staff, vendors, and volunteers. Data should be collected in such a way to enable one to distinguish between demographic characteristics of line staff versus organizational leadership. At the sector levels, there should be agreed upon systems for data collection so data can be aggregated to paint a sector-level picture. This information should be reported on an annual basis and made available online and through annual reports. Information collected should be consistently analyzed and programs and systems should make progressive efforts to increase representation.

Although diversity and inclusion in workforce participation are critically important among service systems and organizations, they are not sufficient in addressing paternalism. An organization can be representative of the population served and still reinforce paternalism. In addition, an organization can lack representation and integrate practices and strategies to mitigate paternalism. However, I would argue that if the organization is truly addressing paternalism, those practices will lead to diversification of staffing. Capacity building should be provided, and organizations should document and collect data on how they authentically engage youth and diverse communities in the design, implementation, and evaluation of services.

Youth Engagement and Community Engagement

The notions of youth engagement and community engagement are not new in scholarship or practice. The last two decades have involved increased scholarship on youth and youth civic engagement, linking the practice to a variety of beneficial outcomes at the individual and community level. According to the Youth Leadership Institute (2009), "Youth engagement in decision-making must first examine and explore the effectiveness of existing structures and processes, and then identify new and different strategies and opportunities to engage diverse youth" (p. 14). Further, effectively preparing young people to become thriving adults will require a significant shift from traditional paternalistic approaches to a framework that strongly and authentically engages youth in their own education (Youth Leadership Institute, 2009). In order to do this effectively, students and others impacted by educational practices must have a voice in the planning process at all levels including conceptualization, strategy development, implementation, and evaluation. The use of youth advice-giving structures or advisory groups has grown over the years, as has research to support and strengthen the practice (Roholt, Baizerman, Rana, & Korum, 2013). The Boston Student Advisory Council (Boston's collective student government body) and its community partners formulated the following definition for engaging students in the education process: "Student engagement is when young people are taken seriously as active participants and valued partners with adults in both their own education and decisions that affect the academic and social climate and culture of their learning environment" (Joselowsky & Aseltine, n.d., p. 8).

This produces a range of benefits for the school, the students, the community, and society as a whole.

Just as engaging youth is important, authentic community engagement is vital to lasting social change efforts. In 1995, the Center for Disease Control and Prevention (CDC) began more fully embracing community involvement as a cornerstone for addressing health issues when they established the Committee for Community Engagement (CDC, 2011). CDC defines community engagement as "the process of working collaboratively with groups of people who are affiliated by geographic proximity, special interest, or similar situations with respect to issues affecting their well being" (CDC, 1997, p. 9).

Truly engaging the community moves beyond initiating transactional interactions to cultivating genuine relationships (Nexus Community Partners, 2014). Nexus Community Partners, an organization based in the Twin Cities of Minnesota, has launched an initiative called Building the Field of Community Engagement. The initiative involves six diverse Twin Cities-based organizational partners that include Casa de Esperanza, Cultural Wellness Center, Hope Community, Lyndale Neighborhood Association, Native American Community Development Institute, and Nexus Community Partners. Central to the mission of the collaborative is to elevate community as a key tool to change the ways resources are invested to solve community issues. The focus on developing relationships takes time; however, it yields longer term benefits. This circular progression of community engagement results in a learning process that is constantly evolving. Authentic engagement of youth and community occurs at four levels: seeking, involving, partnering, and empowering. These concepts are further explored in the text that follows.

Seeking: Soliciting Community Perspectives

The community at large is often eager to provide input concerning the issues, systems, and practices that have a direct impact on their lives. This includes having a voice in decisions that shape policies and practices of systems impacting youth. Students, parents, and others in the community can provide a fresh, first-hand perspective on several elements and strategies for effectively educating and developing youth. This valuable perspective can be lacking when intentional efforts to solicit and incorporate community voice are absent in planning and decision-making. There are a variety of ways to include community voice, including conducting focus groups, convening town halls and community meetings, issuing surveys, and leveraging social media to provide online forums as portals for two-way communication. Regardless of the method, perhaps the most essential element of these interactions is two-fold: (1) each forum must provide a genuine opportunity for community members to express their ideas, concerns, and solutions; and (2) there is a sincere intent on the part of the administration to consider and incorporate viable input into forming solutions.

Involving: Giving Multiple Stakeholders a Voice in Making Decisions

Although providing opportunities for input is important, leaders in areas impacting youth must also allow room at the decision-making table for their constituents. In doing so, deliberate efforts are necessary to ensure inclusion of the stakeholders that represent the diversity of the community that is being served. This includes establishing formalized bodies, such as advisory groups and planning committees, as well as welcoming these stakeholders at the highest levels through practices such as ensuring adequate and equal representation on decision-making boards and in high-level staff positions.

Students, parents, and the community must be afforded genuine opportunities to participate as equal partners in the process. Zeldin, Petrokubi and McNeil (2007) describe the goal of youth-adult partnerships as "integrat[ing] youth into existing forums of decision making that have traditionally been reserved for adults, while also creating new structures for youth to influence important decisions" (p. 4). Educators in the United Kingdom have taken this approach to heart by actively engaging school students in running the school. George Mitchell School in east London has formed a panel of students that serve as advisors to the school, offering feedback and constructive ideas on how to improve lessons, discipline policies, and teaching styles. They are even involved in the decision-making process for staffing the school, including taking part in the interview process for hiring new teachers (Sellgren, 2006).

Partnering: Creating Opportunities for Equal Partnerships

The National Resource Center for Youth Development defines youth-adult partnerships as " . . . relationships in which all parties have equal opportunities to contribute, make decisions, use their skills, and learn from each other. The key to youth/adult partnerships is mutuality" (University of Oklahoma, n.d.). A major way to facilitate equal partnership is through ensuring strong representation of the population served on the boards and staffs of organizations impacting youth. This should be done with intentionality, and proper training should be provided for mainstream staff/boards as well as youth and community members. Nexus Community Partners has also established a Boards and Commissions Leadership Institute. The purpose of the 7-month institute is to train and place members from underrepresented groups on city and county publicly appointed boards and commissions that make major decisions about public resource allocations.

Youthprise, an intermediary that strategically combines funding, capacity building, research, and modeling youth engagement, has been intentional about engaging youth at all levels of its organization. Youthprise strives to include youth in all organizational decision-making and has made a significant commitment to youth-directed giving as a part of its grantmaking portfolio. The organization has three designated youth board slots and has made a commitment to increasing youth board slots as well as having a youth co-chair of every board committee. Resources are also invested directly in young people through employment opportunities and a fellowship program. The Change Fellowship program has strategically placed youth in a learning community with local corporate, nonprofit, and government leadership to shape their ideas for community change.

Empowering: Providing Resources and Opportunities to Lead

Authentic engagement at its highest level involves empowering young people and communities with the agency and resources to develop their own solutions to challenges that exist. The Cultural Wellness Center (CWC) and Allina Heath initiated the Backyard Initiative, which seeks to improve the health of people living in seven neighborhoods in Minneapolis. The initiative, which includes other community-based organizations, involves the community in defining what their needs are and how to address them, making them active partners in improving the health of the community. Youth are also engaged in the community commission on health, playing leadership roles in organizing group meetings and utilizing technology to create efficiencies. The Community Commission on Health established by the CWC and Allina initiative oversee the work of Community Health Action Teams (CHATs) that consistently meet to address specific community health issues.

Youthprise has also seeded an internal Youth Participatory Action Research (YPAR) team to engage young people in critically investigating and addressing issues of their concern. The youth researchers operate from a research justice framework and strive to place knowledge production related to youth in the hands of youth. They have consulted on state-funded projects related to education and health disparities. Funds secured from this work supports the team, and the group has been given resources, as part of Youthprise's commitment to youth philanthropy, to reinvest in other networks of youth interested in engaging in YPAR. The YPAR team has also been commissioned to evaluate the work of Youthprise grantees. Their enterprise model is critical in that they don't want to be dependent on Youthprise funding or be driven exclusively by Youthprise's agenda.

CONCLUSION

Paternalism in youth development and education is one of several factors that impact the quality and effectiveness of services to youth. Although at face value paternalistic practices may be designed to address the needs of marginalized youth and communities, they ultimately perpetuate inequality. The program models and strategies outlined in this chapter that are being developed and applied by organizations can serve as useful examples for school systems, philanthropies, the nonprofit sector, and other youth-serving organizations as they seek to address inequality in youth work. Specifically, the examples demonstrate how to genuinely engage youth and communities of color in the framework of their decision-making process and promote better outcomes for ethnically and racially diverse youth.

As youth of color will continue to comprise a greater share of the youth population, educators and youth-service providers must adopt innovative strategies and practices—like the examples provided in this chapter—that combat paternalism and promote an environment in which youth and their communities are actively and consequentially involved in the planning, design, and implementation of the services and activities that are intended to address their needs. This will increase the probability of more meaningful and useful experiences for young people of color. Moreover, adopting a framework that embraces engagement can yield significant residual benefits to our society and economy by better preparing youth of color for the workforce and equipping them to be productive, skilled, and financially stable citizens who are well able to make positive contributions to society and to the nation's economy.

REFERENCES

The Annie E. Casey Foundation. (2014). *Race for results: Building a path to opportunity for all children*. Baltimore, MD: Author. Retrieved from http://www.aecf.org/resources/race-for-results/

Baker, R.S. (2001). The paradoxes of desegregation: Race, class, and education, 1935–1975. *American Journal of Education, 109*(3), 320–343.

Banerjee, V., & Duflo, E. (2011). *Poor economics: A radical rethinking of the way to fight global poverty*. New York: Public Affairs.

Borman, G., Hewes G., Overman, L., & Brown, S. (2003). Comprehensive school reform and achievement: A meta-analysis. *Review of Educational Research, 73*(2), 125–230.

Burns, C., Barton, K., & Kerby, S. (2012). *The state of diversity in today's workforce*. Policy brief. Washington, DC: Center for American Progress.

Center for Disease Control and Prevention. (1997). *Principles of community engagement: CDC/ATSD Committee on Community Engagement*. Atlanta, GA: Center for Disease Control and Prevention.

Covert, B. (2013). *Only white, male CEOs make the big bucks* [Web log post]. Retrieved from http://thinkprogress.org/economy/2013/10/22/2816041/white-men-ceos/

Duflo, E. (2012). *Human values and the design of the fight against poverty: Paternalism versus freedom?* Paper presented at The Tanner Lectures in Human Values at Mahindra Humanities Center, Harvard University, Cambridge, MA.

Education Trust. (2009). *ESEA: Myths versus Realities. Answers to common questions about the new No Child Left Behind Act*. Washington, DC: Education Trust.

Epple, D., & Romano, R. (2003). Neighborhood schools, choice, and the distribution of educational benefits. In C. Hoxby (Ed.), *The economics of school choice* (pp. 227–286). Chicago, IL: University of Chicago Press.

Incite! Women of color against violence. (2007). *The revolution will not be funded: Beyond the nonprofit industrial complex*. Cambridge, MA: South End Press.

Joselowsky, F., & Aseltine, E. (n.d.). *Students as co-constructors of the learning environment: Building systemic approaches for youth engagement*. Washington, DC: Academy for Educational Development and Youth on Board.

Kania, J., & Kramer M. (2011). Collective impact. *Stanford Social Innovation Review*, 9(1), 36–41.

Klein, D. (1994). *The moral consequences of paternalism: Should government protect us from our vices?* Retrieved from http://www.fee.org/the_freeman/detail/the-moral-consequences-of-paternalism

Kleinig, J. (1983). *Paternalism*. Manchester: Manchester University Press.

Metropolitan Council. (2014, February). *Metro stats—A growing and changing twin cities region: Regional forecast to 2040*. St. Paul: Metropolitan Council.

Mill, J. S. (1859). *On liberty*. London: J.W. Parker and Sons.

Minnesota Compass. (2014a). *Employment gap: White—American Indian—Rank of states* (Data file). Retrieved from http://www.mncompass.org/disparities/race#1–10666-g

Minnesota Compass. (2014b). *Employment gap: White—Southeast Asian—Rank of states* (Data file). Retrieved from http://www.mncompass.org/disparities/race#1–10671-g

Minnesota Compass. (2014c). *Employment gap: White—black—Rank of states, 2010–2012* (Data file). Retrieved from http://www.mncompass.org/disparities/race#1–10679-g

Minnesota Compass. (2014d). *High school students graduating on time by racial and ethnic group* (Data file). Retrieved from http://www.mncompass.org/education/high-school-graduation#1–6084-g

Minnesota Compass. (2014e). *Persons of color as a percent of the total population* (Data file). Retrieved from http://www.mncompass.org/demographics/race#1–5105-g

Minnesota Compass. (2014f). *Population by age and race* (Data file). Retrieved from http://www.mncompass.org/demographics/age#1–5415-g

Minnesota Compass. (2014g). *Rate of homelessness per 10,000 adults (18+) by racial and ethnic group* (Data file). Retrieved from http://www.mncompass.org/housing/homeless-persons#1–10818-g

Minnesota Compass. (2014h). *8th grade students achieving math standards by racial and ethnic group, Minnesota, 2006–2013* (Data file). Retrieved from http://www.mncompass.org/disparities/race#1–10758-d

Minnesota Compass. (2014i). *3rd grade students achieving reading standards by racial and ethnic group, Minnesota, 2006–2013* (Data file). Retrieved from http://www.mncompass.org/disparities/race#1–9516-d

Minnesota Council on Foundations. (2011). *Working towards diversity IV*. Retrieved from http://www.mcf.org/research/diversity

Minnesota Department of Administration, Minnesota State Demographic Center. (2009). *Minnesota population projections by race and Hispanic origin, 2005 to 2035* (Publication No. OSD-09–136). Retrieved from http://www.demography.state.mn.us/ documents/ MinnesotaPopulationProjectionsbyRaceandHispanic-Origin2005to2035.pdf

Minnesota Department of Education. (2013). *Teacher supply and demand: Fiscal year 2013 report to the legislature*. Retrieved from http://education.state.mn.us/MDE/mdeprod /groups/communications/documents/basic/050407.pdf

Minnesota Department of Human Services. (2010). *Minnesota child welfare disparities report*. Retrieved from https://edocs.dhs.state.mn.us /lfserver/Public/DHS-6056-ENG

National Urban League. (2014). *State of black America—One nation underemployed: Jobs rebuild America*. Washington, DC: National Urban League.

Nexus Community Partners. (2014). *The impacts of community engagement*. St. Paul, MN: Nexus Community Partners.

Plato. (1992). *Republic* (G. M. A. Grube, Trans.). Indianapolis: Hackett Publishing Company.

Ramsey County Workforce Investment Board, Blue Ribbon Commission on Reducing Racial Employment Disparities. (2011). *Everybody in: A report to reduce racial employment disparities in the Ramsey County metropolitan area*. Retrieved from http://www.rcwib. org/Aboutus/BRC/BRCReport.pdf

Reagan, S. (2013). Race matters for teachers and students. *Twin Cities Daily Planet*. Retrieved from http://www.tcdailyplanet.net/news/2013/03/22/race-matters-teachers-and-students

Reamer, F. (1983). The free will-determinism debate and social work. *The Social Service Review, 57*(4), 626–644.

Roholt, R., Baizerman, M. L., Rana, S., & Korum, K. (Eds.). (2013). *Transforming youth serving organizations to support healthy youth development: New directions for youth development* (Number 139). Hoboken, NJ: John Wiley & Sons.

Sankowski, E. (1985). Paternalism and social policy. *American Philosophical Quarterly*, 2(1), 1–12.

Sellgren, J. (2006). School where pupils select staff. *BBC News*. Retrieved from http://news.bbc.co.uk/2/hi/uk_news/education/4785538.stm

Soss, J., Fording, R. C., Schram, S. F. (2011). *Disciplining the poor: neoliberal paternalism and the persistent power of race*. Chicago: University of Chicago Press.

Stone, C. (1977). Paternalism among social agency employees. *The Journal of Politics, 39*(3), 794–804.

Taylor, P., & Cohn, D. (2012). *A milestone en route to a minority nation*. Retrieved from http://www.pewsocialtrends.org/2012/11/07/a-milestone-en-route-to-a-majority-minority-nation/?src=rss_main

Tran, J., & Treuhaft, S. (2014). *Minnesota's tomorrow: Equity is the superior growth model*. Oakland, CA: PolicyLink.

University of Oklahoma, National Resource Center for Youth Development. (n.d.). *Youth engagement*. Retrieved from http://www.nrcyd.ou.edu/youth-engagement/youthadult-partnerships

U.S. Department of Health and Human Services, Administration on Aging [HHS]. (2005). *File 2. Interim state projections of population for five-year age groups and selected age groups by sex: July, 1 2004 to 2030*. Retrieved from http://www.aoa.gov/Aging_Statistics/ future_growth/future_growth.aspx#state

Weiss, G. (1985). Paternalism modernized. *Journal of Medical Ethics, 11*, 184–187.

Youth Leadership Institute. (2009). *Education change and youth engagement: Strategies for success*. San Francisco: Youth Leadership Institute.

Zeldin, S., Petrokubi, J., & Mc Neil, C. (2007). *Youth-adult partnerships in community decision making: What does it take to engage adults in the practice?* Chevy Chase, MD: National 4-H Council.

Section IV

Themes and Conclusions

17 From Hope to Wise Action

The Future of Youth Work and Other Global Actions in Education

Michael Heathfield and Dana Fusco

> Social progress is the capacity of a society to meet the basic human needs of its citizens, establish the building blocks that allow citizens and communities to enhance and sustain the quality of their lives, and create the conditions for all individuals to reach their full potential. (Porter, Stern, & Green, 2014, p. 15)

But what happens when social progress is thwarted? When citizens and young citizens are unable to leverage resources to reach their full potential because of a society's incapacity to provide the right structures to ensure they can? In families with greater means, such structural obstacles can be overcome: one family buys a SAT prep book while another relies on an old, tattered, and written-on copy from the local library; one family takes a summer vacation to Puerto Rico, where a young person finds a love of petroglyphs, while another basks in the joys of a public swimming pool, with less exposure to diverse cultural experiences; one family has the resources to make the choice of a highly reputed charter school laden with rich opportunities for learning, while another is limited to the struggling local high school which is a revolving door for young teachers and principals. We do not mean to state that the learning that occurs in lower income families is not of value; in fact, the inherent community nourishment here is often missing in wealthier areas that value independence and compete for accomplishment. However, young people are judged on their academic prowess and achievement; when they start school already behind and then stay there because of a lack of social commitment for equal advancement, inequality grows and society as a whole suffers.

While the adversities resulting from societal failures can be met with hope, resolving inequality requires wise action. Today, inequality is progressively complex, growing rampantly, and increasingly recognized as a global threat in both public and private spheres (IMF Survey, 2015). Youthhood is a pervasive location of inequality, particularly when age is accompanied by other demonized demographics such as blackness, girlness, maleness, queerness, poorness, and the like. In countries around the world, we can find young people struggling against persistent poverty, unemployment, poor educational outcomes, and stunted opportunities for a healthy and happy adulthood. These injustices are not fixed, and we do have the capacity to change them. Engle and colleagues (2014) identify clearly how early childhood interventions in low- and middle-income countries can impact inequalities created by poverty. But the teen years are also critical. Postmodern realities and neoliberal policies have an international reach and frame parallel and differentiated contexts, relationships, and truths for young people. At times in history when young people were more confident in the government, they were also more hopeful about their future (Syvertsen, Wray-Lake, Flanagan, Osgood, & Briddell, 2011). Representation was trusted as a political process. No more. Traditional measures of political and civic engagement have been on the decline among young adults, as has trust in the government overall (Syvertsen et al., 2011). Yet, we can also find young people who are motivated to act on the real concerns for their future pathways. As we have seen here, youth work can and does make a difference for engaging young people. There is global evidence that we can do this differently and change young people's life trajectories.

In this book, we entered the relationship between inequality and youth with an unbridled interest in understanding youth work and other global actions in education as an important approach for not only engaging young people but, more broadly, for making social progress. At the outset we were concerned with the *deeds of dismissal*—the range of tools used by those with power to control and render invisible those judged not worthy of full citizenship, potential, and contribution. It seems to us that the time is now to raise the issues: that youth is a social category decided upon by adults and resting on ageist assumptions, rules, and policies that young people have had no role in designing or deciding upon; that inequality hits young people the hardest, directing and re-directing lifelong and generational trajectories that are often associated with categories of race, ability, sexuality, gender, and class; that at least some young people are tired of the world that their entrusted adults have created and are reclaiming spaces locally and globally so they can transform futures and possibilities; that youth work offers renewed possibility as a credible player in allying with young people to reshape their futures; and that we have found interesting stories globally that tell a complex and fascinating tale that is just one in a larger body of literature currently emerging with inequality in its headlights.

The narratives contained here register numerous voices of young people and their adult allies who, despite vast differences in their geographic, economic, and social contexts, show that adversity can be faced with hope and inequality challenged by action. These are not age-specific qualities, and young people, as citizens now, can and do demonstrate these values and actions across the globe. If we think about these narratives as a collection of 'global actions,' the onus is on us as editors to draw out themes, organize the narratives into some cohesive whole, and pull together a storyline that begins and ends in the voices of the authors (us among them). The onus is also on us to bridge the narratives so that they offer a collective voice for building our field and discipline. We do not take such a task lightly, nor do we believe we achieved the only or even best way to have accomplished this. Each chapter on its own offers a unique and rich perspective, but it is in the totality of this work that we find exciting possibilities for the future of youth work. We conclude this text with a call that illuminating and interrupting inequality be more centrally located as an anchor of strong youth work practice.

ILLUMINATING AND INTERRUPTING INEQUALITY

It is hard to imagine that Socrates was arrested and tried for, among other 'sins,' corrupting youth. In his *Apology* to the court, he stated, "The unexamined life is not worth living." Today, we take for granted that the education of young people includes empowering them to develop their own theories and beliefs, to question existing knowledge, and to discount it when the evidence is not strong. We understand that those who do not examine life as lived cannot fully make informed and ethical decisions. We believe, as did Socrates and many, many since, that young people have an expressed desire and indeed a right to examine the unexamined. There should be no enslavement to knowledge, no entanglement to understanding history, and no politically contrived obstacles to promoting social justice or acting on behalf of equality.

Our learning from the experience and expertise shared amongst our contributors in their deeply contextual writing is that any work committed to improving social justice begins with a communal process of illumination. Inequality is a complex and rough human tapestry. A careful and searching light must be trained to bring to the surface all aspects of inequality within any particular experience. Some aspects need little light and present themselves boldly and brazenly on the surface for all to see; others are deep, hidden, and require a searching multidirectional light for them to be seen in operation. The stories we share here highlight that injustice can always be both simple and complex, but it is only through illuminative processes that these nuances can be examined. Our own American context has provided a number of narratives that indicate these illuminative processes can take a variety of forms. Appreciative interviewing techniques were used in the Matloff-Nieve et al. study of social-justice youth programs in New York City as well as in Gordon's research on adult allies. Deeply personal, reflective narrative was the tool of choice for Hubbard's illuminated experience of beginning a youth council as well as Pope's illumination of overcoming paternalism as a youth worker and funding organization. Gall and Heathfield combined considerable police and public education data with insights from key informants and young people themselves to illuminate systemic injustice. Whatever the methodological approach chosen, illuminating inequality is the needed precursor for the necessary action that must follow.

What we have also learned is that through these varied illuminative processes, a broader socioeconomic and political 'grand narrative' has emerged. This grand narrative seems to involve some form of colonization and subjugation, either through overt control or through the complex interweaving of systems that seem to perpetuate injustice without cause. The fissures of colonialism are deep and wide, reaching beyond geographic and temporal boundaries. Experiences across much of the globe demonstrate both historic and current damage visited on groups of people who are dismissed as mere objects of colonial acquisition. The deliberate unthreading of Indigenous cultures, illegal land acquisitions, and forced destruction of traditional familial and communal nurture, growth, and development practices are indeed global instruments of colonization. In the contextual illumination of these injustices we can also see how an urban or rural location compounds these impacts. These very specific and different sites of injustice provide the complexity that can often derail youth trajectories and the relevant professional services and supports, when they are provided.

As Espinosa explores, young Shipibo students in higher education in Peru face many challenges, not least of which is balancing the nurture and expectations of their Indigenous culture when faced with modern city life and numerous social prejudices. The loss of Indigenous support systems is keenly felt when these young students embark on an urban journey of education that is genuinely intended to secure their future success. Illuminating inequality requires that the dismissal of Indigenous cultural practices, artifacts, and language must be key areas for redress when working with young people whose success resides in successfully bridging lives lived between two cultures. We see strong connections with the parallel work undertaken with the First Nation people in Aotearoa New Zealand. Both stories represent a cultural and structural divide that is difficult for many young people to successfully traverse unsupported. As Baxter and colleagues report, the colonial history of this small nation demonstrates that the destructive forces of expansive capital, initially through trade, were then compounded by the imposition of governance structures and educational segregation frameworks that were hugely disrespectful and disruptive to traditional Indigenous practices that had historically nurtured the young. European colonial masters systematically eradicated long-term relational practices that valued all members of society and transmitted cultural, factual, and esoteric knowledge through communal engagement and responsibility. In this context, it was through youth work association and on-the-ground youth organizing and community mobilization that re-instated long-held but cast-aside Indigenous values and practices. A similar approach was witnessed in Malaysia with BEGUSA's insistent and tireless advocacy of resources for its young people and the broader community in order to break long-held cycles of poverty caused by neglect of a people, a culture, and an entire island.

The resulting destruction of a long-held history of colonial domination and subjugation was illuminated and interrupted in Peru, Aotearoa New Zealand, and Malaysia through tenacious youth and community workers working alongside young people and adult citizens. These local illuminative processes of injustice can also occur on a larger scale. As our Australian example shows, when an authentic issue is identified and genuine partnerships and community expertise are coordinated, resulting in 'joined up' responses, young people's lives can be saved. Positively impacting youth suicide rates demonstrates that significant change can be 'brought to scale' as large institutions are often charged to do. This was a successful national suicide prevention initiative in which youth workers played a strategic role. However, this coordinated strategy had been less effective and had a more complex reach with regard to rural Indigenous Australians and did not achieve equal preventative results. National initiatives cannot escape the dominating impact of the broader social injustice of colonialism without genuine collaboration and creative solutions to youth issues. Government-initiated change almost always has differential impacts and is intersected by class, race, ethnicity, gender, sexual identity, disability, and other significant aspects of human diversity. The necessity of keeping large-scale efforts as close to the ground as possible is a key lesson learned here. Without youth workers' keen understanding of the continued lack of connection to Indigenous young people of this initiative, further re-tuning and impact would not be possible. The breadth of influence that can emanate from large-scale government actions cannot be underestimated when such emergent data from the frontlines is allowed to bubble up through the service structure for more targeted and just efforts.

In Batan's contribution about the plight of Istambays in the Philippines, we see how fairly traditional gender roles and the lack of employment opportunities for specific groups of working-class young men help maintain their subjugated status in a suspended transition to adulthood. The dominant patriarchal breadwinner and provider role is permanently removed from the grasp of these young men. In this illumination, it can also be seen that the role of family and faith provides nurture, hope, and support while simultaneously sustaining this subjugated state. There is no government interruption to this state of being, no service provider or non-governmental interruption to this permanent waiting. Interruption to this inequality is an action also in waiting alongside these young men.

Gender roles and expectations also provide the site of slowly emerging transitions for young women in Portugal as the scouting association opened its doors to girls and young women. The subjugated and secondary role of women is highlighted in the history of global scouting, in which young women were initially excluded but were activists and advocates for their right to similar opportunities for experiential growth and development. As Cunha and Silva recount, young women's subjugated status was originally met with a 'separate but equal' response, but this reactive strategy became unable to sustain itself in the face of the increasing power and expectations of young women in post-modern democracies. This narrative also shows that change can be slow and incremental when long-established institutions carefully protect their history and ideology in the face of social change that seeks more equality and reduced injustice.

In the American context, considerably more illumination is required to surface the issue of subjugation. For instance, while class remains a heavy-weight discriminator, there is an American obsession with making class disappear to shine the light on other facets of human identity that can provide a temporary illusion of change (Côté, 2014). With regard to inequality, while never alone, class matters. In both New York and Chicago, redline zoning perpetuates clear class lines that coincide with school and community resourcing. In addition, the criminal justice system feeds off corrupt school systems and street-located racism from police forces to hugely impact differential outcomes heavily premised on race and class. This is nothing new in a nation founded on racial colonization and the disenfranchisement of Native Americans. Across America, a series of high-profile police officer murders of African American young men have ignited continued street protest across the country. Tragically, deadly outcomes for African American young men are consistently woven into the history of America. But change is possible. Gall and Heathfield show how restorative justice is changing unjust school policies such as discriminatory 'push out' rates for young people of color. In New York, young people have changed citywide policies and made incremental changes in unjust education systems through empowered activism that allows often excluded young people to speak their truths and interrupt the onslaught of abusive power wielded by many placed in systemic positions of judgment.

Neoliberal education reforms prejudice the market over community and have moved further and further away from their moral responsibility for the best education for *all* young people, regardless of their financial and family circumstances. There is an unhealthy and unjust connection between education and criminal justice systems. This symbiotic relationship does not serve the best interests of young people. In protest against this marketization and criminalization of schooling, young people have stood alongside their teachers and parents in objecting to their diminishing voice in what a quality education means. Gordon locates this as a national imperative while noting the challenges that come with some success in resisting this ideological and practical shift in support for basic rights to education.

In short, illuminated through these chapters fairly consistently is how inequalities play out for whole groups of people based on class, race, and gender and how youth work aims explicitly to interrupt such inequities by providing access and opportunities, creating communities of practice, and challenging systems that are not justly serving all young citizens. If we anchor youth work practice in the illumination and interruption of inequality, we must also consider some cautions for the future practice of youth work.

THE FUTURE OF YOUTH WORK FOR ILLUMINATING AND INTERRUPTING INEQUALITY: SOME CAUTIONS

Fusco (2012) argued that the advancing of youth work might rest on understanding the core principles that are the underbelly of good youth work practice. Context, participation, and responsiveness were three principles that emerged consistently across various geographies, contexts, and settings of youth work practice. However, we come back to a point made then, and again in Fusco and Baizerman (2013): The current climate of professionalization of youth work needs to be carefully considered as a strategy for advancing practice. It is too frequently assumed that becoming a 'professionalized' field of practice can only reap advantages for youth workers and the young people they work with. We should use Jones's English contribution as a warning to those rushing headlong to achieve the numerous artifacts of professional status. Statutory youth services that achieve government resources and recognition are thus also subject to savage cuts when austerity measures seek to reduce government spending. Beyond meeting basic human needs, adult interventions in the lives of young people are more likely to be driven by the philosophy and purpose of the provider, not the recipient. Young people are frequently framed as consumers of programs—as objects to be acted upon by those with power to define what is 'needed.' As Pope identifies in this text, young people can rapidly become 'service recipients' when they are selected as the objects of professional interventions. We can find programs across the globe in which young people are over-serviced, under-represented, and subject to the deeds of dismissal even when they are the much prized program participants.

Youth work is both philosophically and practically challenged by professionalism as it is currently articulated through traditional professionalization models and the post-modern dominance of outcome models in human and social services and education. Program models prejudice outcomes over process. Participation should be delivered throughout all aspects of program—from design to delivery. Yet, this is not how most youth programs are created and funded. If a key distinction of youth work is the fact that it centers on a very specific responsive process of engagement with young people, how then can outcomes be externally proscribed at the outset? While we are both vocal advocates for increasing the professional status of youth workers, we also share concerns about how common aspects of professionalization processes may simultaneously run counter to the philosophical and practical tenets of youth work.

One of those tenets, as mentioned, is participation. We see youth work as offering a critical arena for developing voice and agency—both necessary for healthy democracies to flourish. We very much believe that democracy as a form of governance offers a decent, if not 'best,' chance of creating social conditions for human life that are just, fair, and equitable for all (Fusco & Heathfield, 2015). However, we must be aware of domination by 'democracy.' There is certainly a long American history of oppressive behavior that is publically espoused as 'democracy building.' Skalli (this volume) is explicit about the deceptive use of American aid dollars in Morocco and Jordan for 'civics education' in which the curriculum, created in California, serves to tame the prospective pull of terrorist organizations for disenfranchised young people. This colonialist approach to American homeland security has been visited on many nations. There is staggering perversity in the use of U.S. government dollars being spent to train young people in the importance of civic responsibility and citizenship in countries that are modernized feudal kingdoms. Participation in civic behavior is not necessarily a signifier of social justice and equality; indeed, it can have a complex and contradictory range of meanings.

Representative democracy is, and will remain, a prime candidate for interruption for the foreseeable future. This is a global reality that, once contextualized, can become significantly different on the ground. In some contexts, the struggle for a voice and a vote take precedence; in other contexts, the fight to keep these hard-won rights becomes central as those with power and money seek to remove these rights and reinvent inequalities that take social progress backwards. Indeed, representative democracies across the globe are struggling with legitimacy, participation, and the authority to act. Invitations to young people to participate in democratic processes can flounder when young people view traditional democratic processes as futile or fraudulent. This does not always have to be the case, as Scottish young people demonstrated in the 2014 independence vote. When young people have clarity about their future options and know they have been systematically included, they can organize decisively and with considerable impact.

Youth work and youth voice are terms that are wedded at the proverbial hip. Recently, the Council of Europe defined youth work as a practice "guided and governed by principles of participation and empowerment, values of human rights and democracy, and anti-discrimination and tolerance" (2010, p. 2). Of course, we must continually work to detangle the relationships between democracy, youth participation, voice, youth work, and more broadly, education. Hubbard, in this volume, reports about a genuine attempt and structural approach to inclusion, participation, and unusual diversity in co-creating programs alongside young people, indicating, perhaps, that the precursor for this to happen in youth work has to be the expressed intention of the practitioner from the outset. Participation is not a program add-on or an additional imperative but should be a foundational value in work with young people. The program frontline could be conservation, sports, the arts, or any such activity that attracts, engages, and sustains the interest of specific groups of young people, but the foundation must have a participatory structure that includes young people at the outset. Again, this requires some boundary shifting for successful workers. Roles and responsibilities that would normally be allocated through the adult/youth divide and the participant/provider divide must be illuminated and interrupted at the earliest possible programmatic stage. Of course, the parallel accompaniment to participative and communal decision-making is the power to act upon those decisions. When young people are afforded the opportunity to voice their concerns and opinions, adults should be ready to partner on those issues, otherwise 'voice' is simply noise in the background of 'democracy' while those with real power remain in the foreground with key decision-making roles. The definitional frameworks for representative democracy to occur have been provided (e.g., EU Council); now youth workers can seize the opportunity, push the democratic boundaries, and create spaces for young people to lead us out of injustice.

For this to happen, we believe that youth workers must become more adept and articulate at raising up sociological and historical understandings of the human experience to challenge the dominance achieved by psychologically derived disciplinary frames with regard to young people and youth work. Personal development must be liberated from the American default setting of individualism. Young people live in families, peer group networks, neighborhoods and global communities. One's sense of self is a complex amalgam of that which is given from others and that which one chooses to take for oneself to achieve a holistic and connected identity (Solomon, 2013). Consequently, youth work must draw upon and celebrate diverse connectivity at all times. Youth workers must establish significant roles in community and neighborhood groups at every opportunity. Youth work has a proud and important history of communal action, solidarity, and sacrifice in the service of others. Youth workers should always seek to make connections within, across, and between groups because these provide the primary locations in which inequality can be interrupted. It behooves us all to ensure all institutions, including those with disciplinary power, recognize the centrality of communities when policies and actions dismiss community voices and interests. At its heart, youth work remains a communal process of engagement. It is imperative that these historical strengths remain the drivers of new change efforts.

In fact, historically, youth work has always served multiple purposes and been called into action by a range of stakeholders. The driving imperatives of these diverse stakeholders have often been contradictory and remain so today. Perhaps the capacity to adapt and work across and between systems and agencies is a distinctive marker of youth work practice and thus a key element of the youth work contribution to fighting inequality. All professions mark their territory with specific boundaries that separate the worker from those who are 'worked with.' Another distinguishing feature of youth work practice is that youth workers are more likely to transgress some common boundaries. This may be permissible and expected; for example, in dress and language use. It is a practice in which relationships are central and in which closeness and connectivity are highly valued capabilities. There is certainly more license for youth work practitioners to be both bridge builders and boundary crossers when this is necessary to support the young people they work with. The risk in this adaptability is that youth workers become all things to all people and valued by no one. Remaining grounded and committed to illuminating and interrupting injustice could provide the foundational fix that anchors the creative flexibility of strong youth work practice.

CONCLUSION

Differential life outcomes proscribed simply on the basis of one aspect of identity deny the complexity of human existence and allow those with power and status to define the rules of their game. Life and death outcomes premised on race and ethnicities are the realities of life for most young people of color in many global communities. In the U.S., African American young men are 21 times more likely to be shot dead by law enforcement than their age-equivalent white peers (Gabrielson, Growchowski Jones & Sagara, 2014). If we truly lived in a data-driven environment, this fact alone should ignite change on so many levels. And yet, entrenched and embedded power dynamics seek to minimize change to this obscene status quo because ideology remains immune to factual knowledge. As Gordon says in this volume, we must learn to operationalize our outrage.

Youth work has always been a willing partner in challenging the broad range of inequalities that impinge on the lives of many young people. However, as a field there is inconsistency in purpose as well as practice. Such inconsistency has been largely accepted as 'who we are,' a diverse group of individuals, agencies, and organizations with our own differences in how we see and think about and approach the world, a world that includes young people. We, too, have largely accepted our diversity. However, we also more than ever feel the need to take a stance—one that is as much telling of ourselves as educators as it is revealing of our politics. It is a simple stance: Young people as members of communities have experiences, opinions, and beliefs that matter or should matter to other members of communities—in this case, adults. Because of the particular vantage point we each have, only together can we see the world more wholly. Youth work offers a platform for partnership that is centered on illumination and interruption.

We are not alone in envisioning youth work as such a space (Batsleer & Davies, 2010; Belton, 2014; IDYW, 2012; Roholt, Baizerman & Hildreth, 2013; Sallah, 2014). Collectively, there is a growing consensus on youth work as citizen space that is within the reach, role, and responsibility of everyday people as they engage in everyday actions as citizens of the global world. This growing collective dialogue removes the casting of such work as 'radical,' an aim worthy of pursuit. Radicalizing the actors only perpetuates marginalizing groups of people and young people. We would like to remove the 'radical' and instead envision this illumination/interruption as a practice of democracy evoked by everyday citizens for a more just (and healthy) society.

> The aim of civic efficiency has at least the merit of protecting us from the notion of a training of mental power at large. It calls attention to the fact that power must be relative to doing something, and to the fact that the things which most need to be done are things which involve one's relationships with others. ~ John Dewey (1938)

Our view of a healthy society is one in which citizens are aware of social issues which differentially affect the populous, can examine those issues from multiple perspectives and viewpoints, and can act in ways that promote a better society for *all*, not just in ways that serve self-interest. This view is utopian, perhaps, but is a vision needed more and more given the growing inequalities facing our global community. On a social level, such a view might mean that participation in social matters is required among all citizens, not just those with dominant perspectives and capital, to ensure a representative voice and understanding of lived experiences and engagement of those views in political and civic matters. On a personal level, people must develop critical consciousness in which they are capable of deconstructing and reconstructing ideas, strategies, programs, and services at micro- and macro-structural levels to impact inequality.

This would also certainly involve repositioning activism from the fringe to the core of all youth work and reframing what it means to be an activist. Activism can and does operate at multiple locations and layers. We might commonly associate activism with protest, organizing, and taking to the streets to give voice to injustice. We would like to reframe activism for the multiple and complex locales in which it is now most needed. While the primacy of the street should never be overlooked, power moves in numerous ways and can be at its most destructive when it is dishonest and deceptive. Demagogues, dictators, and ideologues have never found problematic the operation of power behind closed doors. Closed-door decision-making by power brokers provide numerous opportunities for illumination and interruption. Young people and their adult allies should be unafraid to open up these sites of injustice to the oxygen of equality.

The diverse narratives we celebrate here establish that intersectionality is not simply a sociological concept; we all live this every day of our lives. Identity and experience, like knowledge, are embodied, embrained, embedded, encultured, and encoded (Blackler, 1995). The urgent charge for youth workers is to develop a diverse and consistent practice that illuminates as many facets of injustice as possible. This should always develop agency and provide relevant partnership actions to interrupt injustice as it impinges on real lives and life chances. If this work is successful, young people and their adult allies (Checkoway, 2011) begin to dim the light on those who seek only to focus on one aspect of identity through which domination and subjugation can occur. While youth work has multiple layers of depth and tolerance for such work, we believe taking even small steps towards such a view can go a long way.

Voice is a precursor of change but only when it speaks with power. As we have seen in this text, a seat at the table has been a traditional and important indicator of acceptance. But it does not necessarily signify that significant decision-making power has shifted to those on the frontlines of injustice. As we have argued elsewhere (Fusco & Heathfield, 2015), placation and tokenism are well-practiced devices to maintain the status quo and silence voices for significant structural change. Youth workers must commit more overtly to an explicit role in coordinating human gifts in the service of social justice. We must celebrate and connect passion with practice by bringing our communal gifts of the heart, head, and hands (Kretzmann & McKnight, 1993) together in the service of social justice. Just like strong impactful youth work practice, this must start where young people are. For some, this will require important work within; for others, this will require the excitement of action that will later lead to reflection and learning. For all, it must immediately connect within and between others who share the same context (McKnight & Block, 2012) and build bridges in our global communities.

We don't always get it right, but we should never repeat wrongs knowingly. Citizens of a democracy are expected to be informed, engaged, and skilled at understanding and examining, indeed illuminating, social issues. What we have learned through working with our colleagues around the world has strengthened our resolve to push forth youth work as a potent strategy for promoting social justice and democracy through exactly this type of examining the unexamined. Historically, the ideas that take hold have utility, social purpose, and help achieve something of value. They also emerge at a time when the ground is prepared to accept the seeds for growth. We hope now is such a time.

REFERENCES

Batsleer, J., & Davies, B. (Eds.). (2010). *What is youth work?* Exeter: Learning Matters.

Belton, B. (Ed.). (2014). *Global perspectives on youth work*. Rotterdam: Sense Publishers.

Blackler, F. (1995). Knowledge, knowledge work and organizations: An overview and interpretation. *Organization Studies, 6*, 1021–1046.

Checkoway, B. (2011). What is youth participation? *Children and Youth Services Review, 33*, 340–345.

Côté, J. (2014). *Youth studies*. New York, NY: Palgrave Macmillan.

Council of Europe (2010, July 7–10). *Declaration of the 1st European Youth Work Convention*. Ghent, Belgium. Retrieved from http://www.coe.int/t/dg4/youth/Source/Resources/Documents/2010_Declaration_European_youth_work_convention_en.pdf

Dewey, J. (1938). *Experience and education.* New York: Macmillan Publishing Company.

Engle, P. L., Fernald, L., Alderman, H., Behrman, J., O'Gara, C., Yousafzai, A., . . . the Global Child Development Steering Group (2014). *Strategies for reducing inequalities and improving inequalities and improving developmental outcomes for young children in low-income and middle-income countries.* Harris School of Public Policy. Chicago, IL: University of Chicago. Retrieved from http://harris.uchicago.edu/sites/default/files/Strategies%20for%20reducing%20inequalities%20and%20improving%20developmental.pdf

Fusco, D. (Ed.). (2012). *Advancing youth work.* New York, NY: Routledge.

Fusco, D., & Baizerman, M. (2013). Professionalization in youth work? Opening and deepening circles of inquiry. *Child & Youth Services, 34,* 89–99.

Fusco, D., & Heathfield, M. (2015). Modeling democracy: Is youth "participation" enough? *Italian Journal of Sociology of Education, 1,* 12–31.

Gabrielson, R., Grochowski Jones, R., & Sagara, E. (2014). *Deadly force: In black and white.* Retrieved from http://www.propublica.org/article/deadly-force-in-black-and-white

IDYW. (2012). *This is youth work: Stories from practice.* London: In Defence of Youth Work.

IMF Survey. (2015, January 20). *Global growth revised down, despite cheaper oil, faster U.S. growth.* Retrieved from: http://www.imf.org/external/pubs/ft/survey/so/2015/NEW012015A.htm

Kretzmann, J., & McKnight, J. (1993). *Building communities from the inside out: A path toward finding and mobilizing a community's assets.* Chicago, IL: ACTA Publications.

McKnight, J., & Block, P. (2012). *The abundant community: Awakening the power of families and neighborhoods.* San Francisco, CA: Berrett-Koehler Publishers.

Porter, M. E., Stern, S., & Green, M. (2014). *Social progress index 2014.* Washington, DC: Social Progress Imperative.

Roholt, R. V., Baizerman, M., & Hildreth, R. W. (2013). *Civic youth work.* Chicago: Lyceum Books.

Sallah, M. (2014). *Global youth work: Provoking consciousness and taking action.* Dorset: Russell House Publishing.

Solomon, A. (2013). *Far from the tree: Parents, children and the search for identity.* New York, NY: Simon & Schuster.

Syvetsen, A. K., Wray-Lake, L., Flanagan, C. A., Osgood, D. W., & Briddell, L. (2011). Thirty-year trends in U.S. adolescents' civic engagement: A story of changing participation and educational differences. *Journal of Research on Adolescence, 21*(3), 586–594.

Contributors

EDITORS

Michael Heathfield is Chair of Applied Sciences at Harold Washington College in Chicago, where he also coordinates youth work and social work programs. He created one of the very few associate degrees in youth work in the United States in 2006. Dr. Heathfield's research and writing, on both sides of the Atlantic, has concentrated on student learning and specifically the education of youth workers. His work with young people has involved numerous youth theaters and youth arts organizations, a drop-in coffee bar for unemployed young people, LGB youth groups, and young men's groups. He moved to America in 1999, studying and working in New York and then Chicago, where he now lives. He was responsible for a number of citywide training and professional education initiatives for youth workers before becoming full-time faculty.

Dana Fusco is a Professor and Department Chair of Education and Youth Studies at City University of New York, York College, in New York, United States. Dr. Fusco began as a youth worker and has since been teaching and studying youth work practice and professional education for over 20 years. She has published extensively on these issues, receiving national and international recognition for her work in creating a discipline of youth work in the United States. Her interest continues to be the expansive need for providing equitable opportunities for the development of young people.

CONTRIBUTORS

Clarence M. Batan is Associate Professor at the Faculty of Arts and Letters, Youth Studies Cluster Head of the Research Center on Culture, Education and Social Issues (RCCESI), and Professorial Lecturer at the Graduate School of the University of Santo Tomas (UST), Manila, Philippines. His academic training in the field of sociology of children and youth started at UST and was further honed at the University of the Philippines-Diliman and Dalhousie University (Canada). He was a Visiting Fellow at Brown University, USA under the Brown International Advanced Research Institutes (BIARI) program. He currently leads the project The Social Investigation on the Lives of Istambays in the Philippines (SILIP) funded by the Commission on Higher Education (CHED). He is Vice President for Asia of the Research Committee 34 —Sociology of Youth of the International Sociological Association, and Chair of the Technical Committee for Sociology of CHED, Philippines.

Rod Baxter is a youth worker in Aotearoa, New Zealand. At the turn of the millennium he joined the team at the Wellington Boys' and Girls' Institute (BGI), a youth development organization founded in the 1880s. After initially studying theater and education, Rod became qualified in youth work and supervision and now teaches youth work students. He formerly chaired the National Youth Workers Network Aotearoa until helping found the national youth development organization Ara Taiohi. Rod's current focuses at BGI are a youth participation team called Link and a crew of emerging street artists painting murals in alleyways.

Manu Caddie is the Director for the Pacific Centre for Participatory Democracy in Aotearoa New Zealand and a consultant on youth and community-led development.

Graham Bidois Cameron has worked in a paid and voluntary capacity in community development in Wellington and Tauranga for the past 15 years. A member of the Ngāti Ranginui, Ngāti Hinerangi, and Ngāti Rangiwewehi tribes of Aotearoa New Zealand, he is a director of the Ngāti Ranginui tribal organization. He currently teaches on the Treaty of Waitangi, Aotearoa New Zealand history, and biculturalism to organizations nationally. He is a married father of four, and he and his family are part of Indigenous education and language revitalisation efforts in his local city and community. He has an undergraduate degree in sociology and an honors degree in Māori studies from Victoria University of Wellington and is currently completing a Master of Theology at the University of Otago.

Brooke Chapman has worked in the youth work sector for over 15 years, with a focus on the southeast corridor of Perth where she worked in the areas of youth homelessness and later in a school for almost seven years as a youth counselor. Brooke is currently the Professional Placement Coordinator of Social Science students and youth work lecturer at Edith Cowan University, Perth Western Australia.

Joy Connolly is Director of Education Program Services at Child Care Council of Nassau, Inc. She holds an MA in educational policy studies from the University of Wisconsin-Madison. Her research interests include critical policy analysis, urban youth policy, equity and diversity. In addition, Joy holds an MPA. from New York University in public policy and nonprofit management, and earned her BA from Wesleyan University.

Trudi Cooper is an Associate Professor at Edith Cowan University (ECU) in Australia, where she leads the Youth Work degree program and the Social Program Innovation Research and Evaluation Group. Trudi specializes in the scholarship of teaching and learning and in collaborative evaluation and research with government and nonprofit organizations. In 2006, she received a Carrick Citation for outstanding contribution to learning and teaching. In 2010, she was recognized as one of ECU's top 20 researchers. In 2014, she received a special commendation for Leadership in Youth Work in Western Australia. Previously, Trudi lectured at Cumbria University in the UK in youth and community work. Before commencing her academic career, Trudi was a youth and community worker, manager, and trainer for ten years, during which time she had a variety of roles that included both center-based youth work and street work.

Shane Cucow is an Australian Youth Worker who specialisms in the use of technology to engage and support young people, with previous experience in street work programs and supported accommodation services. At the time of writing, Shane was the Professionals Manager at ReachOut.com Australia, contributing to the design and development of new systems for online help seeking in Australia. He is passionate about the role technology can play in youth work as a powerful tool for putting help in the places young people look for it. He now lives in France.

Olga Oliveira Cunha is the Educational Methods Deputy National Commissioner for Adult Resources in Corpo Nacional Escutas, (CNE) Portugal, and has been a Scout leader since 1994. Her key roles are project management and the overseeing of the scout trainer of trainers model.
She is a community psychologist and researcher in educational and community fields. She lives in Lisbon, Portugal.

Dzuhailmi Dahalan is a Social Research Officer in the Youth Social Health and Well-being Laboratory, Institute for Social Science Studies, Universiti Putra Malaysia. He has been involved in youth development research for the past seven years. Some of the projects he has worked on include the Implementation of the National Youth Development Policy, the Malaysian Youth Index, and a study on Malaysian youth developmental assets. He is also active in writing on important issues related to Malaysian youth, especially in the area of religiosity, religious tolerance, and national unity.

Oscar A. Espinosa received his doctoral degree in anthropology and historical studies from the New School for Social Research in 2005. He is professor of anthropology in the Department of Social Sciences at the

Pontificia Universidad Católica del Peru. He has also been the Director of the Institute for Ethics and Development at the Universidad Antonio Ruiz de Montoya. He has carried out research in the Peruvian Amazon since 1991, especially among the Ashaninka and the Shipibo-Konibo peoples.

Catherine Ferguson is a Postdoctoral Researcher and Lecturer in the School of Law and Justice at Edith Cowan University in Perth, Western Australia. Cath has been involved in teaching youth in a variety courses and institutions for over 15 years. Her research interests include risk behavior of young people, particularly in relation to driving motor vehicles. Her PhD was based in this area and includes knowledge of risk behaviors', driver behavior, and offending behavior in youth. Cath has also been involved in suicide prevention as project manager of a West Australian suicide prevention strategy.

Judith M. Gall, has been Executive Director of Alternatives, Inc. since 1981 and holds a master's degree in social work from Jane Addams School of Social Work at UIC. Alternatives, Inc. is known for its cutting-edge youth programming in violence and substance abuse prevention, asset-based counseling, workforce development, and out-of-school programming using arts and technology. In the 1980s, Alternatives developed Illinois' first South East Asian Refugee Youth Project. In the 1990s, the agency began spearheading the use of Restorative Justice practices and policies within the Chicago Public Schools. The 2013 creation of the Safe Schools Consortium in partnership with Communities United and Chicago Teacher's Union Quest Center resulted in full-school restorative practices built into the classroom management, curriculum, and policy. Currently, Ms. Gall serves on the Board of Directors for the Illinois Collaboration for Youth; the Chicago Committee on Urban Opportunity; Uptown United's Community Leadership Committee; and is a 1996 fellow of Leadership Greater Chicago.

Hava Rachel Gordon is an Associate Professor of Sociology at the University of Denver in Denver, Colorado, USA. Dr. Gordon specializes in the social construction of inequalities such as gender, race, class, and age; social movements; schooling; and qualitative research methods. Her previous research explored how multiple social inequalities shape youth political movements and is the subject of her book *We Fight to Win: Inequality and the Politics of Youth Activism* (Rutgers University Press) as well as journal articles. Her current research focuses on racial inequality, neoliberalism, and community struggles over urban school reform. She teaches courses on schooling, gender, globalization, and qualitative methods as well as service-learning courses on social movements and youth cultures. Professor Gordon also directs the Gender & Women's Studies Program at the University of Denver

Brian Hubbard is the AmeriCorps Individual Placements Program Coordinator for the Conservation Corps Minnesota and Iowa. In the fall of 2010, he was the Parks and Trails Legacy Strategic Plan Assistant and contributed to youth outreach for the Parks and Trails Legacy Plan. In 2015, he was appointed chair of the Parks and Trails Legacy Advisory Committee. Brian previously served as an English teacher with the Peace Corps in Benin, West Africa, and is certified as an Emergency Medical Technician-Basic. He has participated with the After School Matters Practitioner Fellowship and the Neighborhood Leadership Program. He holds a bachelor's degree in communications and professional writing and a master's degree in education in youth development and leadership from the University of Minnesota.

Helen M.F. Jones is Course Leader BA (Hons) of Youth and Community Work at the University of Huddersfield in West Yorkshire, UK. Her first degree was in English language and literature. She has worked in the voluntary sector in Leeds providing literacy, numeracy, and life and social skills for unemployed young people on government programs. Since 1992, she has worked in higher education. She joined the University of Huddersfield in 1996 and has been Course Leader of the BA Youth and Community Work since the late 1990s.

Steven Eric Krauss is a Research Fellow with the Institute for Social Science Research (IPSAS), Universiti Putra Malaysia (UPM). He originates from the U.S. and has been living and working in Malaysia since 2001. Before joining IPSAS, he was an Associate Professor in the Department of Professional Development and Continuing Education in the Faculty of Educational Studies, UPM. He received his PhD from the Institute for Community & Peace Studies (PEKKA), Universiti Putra Malaysia, in 2005 in the field of youth studies. Prior to his work in academia, he worked in the nonprofit sector in Washington, DC at a national youth development policy organization and a local grassroots philanthropy organization. His research and teaching interests include positive youth development, youth work, Muslim youth religiosity, and qualitative research methods.

Monami Maulik was born in the refugee colonies of Kolkata, India, and grew up in the Bronx, New York. She has been a leader and grassroots organizer in the fields of immigrant, racial justice, youth, and global justice for over 18 years. She holds a bachelor's degree in international development, women's studies, and South Asian studies from Cornell University. In 2000, Ms. Maulik founded DRUM- Desis Rising Up & Moving as one of the first South Asian immigrant workers' membership-based organizations for social justice in the U.S. Since then, she has served as the Executive Director, developing campaigns and leading national and global alliance work. She currently serves as a board member of the National Network for Immigrant and Refugee Rights, the national Dignity in Schools Campaign, the Civil Society Steering Committee for the UN High Level Dialogue on Migration, Immigrant Communities in Action (ICA) in NYC, the NGO Coordinating Committee on Migration, the United National Anti-War Committee, and as an Advisory Board member of the North Star Fund. In 2012, Ms. Maulik launched and now coordinates the Global South Asian Migrant Workers Alliance.

Susan Matloff-Nieves is the Associate Executive Director for Youth Services at the Queens Community House (QCH) in Queens, New York, USA. As a youth worker and community organizer for over three decades with a lifelong passion for social justice, her interests are creating programs that are responsive to youth interests and concerns, development of youth workers as agents of change in young people's lives, and fostering critical thinking and young people's ability to be engaged citizens in the world. Engaging in research and writing with colleagues has provided some of her most rich and meaningful opportunities to reflect upon and deepen practice.

Marcus Pope currently serves as the Director of Partnerships and External Relations for Youthprise. In this role, he builds cross-sector collaborations, oversees research and evaluation, and leads the organization's development efforts. Previous to Youthprise, he served as Associate Director of the Institute on Domestic Violence in the African American Community at the University of Minnesota (U of M). Other experiences include serving as Director of Youth Programs for the Neighborhood Involvement Program in Minneapolis and Academic Advisor for the Youth Studies Department at the U of M School of Social Work. Marcus holds an interdisciplinary undergraduate degree in sociology, youth studies and African American studies and a master's degree from the U of M in education-youth development leadership with an emphasis in program evaluation. He also holds a Mini-MBA in nonprofit management from the University of St. Thomas' Opus College of Business.

Loubna Skalli-Hanna is professor at the School of International Service at the American University, Washington, DC. Her teaching and research examine issues at the intersection of youth, gender, communication, and the politics of development in the Middle East and North Africa (MENA). She designed and taught graduate courses on youth and children in international development and has led the MA concentration in these areas at AU. She has published numerous journal articles and book chapters and co-authored two books in these areas and is completing a third book for Columbia University Press on youth activism and media in MENA. She also works as a consultant with international development agencies on youth and gender issues. Dr. Skalli holds an MA in cultural anthropology from Essex University (England) and a PhD in communication from the Pennsylvania State University, where she was a Fulbright Scholar. She has taught at numerous universities and institutes in Morocco, her native country.

Howard Sercombe has a lifelong involvement in youth affairs as a youth worker, academic, researcher, and media commentator. Born in England and raised in outback Australia, Howard is now Professor of Community Education at the University of Strathclyde, Glasgow, Scotland. He is author of *Youth Work Ethics* (Sage, 2010), co-author of *Youth Studies: an Australian Perspective* (Pearson Education 1998) and *Youth and the Future* (National Youth Affairs Research Scheme 2002), and has written over sixty individual chapters and articles. Dr. Sercombe is first and foremost a youth worker. Trained in social and political theory, media studies, and theology, his current intellectual work is about how our conceptions of young people (including, currently, the conceptions of neuroscience) shape policy and practice and the professional ethics of youth work. He is married to broadcaster Helen Wolfenden and has four sons, aged 34, 32, 29, and 2.

Pedro Duarte Silva is the Educational Methods National Commissioner of the Corpo Nacional de Escutas (the Portuguese Catholic Scout Association). He also participates regularly in several committees and working groups at the International Catholic Conference of Scouting and at the World Organization of the Scout Movement.

Howard Williamson is Professor of European Youth Policy at the University of South Wales. He is also a qualified youth worker and, throughout his life, has combined youth work practice with youth research and youth policy. He ran an open youth center for 24 years. His research work has covered a range of youth policy and lifestyle domains, and his most well-known studies have been of the 'Milltown Boys' (a lifetime study of a group of men he met when they were 13 years old; today they are 54!) and the pioneering research in 1993 on those young people who are now dreadfully referred to as 'NEET.' He has been involved in youth policy in Wales, the UK, the European Commission, the Council of Europe, and the United Nations. He is Organisational Secretary for the International Sociological Association youth research network and was appointed Commander of the Order of the British Empire in 2002 for services to young people.

Shepherd Zeldin is Rothermel Bascom Professor of Human Ecology, University of Wisconsin-Madison, USA. Professor Zeldin has taught in the School of Human Ecology since 1999 and holds a joint appointment with Wisconsin Extension. Prior to becoming a professor, he held leadership roles in the nonprofit and public sectors and directed a grassroots philanthropy organization in the USA. His scholarship centers on the role of youth in strengthening communities and building civil society. His teaching focuses on youth development, community development, and university-community partnership. Professor Zeldin's numerous publications explore issues ranging from community reconciliation to a guidebook on involving youth in organizational change.

Index

0 1341 1569118 7